The C Trilogy

2nd Edition

The C Trilogy

2nd Edition

Eric P. Bloom

Windcrest®/McGraw-Hill

SECOND EDITION
FIRST PRINTING

Library of Congress Cataloging-in-Publication Data

Bloom, Eric P.
   The C trilogy / Eric P. Bloom.—2nd ed.
     p.   cm.
   Includes index.
   ISBN 0-8306-2533-X
   1. C (Computer program language) I. Title.
  QA76.73.C15B56 1991
  005.13'3—dc20   91-24235
                                 CIP

TAB Books offers software for sale. For information and a catalog, please contact
TAB Software Department, Blue Ridge Summit, PA 17294-0850.

Acquisitions Editor: Stephen Moore
Book Editor: David M. McCandless
Director of Production: Katherine G. Brown
Book Design: Jaclyn J. Boone
Cover: Sandra Blair Design and Brent Blair Photography, Harrisburg, Pa.

To Jonathan and Emily

Contents

Introduction   *xi*

_____ PART ONE _____

A C LANGUAGE PRIMER

1 Program design   **3**

Program conceptualization   3
Functional design   3
Technical design   9
Programming   12
Program implementation and maintenance   13
The compilation process   14
Structured programming   15
A conceptual overview   16
The use of the goto statement   19

2 Getting started with C   **21**

Writing a program   21

3 Data types and arithmetic operators   **27**

Variables and constants   27
Valid variable name formats   28
Variable data types   29
Arithmetic expressions and operators   35

4 Control statements   **41**

Conditional logic   41
The conditional operator   49
Looping   50

5 Arrays and character strings   **61**

Numeric arrays   61
Character arrays   65

6   Structures   **75**

Defining structures   75
Initializing structures   77
Arrays of structures   79
Structures within structures   81
Arrays within structures   82
Arrays of structures containing arrays   83

7   Pointers   **85**

Pointers and arrays   88
Pointers to structures   92

8   Functions   **97**

Calling functions   98
Passing and receiving parameters   99
Return values   101
Passing arrays   103
Global variables   105
Automatic and static variables   106
Parameter passing by value and address   108

9   Input and output   **109**

The `printf()` function   109
The `scanf()` function   111
The `putch()` function   113
The `getch()` function   115
Data redirection   115
Special file-handling commands   117
`stdin`, `stdout`, and `stderr`   120
Special IBM-PC inputs and outputs   120

10   Bitwise operations   **125**

The bitwise AND operator   125
The inclusive OR operator   127
The exclusive OR operator   128
The ones complement operator   130
The shift left operator   131
The shift right operator   133
Bit fields   134

11   The C precompiler   **137**

The `#define` directive   137
The `#include` directive   140
Conditional directives   142

12   Using APIs   **145**

Multifunction-based APIs   145
Control-block-based APIs   146
Protocol conversion protocols   146

13   C++ enhancements   **149**

C++ terms   149
C++ keywords and operators   154

PART TWO

A C LANGUAGE REFERENCE

14   Language operators   **159**

15   Storage classes and data types   **199**

16   Compiler directives   **215**

17   Common C statements and functions   **227**

18   C++ operators   **313**

PART THREE

A C TOOLBOX LIBRARY

19   Printer output functions   **325**

20   String functions   **348**

21   Data input functions (C++)   **359**

22   Array manipulation functions (C++)   **378**

23   Measurement conversion functions   **393**

24   Date functions   **414**

25   Mathematical functions   **506**

26   Push-down stacks   **520**

27   Making boxes on the screen   **538**

28   Making lines on the screen   **551**

29 UNIX-like filtering programs   577

Appendix A   Operator precedence   593

Appendix B   Data type conversions   595

Index   597

Introduction

Welcome to *The C Trilogy*. This introductory chapter discusses the book's format and content and provides a brief overview of program design, the compilation and linkage process, and various structured programming concepts.

How to use this book

This book has been designed to assist the programming neophyte, the seasoned computer professional, and all those who fall somewhere between these two polarized extremes. As the word "trilogy" suggests, this book is divided into three related but distinctly different parts.

Part One is a language tutorial designed to take a would-be C programmer by the hand and lead him/her through the maze of functions, rules, and idiosyncrasies that make C a versatile but sometimes hostile language. Additionally, because of its intricate level of detail, it might assist seasoned C programmers in conceptualizing and digesting those one or two concepts that have thus far alluded personal clarification.

Part Two is a generalized C user's reference manual. All too often, a software manufacturer creates an ingenious software compiler or application containing the latest state of the art algorithms but falls short in regard to non-technical, user- oriented software documentation. This section attempts to complement—but certainly not replace—these manufacturer-supplied C reference manuals by providing a less technically oriented explanations in a reference manual format. These explanations will hopefully provide you with the insight needed to understand this more sophisticated manufacturer documentation. In fact, I strongly suggest that you investigate the use of a statement or function using the following steps:

1. Read the function (or statement) explanation provided within your manufacturer-supplied documentation. If additional clarification is required, proceed to the next step.

2. Read the appropriate one-page explanation provided in Part Two of this book. If additional clarification is still needed, proceed to the next step.

3. Turn to the tutorial explanation of that topic within Part One of this book. Note that, where appropriate, the Part Two user reference manual cross references related topics in Part One.

Part Three, the final trilogy section, is a potpourri of ready-to-use functions. These functions can generally be grouped into the following categories:

Chapter 19   Printer output functions
Chapter 20   String manipulation functions
Chapter 21   Data input functions
Chapter 22   Array manipulation functions
Chapter 23   Measurement conversion functions
Chapter 24   Date functions
Chapter 25   Simple mathematical functions
Chapter 26   Push-down stack
Chapter 27   Display boxes on the screen
Chapter 28   Display lines on the screen
Chapter 29   UNIX-like filtering programs

This third part can be used in three primary ways. First, you could purchase a diskette from TAB Books containing these source code libraries. Second, you could create your own library by manually typing in appropriate functions. Last, you could use these functions for reference when writing your own functions.

Part One
A C Language Primer

1
Program design

Developing a program requires more than just sitting down and typing in the code. You must decide ahead of time what the program should do, how it should be structured, and how it should be implemented. To help you, this chapter discusses the program development process that should be followed to ensure the successful implementation of both stand-alone programs and entire applications.

The program development process is divided into these steps: conceptualization, functional design, technical design, programming, implementation, and maintenance.

Program conceptualization

All programs begin as an idea. In this stage, the originator of the idea (if time allows) tends to play mental "what-if" games in an effort to consolidate and refine the program's size and function. If the program still seems worthwhile after these mental exercises are complete, "back-of-the-envelope" analysis begins. In this step, the originator attempts to place thoughts on paper. To this end, s/he starts scratching out notes, report formats, input screens, or just lines and arrows alluding to the flow of data. Once these notes are reasonably complete and the program is conceptually designed in the author's mind, s/he must employ a more formalized and structured design approach: the functional design phase.

Functional design

The functional design phase is the process of formalizing the user's requirements and developing functional documentation. All programs, regardless of the application—whether financial, scientific, or process control—can be described in terms of its inputs, processes, and outputs. *Inputs* are the bits of information entered into a program. *Outputs* are the reports, files, screens, and such that are sent from the program to the users. *Processes* are the step-by-step instructions used to transform these inputs into outputs.

When defining these functional segments, the analyst should first define the program outputs, decide what program inputs are needed to create those outputs, and finally

3

develop the process needed to transform the inputs into the outputs. Many techniques have been developed to assist in this design process, among them being program logic flowcharts, data dictionaries, decision trees, and decision tables.

Program logic flowcharts

Flowcharts are a series of lines, boxes, and circles that graphically represent the logical process contained within a program. This technique is used to assist the analyst in describing the program in a way easily understood and simple to create and modify. The symbols employed by the flowcharting process are shown in Fig. 1-1.

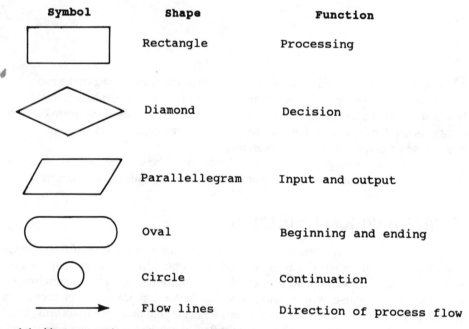

Symbol	Shape	Function
	Rectangle	Processing
	Diamond	Decision
	Parallellegram	Input and output
	Oval	Beginning and ending
	Circle	Continuation
	Flow lines	Direction of process flow

1-1 Most commonly used flowchart symbols.

In the report program logic flowchart example in Fig. 1-2, the files are opened and a record is read from the file. If a record is retrieved, it is formatted, written to the file, and another record is read. This process continues until an end-of-file condition is reached. At that time, the files are closed and the program ends.

This technique can be used to illustrate complex logic in a very simple way. Figure 1-3 shows the process needed to calculate an employee's gross pay.

In the gross pay calculation flowchart, two pay-related questions are asked. First, is the employee paid on an hourly or salaried basis? If the employee is salaried, then the gross pay is calculated as the hourly wage times forty regardless of the number of hours actually worked. If the employee is not salaried (hence hourly), a second question is asked regarding the number of hours worked. If the answer is forty or less, the gross pay is calculated as the hourly wage times the hours worked. Otherwise, the employee is paid for forty hours at the regular wage and time-and-a-half for all hours over forty.

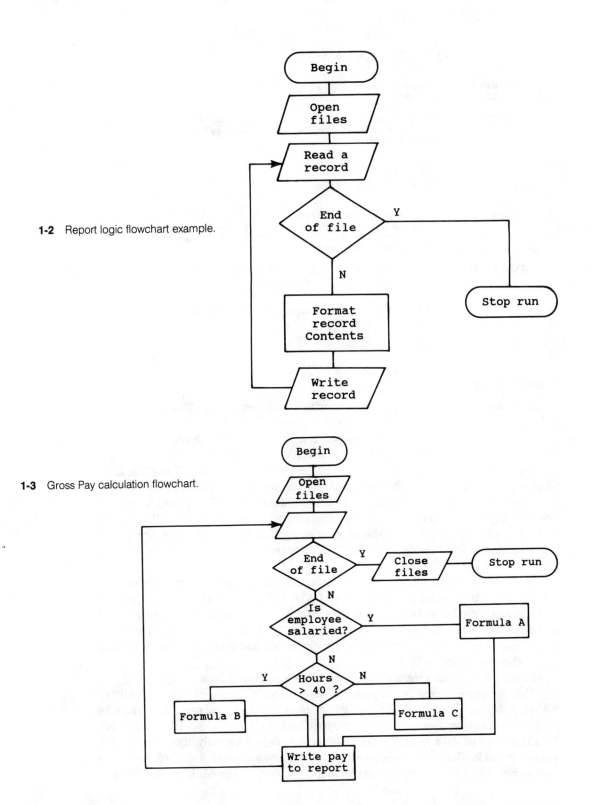

1-2 Report logic flowchart example.

1-3 Gross Pay calculation flowchart.

```
          F I L E   D E S C R I P T I O N   S H E E T


     FILE NAME     : Payroll Master File
     FILE ID       : PAYMAST.DAT

     DESCRIPTION   : This is the main payroll system master file
                     and contains all needed employee payroll
                     information.


     FILE LOCATION: The file is stored on tape and kept in the
                     computer room safe.


     SECURITY      : The data is considered confidential and company
                     proprietary. It may only be removed from the safe
                     for scheduled payroll runs or by the signature of
                     the payroll manager.

     DATA FIELDS   : emp_no, emp_name, emp_address, hourly_wage,
                     no_of_deduct, gross_pay


     MISC          : This file is also used as the main input to the
                     personnel system.
```

1-4   Data dictionary file description example.

Data dictionary

Data dictionaries are used to define the information contained within a data file. This tool is divided into two parts. The first part provides a description of the file including a list of its elements, while the second part contains detailed information about each field. Figure 1-4 shows an example of a fact sheet used to describe each data file.

The FILE NAME line states the name of the file being described. The FILE ID is filled in after the program's technical design is completed and the file is given the name that it will be referred to on disk or tape. The DESCRIPTION field provides a textual description of the file's function within the application being defined. The FILE LOCATION line refers to the file's physical location in regard to the disk drive or tape library where the data actually resides. The SECURITY entry is used to describe any security issues surrounding the files information.

For example, if a payroll master file is being described, then it can state the specific people or departments able to access it. The DATA FIELDS area is used to list the elements included within the data file. This list should be carefully entered because it is used as a cross reference to the data element information to be described shortly. The MISC area is used to place other information of specific interest and does not fit neatly into any of the other categories.

Figure 1-5 is the data element description for the EMP-NO field.

The data element field is comprised of seven specific categories. The ELEMENT NAME is the connection to the file description sheets and is also the name that should be used to describe the data field in the program's DATA DIVISION. The ELEMENT TITLE is a two or three word description of the data field. Generally, the words used in this title coincide with the abbreviations used in the element name. For example, as shown back in Fig. 1-5, EMP-NO has a title of "Employee Name." The SIZE AND FORMAT

```
ELEMENT NAME    : emp_no
ELEMENT TITLE   : Employee Number
SIZE AND FORMAT : char emp_no[6]

DESCRIPTION     : This is the employee identification number used
                  by the payroll system to uniquely identify each
                  employee.

SOURCE          : A number is assigned by personnel to each
                  employee at the time of hire.

UPDATE RULES    : This number should never be changed during the
                  employee's employment with the company and should
                  not be re-used after the employee's termination.

ALIASES         : Badge Number, Payroll Check ID Number.
```

1-5 Data element description example.

line describes the element's length and type in C data type definition format. This format is described in detail within Chapters 3 and 14. The DESCRIPTION explains the element's function or usage within the application. SOURCE describes the location or process from which the data was originally created. This might be a vendor's invoice or the accounting department' control handbook, automatically generated by the computer or other similar beginnings. The UPDATE RULES category specifies the rules and procedures that involve the modification and deletion of the element once it is originally entered into the system. The ALIASES section lists other names for the same element. For example, an employee number is often referred to as a badge number because it is displayed on the employee identification badges.

When applications require many data files, some data elements usually are contained in more than one file. When this is the case, you probably should maintain two separate alphabetic lists—one list containing the file description sheets and the other containing the element description sheets. This will avoid the step of rewriting the element information over and over when it pops up in many files. Additionally, a cross reference from the element description sheets to the data file description can be easily maintained by adding one more category to the former element sheets. This category would list the data files in which the element was used.

Decision trees

A decision tree is a technique defining and documenting the possible options associated with a given situation. One nicety of this definition process is that it is very easy to conceptualize and can therefore be instantly understood by non-technical users. Figure 1-6 shows how a decision tree can be used to illustrate the gross pay calculation previously defined during the flowcharting discussion.

As shown in Fig. 1-6, the decision tree begins with a block stating the problem or question being addressed. Stemming out from the block are two branches alluding to the two possible options of the question being asked, namely, "Is the employee compensated on a salaried or hourly basis?" If salaried, the tree ends and the appropriate gross pay calculation is displayed. However, if the employee is paid hourly, a circle is reached that

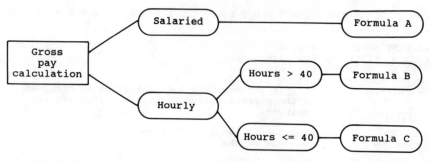

1-6 Decision tree example.

further divides the branch into two new lines. This circle and its newly formed branches are called an *event fork*, showing that one question has been answered but another has yet to be addressed. As with the original branches, each option is marked with its specific criteria and corresponding gross pay calculation.

Decision tables

Decision tables are yet another way to describe the alternatives associated with a given decision. In this technique, two lists are developed. The first, called a *condition list*, contains the criteria that must be evaluated; these questions must be answerable with just a yes or no. The second list contains the possible actions that could be taken.

The process used to connect the questions to the actions can most easily be explained through illustration. Figure 1-7 is a decision table again outlining the gross pay calculation example.

In this decision table example, each question places answers on one or more of three vertical columns. Each of these columns is associated with a particular action as is specified by an "X" in the action's specific row. The first gross pay calculation has an "X" in the first vertical column; therefore, if the answers in column one match the answers for a given employee, then the first formula should be used. For example, if the employee being analyzed was not salary and worked 35 hours, the first question is answered "N," the second is answered "Y," and the third is answered "N." These three responses match the

Condition list

Is the employee paid by salary ?	Y	N	N
Is hours worked greater than 40 ?		Y	N
Is hours worked less than or equal to 40 ?		N	Y

Action list

Formula A	x		
Formula B		x	
Formula C			x

1-7 Decision table example.

second column of the decision table; therefore the calculation `gross_pay = hourly _wage * hours_worked` should be used.

Lastly, note that in the second and third question the first column was left blank. This was done because if the first answer was yes, then the employee was salaried and the number of hours worked has no bearing on the action taken.

Technical design

Technical design is the process of defining a programs structure and detailed logic. To effectively describe this logic, the program being discussed should be divided into bite-size sections called modules. *Modules* are distinct program segments, each of which performs a specific function. The program structure is the way in which these modules interrelate. Detailed logic outlines the steps and algorithms that must be performed within each module to complete its logical function.

Like the design step, this process also contains formalized techniques to assist in the process. The techniques that shall be discussed here are HIPO, pseudocode, and program flowcharts.

HIPO charts

The word HIPO stands for *Hierarchical Input Process Output* technique. This method is comprised of two parts, the first of which is the development of a hierarchical structure chart arranging the program modules in a top-down fashion. The structure chart for a payroll check writing report is shown in Fig. 1-8.

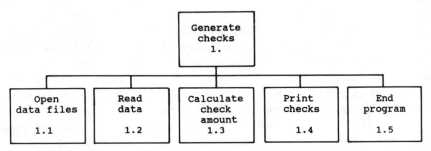

1-8 Example structure chart.

The structure chart in Fig. 1-8 illustrates the modules contained within a check generation program. The top module is Generate Checks, which is used to control the five subordinate level modules: Open Data Files, Read Data, Calculate Check Amounts, Print Checks, and End Program. When the program is executed, GENERATE CHECKS calls the OPEN FILES module. When complete, the program reads a record from the data file, calculates the amount to be paid, prints the check, and returns to module three to retrieve another record. This looping process will continue until the input file is out of records and the sixth module is called to close the files and end the program.

There are times when a single level of module detail will not adequately describe the program's breakdown. In these cases, subordinate modules can be further divided, as shown in Fig. 1-9.

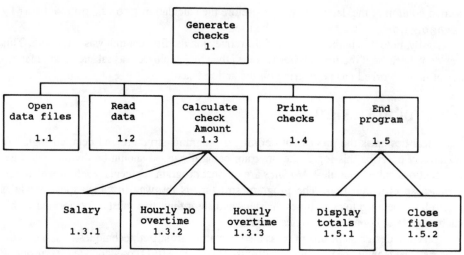

1-9 Second example structure chart.

In Fig. 1-9, additional levels of detail were added to module 1.3 and 1.5. These new levels were designed to provide a finer level of program detail. Remember, these specifications will be used by the programmer as the blueprint of a program's structure. Therefore, the better the design specifications, the easier it is for the programmer.

Note the numbering sequence used to identify the modules; this sequence allows each module to be traced back to its owner. When viewing these modules in a structure chart format, the numbering might seen rather unimportant. However, these numbers will also be placed in the individual module descriptions. There, the numbers will not only serve as a cross reference between the structure chart and module descriptions but will also assist in assessing the relationship between modules when the structure chart is not easily accessible. This numbering scheme also allows easy location of a module on a large complex structure chart. Even if a chart has hundreds of modules, any module can be quickly found by following its numbering sequence from level to level.

The second part of HIPO is the IPO charts. Recall that this stands for *Input/Process/ Output* and is used to provide detailed information about each module identified in the structure chart. Figure 1-10 shows the IPO chart associated with module 1.3 in the second structure chart example.

The IPO chart displayed in Fig. 1-10 is divided into many parts. The SYSTEM NAME is used to place the name of the application being designed. (In this case, the program being designed is part of the payroll system.) PROGRAM NAME is used to record the name of the program being written. The MODULE NAME and MODULE NUMBER are the cross reference to the structure chart. These two fields should be filled out identically to that in the structure chart. The PREPARED BY area specifies the person who completed the IPO form. The DATE field might contain either the date the chart was originally prepared or the date that it was approved. The particular date used will depend on the customs and style of the data processing department doing the work. In some places, both dates are required, and another date field is added to the form.

```
                    I P O   C H A R T

SYSTEM NAME    : Payroll           PREPARED BY  : E. Bloom
PROGRAM NAME   : PRL009.C          DATE         : 8/30/85
MODULE NAME    : Get Check Amount  APPROVED BY  : E. Wells
MODULE NUMBER  : 1.3

CALLED BY : 1. Create checks       IT CALLS : 1.3.1 Salaried
                                              1.3.2 Hourly no overtime
                                              1.3.3 Hourly with overtime

INPUTS : Hourly-wage, Salary-type,      OUTPUTS : Gross-pay
         Gross-pay, Hours-worked

DESCRIPTION : This module decides which gross pay calculation should
              be used and calls the appropriate module.

PROCESS    : If Salary-type = 'salaried'
                 Then do module 1.3.1
             Else
                 If Hours-worked <= 40
                    Then do module 1.3.2
                 Else
                    Do module 1.3.3


LOCAL DATA ELEMENTS : None          MISC : Gross pay is actually
                                           calculated in the submodules;
                                           and the value is passed back to
                                           this module and up to module 1.
```

1-10 IPO chart example.

The next section of the IPO chart describes how the module relates to other modules. The CALLED BY area lists the names and numbers of the modules that call the module being defined. The section IT CALLS states its subordinate modules. The INPUT and OUTPUT blocks list the variables passed to and from the module during processing.

The last chart section explains the processes that will be performed within the module. The DESC area provides a textual description of the modules process. The PROCESS area describes the needed module logic in a C-like format. This near C description is called Structured English and can later be easily transformed into code, thus assisting the programmer in writing the internal program logic. The LOCAL DATA ELEMENTS field is used to list those local variables only referenced within the module and not passed from place to place. Lastly, the MISC section is used to place pertinent information not fitting neatly into any other category.

Pseudocode

Pseudocode is a tool used to design and later document the processes within a module. This is done by using regular English words within a C-like format. The difference between this process and the structured English previously mentioned is that this includes all programming steps needed to execute the module and not just selected pieces of logic. In fact, the format of the pseudocode used on the design of a given application is dictated by the language in which the application will be programmed. However, because pseudocode is so close to the actual program coding, most programmers dislike it. Most programmers generally feel that, because the text being written is almost the actual program, why not just write the actual code? Figure 1-11 is an example of the pseudocode for a small report program.

Three types of commands are used in this pseudocode: functional, conditional logic, and repetition. The *functional* commands are executed in sequence and perform specific functions like opening and closing files, moving values from variable to variable, and doing mathematics. The If commands perform *conditional* logic, function calls allow sub-routining, and For, While, and Do-While facilitate *repetition* through looping. As shall be seen in Chapter 7, these three functions are very closely tied to structured programming ideologies.

```
Start:   Open master file for input
         Open report file for output
         Set record flag to NO
         Read report master file, at end set record flag to Yes
         If record flag is equal to No
            Perform loop until record flag is NO
         Close master file and report file
         Stop run

Loop :   Move master file data to report record
         Write report record to report file
         Read master file, at end move NO to record flag
```

1-11 Pseudocode example.

Programming

The programming phase consists of writing the source code and doing preliminary testing.

Writing the source code

Programs are written and entered into the computer in two different ways. You could first write out the program by hand on either plain lined paper or on some type of special coding form and then key it all into the computer. As an alternative, you could type the program directly into the computer without first writing it on paper (a procedure followed by more experienced programmers). The success of this second method is solely based on the talent of the programmer and the complexity of the application being developed. In either case, proper design specifications greatly assist in the process.

Preliminary testing

During the programming and compilation process, two basic types of programming bugs can and usually do occur: *syntactical errors* and *logical errors*. Syntax errors are easy to find because the program listing created during the compilation process tells the programmer exactly where the error occurred and provide some explanation of the problem. These errors are caused by statements not in the correct C format. For example, the statement while (x < 1) will cause an error because while is not a valid statement and therefore cannot be understood by the compiler.

Once the program being written is free of syntactical problems, logical errors must be identified and corrected. Logical errors are mistakes in the way the program processes the data. These errors are much more difficult to find and might periodically turn up for months or even years depending on the complexity of the program and the thoroughness of the testing process. To identify these errors, the programmer should develop a small set of test data. This data should contain information representative of that used in the application as well as information with out-of-range values and invalid formats. The valid data will assist in the testing of the program's processing logic, while the invalid information will test the program's error checking capabilities.

Program implementation and maintenance

The implementation of a program or system is the final step in the software development process. This step is comprised of final testing/implementation and program maintenance.

The final testing and implementation process

Once the program is completed and seemingly ready for production, it should go through one more round of testing, preferably not by the program's author. The author only should test to see if the program works, while others should test it to find the errors. The difference in mental attitude helps provide a more thorough and complete test. Also, the programmer has presumably tested the program prior to implementation and might therefore take a second round of testing less seriously than someone new.

A very common practice in testing new programs is to develop a testing team consisting of the program's author, a fellow programmer, and a future user of the program. The program's author is present only to provide technical background about the program's development, with the actual testing performed by the second programmer and the user.

This team approach seems to work well because the second programmer can evaluate the program's technical aspects without being hindered by a pride of authorship, and the user has the application knowledge to analyze the program's functional merit. Also, the user has a strong vested interest in that s/he will have to rely on the ability and accuracy of this program for the foreseen future.

Many techniques can be used to test programs; three of the most common are parallel testing, prior testing, and simulation testing.

Parallel testing is the process of running two systems simultaneously. Using this technique requires continuing the old methods and also doing things the new way. This additional responsibility could just be running another report over the weekend or it might mean manually inputting data into two systems. Once complete, the outputs of the two systems are compared. If the results are the same or at least reconcilable, then the new system continues and the old mode of operation is discontinued. If the test results are unsatisfactory, the problems must be discussed and appropriate changes made.

Parallel testing sounds good in theory but in actuality can sometimes be impractical or even impossible to perform, due to a lack of the resources needed to do twice the work or the inability to capture the data in two places at once. Therefore, two alternate approaches were developed that can be performed by just the testing team. The first of these techniques is called *prior testing*. This process uses the same principles as parallel testing, except that it uses data from past months. For example, if a new payroll system is being installed in November, establish the test files as of a few months before, say March. Then, enter April's actual data and compare the test reports to the actual April numbers. Continue this process through October; if all looks good, go with only the new system in November.

Simulation testing is similar to prior testing, except that the test data is strictly simulated. This alternative will not produce as thorough of a test, although it should suffice if the test data is selected carefully. To implement a system using this method, the files being used by the new programs should be copied and converted to the new format; on an appropriate day, the old method is stopped, and the the new method is started.

Program maintenance

Regardless of the implementation method used to operationalize the new program or system, maintenance programming is usually necessary—for many different reasons. Errors that must be corrected might be found in the code. Company policies or procedures might change. Growing firms might outgrow current systems or enhancements might be made to meet new business challenges. Whatever the reason, this task can be made easier if the software being written is well documented, written in a clear and concise structured format, and carefully modified as not to violate structured principles or outdate the documentation.

The compilation process

Once the source code is written and typed into the computer, it must be translated from a human-readable format into computer-readable form. This translation process, known as *compilation*, is illustrated in Fig. 1-12.

To compile a program, the programmer must execute the C compiler and specify the name of the program to be transformed. This process leaves the input source code

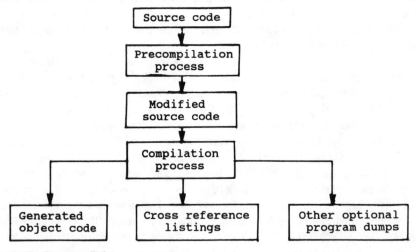

1-12 The compilation process.

unchanged and creates two outputs; a program listing and a file containing the program object code. The program listing is different than the source code listing because it contains information about the compilation, including the number of errors, the error locations, a variable cross reference list, and other similar information that can be used in the program debugging process. The object code is the source code in a computer-readable format (binary). Like many other languages, the C compilation process is performed in two main stages. The first stage is called *precompilation*, which modifies the source code as specified by the compiler directives discussed in Chapters 12 and 15. The second step is the actual compilation, which reads the modified source code, analyzes its syntax for errors, and generates the compiled object code.

After the compilation process is complete, one more step must be performed before the program can be executed—*program linkage*. The linkage process is illustrated in Fig. 1-13.

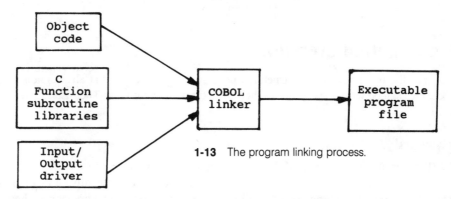

1-13 The program linking process.

The linkage process connects all the various processes needed to successfully execute the program and places them together in one file. In the linkage example, three files are being consolidated. The first file is the program's object code, while the second file contains the object code from a function library like those provided in Part Three of this book. The input/output driver is required by all executing programs regardless of the language in which it was written. This routine connects the program's logic to the terminals, disk drives, and other input or output devices. The particular linker you use will dictate whether this device driver is automatically called in during the linkage process or if it must be explicitly stated.

Structured programming

In the early days of computing, computer hardware was the major contributor to the data processing budget. At that time, with the cost of hardware so high and the cost of programming labor so relatively low, it made good business sense to write applications programs that used sophisticated and complex algorithms in an attempt to minimize the need for additional memory and storage. This programming emphasis saved on hardware acquisition expenditures at the cost of extensive labor hours and the development of complex software. In many cases, this software was so complex that it could not even be modified by the original author.

As the price of hardware began to decline, and the cost per programming hour began to increase, the price of developing and maintaining software became a more significant part of the data processing budget. As a result, a technique called *structured programming* was developed to improve programmer productivity.

When structured programming was implemented, improvements became noticeable in many areas. First, because of the self-documenting nature of structured programming, programs became easier to read and thereby easier to enhance or modify. Second, because the program's structure was generally the same from program to program, less time was spent in the program design phase. In addition, because of a common formalized structure, many programs could be created just by copying and modifying previously written programs (especially prevalent in regard to programs that generated reports). Third, due to the module-like nature of structured programs, they were easier to test and debug. Lastly, as a result of the previously discussed benefits, the software being developed was more reliable and had a longer production life.

A conceptual overview

Conceptually, the developers of structured programming theorized that all programming procedures can be written using one of three structures: sequential, If-Then-Else, and Do-While.

Sequential

The flowchart shown in Fig. 1-14 depicts the sequential processing of statements.

As shown below, the sequential processing structure is the consecutive execution of statements without the interuption of conditional logic or unconditional branching. Figure 1-15 is an example of sequentially processed statements.

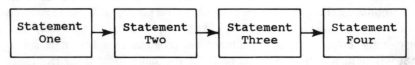

1-14 Sequential processing flowchart.

```
salary = hourly_wage * 40;
total_salary += salary;
printf("\n Employee Salary is %f",salary);
```

1-15 Sequentially processed statements.

There are very few programs that use just a sequentially processed statement. Most programs commonly have a group of statements much like those shown here incorporated into if-then-else logic or within a do-while looping structure.

If-Then-Else

The if-then-else structure is a very powerful and flexible part of the C language and is essential in the development of most business application programs. It defines the program's logic and causes the execution of selected statements based on specified criteria. In other words, IF a particular condition is met, THEN a function or group of functions is performed, ELSE (if the condition is not met) a different set of functions is performed. Figure 1-16 picturally represents the if-then-else logic.

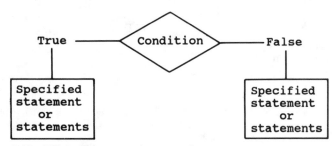

1-16 If-Then-Else processing examples.

Within the C language, this if-then-else structure is performed by the if statement. Even though C does not use the word then in the if statement format, it logically implies its function by the statements that are placed directly after the conditional expression. Figure 1-17 is an example of an if condition.

In the example, a value of 1 will be added to salary_count if pay_type equals "salaried." Otherwise, 1 will be added to the hourly employee counter hourly _count. Note that both these ADD statements will never be executed for the same employee. Therefore, this Then/Else relationship is always an "either/or" scenario.

```
if ( strcmp(pay_type,"salaried") == 0 )
    salary_count +=1;
else
    hourly_count +=1;
```

1-17 If-Then-Else conditional statement.

Do-While

The last of the structured constructs is the do-while format. This format is used for looping and instructs the computer to DO these statements WHILE a particular condition is true. Figure 1-18 shows a flowchart representing the do-while process.

Note in the do-while flowchart that the specified statements are always executed at least once, and then the condition is checked to see if the loop should continue. This processing order will have ramifications from a C perspective in regard to how and when the loop is processed. Figure 1-19 displays this looping process.

C also allows two other structured looping options—the while and for statements. The while statement is very similar to the do-while shown in Fig. 1-19. The two differ in that the statements contained within the while are not automatically executed once prior to assessing the test condition. Thus, if the test condition is not met, then the statements within the while loop will not be executed at all. Figure 1-20 is a flowchart picturally depicting the while looping process, and Fig. 1-21 lists an actual while statement.

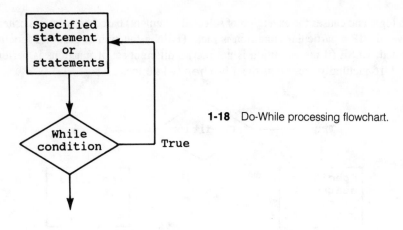

1-18 Do-While processing flowchart.

```
count = 0;
do
 { count++;
   printf("\n I will loop ten times");
 } while ( count < 10 );
```

1-19 Do-While processing example.

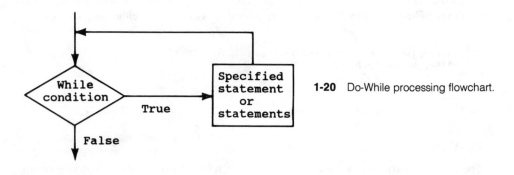

1-20 Do-While processing flowchart.

```
int count = 0;

while ( count < 10 )
 { printf("\n I will also print 10 times");
   count++;
 }
```

1-21 While processing example.

The for statement is yet another variation on the do-while structure. The "for" statement is designed to loop a specified number of times based on an incremented counter. Figure 1-22 describes this looping algorithm, and Fig. 1-23 is an actual C for statement.

18 *A C language primer*

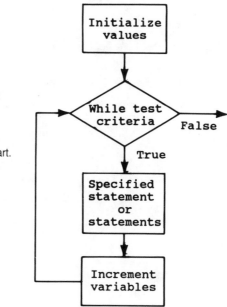

1-22 for processing flowchart.

```
int count;
for ( count=0; count < 10; count++ )
  { printf("\n I will also loop ten times");
  }
```

1-23 for processing example.

The use of the goto statement

Over the years, much debate has occurred over the use of the goto statement in structured programming environment. Many industry specialists believe that this statement has no place in modern programming and should be avoided under all circumstances. The other school of thought believes that goto provides a needed function and may be used if it does not hurt a program's readability and self-documenting nature. In the final analysis, however, the rules for using the goto statement will differ from company to company. Remember the goal is not to avoid goto statements but to write programs that are as clear, reliable, and self-documenting as possible.

2

Getting started with C

This chapter is designed to start you on your voyage through the C language. After reading this chapter, you should have an understanding of many C concepts and statements as well as the knowledge needed to write simple programs.

Writing a program

The only real way to learn a programming language is to write programs. Therefore, let's write a very simple program and expand upon it as new topics are discussed. As its first function, this program will add two numbers together and print their sum on the screen. Let's begin by having the program simply display the words "This program adds up two numbers."

The program doing this is shown in Fig. 2-1.

```
main()
{ printf("This program adds up two numbers");
}
```

2-1 First C program example.

This short program touches on many key points typical of all C programs regardless of their size. First, note that the program begins with the word "main" followed by a set of parentheses. Their combination—namely main()—states that the lines listed below it within the brackets are part of a function called "main." The concept of a function will be fully explained in Chapter 6; but, for now, consider it to be a group of related C statements that perform a specified predetermined task. The parentheses following the function's name are used to pass data values called *parameters* to the function. Even when there is no data to be passed, as is the case with main(), the parentheses are still required. Second, note that the statements (or, in this case, statement) below main() are enclosed within opening and closing curly brackets. These brackets signify the beginning and ending boundaries of the main() function. As shall be seen in later chapters, these brackets signify statement blocks and are required by all functions. Lastly, C, unlike most other programming languages, is case-sensitive and requires that all statement and function names be typed in lowercase (not in capital letters). For example, printf() and PRINTF() are not considered equal; the function must be called using the small letters—printf()—if that is how it was originally defined.

All C programs are (or should be) divided into functions executed when they are referenced within other functions. This referencing is done by placing a function's name within another function. For example, when looking at main(), another function called printf() is contained within main()'s brackets. This reference to printf() will cause the printf() function to execute, thus printing the words "This program adds up 2 numbers" on the screen. This process of executing functions from within other functions does however cause a small problem—namely, which function is executed first. To solve this problem, C requires all programs to have a function named main(); by default, this function is executed first.

Once again, let's turn turn our attention to printf(). This function, as you can well imagine, stands for "print function" and instructs the computer to display the words contained within the quotation marks on the screen. printf() is a standard library print routine supplied with all C ANSI compilers. When examining this function, three key points should be noted. First, the quotation marks are used to specify which characters are to be printed to the terminal. Second, like main(), printf() is followed by both opening and closing parentheses. These required parentheses contain the character string to be printed to the screen and is actually the parameter passed from main() to printf(). Lastly, note that the call to printf() ends with a semicolon. This semicolon is called a statement terminator and must be placed at the end of all C function calls (function references) and all other C statements.

Now that we have written a small C program, let's expand it to include some additional C code. Look at Fig. 2-2.

```
main()
{ int a, c;
  int b = 5;

  a = 10;
  c = a + b;

  printf("The sum of variables A and B is %d",c);
}
```

2-2 Second C program example.

This second program unfolds many new attributes of the C language. Look at the int statement. int stands for integer and is used to declare a, b, and c as variables that may only contain integer values. (Integers are whole numbers and therefore may not have a decimal part.) Table 2-1 shows a list of all standard variable data definition types. int, as well as the other variable type definitions, will be discussed in depth within Chapter 3.

Now examine the first int statements within Fig. 2-2. This first int states that a and c are integer variables. The second int statement defines variable b in a similar fashion to the first int statement. This int, however, has one additional component. This component is the " = 5 " clause. The equal sign followed by a 5 (or whatever value the variable assigned should have) initializes the variable being defined—namely b—to a

Table 2-1 Common data definition types.

Data definition	Data type
char	character
double	double precision floating point
float	floating point
int	decimal signed integer
long	long signed integer
short	short signed integer
unsigned	unsigned decimal integer

value of 5. This procedure can also be used to initialize variables to a value of 0. Unlike many other programming languages, you cannot make the assumption that the initial value of a variable is 0. Therefore, if a variable requires an initial 0 value, as would a counter or totaler, then you must explicitly assign a 0 to that variable. If you do not specifically assign a 0 value, it might by chance be a 0 today and another value tomorrow, causing inconsistent results. Therefore, if a variable is not initialized within its data type declaration statement, as is the case with a in the example, it is often initialized shortly afterwords. This initialization process is also discussed further in Chapter 3.

Once again looking at Fig. 2-2, let's analyze the statement c = a + b;. This is one of the many types of mathematical expressions that will be discussed within the next few chapters. This statement adds together the values contained within variables a and b and places the total in variable c. This mathematical statement is divided into three basic parts: the variable receiving the calculation—c; the equal sign, which causes c to be assigned to the value calculated in the equation; and the equation. In this example, the equation variables a and b are separated by a plus sign; as you might expect, the plus sign denotes addition. Thus, because a has a value of 10 and b has a value of 5, c will be assigned a value of 15.

When looking at the printf() function within Fig. 2-2, notice that some changes were also made within the parentheses. First, a %d was added within the double quotes; this %d, used within many standard C functions, specifies the type of variable being referenced (int, float, etc.) within the function and where the referenced variable should be placed within the printed string. A list of the % variable identifiers and their corresponding variable types is shown in Table 2-2.

Table 2-2 Common data definition "%" types.

Data definition	"%" code
char	%s
double	%lf
float	%f
int	%d
long	%ld

Back in Fig. 2-2, the %d is being used in the `printf()` function to state that c is an integer variable and that its value should be placed on the screen after the word "is," as shown next in Fig. 2-3.

```
The sum of variables A and B is 15
```

2-3 Output form second C program example.

The second addition to the `printf()` example in Fig. 2-2 is the \n clause at the beginning of the words to be printed. This clause instructs the computer to go to a new line before printing the rest of the text. Figure 2-4 shows an example usage of the \n clause, and Fig. 2-5 displays its resulting output.

```
main()
{ printf("\nThis is line 1 \n This is line 2 \n This is line 3");
}
```

2-4 \n programming example.

```
This is line 1
This is line 2      2-5   Output of program in Fig. 2-4.
This is line 3
```

To more completely explain the use of the %d clause within the `printf()` function, examine Fig. 2-6 shown next. In this example, a, b, and c are given the value of 1, 2, and 3 respectively. Then these variables are printed to the terminal via a `printf()` function.

```
main()
{ int a, c;
  int b = 5;

  a = 10;
  c = a + b;

  printf("The values of variables A,B and C are %d, %d and %d "a,b,c);
}
```

2-6 Another printf( ) example.

Note that, unlike the `printf()` function in Fig. 2-2, this example has three %d clauses and three corresponding variable names. The output of this program is shown in Fig. 2-7.

```
The values of variables A,B and C are 10, 5 and 15
```

2-7 Output from program in Fig. 2-6.

Now that we have completed work on our first C program, we must document it. Documentation can be placed directly within the program by placing it between the comment compiler directives—"/*" marks the beginning of a comment and "*/" denotes the end of the comment area and the continuation of C source code. Figure 2-8 shows how the working program discussed in Fig. 2-6 can be documented.

As a final thought, over the years of documenting programs written in C and other languages, programmers have sought to develop techniques that would make their internal program documentation easy to find and read. As a result, many programmers try to highlight their comments by using one of the formats shown in Fig. 2-9.

```
/* ****************************************
 * Program Name : Fig8_6
 * Author       : Eric P. Bloom
 * Description  : This program adds up two
 *                 numbers and prints the
 *                 total on the screen.
 **************************************** */
main()
{ int a, c;
  int b = 5;

  a = 10;
  c = a + b;  /* This line calculates the sum to be printed */

  printf("The values of variables A,B and C are %d, %d and %d "a,b,c);
}
```

2-8 Documented printf( ) example.

```
Ex. 1        j++;       /* on same line as a statement */

Ex. 2        /* Outlining a group of comment lines by
              * placing asterisks at the beginning of
              * each commented line.
              */

Ex. 3        /*
               Just using the beginning and ending
               indicators with no additional asterisk
               blocking.
              */

Ex. 4        /*******************************************
              * Outlining the comments within a four-  *
              * sided asterisk box.                    *
              *******************************************/

Ex. 5        /* Outlining each line of the comments  */
             /* with its own beginning and ending    */
             /* comment indicators.                  */
```

2-9 Documentation examples.

Data types and arithmetic operators

This chapter explains and illustrates the various C data definition types and provides an in-depth discussion of C's wide range of arithmetic operators.

Variables and constants

As a new programmer, the first conceptual hurdle to be overcome is that of constants and variables. *Variables* are labels representing locations in the computer's memory. For example, when you define a variable by entering int a; (as was done in Chapter 2), you are actually reserving a place in memory that can be referenced through a variable named a. Therefore, variable a may only contain integer values that can physically fit in that reserved memory location. Additionally, because the value within a memory location can change, the value of variable a can be changed. A constant, unlike a variable, does not point to a location in memory; it is just a specified value. For example, the number 7 is a constant; and as you can see, the value 7 by definition will never have any other value.

The founders of C developed a concept that closely parallels this idea of variables and constants—the concept of "lvalues" and "rvalues," representing left value and right value (respectively). These values allude to the type of values (variable or constant) that can be on each side of an equation.

Lvalues are variables associated with memory locations and may therefore receive a value. Note that this concept of receiving a value alludes to being on the left side of the equal sign within an equation. For example, in the equation a = b + 7, a will receive the value of the expression b + 7. Note also that the a variable is on the left side of the equal sign—thus, the term "lvalue" is coined. As a result of this idea, lvalues refer to any entity that can logically be placed on the left side of the equal sign within an equation.

Rvalues are constants, functions, and other entities that may only reside on the right side of the equal sign. For example, the equation 7 = x + 1 does not make sense because 7 cannot be set to the value of x + 1. Remember, in C, this equation is not solving the value of x; it is trying to set the number 7 equal to the value of the arithmetic expression x + 1. This inability of the number 7 causes it and all constants to be rvalues because it cannot logically be placed on the left of the equal sign. Table 3-1 provides a list of valid rvalue lvalue types.

Table 3-1 Valid lvalues and rvalues.

Type	lvalue	rvalue
Variables	yes	yes
Constants	no	yes
Functions	no	yes
Math expressions	no	yes

Valid variable name formats

When choosing program variable names, many things must be considered, such as name syntax, reserved words, function names, capitalization of letters, and documentation.

The C language, like all languages, has certain rules that must be followed when constructing a variable's name. These rules specify what characters may be used within the name, how the name must begin, and its minimum and maximum length. In C's case, variable names may contain letters, numbers, and underlines; however, they must begin with either an underline or a letter (i.e., no numbers). Additionally, the length of a variable is categorized in two ways: total length and significant length. Generally, variable names may have a total length of up to thirty characters. However, some older compilers only use the first eight characters and consider any additional letters to be purely documentational. This split rule gives you the flexibility to use long meaningful names but requires that you make the first part of that name unique.

Reserved words are words like if, int, double, and while that have special meaning to the compiler. They should not be used as variable names because it might confuse programmers who must later modify your program. Also, in most instances, a compilation error will occur if you try to use one of these words as a variable.

Function names should also never be used as the name of a variable. Even though this dual naming concept will in many cases compile and execute, it is extremely poor programming practice and can greatly degrade your program's readability. It may also cause future syntax errors if the program is modified in a way that places the variable name and its identically named function in the same program area.

The capitalization of letters within variable names must be carefully employed. Remember, C is case-sensitive. For example, total, Total, and TOTAL are viewed by C as three different and distinct variables. It is strongly suggested within the programming industry that all variables are written using only lower or mixed-case letters, saving upper-case (capitals) for special situations—like within compiler directives.

As a last note, documentation value can be increased by using helpful, descriptive names that explain how a variable is being used. For example, cash_ytd could be the variable used to hold the amount of cash that has been received year to date. However, remember the rules on variable length. total_cash_ytd (total cash received year to date) and total_cash_mtd (total cash received month to date) are seen by the compiler as total_ca and are therefore considered the same variable. To keep your names documented and unique, place the variable's distinguishing feature first. For example, rename total_cash_ytd and total_cash_mtd to ytd_total_cash and mtd_total_cash, thus making them ytd_tota and mtd_tota to the compiler. Table 3-2 list examples of both valid and invalid variable names.

Table 3-2 Valid and invalid variable names.

Valid names	Invalid names
count	1_name
total_pay	name-1
name_1	total$pay
last_name	last name
Help_flag	123
f100_type	100_type
_my_var	

Variable data types

As you now know, variable names are actually pointers (or labels, so to speak) of specified locations in memory. Now let's talk about the format of these locations. Physically, a memory location on the IBM-PC is nothing more than sixteen on/off switches collectively called a *byte* and individually called *bits*. It is up to the software to interpret the meaning of these bits. Therefore, in an attempt to maximize C's flexibility, as is done with many programming languages, you are given many options of how to store the data in these memory areas. This is where variable data types come into play. When you define a variable as an int, float, or other data type, you are actually specifying how the data associated with that variable should be stored in memory. Table 3-3 lists the standard variable data types.

Table 3-3 Common data definition types.

Data definition	Data type
char	character
double	double precision floating point
float	floating point
int	decimal signed integer
long	long signed integer
short	short signed integer
unsigned	unsigned decimal integer

The int data type

The int data type states that the variable being defined may only contain integer values ranging from -32,768 to 32,767. Mathematically speaking, an integer is a numeric value that may possess a negative sign and does not have a fractional (decimal) part. For example, 10 and -10 are valid integer values, while 5.2 is not because of the .2 decimal component. In fact, if you try to move the number 5.2 to an integer variable, the .2 will be truncated and the number will be stored as 5 with the .2 being permanently discarded. Table 3-4 lists both valid and invalid integer values.

The next question at hand is why the integer range is restricted from -32,768 to 32,767. Remember, the IBM PC is a sixteen-bit machine and thus can only create 65,536

Table 3-4 Valid and invalid integers.

Valid integers	Invalid integers
0	.5
5	12.34
10	50000
-15	

(2 to the 16th power) different combinations. However, you do have many options that allow you to easily overcome this limitation. You can use the unsigned int or long int data types if you want to stay with an integer data type or float and double if you are willing to move to a floating point format. These other data types will be discussed soon.

One advantage of integer numbers is the relative ease with which you can print the octal (base 8) and hexadecimal (base 16) equivalents of the current decimal (base 10) number. These alternative numbering systems are very commonly used in the computer world because they can be easily converted to binary (base 2), which is the numbering system ultimately used by all computers. An octal equivalent of a decimal can be displayed by replacing the letter d after the % within the printf() function with the letter o. Alternatively, a decimal's hexadecimal equivalent can be displayed using the printf() function by replacing the d after the % with the letter x. Examples of these alternate print types can be found in Fig. 3-1.

Program
```
main()
{ int a_variable
  a_variable = 45;

  printf("\nThese are values of %d", a_variable)'
  printf("\n    This is decimal     = %d", a_variable);
  printf("\n    This is octal       = %o", a_variable);
  printf("\n    This is hexadecimal = %x", a_variable);
}
```

Output
```
These are values of 45
      This is decimal     = 45
      This is octal       = 55
      this is hexadecimal = 2d
```

3-1 Printing octal and hexadecimal equivalents.

This numeric conversion can also be done in reverse, i.e., from an octal or hexadecimal value to decimal. As shown in Fig. 3-2, if an 0 is placed before the number being assigned, the assigned number will be construed as an octal value. Alternatively, a number may be defined as hexadecimal by placing an 0x before the number being assigned.

The float data type

The float data type states that the variable being defined may contain floating point numeric variables. Floating point numbers are values that may optionally contain whole numbers, decimal values, or both. Additionally, variables defined using the float can

Program
```
main()
{ int a_variable

  a_variable = 055;
  printf("\n Decimal is = %d from octal input", a_variable);

  a_variable = 055;
  printf("\n Decimal is = %d from hex input", a_variable);
}
```

Output
```
Decimal is = 45 from octal input
Decimal is = 85 from hex input
```

3-2 Octal and hexadecimal changed to decimal equivalents.

contain values in scientific notation also known as exponential notation. Table 3-5 lists examples of valid floating point numbers.

Floating point variables can be assigned a value in either standard numeric format (123.45) or in scientific notation (1.2345e2). If the latter is used, then the correct format is the mantissa (1.2345), followed by the letter e, followed by the appropriate exponent (2)—see Fig. 3-3. Additionally, like integers, floating point numbers may be displayed via the printf() function. To print floating point numbers in a standard notation format, use %f; and use %e for scientific notation. This printf() usage is shown also in Fig. 3-3.

Table 3-5   Valid floats.

Valid floats

0
5
-10.5
1.234e6
1.234e-3

Program
```
main()
{ float a_variable;

  a_variable = 12.6e5;
  printf("\n\nValue entered");
  printf("\n      The value is %f",a_variable);
  printf("\n      The value is %e",a_variable);

  a_variable = 12.345;
  printf("\n\nValue entered");
  printf("\n      The value is %f",a_variable);
  printf("\n      The value is %e",a_variable);
}
```

Output
```
Value entered
      The value is 1260000.000000
      The value is 1.260000e+06

Value entered
      The value is 12.345000
      The value is 1.234500e+1
```

3-3 Example floating point program.

The double data type

The double data type stands for double precision floating point and is essentially just a large float. To achieve this larger size, the compiler stores the variable's value in two memory locations instead of one; hence, the term double precision. From a programming perspective, with the exception of the ability to hold large numbers, a double and a float can be treated as the same. In fact, many compilers automatically place floating point numbers in memory using the double precision format. Even though these two data types are very similar, do not use them interchangably because rounding and truncation errors might occur. Figure 3-4 shows an example of the double data type.

Program
```
main()
{ double a_variable;

    a_variable = 12.6e5;
    printf("\n\nValue entered");
    printf("\n       The value is %f",a_variable);
    printf("\n       The value is %e",a_variable);

    a_variable = 12.345;
    printf("\n\nValue entered");
    printf("\n       The value is %f",a_variable);
    printf("\n       The value is %e",a_variable);
}
```

Output
```
Value entered
      The value is 1260000.000000
      The value is 1.260000e+06

Value entered
      The value is 12.345000
      The value is 1.234500e+1
```

3-4 Example double floating point program.

The long data type prefix

The long data type prefix can be placed before int and float and instructs the compiler to store the specified variable across two memory locations instead of one, thus doubling its size. In fact, a double data type is actually a long float. Very often, however, when the word long is followed by a variable name and no data type is specified, the default long data type is an int. Therefore, long a_variable and long int a_variable can be considered equivalent expressions.

As previously discussed, remember that the valid int values ranged from -32,768 to 32,767. When an integer is stored over two memory locations instead of one, the possible range of numbers expands to a range of -2,147,483,648 to 2,147,483,647. One drawback to using long int, however, is that it requires twice as much memory space. Therefore, if memory size is a critical concern in your application, you should use this feature only sparingly.

Figure 3-5 illustrates the use of the long data type prefix.

Program

```
main()
{ long int a_variable;
  long b_variable;

  a_variable = 100;
  printf("\n\nValue entered");
  printf("\n     The value is %d",a_variable);
  printf("\n     The value is %ld",a_variable);

  b_variable = 75;
  printf("\n\nValue entered");
  printf("\n     The value is %d",b_variable);
  printf("\n     The value is %ld",b_variable);
}
```

Output

```
Value entered
     The value is 100
     The value is 100

Value entered
     The value is 75
     The value is 75
```

3-5 long int programming example.

The short data type

The short data type refers specifically to integers and in fact is an abbreviation of short int, which is also valid. The idea behind a short integer is that you can store a number in one half of a memory location, allowing two numbers to be stored in one physical memory address and thus saving memory space. On the IBM PC, however, as you can well imagine, this would only allow for very small numbers. Therefore, most PC-based compilers treat a short integer like a regular int. As a result, short integers are primarily seen on PC's when the software has either come from or is going to a mainframe computer.

Figure 3-6 illustrates the use of the short data type.

Program

```
main()
{ short int a_variable;
  short b_variable;

  a_variable = 100;
  printf("\n\nValue entered");
  printf("\n     The value is %d",a_variable);
  printf("\n     The value is %ld",a_variable);

  b_variable = 75;
  printf("\n\nValue entered");
  printf("\n     The value is %d",b_variable);
  printf("\n     The value is %ld",b_variable);
}
```

Output

```
Value entered
     The value is 100
     The value is 100

Value entered
     The value is 75
     The value is 75
```

3-6 short int programming example.

The unsigned data type

The unsigned data type also refers specifically to integers and is actually short for unsigned int, which may also be used. If you recall from the section on integers (int), a regular integer value may range from -32,768 to 32,767. This was because the IBM-PC is a sixteen-bit machine, meaning that each memory location contains sixteen on/off switches called bits. These sixteen bits can combine to form only 65,546 possible combinations of on/off. Integers divide this range of possible values into three parts; 32,768 combinations to stand for negative numbers, one combination to stand for zero and 32,767 combinations for positive numbers. However, if the compiler knows that there will not be any negative numbers (thus all being either the value 0 or else positive), it can use 65,535 on/off combinations to represent positive numbers and as the one combination to represent 0. This shifting of numeric values makes the valid numbering range 0 to 65,535. Figure 3-7 illustrates the use of the unsigned integer data type.

Program

```
main()
{ unsigned int a_variable;
  unsigned b_variable;

  a_variable = 100;
  printf("\n\nValue entered");
  printf("\n      The value is %d",a_variable);
  printf("\n      The value is %ld",a_variable);

  b_variable = 75;
  printf("\n\nValue entered");
  printf("\n      The value is %d",b_variable);
  printf("\n      The value is %ld",b_variable);
}
```

Output

```
Value entered
      The value is 100
      The value is 100

Value entered
      The value is 75
      The value is 75
```

3-7 unsigned int programming example.

The char data type

The char data type is used to store a single alphanumeric character like "A", "x", "1", and "?". As shall be seen in later chapters, these character fields can be grouped together into strings of characters called arrays. These arrays can then in turn be used to store names, addresses, and other similar alphabetic data.

Technically speaking, a character variable contains the ASCII numeric equivalent of the character being stored. For example, the character "S" is represented by the number 83, and the character "1" is represented by an ASCII value of 49. ASCII stands for *American Standard Code of Information Interchange* and is used within computers to numerically identify the valid computer character set. In simpler terms, consider ASCII to be a coding system similar to Morse code but uses zeros and ones instead of dots and dashes. Thus, as you can see, an integer value of 1 and the ASCII code associated with the character "1" are not the same. This concept will be become more obvious after reviewing Fig. 3-8.

Data can be moved into a `char` variable in four primary ways: by constant, octal constant, decimal value, and octal value. A constant value is moved to a character variable by placing that character within single quotes (`a_char = 'S';`). An octal constant is moved to a character variable by placing a backslash followed by the octal value of the appropriate character within single quotes (`a_char = '\123';`). An integer may also be used to specify the appropriate character by moving the character's decimal character value to the `char` variable (`a_char = 83;`). Lastly, an octal variable may be used to set a character variable by passing the appropriate octal value (`a_char = 0123;`). From a data output perspective, the variable within a `char` data type variable can be printed using the `printf()` function by placing a %c in the print mask and the variable name to be printed in the `printf()` argument list.

These data movements are illustrated in Fig. 3-8.

Program
```
main()
{ char a_char;

    a_char = 'S';
    printf("\n\nValue entered");
    printf("\n        The value is %c",a_char);

    a_char = '\123';
    printf("\n\nValue entered");
    printf("\n        The value is %c",a_char);

    a_char = 83;
    printf("\n\nValue entered");
    printf("\n        The value is %c",a_char);

}
```

Output
```
Value entered
        The value is S

Value entered
        The value is S

Value entered
        The value is S

Value entered
        The value is S
```

3-8 char programming example.

Arithmetic expressions and operators

Like all programming languages, C has the ability to perform mathematical tasks by combining numeric variables and arithmetic operators into mathematical expressions. The numeric variables are defined using the various numeric data types previously discussed. The arithmetic operators are symbols like " + " and " − ", which tell the compiler which mathematical process to perform. These operators are broken down into three types: standard expressions, unary expressions, and increment/decrement.

Standard expressions

There are five standard arithmetic expressions: "+", "−", "*", "/", and "%" standing respectively for addition, subtraction, multiplication, division, and remainder. Table 3-6 lists some examples of the operators and the outcome of their equations.

Table 3-6   Standard expression mathematical examples.

Expression	Before a	b	c	After a	b	c
a = b + c	1	2	3	5	2	3
a = b - c	1	2	3	-1	2	3
a = b * c	1	2	3	6	2	3
a = b / c	1	4	2	2	4	2
a = b % c	1	9	5	4	9	5

When reviewing the examples in Fig. 3-6, you shall see the percent ("%") operator. This operator does not calculate a percent but instead calculates the remainder that would be generated if two integers (those on the left and right of the percent sign) were divided. For example, given the equation a = 3 % 2 ; , a would be given a value of 1.

Figure 3-9 illustrates some examples of this operator.

Program
```
main()
{ int a;
  int b = 3;
  int c = 2;

  a = b % c;

  printf("\n Remainder is = %d",a);

  a = 8 % 5;
  printf("\n Remainder is = %d",a);

  a = 4 % c;
  printf("\n Remainder is = %d",a);

  a = 8 % b;
  printf("\n Remainder is = %d",a);
}
```

Output
```
Remainder is = 1
Remainder is = 3
Remainder is = 0
Remainder is = 2
```

3-9 "%" remainder operator example.

When combining these operators into a single formula, you should take care to ensure that the mathematical processes are performed in the expected order. C evaluates mathematical equations in a way consistent with mathematical principles of precedence. This precedence first processes expressions within parentheses left to right, then multiplication and division left to right, and then addition from left to right.

For example, the equation a = 1 + 2 * 3 will give a a value of 7. First, the 2 and 3 are multiplied, giving a value of 6; then 1 is added to 6, making a total of 7. Therefore, a

= 1 + 2 * 3 and a = 1 + (2 * 3) are equivalent expressions. If however, you want to add the 1 and 2 first and then multiply the sum by 3, the equation should be written a = (1 + 2) * 3. The general rule regarding when to use these parentheses is to always use them, thus forcing the proper order of operation; also, as a by-product, you have improved the formula's documentation.

Table 3-7 lists example formulas and displays their expected result.

Table 3-7 Sample mathematical formulas.

Expression	Result
a = (1 + 2) * 3	9
a = 1 + 2 * 3	7
a = 1 + (2 * 3)	7
a = 2 * (1 + 1) / 2	2
a = 1 + (2 + 6) / 4	3

Unary expressions

Unary expressions perform the same processes as the standard arithmetic operators previously mentioned, the only difference being format, ease of typing, and (most important) the creation of more efficient compiled object code. Table 3-8 lists these unary operations and their standard arithmetic equivalents.

Table 3-8 Sample unary arithmetic operators.

Unary	Standard
a + = b	a = a + b
a + = 2	a = a + 2
a * = 3	a = a * 3
a - = c	a = a - c
a % = b	a = a % b
a / = b	a = a / b
a / = 4	a = a / 4

As can be seen earlier in Fig. 3-8, a unary equation is comprised of three primary parts; the variable being calculated, the unary operator, and the ending variable or constant. The variable being calculated is on the left of the operator. The unary operator specifies the process to be performed, and the variable or constant on the right is the value being used to complete the equation. At first glance, these unary operators seem to be more trouble than they are worth, but they were incorporated into the language for the specific purpose of generating more efficient compiled machine code. More efficient code can be created because the use of a unary operator signifies to the compiler that only one operation will be performed within the equation and that the first variable will be receiving the calculated value. This information allows the compiler to optimize the way it performs the mathematical process, thus generating less machine instructions.

Increment/decrement expressions

The increment and decrement operators are yet another attempt to assist the compiler in the generation of machine code. These operators are "++" and "--". The ++ cause its associated variable to be incremented by 1, thus making a = a + 1 and a++ equivalent equations. This operator however, has one additional feature.

As you review various C programs, you will see that sometimes the ++ is before the variable being incremented and sometimes it is after the variable. When the ++ is before the variable, the increment is performed prior to the execution of the statement or function in which the variable resides. When the ++ is after the variable, the increment is performed after its associated statement or function is performed. In Fig. 3-10, for example, a is set to an initial value of 1 prior to each printf() function call. Additionally, note that in the first printf(), the ++ is before variable a; and in the second printf(), the ++ is after its associated variable.

Program
```
main()
{ int a;

    a = 1;
    printf("\n A has a value of %d with ++ before the a",++a);

    a = 1;
    printf("\n A has a value of %d with ++ after the a",a++);
}
```

Output
```
A has a value of 2 with ++ before the a
A has a value of 1 with ++ after the a
```

3-10 "++" incremental operator example.

The decrement operator -- acts exactly like the ++ operator, with the one exception that it subtracts one from its associated variable's value. Figure 3-11 illustrates the use of this operator.

To sum up the three types of arithmetic operators, Table 3-9 shows all three operator types and, where applicable, highlights equivalent expressions.

Program
```
main()
{ int a;

    a = 1;
    printf("\n A has a value of %d with -- before the a",--a);

    a = 1;
    printf("\n A has a value of %d with -- after the a",a--);
}
```

Output
```
A has a value of 0 with -- before the a
A has a value of 1 with -- after the a
```

3-11 "--" decremental operator example.

Table 3-9 Sample unary arithmetic operators.

Unary	Standard	Increment/Decrement
a + = b	a = a + b	
a + = 2	a = a + 2	a+ +
a * = 3	a = a * 3	
a - = c	a = a - c	a--
a % = b	a = a % b	
a / = b	a = a / b	
a / = 4	a = a / 4	

4

Control statements

All the programs listed and explained thus far begin executing at the first encountered statement or function, continue executing line by line until each line has been executed once, and then end. This type of program is an excellent vehicle to illustrate the usage of a particular statement, function, or operator, but are not very realistic in regard to the functionality that would be required from even the simplest of programs. To create more complex programs, the programmers require the ability to optionally execute statements based on some specified criteria, as well as the ability to optionally repeat the execution of selected statements when performing reiterative processes.

In order to explain the statements needed to perform these complicated tasks, I have divided this chapter into three parts coinciding with the three types of control statements: conditional logic, looping, and transfer of control.

Conditional logic

Conditional logic is the ability to appropriately respond to specified circumstances. In a programming context, this means that the program being executed can determine what tasks to perform by assessing what must be done. In essence, if the test criteria is met, certain statements will be executed. Conversely, if the test is not met, other statements (if present) will be executed. See Fig. 4-1.

Within Fig. 4-1, the user is being asked to enter the type of pay to be calculated. If the person is paid hourly, the user is asked to enter the hourly rate of pay and the number of hours worked. Once entered, the program calculates the gross pay amount. If the person being paid is a salaried employee, the user is just asked to enter the hourly rate. Once entered, the program calculates the gross pay based on an assumed forty hours worked. Then, regardless of the payment type, the gross pay amount is displayed to the user.

Now that we have seen and discussed this procedure from a conceptual viewpoint, let's reshape Fig. 4-1 from a flowchart-type format into one that more resembles a program (see Fig. 4-2).

In this reworded format, note that the first statement is testing for the "hourly" pay type, that being followed by the activities to be performed, if the entered employee is

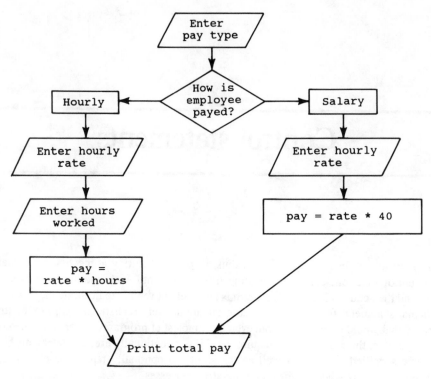

4-1 Conceptual payroll procedural logic.

```
Enter employee's pay type

If the pay type is salaried ( code is 'S' )
  Enter hourly rate
  Gross pay = hourly rate * 40 ( hours )
Else
  Enter hourly rate
  Enter hours worked
  Gross pay = hourly rate * hours worked

Print gross pay
```

4-2 Reworked Gross Pay calculation.

hourly. Then comes the word else, followed by the activities to be executed if the employee is salaried (not hourly). This example parallels the format and structure of the if statement, which is C's primary tool for facilitating conditional logic.

Now that we have seen two conceptual views of the pay calculation, let's move to the actual C program that will perform it.

The IF statement

The IF statement is divided into three sections; conditional logic, positive statements, and else statements. The word if begins the conditional logic section and is followed by the conditions to be examined. Next are the positive statement(s)— commands to be executed

Program

```
main()
 { char pay_type;
   float hours;
   float rate;
   float grosspay;

   printf("\n Enter pay type ( S=salaried, H=hourly) : ");
   scanf("%c",&pay_type);

   if ( pay_type == 'S' )
     { printf("\n Enter hourly rate : ");
       scanf("%f",&rate);
       grosspay = rate * 40;
     }
   else
     { printf("\n Enter hourly rate : ");
       scanf("%f",&rate);
       printf("\n Enter hours worked : ");
       scanf("%f",&hours);
       grosspay = rate * hours;
     }

   printf("\n\n  Gross pay is = %.2f",grosspay);
 }
```

Output

Ex. 1   Enter pay type (S=salaried, H=hourly) : S

         Enter hourly rate : 10

         Gross pay is = 400.00

Ex. 2   Enter pay type (S=salaried, H=hourly) : H

         Enter hourly rate : 7.50

         Enter hours worked : 10

         Gross pay is = 75.00

4-3 Gross Pay calculation program.

if the i f conditions are met. The optional e l se statement(s) begin with the word e l se and are only executed when the i f conditions are not met. Figure 4-4 shows the i f statement format.

Figure 4-5 shows some IF statement examples.

The first i f statement in Fig. 4-5 checks to see if hours_worked is greater than 40. If it is, the condition is satisfied and overtime() is executed. If hours_worked is less than or equal to 40, the i f condition is not met, overtime() is not executed and program control is passed to the next sequential statement.

The second i f statement example is very similar to the first. The difference is that an else clause has been added. This else clause states that if the specified condition (hours_worked > 40) is not true, then execute reg_time().

```
if ( condition )
    statement or statement block
else
    statement or statement block
```

4-4 if statement format.

```
Ex. 1    if ( hours_worked > 40 ) overtime(emp_no);

Ex. 2    if ( hours_worked > 40 )
             overtime(emp_no);
         else
             regular(emp_no);

Ex. 3    if ( employee_status = 'A')
             ;
         else
             error_flay = 'Yº;

Ex. 4    if ( employee_status == 'A' )
             { active(emp_no);
               status_indicator = 'A';
               ++employee_count;
             }
         else  ++error_count
               error_par(emp_no);


Ex. 5    if ( a )
             printf("\n A has a non-zero value");
         else
             printf("\n A has a value of zero");
```

4-5 if statement examples.

The third i f statement tests for employees with a status code of A for active and does nothing if one is. This is coded by placing a semicolon after the i f condition with no corresponding statement, thus serving as a placeholder prior to the e l se clause. In context, the underlying logic is to do nothing if the employee is active but to set an error flag to Y if the employee is not active.

The fourth example in Fig. 4-5 contains two new aspects of the i f statement. First is the option of executing many statements after the conditional logic and e l se clause. When exercising this option, note that the statements are enclosed within brackets; these statements are collectively called a *statement block*. This block informs the compiler that all of the statements within it are to be executed based on the outcome of its associated i f statement. The statement block concept will be seen again when we discuss looping techniques later in this chapter. The second new aspect of the fourth example is the format that should be followed when using multi-line i f statements. This format is designed to ease readability by vertically lining up the words i f and e l se and evenly indenting the condition logic and statements being executed. Also, remember that a semicolon must be placed at the end of each executable statement within the i f.

The fifth and final example in Fig. 4-5 illustrates a new key concept. The i f conditions that we have thus far discussed, like a = = =b and a<b¦¦b>c, perform an evaluation. Once evaluated, the expression produces a zero value if the expression is false and a non-zero value if the condition is true. It is this zero/non-zero value that is used by the i f statement to assess the condition's outcome. Therefore, because the i f statement only requires the presence of a numeric value, you may optionally replace the test expression with an integer variable. This action will cause the i f statement to assess the variable's value using the same zero/non-zero criteria.

Multi-if conditions There are many occasions where a single i f condition cannot completely decide the course of action to be taken. To fill this void, the && (*and*) and ¦¦ (*or*) operators allow for more advanced logic. Figure 4-6 provides examples of these conditions operators.

The first statement in Fig. 4-6 uses the && (*and*) clause to connect two conditions. This clause, states that both conditions must be met for the condition to be true. The second if example uses the || (*or*) option. This connector specifies that only one of the conditions must be met for the "if" to be true.

```
if ( hours > 40 && pay_type == 'H' ) overtime_flag = 'Y';

if ( net_pay < 0 || net_pay > 10000 )
    error(emp_no);

if  ( employee_status = 'A' || ( employee_status == 'L'
      && pay_indicator == 'Y' )
        cut_check(emp_no,net_pay);
```

4-6 Multi-if conditional examples.

The third if statement example contains both && and || operators. In this case, similar to mathematical expressions, there is an order of operation. This order dictates that conditions within parentheses are considered first, then &&, and then ||. Thus, in the statement if (a = = a && b = = b || c = = c), condition a and b are processed first and the outcome of a and b is compared to c. In effect, either a and b must be true or c must be true.

The adding of parentheses could change this scenario, however. In the statement if (a = = a && (b = = b || c = = c)), a must be true and either b or c must also be true. Therefore, within the third if example, the result of (employee_status = = 'L' && pay_indicator = = 'Y') is first decided, and then the outcome is compared to employee_status = 'A'. Also note, that because && is processed before ||, this statement would have executed the same way either with or without the parentheses. Including the parentheses, however, is a good programming practice because it clearly documents the way the if statement will be executed.

Nested if statements C has the ability to define and interpret complex logic by placing if statements within if statements. This "if within an if" is called nesting.

Figure 4-7 shows a nested if example.

```
if ( pay_type == 'H' )
    if ( hours_worked > 40 )
        overtime(emp_no);
    else
        regular_hours(emp_no);
else
    salaried_emp(emp_no);
```

4-7 Nested if example.

In Fig. 4-7, there is an if statement contained within an if statement. The first if asks if the employee pay type is hourly. If the pay type is not hourly, then the else statement is used and salaried_emp() is executed. If the employee is hourly, then a second question is asked pertaining to the number of hours worked. Remember, the inner if will only be reached when pay type is hourly. This inner if statement will call regular_hours() if the employee worked forty hours or less and overtime if more than forty hours were worked.

Figure 4-8 flowcharts the nested if logic.

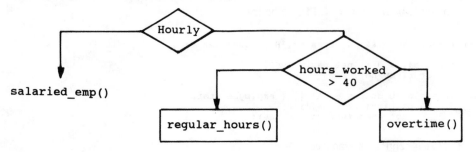

4-8 Flowchart of nested ifs in Fig. 4-7.

Tandem if statements To solve a problem, you sometimes need to ask a group of related questions. For example, suppose that you want to calculate the number of employees making $5,000 – $10,000 and $10,001 – $15,000, and so on up to $100,000. You can employ one of two programming methods to calculate the answer. First, you could type twenty single line if statements as shown in Fig. 4-9A. Also, you could calculate the answer by using tandem if statements as shown in Fig. 4-9B.

The statements of both Fig. 4-9A and Fig. 4-9B will provide the same answer. The questions are "How long will it take to process?" and "How self-documenting is the procedure?" In this case, both A and B are self-documenting. The difference lies in the processing time needed to run the program. When A is executed, all twenty individual if statements will always be executed. Additionally, each if statement has two conditions

```
Part A    if ( salary >=  5000 && SALARY < 10000 ) ++salary5;
          if ( salary >= 10000 && SALARY < 10000 ) ++salary10;
          if ( salary >= 15000 && SALARY < 15000 ) ++salary15;
          if ( salary >= 20000 && SALARY < 20000 ) ++salary20;
          if ( salary >= 25000 && SALARY < 25000 ) ++salary25;
                           .              .              .
                           .              .              .
                           .              .              .
          if ( salary >= 95000 && SALARY < 95000 ) ++salary95;


Part B    if ( salary < 10000 )
              ++salary5;
          else if ( salary < 15000 )
              ++salary10;
          else if ( salary < 20000 )
              ++salary15;
          else if ( salary < 25000 )
              ++salary20;
              .           .           .
              .           .           .
              .           .           .
          else if ( salary < 100000 )
              ++salary95;
```

4-9 Tandem if example.

that must be examined (a greater than and a less than condition). In B, the entire procedure ends when the first conditional statement is met. Thus, all twenty questions are not always asked. Additionally, each question only contains one condition, again minimizing the needed processing.

Figure 4-10 shown below provides additional if statement examples.

```
if ( error_flag == 'Y' ) error(emp_no);

if ( emp_stat == 'A' ) ++active_count;

if ( job_class == '1' || job_class == '2' )
    { ++mgr_count;
      printf("\n %s is a manager",emp_name);
    }
else
    ++support_count;
```

4-10 Additional if statement examples.

The switch statement

The tandem if process previously discussed is so commonly used that the developers of C designed the switch statement to specifically interpret that type of conditional logic. The format of this statement is shown in Fig. 4-11.

```
switch ( expression )
  {
    case value1:
        program statement;
        . . .
        break;

    case value2:
        program statement;
        . . .
        break;

    case value-n:
        program statement;
        . . .
        break;

    default:
        program statement;
        . . .
        break;
```

4-11 switch statement format.

The switch statement is divided into three basic parts; the word switch followed by the expression to be tested, the case sections, and the default section. The expression following the word switch contains the value to be assessed by the case test expression. The case section is comprised of the word case, followed by the value to be compared with the value in the switch clause, that being followed by the statements to be executed if these two values match. The default section contains statements to be executed if none of the case test conditions are satisfied.

See Fig. 4-12 for an example.

Program

```
main()
{ char operator;
  float num_1;
  float num_2;

  printf("\n\nEnter formula : ");
  scanf("%f %c %f",&num_1,&operator,&num_2);

  switch( operator )
    {
      case '+':
        printf("\n\n  Answer is %.2f", ( num_1 + num_2 ) );
        break;

      case '-':
        printf("\n\n  Answer is %.2f", ( num_1 - num_2 ) );
        break;

      case '*':
        printf("\n\n  Answer is %.2f", ( num_1 * num_2 ) );
        break;

      case '/':
        printf("\n\n  Answer is %.2f", ( num_1 / num_2 ) );
        break;

      default:
        printf("\n\n  Unknown operation");
    }
}
```

Output

Ex. 1
```
Enter formula : 10*3

Answer is 30.00
```

Ex. 2
```
Enter formula : 15.5-4

Answer is 11.50
```

4-12 switch statement example.

The program in Fig. 4-12 is an elementary calculator that performs addition, subtraction, multiplication, and division. Note that the second input variable (operator) within the scanf() function receives the symbol of the operation to be performed. This symbol, as specified in the switch expression, is then compared with the case values. If a match is made, the appropriate mathematical process is performed. However, if no match can be ascertained, then the statements following the default label are performed.

Once again, review the switch statement example in Fig. 4-12. Now however, turn your attention to the word break contained within each of the case and default statement list. break will be discussed in depth later in the chapter; for now, it's a C statement that instructs the computer to exit the statement in which break is contained. In the case of the switch statement, break causes switch to be exited and program control to be passed to the next sequential statement.

The conditional operator

The conditional operator is one of the most cryptic features of the C language, performing an If-Then-Else-type procedure. It's formatted in the following manner:

```
condition ? expression1 : expression2
```

The condition is usually a relational test like "a > b." This expression, as discussed in reference to the if statement, produces a value of 0 if the expression is false and a non-zero value if the condition is true. A true response causes the expression after the ? to be evaluated (expression1). If the relational test is false (thus returning a non-zero value), the expression after the : is evaluated. The program contained within Fig. 4-13 illustrates the use of this operator.

Program

```
main()
{ int a;
  int b;
  int c;
  int d;

  a = 1;
  b = 2;

  c = a < b ? 1 : 0;
  printf("\nAnswer is %d",c);

  c = a == b ? 1 : 0;
  printf("\nAnswer is %d",c);

  c = ( (a>b) ? 1 : 0 );
  printf("\nAnswer is %d",c);

  d = 1;
  c = ( d ? 1 : 0 );
  printf("\nAnswer is %d",c);
}
```

Output

```
Answer is 1
Answer is 0
Answer is 0
Answer is 1
```

4-13 Conditional operator example.

Figure 4-13 shows four conditional operator examples. In the first example, a is less than b and thus c is set to the value following the question mark—namely 1. In the second example, a is not equal to b, so c is set to the value after the colon—0. In the third example, parentheses were added. These parentheses are not required as previously seen; however, they greatly assist in the readability of the statement. The fourth and last example has a slightly different twist—it uses an additional variable, d. Remember, a relational test expression (a = = b) returns either a zero or non-zero value, which is the value used by the operational operator. Therefore, because the syntax of the conditional operator only requires the presence of a zero or non-zero value, you may optionally use an integer variable at that location. This technique will cause the operator to assess variable's value using the same zero/non-zero criteria.

Looping

The ability to repeat the execution of selected program statements is a fundamental feature of all computers. It is this ability that allows programmers to write routines that perform reiterative tasks. For example, a company might have thousands of employees and thus prints thousands of payroll checks. The program printing these checks re-executes the same statements when processing each check. Without this reiterative feature (also known as looping), the programmer would be forced to write thousands of check-printing routines, one for each check. As you can imagine, this could make a program prohibitively large.

The C language provides three statements that can perform this vital looping function: while, do-while, and for. Figure 4-14 lists a small program that illustrates these statements.

Program

```
main()
{ int x;

  printf("\n\n The while loop");
  x=1;
  while ( x <= 3 )
    { printf("\n    X has a value of %d",x);
      x++;
    }
  printf("\n\n The do/while loop");
  x=1;
  do
    { printf("\n    X has a value of %d",x);
      x++;
    } while ( x <= 3 );
  printf("\n\n The for loop");
  for (x=1; x <= 3; x++ )
    { printf("\n    X has a value of %d",x);
    }
}
```

Output

```
The while loop
   X has a value of 1
   X has a value of 2
   X has a value of 3

The do/while loop
   X has a value of 1
   X has a value of 2
   X has a value of 3

The for loop
   X has a value of 1
   X has a value of 2
   X has a value of 3
```

4-14 Looping program example.

The while statement

The while statement is designed to repeatedly execute a statement or statements based on a specified test condition. The format of this statement is shown in Fig. 4-15.

The while statement is divided into three parts; the word while, the condition being tested, and the statement or statements being executed. Figure 4-16 provides an example of the while looping process.

```
while ( test expression )
   statement or statement block
```

4-15 while statement format.

Program

```
main()
{ int input;
  int count = 1;
  long int total = 1;

  printf("\n Enter a number for factorial : ");
  scanf("%d",&input);

  while ( input >= count )
   { total *= count;
     printf("\n    Factorial of %d is %ld",count,total);
     ++count;
   }
}
```

Output

```
Enter a number for factorial :
   Factorial of 1 is 1
   Factorial of 2 is 2
   Factorial of 3 is 6
   Factorial of 4 is 24
   Factorial of 5 is 120
   Factorial of 6 is 720
   Factorial of 7 is 5040
   Factorial of 8 is 40320
   Factorial of 9 is 362880
   Factorial of 10 is 3628800
```

4-16 while statement example.

The while statement contained within Fig. 4-16 typifies how this statement is used. Note that it begins with the word while followed by (input < = counter). This expression is the condition tested prior to each reiteration of the statement below it. The proper form of this expression is identical to that used within the if statement test criteria previously mentioned. If the test is true (a non-zero value is produced), the looping process continues. If the test proves to be false (a zero value is produced), the looping ends, the while statement is exited, and program control is passed to the next sequential C statement.

Let's now turn our attention to the reiterated statements within the while loop. First, note (within Fig. 4-16) that the indented statements are enclosed within brackets. Like the if statement previously mentioned, while only associates itself with the one C statement or function call below it. Therefore, if more than one statement is to be contained within the loop, all looping statements must be placed within a statement block. This block instructs the while statement to incorporate the entire blocked group within the loop. The brackets define the beginning and end of the block.

Figure 4-17 provides various while statement examples.

```
x = 10;
while ( x )
  printf("\n X has a value of %d",x--);

x = 1;
while ( x <= 10 )
  { printf("\n X has a value of %d",x);
    x++
  }
```

4-17 Additional while statement examples.

The do-while statement

The do-while statement is very similar to while, the difference occurring when the test condition is evaluated. Remember, while examines the test criteria prior to each execution of the looping statement or statements, and do-while assesses the test criteria after each reiteration of the looping statement. This distinction might seem trivial but in fact causes a key side effect on the statements being executed: unlike with while, the statements within the do-while are always executed at least once. Remember, the test condition is assessed after the loop has executed; then, if the criteria in the test is not met, the loop will not execute a second time.

The format of do-while is shown in Fig. 4-18.

```
do
    statement or statement block
    while ( test expression );
```

4-18 Do-While statement format.

This statement is divided into four parts; the word do, the statement or statement block to be executed, the word while, and the condition to be tested. See Fig. 4-19 for an example of the do-while statement.

When reviewing the program in Fig. 4-19, take special note of the word do, the placement of the statement block, and the word while followed by its associated test criteria. The statement begins with do and, as you can see, is the only word on the line. This convention is not a language syntax rule but is generally done to maximize program readability. do is then followed by the statements to be looped. Like the while statement, if more than one statement or function call is to be looped, then they must be enclosed within brackets, thus creating a statement block. After the looping portion comes the word while and the test criteria. Finally, note that unlike while, this statement must be terminated by placing a semicolon after the test criteria's closing parenthesis.

Figure 4-20 provides some additional "do-while" examples.

Program

```
main()
{ int input;
  int count = 1;
  long int total = 1;

  printf("\n Enter a number for factorial : ");
  scanf("%d",&input);

  do
    { total *= count;
      printf("\n    Factorial of %d is %ld",count,total);
      ++count;
    } while ( input >= count );
}
```

Output

```
Enter a number for factorial :
   Factorial of 1 is 1
   Factorial of 2 is 2
   Factorial of 3 is 6
   Factorial of 4 is 24
   Factorial of 5 is 120
   Factorial of 6 is 720
   Factorial of 7 is 5040
   Factorial of 8 is 40320
   Factorial of 9 is 362880
   Factorial of 10 is 3628800
```

4-19 Do-While statement example.

```
x = 10;
do
  printf("\n X has a value of %d",x--);
  while ( x );

x = 1;
  { printf("\n X has a value of %d",x);
    x++
  } while ( x <= 10 );
```

4-20 Additional Do-While statement examples.

The for statement

The for statement is the last of the looping statements and is designed differently than while and do-while. This statement is primarily used to loop a specified number of times, based on the incrementing of a counter variable. The format of for is shown in Fig. 4-21.

```
for  (initialization test condition incrementation)
   statement of statement block
```

4-21 for statement example.

The for statement is divided into five basic parts: the word for, initialization, test criteria, incrementing, and the statements to be looped. Figure 4-22 shows an example of this statement.

Program

```
main()
{ int input;
  int count = 1;
  long int total = 1;

  printf("\n Enter a number for factorial : ");
  scanf("%d",&input);

  for ( count = 1; input >= count; ++count )
    { total *= count;
      printf("\n    Factorial of %d is %ld",count,total);
    }
}
```

Output

```
Enter a number for factorial :
   Factorial of 1 is 1
   Factorial of 2 is 2
   Factorial of 3 is 6
   Factorial of 4 is 24
   Factorial of 5 is 120
   Factorial of 6 is 720
   Factorial of 7 is 5040
   Factorial of 8 is 40320
   Factorial of 9 is 362880
   Factorial of 10 is 3628800
```

4-22 for statement example.

This statement begins with the word for followed by three control areas enclosed within parentheses followed by the statement of the statement block to be reiterated. The three parenthesized sections deal with the initialization of the appropriate variables, the test condition assessed to see if the loop should repeat, and the statement incrementing the counter variable.

For example, look at the three enclosed areas in Fig. 4-22. The count = 0; is initializing the counter variable to zero, the count <= input; is testing to see if the loop should continue to reiterate, and the count + + is incrementing the count variable by 1 after each execution of the loop—bringing it closer to satisfying the test criteria.

Lastly, like while and do-while, a single statement can be repeated by just placing it after the for, or alternatively, many statements can be reiterated by placing them within a statement block. Figure 4-23 provides additional for statement examples.

```
for ( x=10; x > 0; x-- )
  printf("\n X has a value of %d",x);

for ( x=1; x <= 10; x++ )
  { printf("\n X has a value of %d",x);
  }
```

4-23 Additional Do-While statement examples.

Nested loops

When automating a procedure, the programmer must sometimes place a loop within a loop. This loop-in-a-loop is called (as you might expect) a *nested loop*. When this procedure is used, the inner loop processes to completion during each reiteration of the outer loop. This looping process is illustrated in Fig. 4-24.

The program in Fig. 4-24 has a for statement within a for statement and uses two variables: outer and inner, both of which loop within their respective for statements. When executed (as can also be seen in Fig. 4-24), the inner loop processes to completion each time the outer loop increments.

Program

```
main()
{ int outer;
  int inner;

  for ( outer = 0; outer < 3; ++outer )
    { printf("\n Outer loop -> %d",outer);
      for ( inner = 0; inner < 4; ++inner )
  { printf("\n    Inner loop -> %d",inner);
        }
    }
}
```

Output

```
Outer loop -> 0
    Inner loop -> 0
    Inner loop -> 1
    Inner loop -> 2
    Inner loop -> 3

Outer loop -> 1
    Inner loop -> 0
    Inner loop -> 1
    Inner loop -> 2
    Inner loop -> 3

Outer loop -> 2
    Inner loop -> 0
    Inner loop -> 1
    Inner loop -> 2
    Inner loop -> 3
```

4-24 Nested loop example.

Figure 4-25 also dramatizes the nested loop concept by printing a picture of a right-angle triangle.

In Fig. 4-25, the inner loop is repeating based on the value of the counter in the outer loop (look in the test criteria section in the inner loop for clarification). Also, once again, the inner loop processes to completion during each reiteration of the outer loop.

Associated looping statements

Two other C statements also are associated with the looping process but do not perform looping functions: break and continue.

The break statement is used to immediately terminate the looping process, regardless of the looping test criteria. Figure 4-26 illustrates this statement by listing a program containing two loops and the program's respective output. The first loop is a single for statement containing a printf() function displaying the counter's value. In contrast,

Program

```
main()
{ int outer;
  int inner;

  for ( outer = 1; outer <= 10; ++outer )
    { for ( inner = 1; inner <= outer; ++inner )
      { printf("*");
    }
      printf("\n");
    }
}
```

Output

```
*
**
***
****
*****
******
*******
********
*********
**********
```

4-25 Additional nested loop example.

Program

```
main()
{ int count;

  printf("\n\n First loop");
  for ( count = 1; count <= 5; count++)
    { printf("\n    Count is %d",count);
    }

  printf("\n\n Second loop");
  for ( count = 1; count <= 5; count++)
  { printf("\n    Count is %d",count);
    if ( count == 3 ) break;
  }
}
```

Output

```
First loop
   Count is 1
   Count is 2
   Count is 3
   Count is 4
   Count is 5

Second loop
   Count is 1
   Count is 2
   Count is 3
```

4-26 break statement example.

the second for loop is identical with the exception of an if statement causing the loop to break when the counter equals 3. When reviewing the output of this program (also shown in Fig. 4-26), the first loop repeats 5 times and the second loop repeats 3 times, indicating that the break statement does in fact end execution of the loop.

Similar but not identical to break, the continue statement causes the statements within a looping control block to skip a reiteration. Figure 4-27 illustrates this process.

When viewing the output contained within Fig. 4-27, note that count is 3 is missing from the second loop, but count 4 and 5 are present. This skipped count is 3 is the work of the continue statement. Within the program, the statement if (count == 3) continue; is contained in the second for loop and instructs the program to execute the continue statement when the counter variable is equal to 3. This continue statement in turn instructs the computer to skip the execution of all the remaining statements within the loop's control block and to proceed directly to the next loop reiteration. Thus, the printf() function call has skipped.

Program

```
main()
{ int count;

  printf("\n\n First loop");
  for ( count = 1; count <= 5; count++)
    { printf("\n    Count is %d",count);
    }

  printf("\n\n Second loop");
  for ( count = 1; count <= 5; count++)
    { if ( count == 3 ) continue;
      printf("\n    Count is %d",count);
    }
}
```

Output

```
First loop
    Count is 1
    Count is 2
    Count is 3
    Count is 4
    Count is 5

Second loop
    Count is 1
    Count is 2
    Count is 4
    Count is 5
```

4-27   continue statement example.

Finally, the continue statement only suppresses the execution of statements after the continue; the statements before continue within the loop will still execute. For example, in Fig. 4-28, the for loop contains two printf() function calls separated by a continue statement. As you can see by reviewing the program's output, the first printf() always executes and the second one is never called.

The goto statement

The goto statement is used to permanently transfer control from the statement being executed to a specified label name somewhere else within the function.

Since the concept of structured programming was introduced as a method of standardized programming techniques, the goto statement has somewhat fallen from grace. As

Program

```
main()
{ int count;

    printf("\n\n First loop");
    for ( count = 1; count <= 5; count++)
      { printf("\n    Count is %d",count);
      }

    printf("\n\n Second loop");
    for ( count = 1; count <= 5; count++)
      { if ( count == 3 ) continue;
        printf("\n    Count is %d",count);
      }
}
```

Output

```
This is the first printf()
This is the first printf()
This is the first printf()
This is the first printf()
This is the first printf()
```

4-28 Another continue statement example.

discussed in Chapter 1, structured programming relies heavily on subroutining through function calls as the preferred branching process. However, goto is still a commonly used programming option.

Figure 4-29 outlines the goto statement format.


```
goto label-name;
```

4-29 goto statement format.

The goto statement consists of two parts: the word goto and a label name. For the statement to function correctly, the specified label name must exist in a valid format somewhere within the same function as the goto.

Figure 4-30 illustrates the use of the goto statement.

The program example in Fig. 4-31 illustrates the classic justification for using the goto statement. Within the first program example, the goto statement is contained within the nested loop. When both looping counters have a value of 3, the loops will be exited via the goto statement, with program control being passed directly to the label: statement placed below the loop. This program in itself is not very useful but still illustrates a simple and efficient way to exit from the depths of a nested loop.

The program in Fig. 4-31 exits the looping process by a more structured approach—namely, by two break statements and the assistance of an if statement and an additional variable. Note that both techniques will get the job done, but the program using the goto is a tad more efficient (it uses less program statements and one less variable) and easier to read. This situation however, is the exception rather than the rule. Thus, for many reasons, the goto statement should be used with discretion.

Program

```
main()
{ int outer;
  int inner;

  for ( outer=1; outer < 5; outer++ )
    { for ( inner=1; inner < 5; inner++ )
        { printf("\n Outer is %d, inner is %d",outer, inner);
      if ( outer == 3 && inner == 3 ) goto skipout;
        }
    }
  skipout:
    printf("\n I skipped out");
}
```

Output

```
Outer is 1, inner is 1
Outer is 1, inner is 2
Outer is 1, inner is 3
Outer is 1, inner is 4
Outer is 2, inner is 1
Outer is 2, inner is 2
Outer is 2, inner is 3
Outer is 2, inner is 4
Outer is 3, inner is 1
Outer is 3, inner is 2
Outer is 3, inner is 3
I skipped out
```

4-30 goto statement example.

Program

```
main()
{ int outer;
  int inner;
  int flag = 0;

  for ( outer=1; outer < 5; outer++ )
    { for ( inner=1; inner < 5; inner++ )
        { printf("\n Outer is %d, inner is %d",outer, inner);
      if ( outer == 3 && inner == 3 )
        { flag = 1;
          break;
        }
    }
        if ( flag == 1 ) break;
    }
    printf("\n I skipped out");
}
```

Output

```
Outer is 1, inner is 1
Outer is 1, inner is 2
Outer is 1, inner is 3
Outer is 1, inner is 4
Outer is 2, inner is 1
Outer is 2, inner is 2
Outer is 2, inner is 3
Outer is 2, inner is 4
Outer is 3, inner is 1
Outer is 3, inner is 2
Outer is 3, inner is 3
I skipped out
```

4-31 "Not using a goto" example.

5

Arrays and character strings

An *array* is a collection of related data items stored under a common name. These arrays, also known as tables, might contain the days of the week, months of the year, a list of valid employee numbers, or any other group of related information. This chapter describes the role that these arrays can play as a programming tool, covering topics such as the validation of data entry, statistical manipulation, character array manipulation, and other specific techniques and procedures that can be easily incorporated into any application.

Numeric arrays

Data can be loaded into a table either as part of the array definition process or by being assigned to the proper array location during the execution of the program. Both methods are equally popular. In fact, the method chosen for loading an array is usually dictated by the ultimate use of the array and the type of data within it, as opposed to a matter of programming style. In most cases, if the information placed in the table does not change from day to day—for example, the number of days in each month (as shown in Fig. 5-1—the data can be permanently placed in the program within the array definition statement.

```
main()
{ static int months[] = { 31,28,31,30,31,30,31,31,30,31,30,31 };
  int count;
  for ( count=0; count <= 11; count++ )
    printf("\n [%d] = %d",count,months[count]);
}
```

5-1 First array loading example.

I should mention a few key points of Fig. 5-1. First, the integer number months is followed by [ ]. These braces state that the variable being defined is an array. Second, the array definition is followed by an equal sign and a list of numbers enclosed within brackets ({}). When this loading procedure is used, the size of the array is automatically calculated by the compiler by counting the number of array elements listed between the brackets. Figure 5-2 illustrates conceptually how the array elements defined in Fig. 5-1 are viewed

months[1]	31
months[2]	28
months[3]	31
months[4]	30
months[5]	31
months[6]	30
months[7]	31
months[8]	31
months[9]	30
months[10]	31
months[11]	30
months[12]	31

5-2 Conceptual view of months array.

within the computer's memory. When reviewing this figure, take special notice that the array begins at position [0], not [1]—therefore, the value for January will be in month[0], February will be in months[1], and so on.

Let's turn our attention back to the printf() function in Fig. 5-1. The array months[ ] is being subscripted by the variable count, causing the array to be written as months[count]. This procedure will cause the printf() function to print the contents of a particular location of the months[ ] array as specified by the value of the variable count. For example, if count has a value of 3, then months[count] translates to month[3], thus printing April's value of 30. (Remember, the array starts at location 0, not 1; thus, the monthly values are in locations 0 through 11, not in locations 1 through 12.)

Figure 5-3 is an expanded version of the program previously discussed in Fig. 5-1. Note that this program includes the printing of headings and the numbers of the associated memory locations being printed.

The program in Fig. 5-3 contains one new major point of interest. The printf() function within the for loop was modified by taking out the open and close brackets from around the %d associated with count, deleting the equal sign, and (most particularly) changing the first printed value from count to count + 1. Once again, remember that the array begins with 0; thus, when 1 is added to the value of count prior to printing, the month's number (1 = January, 2 = February, etc.) and its corresponding numbers line up correctly.

The second array loading option, as alluded to earlier, reads the information from a data file or the user's keyboard. This process is primarily used in applications that should not have the information hard-wired into the program. For example, a payroll system might contain thirty programs using employee status information. If all thirty programs

Program

```
main()
{ static int months[] = { 31,28,31,30,31,30,31,31,30,31,30,31 };
  int count;
  printf("\n       Month   No. of Days");
  printf("\n       -----   -----------");
  for ( count=0; count <= 11; count++ )
  printf("\n         %d           %d",count+1,months[count]);
}
```

Output

```
Month   No.   of Days
-----   -----------
  1         31
  2         28
  3         31
  4         30
  5         31
  6         30
  7         31
  8         31
  9         30
 10          31
 11          30
 12          31
```

5-3 Expanded array program.

had the codes explicitly written in the program, then the addition of a new code would cause all the programs to be edited and recompiled. However, if these programs read the codes from a small sequential disk file into memory, then only the small file would require modification. The program listed in Fig. 5-4 shows how an array can be loaded from the keyboard. Loading an array from a file will be discussed in Chapter 9 on file input and output.

When reviewing Fig. 5-4, note that a second for loop has been added. This loop causes "Enter value of month : " to be displayed and allows the user—via a scanf() function—to enter the number of days in each month. Also note that the word static and the twelve monthly values were deleted from the int statement where months[ ] was defined. Additionally, the number 12 was placed within the array brackets (int months[12];). This 12 specifies that array months[ ] will be 12 members long, with array locations ranging from 0 to 11. Remember, when array values were listed within the int statement, the 12 was not needed because the compiler could figure out the appropriate array size by counting the number of elements.

Figure 5-5 converts the previously explained array examples into a useful date validation routine. This program asks the user to enter a date in a specified format, assesses its value, and displays a message stating if the entered date was valid or invalid. One caution, however: if you try to use this program as a real application, you will have to make allowance for leap year; I didn't implement it when developing the validation logic because I wanted to simplify the example.

The next programming example, shown in Fig. 5-6, allows a teacher to enter student grades. Once the grades are entered, the program calculates and prints the average grade value. This program in itself is only marginally useful; however, it illustrates how arrays can be used to analyze and manipulate numerically oriented statistical data.

Program

```
main()
{ int months[12];
  int count;

  for ( count=0; count <= 11; count++ )
    { printf("\nEnter value of month %d : ",count+1);
      scanf("%d",&months[count]);
    }
  printf("\n    Month    No. of Days");
  printf("\n    -----    -----------");
  for ( count=0; count <= 11; count++ )
    printf("\n      %d        %d",count+1,months[count]);
}
```

Output

Month	No. of Days
1	31
2	28
3	31
4	30
5	31
6	30
7	31
8	31
9	30
10	31
11	30
12	31

```
Enter value of month 1 : 31
Enter value of month 2 : 28
Enter value of month 3 : 31
Enter value of month 4 : 30
Enter value of month 5 : 31
Enter value of month 6 : 30
Enter value of month 7 : 31
Enter value of month 8 : 31
Enter value of month 9 : 30
Enter value of month 10 : 31
Enter value of month 11 : 30
Enter value of month 12 : 31
```

5-4 Array loading program.

Program

```
main()
{ static int months[] = { 31,28,31,30,31,30,31,31,30,31,30,31 };
  int count;
  int month;
  int day;
  int year;
  char dummy;

  printf("\n Enter date in format MM/DD/YY : ");
  scanf("%d%c%d%c%d",&month,&dummy,&day,&dummy,&year);

  if ( day >= 1 && day <= months[month-1] )
    printf("\n    Date is valid");
  else
    printf("\n    Date is not valid");
}
```

Output

Ex. 1

```
Enter date in format MM/DD/YY : 12/23/86

    Date is valid
```

Ex. 2

```
Enter date in format MM/DD/YY : 02/31/86

    Date is not valid
```

Ex. 3

```
Enter date in format MM/DD/YY : 06/06/87

    Date is valid
```

5-5 Date validation program.

Program

```
main()
{ int grades[30];
  int count;
  int total = 0;
  int ave_grade;

  for ( count=0; count <= 11; count++ )
    { printf("\nEnter grade for student number %d : ",count+1);
      scanf("%d",&grades[count]);
      if ( grades[count] == -1 ) break;
    }
  for ( count=0; grades[count] != -1; count++ )
    { total += grades[count];
    }
  ave_grade = total / count;
  printf("\n Average is = %d",ave_grade);
}
```

Output

```
Enter grade for student number 1 : 100
Enter grade for student number 1 : 90
Enter grade for student number 1 : 80
Enter grade for student number 1 : 85
Enter grade for student number 1 : 95
Average is = 90
```

5-6 Student grading example.

The grading program in Fig. 5-6 is divided into four parts; variable initialization, data entry, array manipulation, and final calculation with output. Take special note of the array manipulation section (the second for loop). This for statement is analyzing the contents of the grades[ ] array by summing the grades in preparation for calculating an average. Figure 5-7 is a little more complex than the example in Fig. 5-6. This program also allows for the input of student grades but now calculates the maximum grade, minimum grade, and arithmetic mean as well.

Character arrays

Arrays are very commonly used in C to store ASCII character strings, such as names and addresses. Unlike many other computer programming languages, C requires the programmer to treat character strings as a character array and not as a single character variable. This seemingly small difference in representation has a dramatic effect in the way alphabetic data is stored, accessed, and modified.

To find uses for character strings, let's go back to our first C program, shown once more in Fig. 5-8.

Recall from the previous discussion of Fig. 5-8 that the phrase "Hi there" is called a character string and must be enclosed within double quotes. These double quotes perform two main functions. First and most obvious, they specify the beginning and ending points of the string. Second, they instruct the compiler to place a special character called a *null string terminator* at the end of the string. Remember, in C, a character string is just an array of individual letters. The null terminator specifies where these letters end. Let's now

Program

```
main()
{ int grades[30];
  int count;
  int total = 0;
  int ave_grade;
  int mean_val;
  int max_val;
  int min_val;

  for ( count=0; count <= 11; count++ )
    { printf("\nEnter grade for student number %d : ",count+1);
      scanf("%d",&grades[count]);
      if ( grades[count] == -1 ) break;
    }
  max_val = grades[0];
  min_val = grades[0];
  for ( count=0; grades[count] != -1; count++ )
    { total += grades[count];
      if ( max_val < grades[count] ) max_val = grades[count];
      if ( min_val > grades[count] ) min_val = grades[count];
    }
  ave_grade = total / count;
  mean_val = ( max_val + min_val ) / 2;

  printf("\n Average is = %d",ave_grade);
  printf("\n Maximum is = %d",max_val);
  printf("\n Minimum is = %d",min_val);
  printf("\n Mean    is = %d",mean_val);
}
```

Output

```
Enter grade for student number 1 : 100
Enter grade for student number 1 : 90
Enter grade for student number 1 : 80
Enter grade for student number 1 : 85
Enter grade for student number 1 : 95
Average is = 90
Maximum is = 100
Minimum is = 80
Mean    is = 90
```

5-7 Expanded student grading example.

```
main()
{ Printf("Hi there");
}
```

5-8 First example program.

modify Fig. 5-8 in an attempt to better analyze the null terminator concept. See Fig. 5-9 for the reworked program.

This reworded program assigns the value "Hi there" to a character array string called a_string. Then, the printf() function prints the value contained within a_string—namely, "Hi there." Also note that when using the printf() function to print character strings, the symbol %s is used to denote the printing of a string. Now let's once again expand the program to shed further light on the character manipulation process (see Fig. 5-10).

```
main()
{ static char a_string[] = { "Hi there" };

  printf("\n %s",a_string);
```

5-9 Expanded printf example program.

Program

```
main()
{ static char a_string[] = { "Hi there" };
  int count;

  printf("%s",a_string);

  for ( count = 0; count < 9; count++ )
      printf("\n a_string[%d] = %c = %d"
    ,count,a_string[count], a_string[count] );

}
```

Output

```
Hi there
 a_string[0] = H = 72
 a_string[1] = i = 105
 a_string[2] =   = 32
 a_string[3] = t = 116
 a_string[4] = h = 104
 a_string[5] = e = 101
 a_string[6] = r = 114
 a_string[7] = e = 101
 a_string[8] =   = 0
```

5-10 Another expanded printf example program.

The second expanded program contains an additional routine that prints the value of each individual memory location within the a_string array. When reviewing this program, pay close attention to the new printf() function. In particular, note that three values are being printed; count, which is the variable used as the array subscript; the character decimal value of the array contents; and the ASCII decimal value of the array contents. As you can see, the ASCII value of a_string[8] is 0, this 0 value is the null terminator specifying the end of the string. The other numeric values are the ASCII equivalent of the characters on the associated line.

Calculating string length

The program shown in Fig. 5-11 calculates the size of a character string (also known as a *string array* or *character array*) and typifies how these strings must be handled. Do not worry, though—all C compilers provide prewritten functions that copy, compare, test, and manipulate this type of data.

The use of the while statement in this program is particularly noteworthy. It is constructed in a manner that increments the variable count until the referenced array location contains a value of ' \0.' This value, as you recall, is called a string terminator and signifies the end of the character string. Without this terminator, the length testing will

Program

```
main()
{ static char a_string[15] = {"aaaaaaaa"};
  int the_len;

  the_len = length(a_string);
  printf("\n The length of a_string is %d",the_len);
}

int length(s1)
  char s1[];
{ int x = 0;
  while ( s1[x] )
      ++x;
  return(x);
}
```

Output

```
    The length of a_string is 8
```

5-11 String length program example.

read past the end of the array and access whatever values happen to be in the next sequential memory location. As you can well imagine, this error could, and probably will, produce inconsistent and often strange results.

The '\0' notation is comprised of three basic parts; the single quotation marks (the apostrophes), the backslash, and the 0. The backslash states that the number placed after it is the ASCII value of the character to be referenced. The 0 is the number following the backslash. Therefore, the expression '\0' is a representation of the character with an ASCII value of 0—the null string terminator. Lastly, the single quotation mark can best be explained by comparing it with the double quotation mark. The double quotation, as previously discussed, is used to enclose character string literals and instructs the compiler to place a null terminator at the end of the string. The single quotation mark also encloses a character or group of characters but does not instruct the compiler to place a null after the string.

The standard C function that performs this task is named strlen() and is shown in Fig. 5-12.

Program

```
main()
{ static char a_string[15] = {"aaaaaaaa"};
  int the_len;

  the_len = strlen(a_string);
  printf("\n The length of a_string is %d",the_len);
}
```

Output

```
    The length of a_string is 8
```

5-12 strlen( ) program example.

Comparing string equality

Character strings cannot be compared in the same manner as variables are compared, namely a_string == b_string. Strings must be compared by assessing the equality of each pair of corresponding array location. Figure 5-13 illustrates this process. As with string length, don't worry—all compilers provide a built-in function to perform this task.

Program

```
main()
{ char a_string[15];
  char b_string[15];
  int x;

  scanf("%s",a_string);
  scanf("%s",b_string);

  if ( equals(a_string,b_string) == 0 )
      printf("\n Strings are equal");
  else
      printf("\n Strings are not equal");
}

int equals(s1,s2)
char s1[], s2[];
{ int x = 0;
  while ( s1[x] == s2[x] )
      if ( s1[x++] == '\0' ) return(0);
  return(s1[x] - s2[x]);
}
```

Output

Ex. 1
```
Hello
Hi
  Strings are not equal
```

Ex. 2
```
Hello
Hello
  Strings are equal
```

Ex. 3
```
Hello
Hellox
  Strings are not equal
```

5-13 String equality example.

Figure 5-13 brings forward a C feature that has thus far only been mentioned in passing—the creation and execution of a function. A *function* is a group of associated statements grouped under a common name. For example, when you say printf("Hello");, you are actually running a group of C statements collectively bundled under the name printf(). This concept is completely discussed in Chapter 8; but, for now, you only need to know that when the function equals() is called in Fig. 5-13, the value of a_string and b_string are passed to variables s1 and s2 (respectively) and that the return statement passes a numeric value from the equals() function back to the main program.

Within the equals() function, each array location in s1[ ] is compared to the corresponding array location in s2[ ]. If the two locations are equal, the while statement within which the comparison is being made will continue to process. During the reiteration of this loop, the if statement within the loop increments the counter x and tests for a null terminator. If s1[x] is null, then the two strings are equal and a 0 value is returned to the main program, thus signifying equality. Remember, because you are still within the loop, s2[x] must also be equal to '\0' because the looping criteria states that the two locations must be equal. Also, because they are equal to this point and have both ended—as specified by the null terminators— the two arrays must then contain identical information.

If the two locations do not match, then the loop will be terminated and the return statement below the loop will be executed. This return will perform two activities. First, it will subtract the ASCII value of s2[x] from the ASCII value of s1[x], Second, the value just calculated will be passed back to the main program and, being a non-zero value, will signify that the strings are not equal.

This ASCII subtraction has an interesting by-product. If the calculated return value is positive, then s1[ ] is greater then s2[ ]. Conversely, if the returned value is negative, then s1[ ] is less than s2[ ]. Figure 5-14 illustrates this greater than/less than by-product.

The standard C function performing this task is named strcmp() and is shown below in Fig. 5-15.

Program

```
main()
{ static char a_string[15] = {"string-a"};
  static char b_string[15] = {"string-b"};
  static char c_string[15] = {"string-c"};
  static char d_string[15] = {"string-d"};
  int x;

  x = equals(a_string,b_string);
  printf("\n equals function returned a value of ==> %d",x);

  x = equals(b_string,a_string);
  printf("\n equals function returned a value of ==> %d",x);

  x = equals(a_string,d_string);
  printf("\n equals function returned a value of ==> %d",x);

  x = equals(a_string,a_string);
  printf("\n equals function returned a value of ==> %d",x);

}

int equals(s1,s2)
  char s1[], s2[];

{ int x = 0;
  while ( s1[x] == s2[x] )
    if ( s1[x++] == '\0' ) return(0);
  return(s1[x] - s2[x]);
}
```

Output

```
equals function returned a value of ==> -1
equals function returned a value of ==> 1
equals function returned a value of ==> -3
equals function returned a value of ==> 0
```

5-14 Additional equality example.

Program

```
main()
{ char a_string[15];
  char b_string[15];
  int x;

  scanf("%s",a_string);
  scanf("%s",b_string);

  if ( strcmp(a_string,b_string) == 0 )
      printf("\n Strings are equal");
  else
      printf("\n Strings are not equal");
}
```

Output

Ex. 1
```
Hello
Hi
  Strings are not equal
```

Ex. 2
```
Hello
Hello
  Strings are equal
```

Ex. 3
```
Hello
Hellox
  Strings are not equal
```

5-15   strcmp( ) program example.

Copying a character string

String copying, like string equality testing, also cannot be performed by using a simple assignment operator, namely, a__string = b__string. This task also requires each element of the array to be individually copied from the old array to the appropriate location in the new array. Figure 5-16 illustrates this process.

Figure 5-16 begins by defining and initializing two character strings, one with a value of "aaaaaaaa" and the other with a value of "bbb." Then the function copy() is

Program

```
main()
{ static char a_string[15] = {"aaaaaaaa"};
  static char b_string[15] = {"bbb"};

  copy(a_string,b_string);
  printf("\n a_string = %s,    b_string = %s",a_string,b_string);
}

void copy(s1,s2)
 char s1[], s2[];

{ int x = 0;
  while ( s1[x] = s2[x++] )
     ;
}
```

Output

```
a_string = bbb, b_string = bbb
```

5-16   String copying example.

called, transferring control to that function. Note that here, as in Fig. 5-12 (string comparison), the string arrays a__string and b__string are then being passed to arrays s1[ ] and s2[ ] respectively. Once passed, the variable x is defined, and a while loop is entered. This while loop appears unfinished but is in fact performing the entire string copy.

Note that the test expression within the parentheses is actually an assignment operator " = " and not the equality test operator " = = ". Also note that variable x is being incremented within the assignment. This combination allows three crucial things to happen at once. First, the loop will repeat until s2[x] has a value of 0—the value of a null terminator that also happens to signify the end of the string to be copied. Second, while the loop is waiting for the zero value, it is copying each encountered s1[x] array to the corresponding s2[x] location. Third and last, after the s2[x] value is moved to s1[x] and the expression is tested for a null terminator, the + + adds 1 to x, thus moving to the next array location.

The standard C function that performs this task is named strcpy() and is shown in Fig. 5-17.

Program

```
main()
{ static char a_string[15] = {"aaaaaaaa"};
  static char b_string[15] = {"bbb"};

  strcpy(a_string,b_string);
  printf("\n a_string = %s,    b_string = %s",a_string,b_string);
}
```

Output

```
a_string = bbb, b_string = bbb
```

5-17   strcpy copying example.

Concatenating two strings

So far, we have examined the comparison and copying of strings; now let's examine their *concatenation*—the adding of one string array's value to the end of another. Figure 5-18 illustrates how concatenation is performed.

The program within Fig. 5-18 begins in a manner similar to string comparison and copying, with the only difference being the calling and execution of the concat function. This concatenation begins by defining and initializing the variables x and y. x will be used to subscript s1[ ] and y will be used to subscript s2[ ]. Once defined, the first while statement will scan the s1[ ] array in search of its null terminator. When reached, the value of x will contain a value one greater than the location of the null terminator within the array. This occurs because x is automatically incremented after the while test criteria is evaluated as specified by the + + operator. Therefore, 1 must be subtracted from the x to ensure that the null value is overwritten by the first character of the array being added. Lastly, the second while loop copies the s2[ ] characters to the end of s1[ ] using a process similar to that discussed for string copying.

The standard C function that performs this task is named strcat() and is shown in Fig. 5-19.

Program

```
main()
{ static char a_string[15] = {"aaaa"};
  static char b_string[15] = {"bbb"};

  concat(a_string,b_string);
  printf("\n a_string = %s,    b_string = %s",a_string,b_string);
}

void concat(s1,s2)
  char s1[], s2[];

{ int x = 0;
  int y = 0;

  while ( s1[x++] )
     ;
  x--;

  while ( s1[x++] = s2[y++] )
     ;
}
```

Output

```
a_string = aaaabbb, b_string = bbb
```

5-18   String concatenation example.

Program

```
main()
{ static char a_string[15] = {"aaaa"};
  static char b_string[15] = {"bbb"};

  strcat(a_string,b_string);
  printf("\n a_string = %s,    b_string = %s",a_string,b_string);
}
```

Output

```
a_string = aaaabbb, b_string = bbb
```

5-19   strcat program example.

6

Structures

From the explanation of arrays in Chapter 5, you learned how to group together related elements of data. C provides yet another facility called a *structure* to perform this task. Unlike arrays, however, structures can bring together data of different data types, data sizes, and even data arrays. I will present two primary examples that illustrate how structures will be used: the first example is the definition of a date, while the second is the definition of a structure within a structure.

Defining structures

The program in Fig. 6-1 uses a struct (for *struct*ure) statement to define the format of a date. Once defined, this date variable will be given a value and printed to the screen via a printf() function.

Program

```
main()
{
    struct date_format
        { int month;
          int day;
          int year;
        };

    struct date_format date;

    date.month = 4;
    date.day   = 9;
    date.year  = 1987;

    printf("\n Month is = %d",date.month);
    printf("\n Day is   = %d",date.day);
    printf("\n Year is  = %d",date.year);

}
```

Output

```
Month is = 4
Day is   = 9
Year is  = 1987
```

6-1   First array example.

The structure programming example in Fig. 6-1 is divided into four parts: the structure definition, the structure allocation, the variable assignment, and the printing of defined values. The first section begins with the word `struct` and is explained in the first structure format shown next in Fig. 6-2.

```
struct template-name
  { data-type data-name;
    date-type date-name;
      . . .
    date-type date-name;
  };
```

6-2 First struct format.

The `struct` statement stands for structure and begins as you would expect—with the word `struct` followed by the name of the structure being defined. This name is then followed by the definition of the variables to be contained within the structure. For example, back in Fig. 6-1, the structure is named `date_format` and contains the three integer variables named `month`, `day`, and `year`. Also note that this variable list is contained within brackets {} and is followed by an ending semicolon. This punctuation is required and is considered to be part of the format.

Before moving on to the second `struct` statement back in Fig. 6-1, let's examine the purpose of the first `struct`. The first `struct` did not create a usable data area or allocate memory for the variables `month`, `day`, and `year`. This first statement only defined the format (also known as a *template*) by which a structure might be defined. The second `struct` statement then uses this template to state that a structure called `date` should be created and allocated memory space, based on the the format of `date_format`, which has been previously defined. Thus, within Fig. 6-1, the `date` structure has an identical format to the `date_format` structure template, with the difference being that `date` is associated with actual memory locations and can be used to store data, while `date_format` is just a structure template from which usable structures may be defined.

The format of this second `struct` statement is shown in Fig. 6-3.

```
struct template-name structure-name, structure-name ...
```

6-3 Second struct format.

As shown in the second `struct` format, it begins with the word `struct` followed by the name of the structure format (also known as a *structure template*), that being followed by the name(s) of the structure(s) to be defined.

Thus far in Fig. 6-1, we have defined a structure format named `date_format` and a usable structure named `date`. Now, let's look at the usage of the variables within the `date` structure. First, you must understand that the variables defined within a structure must always be referenced in association with its structure. This association is made by prefixing the variable name with its structure name, followed by a period (`structure_name.variable_name`). For example, within Fig. 6-1, the `month`, `day`, and `year` variables are prefixed with `date.`, thus making then `date.month`, `date.day`, and `date.year` respectively. Other than this required prefix, however, the variables may be used like regular non-structured variables.

Now that we have examined the structure definition process used in Fig. 6-1, let's look at an alternative definition process (see Fig. 6-4).

The alternative structure definition process used in Fig. 6-4 combines the two struct formats used in Fig. 6-1 into one statement. Note that within this combined definition, the date structure (the structure that actually has associated memory locations) is named after the closing bracket of the variable name list and before the ending semicolon of the struct statement. This format is commonly used when the defined structure template is only used in association with one memory allocated structure. The format of this struct statement is shown next in Fig. 6-5.

Program

```
main()
{
    struct date_format
        { int month;
          int day;
          int year;
        } date;

    date.month = 4;
    date.day   = 9;
    date.year  = 1987;

    printf("\n Month is = %d",date.month);
    printf("\n Day is   = %d",date.day);
    printf("\n Year is  = %d",date.year);

}
```

Output

```
    Month is = 4
    Day is   = 9
    Year is  = 1987
```

6-4 Second struct program example.

```
struct template-name
  { data-type data-name;
    date-type date-name;
        . . .
    date-type date-name;
  } structure-name;
```

6-5 First struct format.

Initializing structures

Structures may be initialized in two main ways, the first of which you have already seen in Fig. 6-1 and Fig. 6-4: by the use of an assignment operator (e.g., date.month = 9;). The second initialization process is shown here in Fig. 6-6.

The structure initialization example in Fig. 6-6 differs from the other structure program examples in three ways.

First, the word static was placed before the struct statement. Second, the numbers 9, 4, and 1987 are listed after the word date following an equal sign and within

Program

```
main()
{
  struct date_format
  { int month;
    int day;
    int year;
  };

  static struct date_format date = { 4, 9, 1987 };

  printf("\n Month is = %d",date.month);
  printf("\n Day is   = %d",date.day);
  printf("\n Year is  = %d",date.year);

}
```

Output

```
Month is = 4
Day is   = 9
Year is  = 1987
```

6-6   Structure initialization example.

brackets. Note that the numbers are in the same order as the structure's variable list; this ensures that the C compiler places the correct value in each variable. Also note that this initialization format is similar to that used when initializing arrays and regular variables. Third, notice that the three assignment statements used in Fig. 6-1 and Fig. 6-4 have been deleted. This deletion was essential because the structure was defined as static and thus its contents need not be set because the structure has already been initialized to its appropriate values.

As an additional point, this initialization process can also be employed when used on the alternative structure definition process shown in Fig. 6-4. This alternative process is shown in Fig. 6-7.

Program

```
main()
{
  static struct date_format
    { int month;
      int day;
      int year;
    } date = { 4, 9, 1987 };

  printf("\n Month is = %d",date.month);
  printf("\n Day is   = %d",date.day);
  printf("\n Year is  = %d",date.year);
}
```

Output

```
Month is = 4
Day is   = 9
Year is  = 1987
```

6-7   Alternate initialization process.

Now that we have discussed and examined various structure definition alternatives, Fig. 6-8 provides a useful programming example of how structures may be effectively used. In fact, to assist in contrasting the use of regular and structured variables, Fig. 6-8 is a rework of the date validation program examined back in Fig. 5-5.

Program

```
main()
{ static int months[] = { 31,28,31,30,31,30,31,31,30,31,30,31 };
  int count;
  char dummy;

  struct date_format
   { int month;
     int day;
     int year;
   };

  struct date_format date;

  printf("\n Enter date in format MM/DD/YY : ");
scanf("%d%c%d%c%d",&date.month,&dummy,&date.day,&dummy,&date.year);

  if ( date.day >= 1 && date.day <= months[date.month-1] )
     printf("\n     Date is valid");
  else
     printf("\n     Date is not valid");
}
```

Output

```
Enter date in format MM/DD/YY : 12/23/86
    Data is valid

Enter date in format MM/DD/YY : 12/33/86
    Date is not valid
```

6-8 Date validation program.

Arrays of structures

Now that we have determined the use of arrays and the use of structures, let's examine arrays of structures. Figure 6-9 illustrates this concept by asking the user to enter five names and birthdays, facilitating their input, and printing out a formatted list.

The program in Fig. 6-9 defines a structure template named date_format, which in turn is used to define the date structure. This process, as you might recall, resembles the process used in Fig. 6-4. This example, however, has one additional attribute—the [10]. Like the definition of a character string, the [10] states that the entity being suffixed is an array. It just so happens that, in this case, it is a structure and not an individual variable. Next, the user is asked to enter five sets of names and dates by a combination of printf() and scanf() functions. Take special note that within the scanf() function, the month variable is referenced as date[count].month. The variable within the braces, like all other arrays, specifies which date array location should be referenced. Figure 6-10 illustrates how an array of structures is stored within memory.

Program

```
main()
{ int count;
  char dummy;
  int no_names;

  struct date_format
    { char name[15];
      int month;
      int day;
      int year;
    } date[5];

  for ( count=0; count < 5; count++ )
    { printf("\n Enter Last Name : ");
      scanf("%s",&date[count].name);

      printf("\n Enter date in format MM/DD/YY : ");
      scanf("%d%c%d%c%d",&date[count].month,&dummy,
        &date[count].day,&dummy,&date[count].year);
    }
  printf("\n\n   Names and Birthday");
  printf("\n   ------------------");

  for ( count=0; count < 5; count++ )
    { printf("\n  %s       %d/%d/%d",date[count].name,
        date[count].month, date[count].day, date[count].year);
    }
}
```

Output

```
Enter last name : Bloom
Enter data in format MM/DD/YY : 06/06/87
Enter last name : Tanner
Enter data in format MM/DD/YY : 04/09/87
Enter last name : Wells
Enter data in format MM/DD/YY : 07/08/83
Enter last name : Tobin
Enter data in format MM/DD/YY : 10/06/88
Enter last name : Gasman
Enter data in format MM/DD/YY : 03/05/87

Names and Birthday
------------------

Bloom     06/06/87
Tanner    4/9/87
Wells     7/8/83
Tobin     10/6/88
Gasman    3/5/87
```

6-9 Array of structures example.

6-10 View of an array of structures.

Structures within structures

Sometimes it is advantageous to place structures within structures. The previously discussed `date` structure is the classic example illustrating this concept. Like many applications, the program listed in Fig. 6-11 has two dates associated with an individual name—the birthday and the wedding anniversary.

Program

```
main()
{
  struct date_format
    { int month;
      int day;
      int year;
    };

  struct info_format
    { char name[20];
      struct date_format birth;
      struct date_format wedding;
    } info;

  strcpy(info.name,"Kim S. Bloom");

  info.birth.month = 4;
  info.birth.day   = 9;
  info.birth.year  = 1958;

  info.wedding.month = 11;
  info.wedding.day   = 2;
  info.wedding.year  = 1980;

  printf("\n Name : %s",info.name);
  printf("\n   Birth   : %d/%d/%d",info.birth.month,
    info.birth.day, info.birth.year);

  printf("\n   Wedding : %d/%d/%d",info.wedding.month,
    info.wedding.day, info.wedding.year);

}
```

Output

```
Name : Kim S. Bloom
  Birth   : 4/9/1958
  Wedding : 12/2/1980
```

6-11   Structure within a structure example.

Figure 6-11 begins by defining a structure template called `date_format`. Once defined, the program then defines a second structure template named `info_format`. In this case however, the word `info` is placed after the structure variable list, thus assigning space in memory as discussed earlier in the chapter. The variable list within the second structure contains the character variable `name` and two `date_format` structures named `birth` and `wedding`, thus alluding to the person's birthday and wedding anniversary, respectively.

Now that the variables and structures have been defined, note the way in which the variables within the structure are referenced. The `name` variable, as you would expect from prior discussion, is referenced by prefixing it with the name of the structure in which it resides—info. Remember, the structure's contents are always associated with info and not info_format, the name of the structure template. Now, take special notice of how the date variables are referenced. As an example, the birthday's month field is written as info.birth.month. info refers to the main structure, birth refers to the structure defined within info using the date_format template, and month is the variable's name. After a quick examination, you will see that this naming convention typifies the process used for referencing the other date variables.

Arrays within structures

The program in Fig. 6-12 provides an example of how to define and use arrays placed within structures.

Within Fig. 6-12, the structure info contains the integer array grades[ ]. This array, may be used like any non-structured variable array, with the exception that—like all structure variables—it must be prefixed with the name of its associated structure. For example, within Fig. 6-12, grades[ ] is always referenced as info.grades[ ].

Program

```
main()
{ int count;

  struct info_format
   { char name[20];
     int grades[5];
   } info;

  printf("\n Enter name : ");
  scanf("%s",info.name);

  for ( count=0; count<5; count++ )
    { printf("\n Enter grade %d : ",count);
      scanf("%d",&info.grades[count]);
    }

  printf("\n\n Grades for %s are \n",info.name);
  for ( count=0; count<5; count++ )
    { printf("\n   Grade %d = %d: ",count,info.grades[count]);
    }
}
```

Output

```
Enter name : Bloom
Enter grade 0 : 100
Enter grade 1 : 95
Enter grade 2 : 80
Enter grade 3 : 90
Enter grade 4 : 85

Grades for Bloom are :

  Grade 0 = 100
  Grade 1 = 95
  Grade 2 = 80
  Grade 3 = 90
  Grade 4 = 85
```

6-12 Arrays within a structure program example.

Figure 6-13 shows how this array and structure is stored within memory. When reviewing this conceptual view, note that the name[ ] string is an array and is stored in the same manner as grades[ ].

info

| name[0] |
| name[1] |

. . .

| name[9] |
| grades[0] |
| grades[1] |
| grades[2] |
| grades[3] |
| grades[4] |

6-13   View of an array within a structure.

Arrays of structures containing arrays

When discussing various structure and array usages, it is inevitable that someone will be forced to place an array of variables within an array of structures. To perform this task, you must define the structure to be an array, as well as define the appropriate variables as arrays (see Fig. 6-14).

Program

```
main()
{ int bigloop;
  int count;

  struct info_format
    { char name[20];
      int grades[5];
    } info[5];

  for ( bigloop=0; bigloop<3; bigloop++ )
    { printf("\n Enter name : ");
      scanf("%s",info[bigloop].name);

      for ( count=0; count<5; count++ )
        { printf("\n Enter grade %d : ",count);
          scanf("%d",&info[bigloop].grades[count]);
        }
    }
  for ( bigloop=0; bigloop<3; bigloop++ )
    { printf("\n\n Grades for %s are : \n",info[bigloop].name);
      for ( count=0; count<5; count++ )
        { printf("\n      Grade %d = %d:",
            count,info[bigloop].grades[count]);
        }
    }
}
```

6-14   Array of structures containing arrays.

Figure 6-14 begins by defining two integer variables—bigloop and count. Big loop will be used to subscript the structure info; count, as before, will be used to subscript the grades[ ] array.

Next, the info structure is defined as an array by placing info[ ] after the structure's variable list. Once the variable and array definitions are complete, the program loops three times, asking the user to enter a name and five associated grades. Note that, within this loop, names[ ] is referenced as info[bigloop].names and the grades[ ] array is referenced as info[bigloop].grades[count], thus in both cases stating which array location within info is being referenced. Additionally, in the case of grades[ ], the array is further defined by the use of count.

This double array definition process is stored in memory in the order shown in Fig. 6-15.

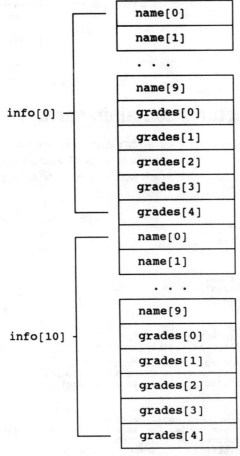

6-15 View of an array of structures with arrays.

7
Pointers

This chapter examines a feature of C not only distinguishing C from virtually all other high level programming languages but also providing it with incredible power and flexibility—*pointers*. These pointers can assist in the manipulation of arrays, the passing of data between functions, the definition of complex data structures, and the tracking of allocated computer memory.

To understand this feature, you must first understand the concept of indirection. Indirection can best be explained using the non-technical example of a telephone book (yes, a telephone book!) The friend you are calling does not physically live in the book; however, the telephone book provides you with the address and phone number of where your friend can be found. Therefore, the phone book is acting as a pointer to your friend. Within C, a pointer performs a similar function—it contains the memory location of where its associated data physically resides. Figure 7-1 illustrates this concept.

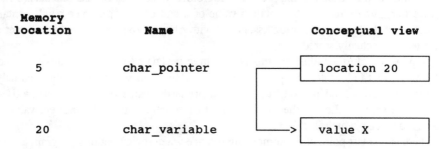

7-1 Conceptual view of a pointer.

When reviewing Fig. 7-1, note that char_pointer is physically located in memory location 5 and char_variable is physically located in memory location 20. Furthermore, note that char_variable has a value of x and char_pointer has a value of 20. This 20, as can be seen in the diagram, specifies where the value within char_variable can be found—namely, location 20. This process within a C program can be seen in Fig. 7-2.

Program

```
main()
{ char *char_pointer;
  char char_variable;

  char_variable = 'x';
  char_pointer = &char_variable;

  printf("\n The pointer value of char_pointer is %x",char_pointer);
  printf("\n The value of char_pointer is %c",*char_pointer);
  printf("\n The value of char_variable is %c",char_variable);
}
```

Output

```
The pointer value of char_pointer is 1d
The value of char_pointer is x
The value of char_variable is x
```

7-2   First pointer example.

Like Fig. 7-1, Fig. 7-2 contains a character variable and a pointer to a character variable—char_variable and char_pointer, respectively. As you might surmise, the asterisk within the char statement prefixing char_pointer instructs the compiler to treat its associated variable as a pointer and not a regular variable. This is an important distinction because character data and pointers are stored differently within memory. In fact, they sometimes even require different amounts of memory space. As a result, an attempt to incorrectly use their data types could cause very strange results.

Once defined, char_variable is set to a value of x and the pointer char_pointer is given the memory address of where char_variable is stored. This is done by placing an ampersand & before char_variable within the assignment statement. The & is called the address operator and instructs the compiler to pass the address, not the value, of the variable being prefixed. Therefore, once these two statements are executed, char_variable will contain a value of x and char_pointer will contain the address of the memory location associated with char_variable, which in fact is where the x is actually stored.

To prove and further illustrate this point, three printf() function calls are used. The first printf() statement prints the memory location where x resides—namely, location 1d. The second printf() function prints the value of char_variable, which is the value x. Lastly, the third printf() function prints the indirect value of char_pointer which is also x.

There is one last point of the utmost importance when reviewing this program and all other programs that use pointers: all pointers are not the same. Namely, a pointer that points to a char variable must be defined as a char, and a pointer that points to an int or double should be defined as an int pointer or double pointer, respectively. For example, the pointer used to reference char char_pointer must be defined as char *pointer, and a pointer to int an_integer must be defined as int *pointer.

Figure 7-3 expands the first pointer example and sheds additional light on the use of pointers.

The program in Fig. 7-3 begins in a manner similar to Fig. 7-1 by defining a character variable and a pointer to a character variable. From there, a third variable named

Program

```
main()
{ char *char_pointer;
  char char_variable;
  char val_of_x;

  val_of_x = 'x';

  char_pointer = &val_of_x;
  char_variable = *char_pointer;

  printf("\n The value of char_variable is %c",char_variable);
}
```

Output

```
The value of char_variable is x
```

7-3   Expanded pointer example.

val_of_x is also defined. This variable, as you might expect, is set to a value of x immediately after being defined. The next line—char_pointer = &val_of_x— causes the address of val_of_x (as specified by the &) to be passed to the pointer value char_pointer. Then, in the statement char_variable = *char _pointer, char_variable is set to the value contained in the memory location specified by char_pointer, which in fact is the value x. Remember, the asterisk before char_pointer causes the indirection to val_of_x. If the * was not present, then char_variable would be set equal to the value in char_pointer, which is the address of val_of_x. This accidental error is shown in Fig. 7-4.

Program

```
main()
{ char *char_pointer;
  char char_variable;
  char val_of_x;

  val_of_x = 'x';

  char_pointer = &val_of_x;
  char_variable = char_pointer;

  printf("\n The value of char_variable is %c",char_variable);
  printf("\n The value of char_variable is %x",char_variable);
}
```

Output

```
The value of char_variable is
The value of char_variable is 20
```

7-4   Pointer programming error example.

The erred program in Fig. 7-4 incorrectly passes a character pointer to a non-pointer variable in the statement char_variable = char_pointer. This program moves the contents of char_pointer and not the indirect value of char_pointer to char_variable. As shown in the output of the program, you can see that the ASCII value is non-printable; thus, it could not possibly be x.

Up to now, pointers have been used in cooperation with regular variables; as can be seen in Fig. 7-5, pointer values can be passed from pointer to pointer.

Program

```
main()
{ char *point_1;
  char *point_2;
  char var_1;
  char var_2;

  var_1 = 'x';

  point_1 = &var_1;
  point_2 = point_1;

  var_2 = *point_2;

  printf("\n The value of var_1 is %c",var_1);
  printf("\n The value of var_2 is %c",var_2);
  printf("\n The indirect value of point_1 is %c",*point_1);
  printf("\n The indirect value of point_2 is %c",*point_2);
  printf("\n The address value of point_1 is %d",point_1);
  printf("\n The address value of point_2 is %d",point_2);
}
```

Output

```
The value of var_1 is x
The value of var_2 is x
The indirect value of point_1 is x
The indirect value of point_2 is x
The address value of point_1 is 33
The address value of point_2 is 33
```

7-5 Passing pointer address example.

The program in Fig. 7-5 set var__1 to a value of x and sets pointer point__1 to the address of var__1. Then, the statement point__2 = point__1 makes point__2 point to the same location as point__1—namely, var__1. Next, now that pointer point__2 points to variable var__1, the statement var__2 = *point__2 gives var__2 the value of x.

This four statement scenario is proven by the ending printf() calls. In particular, note that the contents of both variables is x, that both pointers contain the same indirect value of x (both point to var__1), and that both pointers point to the same indirect memory location.

The program in Fig. 7-6 displays yet another introductory pointer program. This program, however, illustrates that many pointers can point to the same memory location and can thus all be initialized at one time.

In Fig. 7-6, all five pointers are directed to the memory location associated with char__variable. Thus, when char__variable is set to x, the indirect value of all five pointers is also set to x.

Pointers and arrays

Pointers are most commonly used to manipulate arrays, basically for three reasons; program efficiency, ease of writing, and C snob appeal. Program efficiency can be improved because compilers tend to generate better machine code from pointer notation than from

Program

```
main()
{ char *point_1;
  char *point_2;
  char *point_3;
  char *point_4;
  char *point_5;
  char char_variable;

  point_1 = &char_variable;
  point_2 = &char_variable;
  point_3 = &char_variable;
  point_4 = &char_variable;
  point_5 = &char_variable;

  char_variable = 'x';

  printf("\n The indirect value of point_1 is %c",*point_1);
  printf("\n The indirect value of point_2 is %c",*point_2);
  printf("\n The indirect value of point_3 is %c",*point_3);
  printf("\n The indirect value of point_4 is %c",*point_4);
  printf("\n The indirect value of point_5 is %c",*point_5);
}
```

Output

```
The indirect value of point_1 is x
The indirect value of point_2 is x
The indirect value of point_3 is x
The indirect value of point_4 is x
The indirect value of point_5 is x
```

7-6 Additional pointer example.

array notation. This advantage, however, is starting to diminish as compiler optimization techniques improve. In fact, many compilers automatically convert array notation to pointer notation during the compilation process. Moving to the second reason, people find pointer notation easier to type. Lastly, and especially with arrays, is C snob appeal. This idea being, that if you are not going to take advantage of C's strengths and format, why use C at all.

To illustrate the use of array pointers, Table 7-1 illustrates equivalent array and pointer notation.

**Table 7-1 Equivalent
array and pointer notation.**

Array notation	Pointer notation
an_array	a_pointer
an_array [0]	*a_pointer
an_array [2]	*(a_pointer + 2)

In Table 7-1, the expressions on the left use the traditional array notation discussed in Chapter 5, while the expressions on the right show their equivalent pointer expression. When reviewing this table, you must remember one fact that shall greatly increase your understanding of these examples: when an array name (e.g., grades) is used alone without its subscript [ ], it is considered to be a pointer to the array's first memory location.

Thus, the expressions &grade[0] and grades are equivalent, and both produce the address of the first array location. In the first example of Table 7-1, a__pointer is being given the address of the first grades[] array location. The second and third examples are referencing various locations within the grades[] array.

Figure 7-7 provides the first example of this alternate array notation.

Program

```
main()
{ static char alphabet [] = {"abcdefghijklmnopqrstuvwxyz"};
  int count;

  count = 0;

  printf("\n Value of grades[0] = %c",alphabet[0]);
  printf("\n Value of *grades   = %c",*alphabet);

  printf("\n Pointer to grades[0] is address   %d",&alphabet[0]);
  printf("\n Pointer to grades is address      %d",alphabet);
}
```

Output

```
Value of grades[0] = a
Value of *grades   = a
Pointer to grades[0] is address   15
Pointer to grades is address      15
```

7-7   First array pointer example.

Figure 7-7 contains two sets of print statements: the first set prints the value of the first alphabet[] array location (namely, the value a), while the second set prints the memory location where the a value previously printed physically resides. Note that, in both sets, the same value is printed; this proves the equivalency of the two notations.

Figure 7-8 expands on the previous example by adding a loop to print the alphabet in both standard and pointer notation.

The example following in Fig. 7-9 introduces a new concept called *pointer arithmetic*, which allows you to move from array location to array location by incrementing or decrementing a pointer's value.

The program in Fig. 7-9 employs pointer arithmetic to print the alphabet. Within this program, c__pointer is given the starting address of the alphabet array in the statement c__pointer = alphabet. This assignment is necessary because if you modify the pointer value within alphabet, you will lose the starting position of the alphabet array. Also, many compilers will give an error or warning if you attempt to modify that value.

Next, after printing the words "The alphabet," the while loop causes the repeated execution of printf(). Within this function, the clause *(c__pointer + +) is referencing the memory location to be printed and is then incrementing c__pointer, causing it to point to the next array location.

To further illustrate this process, Fig. 7-10 not only prints the alphabet array but also prints its associated memory addresses. Note that the pointer value within c__pointer is incremented by 1 after each reiteration of the loop.

Program

```
main()
{ static char alphabet [] = {"abcdefghijklmnopqrstuvwxyz"};
  int count;

  count = 0;

  printf("\n Letters of the Alphabet");
  printf("\n -----------------------");
  for ( count = 0; count < 26; count++ )
    printf("\n           %c            %c",
    alphabet[count], *(alphabet + count) );
}
```

Output

```
Letters of the Alphabet
-----------------------
          a           a
          b           b
          c           c
          d           d
          e           e
          f           f
          g           g
          h           h
          i           i
          j           j
          k           k
          l           l
          m           m
          n           n
          o           o
          p           p
          q           q
          r           r
          s           s
          t           t
          u           u
          v           v
          w           w
          x           x
          y           y
          z           z
```

7-8 Expanded array pointer example.

Program

```
main()
{ static char alphabet [] = {"abcdefghijklmnopqrstuvwxyz"};
  char *c_pointer;

  c_pointer = alphabet;

  printf("\n The Alphabet : ");

  while ( *c_pointer )
  { printf("%c", *(c_pointer++) );
  }
}
```

Output

```
The Alphabet : abcdefghijklmnopqrstuvwxyz
```

7-9 Pointer arithmetic example.

Program

```
main()
{ static char alphabet [] = {"abcdefghijklmnopqrstuvwxyz"};
  char *c_pointer;

  c_pointer = alphabet;

  printf("\n The Alphabet");
  printf("\n ------------");

  while ( *c_pointer )
    { printf("\n    %c  %d", *(c_pointer), c_pointer++ );
    }
}
```

Output

```
The Alphabet
------------
   a   2
   b   3
   c   4
   d   5
   e   6
   f   7
   g   8
   h   9
   i  10
   j  11
   k  12
   l  13
   m  14
   n  15
   o  16
   p  17
   q  18
   r  19
   s  20
   t  21
   u  22
   v  23
   w  24
   x  25
   y  26
   z  27
```

7-10 Incrementing a pointer example.

As you might expect, a pointer value may also be decremented using the – operator (see Fig. 7-11).

Figure 7-11 performs two types of pointer arithmetic. First, in the statement c_pointer = alphabet + 25, c_pointer is being pointed to the 25 memory locations after the beginning of the alphabet—namely, the location of z. The second type of pointer arithmetic is employing the—to move the pointer back one memory location with each loop reiteration.

Pointers to structures

Thus far, we have examined how pointers can be used to manipulate regular variables and arrays. As shall soon be seen, pointers can be used in the processing of structures. Figure 7-12 offers an example of this manipulation.

Program

```
main()
{ static char alphabet [] = {"abcdefghijklmnopqrstuvwxyz"};
  char *c_pointer;

  c_pointer = alphabet + 25;

  printf("\n The Alphabet");
  printf("\n ------------");

  do
    { printf("\n      %c  %d", *(c_pointer), c_pointer-- );
    } while ( c_pointer >= alphabet );
}
```

Output

```
The Alphabet
------------
  z   28
  y   27
  x   26
  w   25
  v   24
  u   23
  t   22
  s   21
  r   20
  q   19
  p   18
  o   17
  n   16
  m   15
  l   14
  k   13
  j   12
  i   11
  h   10
  g   9
  f   8
  e   7
  d   6
  c   5
  b   4
  a   3
```

7-11 Decrementing a pointer example.

Figure 7-12 begins by defining the date_format structure template using the struct format as in Fig. 6-2. Once defined, a second struct statement defines a usable structure named date and a pointer to the date structure named *date_pointer. When defining a pointer to a structure, it is imperative that the pointer being defined is not only defined within a struct statement but is defined using the same structure template as the structure it will be referencing.

In the case of Fig. 7-12, note that both date and date_pointer are defined using the date_format template. Once defined, like other pointers, date_pointer must be passed the address of the structure it will be defined as—namely, date. Next, note the format used to reference the month variable: the pointer name, followed by – >, that being followed by the variable being referenced. Therefore, the statement date.month = 4 can be written in the format date_pointer – >month = 4.

Program

```
main()
{
  struct date_format
    { int month;
      int day;
      int year;
    };

  struct date_format date, *date_pointer;
  date_pointer = &date;

  date_pointer->month = 4;
  date_pointer->day   = 9;
  date_pointer->year  = 1987;

  printf("\n Month is = %d",date_pointer->month);
  printf("\n Day is   = %d",date_pointer->day);
  printf("\n Year is  = %d",date_pointer->year);
}
```

Output

```
Month is = 4
Day is   = 9
Year is  = 1987
```

7-12 Pointer to a structure example.

As mentioned in previous chapters, C supports the concept of arrays or structures. Therefore, because pointers can be used interchangably with standard array notation, array structures can also be referenced through pointers in a manner similar to the process used to reference variables and arrays. Figure 7-13 illustrates this concept.

The program in Fig. 7-13 is a rewording of the array program shown in Fig. 6-9 and is explained within Chapter 6. When reviewing this figure, take special note as to how the structure's array locations are referenced. For example, the month variable is referenced as (date_pointer + count) ->month. This format encloses the pointer name and offset, namely date_pointer and count, respectively, within the parentheses to ensure that the compiler correctly understands the order of operations. This is followed by the - > operator and the structure variable being referenced.

Program

```
main()
{ int count;
  char dummy;
  int no_names;

  struct date_format
    { char name[15];
      int month;
      int day;
      int year;
    } date[5];

  struct date_format *date_pointer;
  date_pointer = &date;
```

7-13 Pointer to an array of structures example.

```
   for ( count=0; count < 5; count++ )
     { printf("\n Enter Last Name : ");
       scanf("%s",&(date_pointer + count )->name);

       printf("\n Enter date in format MM/DD/YY : ");
       scanf("%d%c%d%c%d",&( date_pointer + count )->month,&dummy,
          &( date_pointer + count )->day,&dummy,
          &( date_pointer + count )->year);
     }

   printf("\n\n   Names and Birthday");
   printf("\n   ------------------");

     for ( count=0; count < 5; count++ )
     { printf("\n  %s      %d/%d/%d",( date_pointer + count )->name,
          ( date_pointer + count )->month,
          ( date_pointer + count )->day,
          ( date_pointer + count )->year);
     }
}
```

Output

```
Enter Last Name : Bloom
Enter date in format MM/DD/YY : 01/01/87
Enter Last Name : Tanner
Enter date in format MM/DD/YY : 02/02/87
Enter Last Name : Wells
Enter date in format MM/DD/YY : 03/03/87
Enter Last Name : Gagne
Enter date in format MM/DD/YY : 04/04/87
Enter Last Name : Kalish
Enter date in format MM/DD/YY : 05/05/87

  Names and Birthday
  ------------------
  Bloom      1/1/87
  Tanner     2/2/87
  Wells      3/3/87
  Gagne      4/4/87
  Kalish     5/5/87
```

8

Functions

Thus far, functions have been used and manipulated as needed to illustrate other topics. But, as promised within those illustrations, I will now present functions in detail.

A *function* is nothing more than a label that allows a defined list of statements to be grouped under a common name. Thus, allowing these statements to be executed simply by referencing the specified label. To illustrate this process, let's once again turn to our first C program reshown in Fig. 8-1.

Program

```
Main()
{ Printf("Hello There");
}
```

8-1   First C program.

This program brings forward some key points that have not yet been discussed. First, note that the program begins with the word main followed by a set of empty parentheses. This combination, main(), states that the lines listed below it within the brackets are part of a function called main. The parentheses are used to pass data values called *parameters* from function to function. Even when there is no data to be passed, as is the case with main(), the parentheses are still required.

All C programs are—or should be—divided into these functions that are executed when their name is referenced within other functions. This referencing concept can be seen by reviewing the way in which the printf() function was executed within Fig. 8-1.

This process of executing functions within other functions, however, presents the small problem of which function should be executed first. Therefore, to alleviate this situation, C requires all programs to have a function called main(); and by default, this function is automatically executed first.

Calling functions

Now turn your attention to the `printf()` function call within `main()` of Fig. 8-1. When reviewing this function call, you should notice three things. First, quotation marks are used to specify which characters are to be printed to the terminal. Second, just like `main()`, `printf()` is followed by opening and closing parentheses. These parentheses contain the string to be passed from `main()` to `printf()`. Lastly, the `printf()` function call ends with a semicolon, which is not part of the function call but is just a statement terminator like that at the end of all C statements. As you shall see in Fig. 8-2 through Fig. 8-4, functions are often called within statements, mathematical formulas, and even within other functions. In these cases, the semicolon is placed at the end of the line and not at the end of the function call.

Figure 8-2 illustrates how functions can be called from within C statements.

Program

```
main()
{ static char a_string[] = {"Hello there"};
  static char b_string[] = {"Hello there"};

  if ( strcmp(a_string, b_string) == 0 )
     printf("\n The two strings are equal");
  else
     printf("\n The two strings are not equal");
}
```

Output

```
The two strings are equal
```

8-2 Function call within an if statement.

The program in Fig. 8-2 employs the `strcmp()` function that compares the equality of character strings. (This function is discussed in length within Chapter 5.) Note that this function is called from within an `if` statement. When this technique is used, the value returned by the function, not the function itself, is used by the `if` statement. For example, within Fig. 8-2, character strings `a_string` and `b_string` are compared. Because they have equal values, `strcmp()` returns a zero (stating equality). It is this zero that is used for comparison within the `if` statement.

Figure 8-3 illustrates how a function can be called from within a mathematical formula.

The program shown in Fig. 8-3 defines the variables `x`, `y`, and `z`. Once defined, `x` is set to 9, `y` is set to 10, and `z` is set equal to the square of `x` plus the value of `y`.

This program has three noteworthy points. First, note the presence of the `#include` statement. This statement is called a *compiler directive* and is discussed fully in Chapter 11. For now, however, just consider it to be a requirement of the square root function.

Second, note that `x` and `y` were set to the values 9.0 and 10.0, not 9 and 10. This .0 instructs the compiler to pass the values 9 and 10 in a floating point format and not as an integer. Remember, C is very particular in regard to the format of data variable values. Without the .0, the 9 and 10 would be construed as integers and would be incorrectly placed in `x` and `y`.

Program

```
#include "c:\lc\math.h"

main()
{ double x;
  double y;
  double z;

  x = 9.0;
  y = 10.0;

  z = sqrt(x) + y;

  printf("\n The value is %4.2f",z);
}
```

Output

```
The value is 13.00
```

8-3   Function call within a formula.

Lastly, and most important to this discussion, the formula uses the square root value within the formulation of z.

As previously mentioned, functions can be called from within functions. This process is illustrated in Fig. 8-4.

Like Fig. 8-2 and Fig. 8-3, when a function is called from within a function, the return value of the inner function is used by the outer function. For example, in Fig. 8-4, the strlen() function is called from within a printf() function. strlen() calculates the number of characters in a character string and returns that calculated value. The printf() function then displays this returned value on the screen as shown in the program's output.

Program

```
main()
{ static char a_string[] = {"Hello there"};

  printf("\n a_string is %d characters long",strlen(a_string) );
}
```

Output

```
a_string is 11 characters long
```

8-4   Function call within a function.

Passing and receiving parameters

Thus far, we have examined how values are passed to functions. Now let's determine how the functions being called deal with these passed values (see Fig. 8-5).

The program listed in Fig. 8-5, defines and calls a function named square(), which calculates and prints the square of a number. When reviewing this function, note the way in which variables a and b are defined. In particular, note that a is defined before

Program

```
main()
{ int x;

  x = 3;

  square(x);
}

square(a)
int a;
{ int b;
  b = a * a;
  printf("\n The square of %d is %d", a, b);
}
```

Output

```
The square of 3 is 9
```

8-5 First parameter example.

the function's open bracket and that b is defined after the opening bracket. This placement indicates that a is a variable into which a parameter is passed. On the other hand, b is called an *automatic variable* and instructs the compiler that b will only be used within the function.

Now let's modify our program to multiply two numbers together and print the calculated value. Look at Fig. 8-6.

Program

```
main()
{ int x;
  int y;

  x = 2;
  y = 3;

  times(x,y);
}

times(a,b)
int a;
int b;
{ int c;
  c = a * b;
  printf("\n The product of %d times %d is %d", a, b, c);
}
```

Output

```
The product of 2 and 3 is 6
```

8-6 Second parameter example.

The program in Fig. 8-6 defines and calls the t imes () function, which accepts two integer parameters, multiplies them together, and then prints the total. As shown in the program, each passed parameter has a variable into which it can be placed. Also, note that these parameters are passed positionally, this meaning that the first passed parameter is placed in the first listed, the second parameter is placed in the second variable listed, and so on. In the case of the times() function in Fig. 8-6, for example, the value of x will be passed into variable a and the value of y is placed in variable b.

This concept of positionally passed values has one additional component—the consistency of the data types of the values being passed. In Fig. 8-6, both x and a are defined as integers. This data type consistency is required because, without it, the called function would not know the format of the incoming data and thus could not interpret it correctly.

Figure 8-7 further illustrates this concept of data type consistency.

Program

```
main()
{ int     an_int;
  double a_double;
  long    a_long_int;
  char    a_char;

  an_int = 1;
  a_double = 2;
  a_long_int = 3;
  a_char = 'A';

  dummy(an_int, a_double, a_long_int, a_char);
}

dummy(a, b, c, d)
  int a;
  double b;
  long c;
  char d;
{
  printf("\n The integer   is %d", a);
  printf("\n The double    is %f", b);
  printf("\n The long      is %ld", c);
  printf("\n The character is %c", d);
}
```

Output

```
The integer   is 1
The double    is 2
The long      is 3
The character is A
```

8-7 Data type consistency example.

Return values

Figure 8-8 is a modification of the program in Fig. 8-6; the printf() function has been moved out of times() and placed within main(). Also, a return statement has been placed in the times() function; this statement will pass the value contained within it (namely, c) back to the equation where times() was called. This process will instruct the compiler to give the times() function the variable-like property of containing a value (this value being the value of the variable in the return statement).

For example, within Fig. 8-8, times() is called in the statement z = times(x, y). Within times(), a value is calculated and placed in c. The value within c is then passed back to z = times(x, y) via the return statement, giving the effect of being z = 6. This 6 is then printed on the screen.

Program

```
main()
{ int x;
  int y;
  int z;

  x = 2;
  y = 3;

  z = times(x,y);
  printf("\n The product of %d times %d is %d", x, y, z);
}

int times(a,b)
 int a;
 int b;
 { int c;
   c = a * b;
   return (c);
 }
```

Output

8-8 First return code example.

Now that we have examined the process of returning values from a function, an additional type of data consistency is required between the data type of the value in the `return` statement and the data type of the function. Look at Fig. 8-9.

Figure 8-9 presents two types of consistency. The first, discussed previously, deals with parameter passing. As can be seen, the value being passed—namely x—and the variable into which x will be received—namely a—are both defined as integers.

The second data consistency involves the process used to return a value from the called function and appears in four areas, two being within the calling function and two

Program

```
main()
{ int x;
  double y;
  double square();

  x = 4.0;

  y = square(x);
  printf("\n The square of %d is %4.2f", x, y);
}

double square(a)
 int a;
{ double b;
  b = a * a;
  return(b);
}
```

Output

```
The square of 4 is 16.00
```

8-9 Data consistency example.

being within the function being called. Within the calling function—main()— are two double data type definitions. The first—double y—defines the data type of the variable that will be receiving the returned value of the square() function. The second double statement states that the function square will be returning a value defined as a double. In the square() function itself, the name is prefixed by the data type that it shall return. Lastly, in the statement double b, b is defined as a double. b is the variable referenced within the return statement.

Figure 8-10 further illustrates this required return value data type consistency.

Program

```
main()
{ int a;

  double d;
  double dbl_function();

  int i;
  int int_fucntion();

  a = 5;

  d = dbl_function(a);
  printf("\n The double function returned a %f", d);

  i = int_function(a);
  printf("\n The double function returned a %d", i);
}

double dbl_function(x)
  int x;
{ double y;
  y = x * 3.14;
  return(y);
}

int int_function(x)
  int x;
{ int y;
  y = x * 3.14;
  return(y);
}
```

Output

```
The double function returned a 15.7000000
The double function returned a 15
```

8-10 Additional data return example.

Passing arrays

Like regular variables, arrays can also be passed to a function. This array passing, however, is different from that done with regular variables. With regular variables, the value of the specified variable is passed; with arrays, the address of the first array memory location is passed (e.g., an array pointer). Once passed to the function, you may manipulate that array using either array or pointer notation.

As a first example of this process, Fig. 8-11 passes a character array to the function `length()`. This function is similar to the `strlen()` function supplied on most compilers and illustrates how to receive an array pointer in a way that facilitates the use of standard array notation.

Program

```
main()
{ static char a_string[15] = {"Hi There"};
  int the_len;

  the_len = length(a_string);
  printf("\n The length of a_string is %d",the_len);
}

int length(s1)
 char s1[];
{ int x = 0;
  while ( s1[x] )
  ++x;
  return(x);
}
```

Output

```
The length of a_string is 8
```

8-11 First array passing example.

The program listed in Fig. 8-11 is discussed at length within Chapter 5; basically, it counts the number of characters in a character array by searching for its ending string terminator. Within this program, the starting address of the a_string character array is passed to `length()` in the statement the_len = `length(a_string)`. Remember, as discussed in Chapter 7, when an array's name is used without a suffixed [], the name is considered a pointer to the array's first location. Within the called function `length()`, an array named s1[] is positioned to receive the pointer and establish the array within the function. Once defined, it may be used like any other array. One note of caution, however: because the array address (*not* the array values) was passed, you are accessing the same memory area as the original array; and, thus, any changes made to the passed array are permanently changed in the original array.

Figure 8-12 performs the same task as that discussed in Fig. 8-11, the difference being that `length()` is using pointer instead of array notation.

In Fig. 8-12, the process used to call functions is identical with that used in Fig. 8-11. The difference is completely within the `length()` function. Note that, within `length()`, the pointer received from a_string[] is placed in a character pointer defined as char *s1. Once defined as a pointer, the array may be manipulated using pointer notation.

Alternatively, you may define the incoming pointer as an array for documentation purposes and then pass the array address to a pointer and use pointer notation (see Fig. 8-13).

Program

```
main()
{ static char a_string[15] = {"Hi There"};
  int the_len;

  the_len = length(a_string);
  printf("\n The length of a_string is %d",the_len);
}

int length(s1)
 char *s1;
{ int x = 0;
  while ( *s1++ )
  ++x;
  return(x);
}
```

Output

```
The length of a_string is 8
```

8-12 Second array passing example.

Program

```
main()
{ static char a_string[15] = {"Hi There"};
  int the_len;

  the_len = length(a_string);
  printf("\n The length of a_string is %d",the_len);
}

int length(s1)
 char s1[];
{ char *s_point;
  int x = 0;

  s_point = s1;
  while ( *s_point++ )
  ++x;
  return(x);
}
```

Output

```
The length of a_string is 8
```

8-13 Alternate array processing example.

Global variables

Sometimes it is necessary to reference the same variable from within many functions, one such classic case being the line counter in a report program. These variables are known as *global variables* and are defined by placing the variable's definition before the main() function (see Fig. 8-14).

Program

```
int line_count = 0;
main()
{ print1();
  print2();
  print3();
  print4();
  print5();
}
print1()
{ line_count++;
  printf("\n This is print1, line_count is %d",line_count);
}

print2()
{ line_count++;
  printf("\n This is print2, line_count is %d",line_count);
}

print3()
{ line_count++;
  printf("\n This is print3, line_count is %d",line_count);
}

print4()
{ line_count++;
  printf("\n This is print4, line_count is %d",line_count);
}

print5()
{ line_count++;
  printf("\n This is print5, line_count is %d",line_count);
}
```

Output

```
This is print1, line_count is 1
This is print2, line_count is 2
This is print3, line_count is 3
This is print4, line_count is 4
This is print5, line_count is 5
```

8-14 Global variable example.

In Fig. 8-14, the integer variable line_count is defined prior to the beginning of the main() function. This simple action of not placing a variable within a particular function makes it usable by all functions. To illustrate this point, main() calls five functions, each of which increments line_count and prints its value on the screen. As you can see, line_count is not defined within any of these functions and keeps its value as it moves from function to function.

Automatic and static variables

By a quick review of the programming examples in this and other chapters, you will see that some variable definitions (e.g., int x) begin with the word "static" and some do not. Those variables defined by using the word "static" are called *static variables*. Variables defined without the word "static" are considered to be automatic variables. Automatic variables may be defined by prefixing the data definition with the word "auto" (Ex. auto int x). However, because "auto" is the default and not required, it is barely ever used.

During program execution, automatic variables are created and allocated memory when the function in which they reside is executed. When the function is terminated, the memory associated with these variables are released; hence, in a manner of speaking, the variables disappear. This automatic creation and deletion of variables facilitates an efficient use of memory because only the variables currently in use require space. The drawbacks of this process are that the variables must be created and initialized each time its function is called; additionally, because the variable is being recreated, it loses its prior value.

Static variables are not created and deleted in accordance with its host function. If a variable is defined as static, its memory space is allocated and initialized when the program begins and remains in memory until the program terminates. The advantage of this approach is that, because the memory space associated with the variable is not lost, the variable's value from the prior execution is still present if the function is called a second time. The major drawbacks of static variables are that they take up memory space for the entire execution of the program and their values are only reinitialized once. Therefore, if the first execution of the function modifies its value, the second execution of that function will begin with modified data.

Figure 8-15 illustrates the difference between these two variable types.

Program

```
main()
{ int count;
  for (count = 0; count < 5; count++)
    { printf("\n\n Loop %d",count);
      loop_function();
    }
}

loop_function()
{ static int stat_var = 0;
  int auto_var = 0;

  stat_var++;
  auto_var++;

  printf("\n    The stat_var variable = %d",stat_var);
  printf("\n    The auto_var variable = %d",auto_var);
}
```

Output

```
Loop 0
    The stat_var variable = 1
    The auto_var variable = 1

Loop 1
    The stat_var variable = 2
    The auto_var variable = 1

Loop 2
    The stat_var variable = 3
    The auto_var variable = 1

Loop 3
    The stat_var variable = 4
    The auto_var variable = 1

Loop 4
    The stat_var variable = 5
    The auto_var variable = 1
```

8-15 Static and automatic variable example.

As shown in Fig. 8-15, variable stat__var, a static variable, held its value from execution to execution. auto__var, an automatic variable, was continually reinitialized.

Parameter passing by value and address

All data passed from one function to another is passed either by value or by address. When a parameter is passed by value, the actual value of the variable is sent. When a parameter is passed by address, a pointer is passed stating where in memory the needed value can be found. Figure 8-16 shows the process and implications of these two different methods.

Program

```
main()
{ int a_variable;
  int *a_pointer;
  int b_variable;

  a_variable = 10;
  b_variable = 10;
  a_pointer = &a_variable;

  dummy(a_pointer, b_variable);

  printf("\n A_variable has a value of %d",a_variable);
  printf("\n B_variable has a value of %d",b_variable);
}

dummy(a_point, b_var)
  int *a_point;
  int b_var;
{ *a_point = 5;
  b_var = 5;
}
```

Output

```
A_variable has a value of 5
B_variable has a value of 10
```

8-16 Value and address parameter passing example.

As shown in Fig. 8-16, two parameters are being passed to the function called dummy(). The first is a pointer, while the second is a regular variable. When a regular variable is passed, C automatically sets up a memory location for the received value in the format specified in the parameter definition (e.g., int b__val). Therefore, because this received value resides in its own memory location, changes made to this value do not affect the original variable—a__variable. When a pointer is passed, as is the case with a__pointer, the called function—dummy()—is accessed using the same memory locations as the original pointer—a__pointer. Therefore, changes made to a variable within the called function permanently affect the value of the variable in the calling function—a__pointer and a__variable in main().

9

Input and output

All of the programs presented in prior chapters received their input from the keyboard via the scanf() function and displayed their output on the screen using printf(). These capabilities are sufficient for some software projects, but most applications require the additional ability to access and manipulate data stored on floppy disks or other storage media. As you might expect, C provides this ability; however, C—unlike most other programming languages—does not contain any input/output statements like read, write, input, print, or display. All I/O is performed by calling functions similar to scanf() and printf() supplied by the compiler manufacturer.

Let's begin our scrutiny of program input and output by analyzing the functions that we are most familiar with—namely, scanf() and printf().

The printf( ) function

The printf() function is used to display text and variable values on the screen or other specified output device. The format of this function is shown in Fig. 9-1.

```
printf(print-mask, variable-list)
```

9-1 printf( ) function format.

The printf() function is divided into three parts; the word printf, the print mask, and (if applicable) the list of variables to be printed. The *print mask* is an intertwined combination of the text that will be printed as shown in the mask and variable definition types. As shall soon be seen, these definition types are used to specify the data type of the variable being printed, as well as their location within its surrounding verbiage. The *variable list* is the list of variables to be printed in accordance with the variable definition types in the print mask.

Figure 9-2 shows an example of the printf() function.

The program in Fig. 9-2 brings forth many key points about the printf() function, namely the \n, %d, the text within the double quotes, and the x variable placed after the

Program

```
main()
{ int x = 5;
  printf("\n The variable x has a value of %d",x);
}
```

Output

```
The variable x has a value of 5
```

9-2 First printf( ) example.

closing quote and comma. The \n is called an *escape sequence* and causes the text following it to begin on a new line. Figure 9-3 further illustrates this process.

As can be seen when reviewing the program output in Fig. 9-3, each time a \n was encountered, the X's began printing on a new line. Without the \n values, the X's would just print horizontally on one line. The \n, however, is not the only escape sequence option. Table 9-1 offers some other options.

Program

```
main()
{ printf("\n x \n xx \n xxx \n xxxx \n xxxxx");
}
```

Output

```
*
**
***
****
*****
```

9-3 New line escape sequence example.

Table 9-1   Escape sequence options.

Type	Sequence
Backslash	\\
Backspace	\b
Bit pattern	\ddd
Carriage return	\r
Form feed	\f
Horizontal tab	\t
New line	\n
Single quote	\'

Figure 9-4 illustrates the use of other selected escape sequence characters.

Looking back to Fig. 9-2, the %d is called a *data type identifier*. This identifier serves two purposes: it identifies the data type of its associated variable, and it states where that variable's values should be printed (see Fig. 9-5).

Program

```
main()
{ printf("\n tab \t tab \t tab \t tab");
  printf("\n backslash \\ backslash \\ backslash");
  printf("\n quote \' quote \' quote \'");
}
```

Output

```
        tab     tab       tab      tab
        backslash \ backslash \ backslash
        quote ' quote ' qoute
```

9-4 Other escape sequence examples.

Program

```
main()
{ int    i = 1;
  float  f = 2.0;
  char   c = 'A';

  printf("\nThe integer is %d, float is %f, character is %c",i,f,c);
}
```

Output

```
        The integer is 1, float is 2.0000000, character is A
```

9-5 Data type identifier example.

In Fig. 9-5, three variables are defined— i as an integer, f as a floating point, and c as a character. When reviewing this program, notice that these variables were printed in the order that they were listed within the function. Also, the data type identifiers within the print mask are placed in the same order as the variable list. As you can see, %d is used for integers, %f is used for floating points, and %c is used for characters. A complete list of these symbols can be found in Table 9-2.

Table 9-2   Data type identifiers.

Character	Purpose
c	Prints the value of a character.
d	Prints the decimal value of an integer number.
e	Prints a number in an exponential notation format.
f	Prints a floating point number in floating point format.
g	Prints a floating point number in either *e* or *f* format based on the number being printed.
o	Prints the octal value of an integer number.
u	Prints the value of an unsigned integer.
x	Prints the hexadecimal value of an integer number.

The scanf( ) function

The scanf() function is used to input data from the keyboard or other specified input device and place this entered value in the appropriate variable or variables. The format of this function is shown in Fig. 9-6.

```
scanf(input_control_list, variable_list)
```

9-6   scanf( )function format.

The `scanf()` function is divided into three primary parts: the word `scanf`, the input control list, and the variable list. The control list contains the data type identifiers associated with the variables being read. The variable list contains the list of these variables. Figure 9-7 provides an example of this function.

The program listed in Fig. 9-7 asks the user to input a date and then prints that date back to the screen. The display to the user is done by the `printf()` function already discussed and the date input was done via a `scanf()`. The input control list within the `scanf()`—%d/%d/%d—states that three integer values will be entered as specified by the three %d clauses. The slashes between the %d clauses further state that the entered numbers will be delimited by backslashes. The variable list after the control list defines the memory address of the variables into which these integer values should be placed. Remember from Chapter 8 that integers are passed by value, and thus their original values cannot be modified. By placing an ampersand before the variable, you are passing the variable's memory address to `scanf()` and not its value. Once it has this address, `scanf()` can then modify the variable's value by setting it equal to the value entered from the keyboard.

Program

```
    main()
    { int year;
      int month;
      int day;

      printf("\n Enter the date in the format MM/DD/YY : ");
      scanf("%d/%d/%d",&month, &day, &year);

      printf("\n Date is %d:%d:%d",month,day,year);
    }
```

Output

```
        Enter the date in the format MM/DD/YY : 12/23/87

        Date is 12/23/87
```

9-7   scanf( ) function example.

Like the `printf()` function, `scanf()` must specify the data type of the variables being entered. These data types are specified using the same % identifiers as `printf()` and are listed in Table 9-2.

When defining the input control list, you should take special notice as to where you place spaces, dashes, and other characters. These non-data type identifiers are construed as field delimiters by some compilers and can produce unexpected results. In all cases, however, a space is considered a delimiter. For example, in Fig. 9-8, last name and first name end up in different variables because they were entered with a space between them.

Thus far, all of the programs examined in this and prior chapters have used the `scanf()` function for input and the `printf()` function for output. As we have learned,

Program

```
main()
{ int age;
  char f_name[10];
  char l_name[10];

  printf("\n   Enter name : ");
  scanf("%s %s",f_name, l_name);
  printf("\n    Your first name is %s",f_name);
  printf("\n    Your last name is   %s",l_name);
}
```

Output

```
Enter Name : Eric Bloom

  Your first name is Eric
  Your last name is  Bloom
```

9-8 Second scanf( ) function example.

these functions facilitate the input and output of integers, strings, and other data types. However, they are not the only input option. Another class of less sophisticated functions receives or sends one character of data at a time, thus allowing you the ability to write your own input and output routines and have full control over your input and output procedures. These functions are getch(), which gets a character from the keyboard or other designated input device, and putch(), which puts (or writes) a single character on the screen.

The putch( ) function

The putch() function is used to output a character to the screen. Its format is shown in Fig. 9-9.

```
putch (integer-value)
```

9-9 putch( ) function format.

This function consists of two parts: the word putch, and the integer variable or integer constant containing the ASCII value of the character to be printed. Examples of this process are shown in Fig. 9-10.

Program

```
main()
{ int x;
  x = 65;

  putch(x);
  putch(66);
}
```

Output

```
AB
```

9-10 First putch( ) function example.

The program listed in Fig. 9-10 contains two putch() functions. The first prints the letter "A," which has an ASCII value of 65, and illustrates how a variable can be used to specify the character being output. The second putch() function illustrates how an integer constant can be passed, causing the letter "B" to print.

Figure 9-11 shows a trick that can be used to print character values on the screen. To understand this trick, however, you must understand that integers and characters are treated very similarly by C. In fact, characters are stored in memory as numbers, these numbers being the ASCII value associated with the character being stored. Therefore, as seen in Fig. 9-11, you may pass character values to the putch() function and it will work correctly. As a word of caution when using this technique, however, read your compiler's documentation to ensure that characters and integers are stored in identical formats.

Program

```
main()
{ char a_char;
  a_char = 'Y';

  putch(a_char);
  putch('Z');
}
```

Output

```
YZ
```

9-11 Second putch( ) function example.

In Fig. 9-11, the first putch() function call prints the value Y as specified by a_char. The second putch() function prints the letter Z as specified by the character constant passed as a parameter.

Now that we have seen the putch() function work on the output of individual characters, let's employ it to print the character string as shown in Fig. 9-12.

Within Fig. 9-12, the putch() function is placed within a loop that causes putch() to execute continually until the null indicator at the end of a_string is reached. Remember, the ++ in *a_pointer++ is performing pointer arithmetic, thus moving the pointer to the next memory location after the current value is printed.

Program

```
main()
{ static char a_string[] = {"Hello there "};
  char *a_pointer;

  a_pointer = a_string;

  while ( *a_pointer )
    { putch(*a_pointer++);
    }
}
```

Output

```
Hello There
```

9-12 Looping putch( ) function example.

The getch( ) function

The getch() function is used to get a single character from the keyboard and place the ASCII value associated with that character into an integer variable. The format of this function is shown in Fig. 9-13.

```
int-variable = getch();
```

9-13   getch( ) function format.

The getch() function is extremely simple in format, just consisting of the function name preceded by the variable into which the retrieved character should be placed. Figure 9-14 provides a first example of this function.

Program

```
main()
{ int an_int;

  an_int = getch();
  putch(an_int);
}
```

Output

A

9-14   First getch( ) function example.

The program in Fig. 9-14 defines an__int as an integer variable, gets a character from the keyboard via the getch() function, and then prints that character on the screen by use of putch(). Note that, when reviewing the output of this program, only one character is printed because the getch() function only reads a character from the keyboard and does not automatically echo that character to the screen. Therefore, the putch() function is needed to allow the user to view his entered keystrokes. Figure 9-15 expands on this procedure and illustrates how an entire character string can be entered using these two single character functions.

In Fig. 9-15, the getch() statement is placed within a Do-While loop. This loop will continue to execute until the carriage return key (\15) is hit. At this time, one is subtracted from the pointer in the statement a_pointer-; and the \15 is replaced with a null \0. Lastly, a printf() function is called just to illustrate that the input process worked correctly.

Data redirection

The MS-DOS environment has two processes that allow you to redirect a program's input and output from the keyboard and screen defaults to other specified programs and devices: *piping* and *filtering*. Piping lets you read or write data to or from a file without changing

Program

```
main()
{ char a_string[20];
  char *a_pointer;

  a_pointer = &a_string;

  do
    { *a_pointer = getch();
      putch(*a_pointer);
    } while ( *a_pointer++ != '\15' );

  a_pointer--;
  *a_pointer = '\0';

  printf("\n\n a_string = %s", a_string);
}
```

Output

```
Hello There

a_string = Hello There
```

9-15 Looping getch( ) function example.

the program, while filtering allows you to specify that the output from program should be used as the input of another program.

Piping

If you want to write the output of your program to a data file, attached printer, or other appropriate device, you can do so by placing a greater than sign after the program name having output to be redirected and then the device or filename to receive the data. Table 9-3 lists and explains various piping alternatives.

Table 9-3 Piping examples.

Command	Effect
dir > xyz	Writes a directory to file xyz.
file1 | prog1	Uses file1 as input to program prog1.
files | sort > file1	Sorts file1 and places the output in file2.

Filtering

Filtering is the process of using the output of one program as the input of another program and is performed by placing a ¦ between the two programs being employed. Table 9-4 lists and explains various filtering examples.

Table 9-4 Filtering examples.

Command	Effect
dir ¦ sort	Prints a directory in sorted order.
prog1 ¦ prog2	Uses prog1 as input to program prog2.
dir ¦ sort ¦ file1	Writes a sorted directory to file file1.

Special file-handling commands

Many applications require the ability to read, write, and manipulate data files in ways not easily handled using piping techniques. As a result, virtually all C compilers come equipped with predefined functions to facilitate data manipulation.

The fopen( ) function

When attempting to manipulate data within a file, you must first tell the program what file is to be accessed and the type of processing that will be performed on that file. This information is provided by the fopen() function, whose format is shown in Fig. 9-16.

```
file-pointer = fopen(filename, file mode)
```

9-16   fopen( ) function format.

This function is divided into four parts: the word fopen, standing for "file open," the name of the file to be opened, the mode of the file (read, write, append, etc.), and the pointer variable that will be used to identify the file in all file- related procedures. See Fig. 9-17 for an example.

The partial program listed in Fig. 9-17 consists of four lines: the #include statement, the FILE statement, the fopen() function, and the fclose() function. The #include statement is a compiler directive (see Chapter 11) that causes the file stdio.h to be included in your compiled program. stdio.h, called a *header file*, contains all the standard input and output definitions needed to access files (see Chapter 11 for more information). The FILE statement is defined within this stdio.h file and is used to declare the file pointer's data type and the date type of the fopen() function's return value. The fopen() function actually opens the file, sets up the internal file data buffers, and returns a pointer stating where the file information and buffers can be found. This returned pointer value is then placed in the file variable input_file. Lastly, the fclose() function is used to close the file previously opened.

```
#include "stdio.h"
FILE *input_file, *fopen();
*input_file = fopen("infile.dat,"r");
   . . .
   . . .
fclose(input_file);
```

9-17   fopen( ) function example.

The fgets( ) function

The fgets() function is used to retrieve information from an open file and place the retrieved data in a specified variable. The format of this function is shown in Fig. 9-18.

```
fgets(string, size, file-pointer)
```

9-18   fgets( ) function format.

The fgets() function is divided into four parts: the word fgets, the name of the character string array that will be receiving the data, the number of characters to be retrieved, and the file pointer identifying which file should be read. The use of this function is illustrated in Fig. 9-19. As can be seen, this program reads a file named data9.dat and prints the retrieved data on the screen.

The fgets() function in Fig. 9-19 is instructing the compiler to read 10 characters from the file associated with file pointer input__file and place the retrieved characters in the character string a__string.

Program

```
#include "c:\lc\stdio.h"

main()
{ FILE *input_file, *fopen();
  char a_string[11];

  input_file = fopen("data9.dat","r");

  while ( fgets(a_string, 11, input_file) != NULL )
    printf("\ndata is ==> %s",a_string);

  close(input_file);

}
```

Output

```
1234567890
abcdefghij
klmnopqrst
```

9-19 Example file reading program.

The fputs( ) function

The fputs() function is used to place data in a file. The format of this function is shown in Fig. 9-20.

The fputf() function is divided into three parts: the word fputf, the name of the variable string to be printed, and the pointer value associated with the file being written. Figure 9-21 lists a program illustrating the use of this function. This listed program receives input from the screen via a scanf() function and writes the entered data in a file.

fputf(string, *file-pointer*)

9-20 fputf( ) function format.

The fscanf( ) and fprintf( ) functions

The fscanf() and fprintf() file manipulation functions are very similar to their keyboard and screen counterparts, the difference being that fscanf() and fprintf() receive and send their data to and from a specified data file. Examples of these functions can be found in Fig. 9-22.

Program

```
#include "c:\lc\stdio.h"

main()
{ FILE *output_file, *fopen();
  char a_string[11];

  output_file = fopen("data9.dat","w");

  printf("\n Enter name : ");
  scanf("%s",a_string);
  while ( strcmp(a_string,"end") != 0 )
    { fputs(a_string, output_file);
      printf("\n Enter name : ");
      scanf("%s",a_string);
    }
  close(output_file);
}
```

Output

```
Enter name : Bloom
Enter name : Tanner
Enter name : Wells
Enter name : Gagne
Enter name : Kalish
```

9-21 fputf( ) function example.

```
fprintf(out_file, "Hello There ");
fprintf(out_file, "The answer is %d", x);
fprintf(out_file, "%f plus %f is %f", x, y, z);

fscanf(in_file,"%s",a_string);
fscanf(in_file,"%f%s",a_float, a_string);
```

9-22 fscanf( ) and fprintf( ) examples.

The fgetc( ) and fputc( ) functions

The fgetc() and fputc() file functions are also very similar to their interactive partners—getch() and putch(). They differ in that fgetc() and fputc() require an additional parameter specifying the file that should be accessed. As with all file manipulation functions, the file being referenced by this pointer must be opened in an appropriate file mode using the fopen() function. For example, a fputc() function call (which writes a character to a file) cannot be used on a file opened for read-only access.

Figure 9-23 provides examples of these functions.

```
fgets(a_string, 7, file_pointer);
fgets(b_string, 4, in_file);

fputs(a_string, file_pointer );
fputs(b_string, file_pointer );
```

9-23 fgets( ) and fputs( ) examples.

The fclose( ) function

Once you have finished the processing of a particular file, that file should be closed by calling the `fclose()` function, which consists of the word `fclose` followed by the file pointer associated with the file to be closed. An example of this function can be seen in Fig. 9-24.

```
fclose(input_file);
```

9-24   fclose( ) function format.

If by chance you forget to close your files, they will automatically be closed when the program terminates; still, not closing your files yourself is considered to be a poor programming practice.

stdin, stdout, and stderr

When a C program is executed, three file channels are automatically opened: `stdin`, `stdout`, and `stderr`. `stdin` is the standard input file defaulting to the keyboard, `stdout` is the standard output channel defaulting to the screen, and `stderr` is the standard error message area where most of the error messages are printed. (`stderr` is also sent to the screen.)

This concept of standard input and standard output facilitates the use of the piping and filtering techniques previously discussed. In fact, because `stdin` and `stdout` are considered files, you can use any of your file manipulation functions like `fscanf()` and `fputc()` to perform keyboard input or screen output simply by using the words `stdin` and `stdout` as your file pointer. Examples of this process are shown in Fig. 9-25.

```
fprintf(stdout, "Hello There ");
fprintf(stdout, "The answer is %d", x);
fprintf(stdout "%f plus %f is %f", x, y, z);

fscanf(stdin, "%s",a_string);
fscanf(stdin, "%f%s",a_float, a_string);
```

9-25   stdin( ) and stdout( ) examples.

Special IBM-PC inputs and outputs

One advantage of writing software for a particular computer or class of computers is that you can capitalize on the particular attributes of the machine being used. In particular, we will be discussing screen formatting, the input of function keys, and printer commands.

Formatting screen outputs

Screen attributes like reverse video, screen brightness, background color, cursor placement, and screen clearing can be controlled in two ways. First, you could use assembly language subroutines to access and modify the area in memory that stores screen information. However, this method is very complicated and outside the scope of this book. Alternately, you can use the `printf()` function to pass special video control commands to the screen (which seems much more plausible). In fact, Chapter 22 of this book provides ready-to-use functions to help you modify screen attributes. First, let's examine the clear screen function shown in Fig. 9-26.

```
e_screen()
{ printf("%c"[2J", '\33');
}
```

9-26 Erase screen function.

The `printf()` function in Fig. 9-26 sends a stream of characters to the screen. Note that the first character of this stream is a `\33` and is defined as a character (c) in the print mask. This `\33` is the octal ASCII value for the escape key, which informs the screen that the characters following are screen instructions and should not be printed on the screen. The characters following the escape character are [2J, which together form the screen clear command. Then, once the command is completed, the screen automatically reverts back to character printing mode.

For a list of additional screen command strings, refer to Chapter 22.

Printer output

Like video screens, most PC printers can receive and interpret commands from your program by sending escape sequences similar to those discussed for screens. Figure 9-27 illustrates this process.

The function shown in Fig. 9-27 is designed for an Epson FX100 printer and is using an escape sequence command instructing the printer to turn off double strike printing mode (which presumably has been previously turned on). When reviewing this function, note that an `fopen()` function is being employed to open a file called prn. This file name is a key word and stands for the printer port on the back of your PC. Therefore, when you send the escape sequence via an `fprintf()` function call to the file, you are actually sending it out the printer port to the printer. As an additional note, you can also use this printer/file technique to send text and graphical data to your printer. Lastly, like with all opened files, you should call an `fclose()` function to close the file when you are done printing.

```
ds_off()
{ FILE *prn_file, *fopen();
  prn_file = fopen("prn","w");
  fprintf(prn_file,"%cH", '\033');
  fclose(prn_file);
}
```

9-27 First printer command example.

Figure 9-28 shows the printer command stream used to set an Epson FX100 printer into compressed printing mode. Note in this case, however, that an escape character is not used—just the octal value 22. Printers, unlike screens, often have some commands that do not contain escape characters. This can be done as long as the first character in the command sequence is not a printable character.

```
comp_off()
{ FILE *prn_file, *fopen();
  prn_file = fopen("prn","w");
  fprintf(prn_file,"%c", '\022');
  fclose(prn_file);
}
```

9-28 Second printer command example.

One note of caution when using these printer command streams: each printer manufacturer uses its own set of escape command strings. Therefore, refer to your printer's reference manual for the correct command formats.

Lastly, the two printer functions just discussed (as well as many others) can be found
in Chapter 16.

Function key input

When you press a function key on your PC keyboard, you are sending two characters to
your program. The first character is a null \0, which signifies that a function key or other
special key was hit. The second character specifies which key was entered.

Table 9-5 lists the function keys and their associated transmitted characters. As you

Table 9-5 Function key ASCII codes.

Second ASCII code	Key
3	Null
15	Shift-Tab
16-25	Alt - Q,W,E,R,T,Y,U,I,O,P
30-38	Alt - A,S,D,F,G,H,J,K,L
44-50	Alt - Z,X,C,V,B,N,M
59-68	F1-F10
71	Home
72	Cursor Up
73	PgUp
75	Cursor Left
77	Cursor Right
79	End
80	Cursor Down
81	PgDn
82	Ins
83	Del
84-93	Shift - F1-F10
94-103	Ctrl - F1-F10
104-113	Alt - F1-F10
114	Ctrl-PrtSc
115	Previous Word
116	Next word
117	Ctrl-End
118	Ctrl-PgDn
119	Ctrl-Home
120-131	Alt - 1,2,3,4,5,6,7,8,9,0,-,=
132	Ctrl-PgUp

can see when reviewing this list, the Alt keys and arrow keys also employ this two-part character code.

When analyzing the program in Fig. 9-29, note that a getch() function call places the first received character into the variable char_1. If that character is a null, the function what_key() is called. Otherwise, a message prints on the screen stating that the entered key was not a special key. If what_key() is called, the second character is pulled from the buffer and placed in variable char_2. char_2 is then compared against the octal value of various ASCII characters. If a match is made, the appropriate message is printed.

The example in Figure 9-29 searches for the function keys F1 through F10 and for the four arrow keys. However, it could be easily expanded to include the other special keys listed in Table 9-5.

Program

```
main()
{ char char_1;

  printf("\n Hit a function key : ");
  char_1 = getch();

  if ( char_1 != '\0' )
    printf("\n\n That was not a function key");
  else
    what_key();
}

what_key()
{ char char_2;

  char_2 = getch();

  if ( char_2 == '\073') printf(" ==> You hit the F1 key");
  if ( char_2 == '\074') printf(" ==> You hit the F2 key");
  if ( char_2 == '\075') printf(" ==> You hit the F3 key");
  if ( char_2 == '\076') printf(" ==> You hit the F4 key");
  if ( char_2 == '\077') printf(" ==> You hit the F5 key");
  if ( char_2 == '\100') printf(" ==> You hit the F6 key");
  if ( char_2 == '\101') printf(" ==> You hit the F7 key");
  if ( char_2 == '\102') printf(" ==> You hit the F8 key");
  if ( char_2 == '\103') printf(" ==> You hit the F9 key");
  if ( char_2 == '\104') printf(" ==> You hit the F10 key");

  if ( char_2 == '\110') printf(" ==> You hit the up arrow");
  if ( char_2 == '\113') printf(" ==> You hit the left arrow");
  if ( char_2 == '\115') printf(" ==> You hit the right arrow");
  if ( char_2 == '\120') printf(" ==> You hit the down arrow");
}
```

Output

```
Hit a function key :

    You hit the up arrow
```

9-29 Function key analysis program.

10

Bitwise operations

When the C language was initially designed and developed, it was earmarked for use as a way of developing operating systems and other system-level applications. As a result, it was given the ability to analyze and manipulate the individual bits within a given memory location. This chapter discusses the various operators associated with this feature and provides insight into their usage. Table 10-1 lists these bit manipulation commands, called *bitwise operators*.

The bitwise operators shown in Table 10-1 can be used on any integer variable. (i.e., on any variable defined using int, short, long, or unsigned). Also, with the exception of the ~ (which is the ones compliment operator), they can be used in a unary or binary equation (e.g., x &= y or x = x & y, respectively).

Table 10-1 Bitwise operators.

Operator	Name
&	AND operator
|	Inclusive OR operator
^	Exclusive OR operator
~	Ones compliment operator
<<	Shift-left operator
>>	Shift-right operator

The bitwise AND operator

The bitwise operator & is used to combine two lists of bits using the same Boolean principles as the && operator used in if statements. In particular, the condition is only true (a value of 1) if both compared bit values are true. Otherwise, the outcome is false (a value of 0). Table 10-2 lists the True/False alternatives.

The program listed in Fig. 10-1 illustrates the use of the AND operator. When reviewing this program, just concentrate on the statements within main(). The bit_print() function will be explained later in the chapter during the discussion of bit fields. In particular, within main(), note the statement int_value = int_value & -50;. This

125

statement is instructing the compiler to compare the bits in int_value with the bit placement associated with the number −50. The outcome of this comparison is then placed back
within int_value.

When reviewing the output from this process, as shown by the use of the bit
_print function, only one bit combination proved to be true (both bits had a value of
1), all other bit pairs were either 0 and 1, 1 and 0 or 0 and 0. These pairs (as shown in
Table 10-2) are not construed as true and produce a 0 value.

Table 10-2 List of AND alternatives.

Bit 1	Bit 2	Outcome
0	0	0
0	1	0
1	0	0
1	1	1

Program

```
main()
{ int int_value = 50;

   printf("\n                       Bitwise AND    ");
   printf("\n");
   bit_print(int_value);
   bit_print(-50);
   printf("\n                 ----------------");
   int_value = int_value & -50;
   bit_print(int_value);
}

bit_print(value_in)
  int value_in;
{ struct bit_mask
    { unsigned bit_1   :1;
      unsigned bit_2   :1;
      unsigned bit_3   :1;
      unsigned bit_4   :1;
      unsigned bit_5   :1;
      unsigned bit_6   :1;
      unsigned bit_7   :1;
      unsigned bit_8   :1;
      unsigned bit_9   :1;
      unsigned bit_10  :1;
      unsigned bit_11  :1;
      unsigned bit_12  :1;
      unsigned bit_13  :1;
      unsigned bit_14  :1;
      unsigned bit_15  :1;
      unsigned bit_16  :1;
    };

  union
    { struct bit_mask bits;
      int int_mask;
    } bit_union;

  bit_union.int_mask = value_in;
    printf("\n bit mask is : ");
    printf("%d",bit_union.bits.bit_1);
```

10-1 Bitwise AND program example.

```
        printf("%d",bit_union.bits.bit_2);
        printf("%d",bit_union.bits.bit_3);
        printf("%d",bit_union.bits.bit_4);
        printf("%d",bit_union.bits.bit_5);
        printf("%d",bit_union.bits.bit_6);
        printf("%d",bit_union.bits.bit_7);
        printf("%d",bit_union.bits.bit_8);
        printf("%d",bit_union.bits.bit_9);
        printf("%d",bit_union.bits.bit_10);
        printf("%d",bit_union.bits.bit_11);
        printf("%d",bit_union.bits.bit_12);
        printf("%d",bit_union.bits.bit_13);
        printf("%d",bit_union.bits.bit_14);
        printf("%d",bit_union.bits.bit_15);
        printf("%d",bit_union.bits.bit_16);
    }
```

Output

```
                    Bitwise AND

    bit mask is : 0000000000110010
    bit mask is : 1111111111001110
                  ----------------
    bit mask is : 0000000000000010
```

The inclusive OR operator

The inclusive OR operator | also compares two fields of bits but in this case uses an OR condition similar to the || operator used in i f statements. Table 10-3 provides a list of the possible | comparison alternatives.

**Table 10-3   List of
Inclusive OR alternatives.**

Bit 1	Bit 2	Outcome
0	0	0
0	1	1
1	0	1
1	1	1

The program shown in Fig. 10-2 is similar to that used when explaining the AND operator. In this case, however, note that the | operator is now being used in the statement int_value = int_value| –50 within the main() function.

When reviewing the output produced by the program in Fig. 10-2, note that only the rightmost bit combination was false (both bits had a 0 value) and resulted in a 0 value. All the other combinations contained at least one 1 value and was therefore made true.

Program

```
main()
        { int int_value = 50;

            printf("\n                      Inclusive OR    "
            printf("\n");
            bit_print(int_value);
```

10-2   Bitwise Inclusive OR program example.

```
      bit_print(-50);
      printf("\n               ----------------")
      int_value = int_value | -50;
      bit_print(int_value);
}

bit_print(value_in)
  int value_in;
{ struct bit_mask
    { unsigned bit_1  :1;
      unsigned bit_2  :1;
      unsigned bit_3  :1;
      unsigned bit_4  :1;
      unsigned bit_5  :1;
      unsigned bit_6  :1;
      unsigned bit_7  :1;
      unsigned bit_8  :1;
      unsigned bit_9  :1;
      unsigned bit_10 :1;
      unsigned bit_11 :1;
      unsigned bit_12 :1;
      unsigned bit_13 :1;
      unsigned bit_14 :1;
      unsigned bit_15 :1;
      unsigned bit_16 :1;
    };

  union
    { struct bit_mask bits;
      int int_mask;
    } bit_union;

  bit_union.int_mask = value_in;
    printf("\n bit mask is : ");
    printf("%d",bit_union.bits.bit_1);
    printf("%d",bit_union.bits.bit_2);
    printf("%d",bit_union.bits.bit_3);
    printf("%d",bit_union.bits.bit_4);
    printf("%d",bit_union.bits.bit_5);
    printf("%d",bit_union.bits.bit_6);
    printf("%d",bit_union.bits.bit_7);
    printf("%d",bit_union.bits.bit_8);
    printf("%d",bit_union.bits.bit_9);
    printf("%d",bit_union.bits.bit_10);
    printf("%d",bit_union.bits.bit_11);
    printf("%d",bit_union.bits.bit_12);
    printf("%d",bit_union.bits.bit_13);
    printf("%d",bit_union.bits.bit_14);
    printf("%d",bit_union.bits.bit_15);
    printf("%d",bit_union.bits.bit_16);
}
```

Output

```
              Inclusive OR

bit mask is : 0000000000110010
bit mask is : 1111111111001110
              ----------------
bit mask is : 1111111111111110
```

10-2 Continued.

The exclusive OR operator

The exclusive OR operator ^ is similar to the inclusive OR | operator with the exception that only one (but not both) of the bits being compared must be true (a 1 value). A list of the possible comparative outcomes are shown in Table 10-4.

Table 10-4   List of
Exclusive OR alternatives.

Bit 1	Bit 2	Outcome
0	0	0
0	1	1
1	0	1
1	1	0

Like the prior operator, the program and program output in Fig. 10-3 illustrates the use and output of the exclusive OR operator.

When reviewing the output of Fig. 10-3, note that the bit combinations that contained both a 0 and a 1 proved to be true and thus produced a 1 value. But, the bit pairs that were both of the same type, proved false and a 0 value resulted.

Program

```
main()
{ int int_value = 50;

  printf("\n                        Exclusive OR    ")
  printf("\n");
  bit_print(int_value);
  bit_print(-50);
  printf("\n                     ----------------");
  int_value = int_value ^ -50;
  bit_print(int_value);
}

bit_print(value_in)
 int value_in;
{ struct bit_mask
    { unsigned bit_1  :1;
      unsigned bit_2  :1;
      unsigned bit_3  :1;
      unsigned bit_4  :1;
      unsigned bit_5  :1;
      unsigned bit_6  :1;
      unsigned bit_7  :1;
      unsigned bit_8  :1;
      unsigned bit_9  :1;
      unsigned bit_10 :1;
      unsigned bit_11 :1;
      unsigned bit_12 :1;
      unsigned bit_13 :1;
      unsigned bit_14 :1;
      unsigned bit_15 :1;
      unsigned bit_16 :1;
    };

  union
    { struct bit_mask bits;
      int int_mask;
    } bit_union;

  bit_union.int_mask = value_in;
  printf("\n bit mask is : ");
  printf("%d",bit_union.bits.bit_1);
  printf("%d",bit_union.bits.bit_2);
  printf("%d",bit_union.bits.bit_3);
  printf("%d",bit_union.bits.bit_4);
```

10-3   Bitwise Exclusive OR program example.

```
    printf("%d",bit_union.bits.bit_5);
    printf("%d",bit_union.bits.bit_6);
    printf("%d",bit_union.bits.bit_7);
    printf("%d",bit_union.bits.bit_8);
    printf("%d",bit_union.bits.bit_9);
    printf("%d",bit_union.bits.bit_10);
    printf("%d",bit_union.bits.bit_11);
    printf("%d",bit_union.bits.bit_12);
    printf("%d",bit_union.bits.bit_13);
    printf("%d",bit_union.bits.bit_14);
    printf("%d",bit_union.bits.bit_15);
    printf("%d",bit_union.bits.bit_16);
}
```

Output

```
                    Exclusive OR

bit mask is : 0000000000110010
bit mask is : 1111111111001110
              ----------------
bit mask is : 1111111111111100
```

10-3 Continued.

The ones complement operator

The ones complement operator, ~, is used to change all the 1 values to 0 and all the 0 values to 1, thus in a manner of speaking flip-flopping the values. An example of this process can be seen in Fig. 10-4.

Program

```
main()
{ int int_value = 50;

  printf("\n                  Ones Complement ");
  printf("\n");
  bit_print(int_value);
  printf("\n                  ----------------");
  int_value = int_value;
  bit_print(int_value);
}

bit_print(value_in)
 int value_in;
{ struct bit_mask
   { unsigned bit_1  :1;
     unsigned bit_2  :1;
     unsigned bit_3  :1;
     unsigned bit_4  :1;
     unsigned bit_5  :1;
     unsigned bit_6  :1;
     unsigned bit_7  :1;
     unsigned bit_8  :1;
     unsigned bit_9  :1;
     unsigned bit_10 :1;
     unsigned bit_11 :1;
     unsigned bit_12 :1;
     unsigned bit_13 :1;
     unsigned bit_14 :1;
     unsigned bit_15 :1;
     unsigned bit_16 :1;
   };
```

10-4 Bitwise Ones Complement program example.

```
union
  { struct bit_mask bits;
    int int_mask;
  } bit_union;

bit_union.int_mask = value_in;
 printf("\n bit mask is : ");
 printf("%d",bit_union.bits.bit_1);
 printf("%d",bit_union.bits.bit_2);
 printf("%d",bit_union.bits.bit_3);
 printf("%d",bit_union.bits.bit_4);
 printf("%d",bit_union.bits.bit_5);
 printf("%d",bit_union.bits.bit_6);
 printf("%d",bit_union.bits.bit_7);
 printf("%d",bit_union.bits.bit_8);
 printf("%d",bit_union.bits.bit_9);
 printf("%d",bit_union.bits.bit_10);
 printf("%d",bit_union.bits.bit_11);
 printf("%d",bit_union.bits.bit_12);
 printf("%d",bit_union.bits.bit_13);
 printf("%d",bit_union.bits.bit_14);
 printf("%d",bit_union.bits.bit_15);
 printf("%d",bit_union.bits.bit_16);
}
```

Output

```
            Ones Complement

bit mask is : 0000000000110010
              ----------------
bit mask is : 1111111111001101
```

When reviewing Fig. 10-4, take special note of the statement int_value = int_value within main(). This statement instructs the computer to invert the bits in variable int_value (i.e., take the ones complement) and place this inverted bit pattern back in variable int_value. Additionally, when reviewing the output of Fig. 10-4, note that all 0 values have become 1 and all 1 values have become 0.

The shift left operator

The shift left operator < < causes the bits within the variable to be shifted to the left a specified number of characters. Figure 10-5 illustrates the use of this operator.

Program

```
main()
{ int int_value = 50;

  printf("\n                     Shift Left  ");
  printf("\n");
  bit_print(int_value);
  printf("\n                     ----------------");
  int_value = int_value << 2;
  bit_print(int_value);
  printf("\n                     ----------------");
  int_value = int_value << 3;
  bit_print(int_value);
}
```

10-5 Bitwise Shift-left program example.

```
bit_print(value_in)
int value_in;
{ struct bit_mask
    { unsigned bit_1  :1;
      unsigned bit_2  :1;
      unsigned bit_3  :1;
      unsigned bit_4  :1;
      unsigned bit_5  :1;
      unsigned bit_6  :1;
      unsigned bit_7  :1;
      unsigned bit_8  :1;
      unsigned bit_9  :1;
      unsigned bit_10 :1;
      unsigned bit_11 :1;
      unsigned bit_12 :1;
      unsigned bit_13 :1;
      unsigned bit_14 :1;
      unsigned bit_15 :1;
      unsigned bit_16 :1;
    };

  union
    { struct bit_mask bits;
      int int_mask;
    } bit_union;

  bit_union.int_mask = value_in;
    printf("\n bit mask is : ");
    printf("%d",bit_union.bits.bit_1);
    printf("%d",bit_union.bits.bit_2);
    printf("%d",bit_union.bits.bit_3);
    printf("%d",bit_union.bits.bit_4);
    printf("%d",bit_union.bits.bit_5);
    printf("%d",bit_union.bits.bit_6);
    printf("%d",bit_union.bits.bit_7);
    printf("%d",bit_union.bits.bit_8);
    printf("%d",bit_union.bits.bit_9);
    printf("%d",bit_union.bits.bit_10);
    printf("%d",bit_union.bits.bit_11);
    printf("%d",bit_union.bits.bit_12);
    printf("%d",bit_union.bits.bit_13);
    printf("%d",bit_union.bits.bit_14);
    printf("%d",bit_union.bits.bit_15);
    printf("%d",bit_union.bits.bit_16);
}
```

Output

```
                    Shift Left

    bit mask is : 0000000000110010
                  -----------------
    bit mask is : 0000000011001000
                  -----------------
    bit mask is : 0000011001000000
```

10-5 Continued.

When reviewing the program listed in Fig. 10-5, you will see that the bit shifting is performed twice. The first shift, performed in the statement int_value = int_value << 2, causes the sixteen bits originally in int_value to move two places to the left. When this shift is performed, the two leftmost bits are shifted out the left side of the variable and are lost. Also notice that the two bit places on the right that were left vacant by the shift were filled with zeros. The second shift left statement moves the bits three more places to the left, again causing the three leftmost bits to be lost, the remaining bits to be shifted three positions, and the vacated bit locations to be filled with zeros.

The shift right operator

The shift right operator > > causes the bits within the variable to be shifted to the right a specified number of characters. Figure 10-6 illustrates the use of this operator.

When reviewing the program listed in Fig. 10-5, you will see that the bit shifting is performed twice. The first shift, performed in the statement int_value = int_value << 2, causes the sixteen bits originally in int_value to move two places to the right. When this shift is performed, the two rightmost bits are shifted out the right side of the variable and are lost. Also notice that the two bit places that were left vacant by the shift were filled with zeros. The second shift right statement moves the bits three more places to the right, again causing the three rightmost bits to be lost, the remaining bits to be shifted three positions, and the vacated bit locations to be filled with zeros.

Program

```
main()
{ int int_value = 50;

    printf("\n                      Shift Right ");
    printf("\n");
    bit_print(int_value);
    printf("\n               ----------------");
    int_value = int_value >> 2;
    bit_print(int_value);
    printf("\n               ----------------");
    int_value = int_value >> 3;
    bit_print(int_value);
}

bit_print(value_in)
  int value_in;
{ struct bit_mask
    { unsigned bit_1  :1;
      unsigned bit_2  :1;
      unsigned bit_3  :1;
      unsigned bit_4  :1;
      unsigned bit_5  :1;
      unsigned bit_6  :1;
      unsigned bit_7  :1;
      unsigned bit_8  :1;
      unsigned bit_9  :1;
      unsigned bit_10 :1;
      unsigned bit_11 :1;
      unsigned bit_12 :1;
      unsigned bit_13 :1;
      unsigned bit_14 :1;
      unsigned bit_15 :1;
      unsigned bit_16 :1;
    };

  union
    { struct bit_mask bits;
      int int_mask;
    } bit_union;
```

10-6 Bitwise Shift-left program example.

```
        bit_union.int_mask = value_in;
      printf("\n bit mask is : ");
      printf("%d",bit_union.bits.bit_1);
      printf("%d",bit_union.bits.bit_2);
      printf("%d",bit_union.bits.bit_3);
      printf("%d",bit_union.bits.bit_4);
      printf("%d",bit_union.bits.bit_5);
      printf("%d",bit_union.bits.bit_6);
      printf("%d",bit_union.bits.bit_7);
      printf("%d",bit_union.bits.bit_8);
      printf("%d",bit_union.bits.bit_9);
      printf("%d",bit_union.bits.bit_10);
      printf("%d",bit_union.bits.bit_11);
      printf("%d",bit_union.bits.bit_12);
      printf("%d",bit_union.bits.bit_13);
      printf("%d",bit_union.bits.bit_14);
      printf("%d",bit_union.bits.bit_15);
      printf("%d",bit_union.bits.bit_16);
    }
```

Output

```
                    Shift Right
    bit mask is : 0000000000110010
                  ----------------
    bit mask is : 0000000000001100
                  ----------------
    bit mask is : 0000000000000001
```

10-6   Continued.

Bit fields

The bitwise operators examined so far have caused a particular process to be performed on all sixteen bits within the variable. Sometimes, however, you will only want to manipulate selected bits within a variable. Likewise, because of memory constraints, you might be forced to place your data in memory as compactly as possible. Both of these situations can be addressed through the use of bit fields. A *bit field* is a structure (or struct) used to assign variable names to the bits contained within a variable. An example of this process is shown in Fig. 10-7.

Program

```
    main()
    { struct date_format
        { unsigned day      :5;
          unsigned month    :4;
          unsigned year     :7;
        } date;

      date.day = 31;
      date.month = 12;
      date.year = 87;

      printf("\n The month is = %d",date.month);
      printf("\n The day   is = %d",date.day);
      printf("\n The year  is = %d",date.year);
    }
```

10-7   Bit field program example.

Output

```
The month is = 12
The day   is = 31
The year  is = 87
```

When reviewing the program in Fig. 10-7, note that the definitions of the day, month, and year include a colon followed by an integer number. The colon signifies that the variable being suffixed is a bit field and not a regular variable, while the number following the colon specifies the number of bits contained within the field.

For example, the month variable is defined by unsigned month : 4;, stating that month is an unsigned integer that will be stored using four bits. Remember, however, that a four-bit field can only contain a range of sixteen numbers (i.e., 0 through 15). This limitation is acceptable, however, because there are only 12 months. Next, notice that the three bit fields defined in the date_format structure add up to 16 bits—one memory location. This memory location is conceptually shown in Fig. 10-8.

As you can see when reviewing Fig. 10-8, the 16 bits within the displayed byte is divided into three parts; 5 bits for day, 4 bits for month, and 7 bits for year.

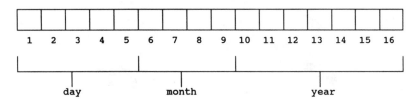

10-8 Bit field conceptual view.

11

The C precompiler

Unlike most programming languages, the C compilation process is performed in two steps. The first step adjusts and modifies the source code based on specific instructions called *compiler directives* inserted into the source code by the programmer. These directives all begin with a number sign # and will be discussed at length within this chapter. The second step of the compilation process reads this modified source code and performs traditional compilation activities.

The #define directive

The #define directive serves two purposes. First, it allows you to assign symbolic names to program constants, thus improving program readability. Second, it provides the ability to define small function-like procedures called *macros*. These two uses will be explained next.

Simple text replacement

One of the most common uses of the *#define* directive is to perform simple text replacement through the use of symbolic names. For example, the statement

    #define TRUE 1

states that the word TRUE has a symbolic value equaling the number 1. Therefore, during precompilation, all occurrences of the word TRUE are replaced with a 1. Table 11-1 provides some examples of this substitution process.

The #define directive can also be used to alter the format of the C language. For example, if you want to add the word THEN to your if statements, place the word LET before your assignment statements, and change the equality operator = = to the word EQUALS, you can do so using the process shown in Fig. 11-1.

When reviewing the program in Fig. 11-1, note that there are three #define statements. The first statement assigns the word EQUALS a value of " = =," causing the precompiler to replace EQUALS with " = =" during precompilation. The second and third

Table 11-1   #define substitution examples.

Define statement	Before substitution	After substitution
#Define FALSE 0	if(x = = FALSE)	if(x = = 0)
#Define TRUE 1	if(x = = TRUE)	if(x = = 1)
#Define RED 26	WindowColor = RED;	WindowColor = 26;

```
#define EQUALS ==
#define THEN
#define LET

main()
{ int a_number;

  LET a_number = 5;

  if ( a_number EQUALS 5 )
  THEN printf("\n\n The number equals 5");

  if ( a_number EQUALS 6 )
  THEN printf("\n\n The number equals 6");
}
```

11-1   First #define directive example.

#define statements set the words THEN and LET equal to a space, thus telling the compiler to replace those words with a nothing. In effect, this procedure is instructing the compiler to delete them from the source code prior to compilation.

Still, even though the #define directive can be used in this manner to alter the appearance of C statements, actually doing so is frowned upon by most programmers. If you are going to program in C, then make your programs look like C and not like some other language.

Defining macros

The #define directive can also be used to define small function like procedures called macros. An example of this process is shown in Fig. 11-2.

```
#define TIMES_TWO(x) ( x * 2 )

main()
{ int a_number;
  int b_number;

  a_number = 5;
  b_number = TIMES_TWO(a_number);

  printf("\n b_number has a value of %d, b_number);
}
```

11-2   Second #define directive example.

The #define statement in Fig. 11-2 defines a macro called times_two. As you might expect, it takes a number and multiplies it by the value 2.

When this macro, namely

b-number = times_two(a_number)

is passed through precompilation, it will be converted to

b-number = a_number * 2

thus replacing the macro call with the macro's process as specified within the parentheses of the #define statement.

Lastly, note that the transformation of (x * 2) to

a_number * 2

was made by associating the x parameter in the define statement with the a_number parameter in the macro call. To expand this macro call transformation, Fig. 11-3 defines a macro using two parameters.

```
#define multiply(x,y) ( x * y )

main()
{ int a_number;
  int b_number;
  int c_number;

  a_number = 2;
  b_number = 3;
  c_number = multiply(a_number, b_number)
  printf("\n %d times %d is %d", a_number, b_number, c_number);
}
```

11-3 Third #define directive example.

As shown in Fig. 11-3, the multiply macro uses two variables: x and y. Also note that two variables are used when referencing multiply: a_variable and b_variables. When this program is precompiled, the C source code will be modified from

c_number = multiply(a_variable, b_variable)

to the statement

c_number = a_variable * b_variable

thus, associating a_variable with x and b_variable with y.

The last #define example is shown in Fig. 11-4 and contains an added twist: rather than defining a formula, as previously discussed, the #define directive is defining an if condition using the equation operator.

The is_int macro, defined in Fig. 11-4, tests to see if the character defined within a_character is a numeric digit. Like previous examples, the passed parameter (a_character) is used to replace the x variable in the macro formula from the statement

if(is_int(a_character))

```
#define is_int(x) ( ( x >= '0' && x <= '9' ) ? 1: 0 )

main()
{ char a_character;

  a_character = '4';
  if ( is_int(a_character) )
    printf("\n a_character is not an integer");
  else
    printf("\, a_character is an integer");
```

11-4 Forth #define directive example.

to the statement

> if ((a_variable > = '0' && a_variable < = '9') ? 1 : 0).

It is this transformed line that will actually be compiled into executable code.

Like all programming options, using #define macros has advantages and disadvantages. The advantages are that hard-to-type procedures like that used in Fig. 11-4 can be written and debugged once and then referenced as needed throughout the rest of the program. Also, because macros can be given descriptive names, it improves the readability of the program. Lastly, macros do not require the processing overhead associated with functions and as a result are processed more efficiently.

The disadvantages are three-fold. First, if macros are not referenced correctly, the source code transformed by the precompiler might be modified incorrectly. Even worse, these errors cannot be seen when reading the original source code, thus making it harder to debug. Second, because the macro is actually copied into the source code each time it is referenced, it can expand the size of your executable code if used often and thus requires more computer resources to store and execute. Lastly, unlike functions, the variable's name and not the variable's value are passed to the macro. Therefore, if you attempt to pass a parameter in the form of an expression (e.g., x + 5), the expression and not the value of the expression will be placed in the precompiled source code. As an other example, the #define statement

> #define TIMES_TWO(x * 2)

when referenced by the statement

> c_number = TIMES_TWO(a_variable + 5)

will generate a source code statement of

> c_variable = a_variable + 5 * 2

and not the expected result of the value of a_variable plus 5.

The #include directive

The #include directive is used to instruct the preprocesser to read the C code contained within a specified file (known as a *header file*) and place its contents within the program being compiled. For example, once you have written a list of #define macros and symbolic names, like those previously discussed, you can place these definitions in their own file and have them automatically called into your C program during precompilation. The advantage of the technique is that, because your #define directives can be centrally located and not physically placed in each program, modifying your definitions becomes easier because you only have to make the change in one place. Figure 11-5 lists an example file that can be referenced by an #include directive.

```
#define NULL '\0'
#define TRUE 1
#define FALSE 0
#define EOF -1
```

11-5 Example header definition file.

When reviewing the definition file in Fig. 11-5, note that the file name mydefs.h ends with an extension of .h, which stands for "header file." Although the file does not need to be marked as such, the programming industry considers header files with a .h extension to be a standard convention. In fact, when you buy a C compiler, it comes with various definition header files using the .h naming convention.

Additionally, also note that the file does not contain any procedural statements like for and while. By convention, header files should only be used for the definition of #define macros, external variables, and symbolic names. Figure 11-6, illustrates how the #include statement is used to reference the mydefs.h file.

```
#include <mydefs.h>

main()
{ char a_character;

  a_character = '4';
  if ( is_int(a_character) == TRUE )
    printf("\n a_character is an integer");

  if ( is_int(a_character) == FALSE )
    printf("\n a_character is not an integer");
```

11-6 #include directive program example.

When the program in Fig. 11-6 is precompiled, it will first be transformed into the program shown in Fig. 11-7. When reviewing this modified program, note that the #include directive is gone and the symbols TRUE and FALSE were replaced by the their symbolic values as specified in the header file mydefs.h.

```
main()
{ char a_character;

  a_character = '4';
  if ( is_int(a_character) == 1 )
    printf("\n a_character is an integer");

  if ( is_int(a_character) == 0 )
    printf("\n a_character is not an integer");
```

11-7 Precompiled C program example.

Conditional directives

In addition to having the ability to symbolically modify your source code via the #define and #include directives, you can also employ conditional logic. This logic can be used to decide which #define and #include directives are used by the precompiler, as well as even which sections of your source code are compiled. The directives facilitating these conditional options are discussed next.

The #ifdef directive

The #ifdef directive instructs the precompiler to conditionally compile statements of other directives based on whether a specified name has been defined by a #define directive (see Fig. 11-8).

```
#ifdef TESTRUN
  #define TESTFLAG 1
  printf("\n This is a test");
#endif
```

11-8 #ifdef directive program example.

The partial program shown in Fig. 11-8 checks to see if the symbolic name TESTRUN has been defined via a #define directive. If it has, the two lines below it are used; otherwise, the two lines are not used. Additionally, note that the #ifdef directive ends with #endif. #endif is required when using any of the conditional directives and signifies the end of the conditional expression.

The #ifndef directive

The #ifndef directive instructs the precompiler to conditionally use statements of directives based on whether a specified identifier has not been defined by a #define directive. In fact, this directive is the opposite of the #ifdef directive. Figure 11-9 illustrates the use of this directive.

```
#ifndef TESTRUN
  #define TESTFLAG 0
  printf("\n This is not a test");
#endif
```

11-9 #ifndef directive program example.

When reviewing the program in Fig. 11-9, note that the lines between the #ifndef directive and its associated #endif directive will only be executed if TESTRUN has not been defined via a #define directive.

The #if directive

The #if directive provides the ability to compile or not compile sections of source code and directives based on the value of a specified symbolic name. If the symbolic name being tested has a value of zero, the expression is considered false. If the symbolic name has a non-zero value, then it is considered true. Figure 11-10 illustrates the use of this directive.

When reviewing this program, note that the lines between #if and its associated #endif directive will only be executed if TESTRUN has a non-zero value.

```
#if TESTRUN
  #define TESTFLAG 1
  printf("\n This is a test");
#endif
```

11-10 #if directive program example.

The #else directive

The #else compiler directive is used to provide the #if, #ifdef, and #ifndef directives with an if-then-else capability. This directive is optional and should only be used when it will be containing associated lines. Also note that this directive does not take the place of an #endif. The #endif is still required and must be placed after the #else directive if one is present. Figure 11-11 illustrates the use of this function.

```
#if TESTRUN
  #define TESTFLAG 1
  printf("\n This is a test");
#else
  #define TESTFLAG 0
  prinf("\n This is not a test");
#endif
```

11-11 #else directive program example.

When reviewing the partial program in Fig. 11-11, note that the #else directive was placed after the conditional directive and before the #endif. Also note that the lines within the conditional expression are indented in a manner similar to that used with the C if statement. This format is not required but helps make the program more readable.

The #undef directive

The #undef directive is used to undefine a symbolic name or define macro that has previously been defined using the #define directive. An example of the #undef directive is shown in Fig. 11-12.

```
#define TRUE
  . . .
  . . .
#undef TRUE
```

11-12 #undef directive example.

When reviewing the partial program in Fig. 11-12, note that the word TRUE was assigned a value of 1; then, TRUE became unassigned by executing the #undef command.

12

Using APIs

An Application Programming Interface (API) is a facility that allows computer applications (like EXCEL by Microsoft), software development platforms (like Clipper and DB2), and communications products (like IRMA boards and LAN networks) to be controlled programmatically by logic in your C programs.

APIs link an object code library (an .OBJ file) to your C program, with the .OBJ file being supplied by the vendor of the product with which you want to link. Then, from within your C program, you can call functions contained in this .OBJ file.

All APIs generally fall into one of two general categories: *multifunction-based* APIs and *control-block-based* APIs. To help illustrate the difference between these two approaches, I've included an API example under both the multifunction and control-block API discussions. The sample library being shown is capable of adding or subtracting two numbers. In both cases, the APIs and the calling functions are contained within the same program. In "real-life," they would be physically placed in separate program files.

Multifunction-based APIs

Multifunction-based APIs are very similar to the function code libraries provided with your C compiler. For example, the functions used within C for standard file I/O (`fopen`, `fclose`, etc.) are an example of a multifunction-based API. These file manipulation functions (discussed in Chapter 9) provide you with an interface to the operating system's file management facilities. In fact, most database products on the market (Oracle, DB2, etc.) provide a multifunction interface very similar to these standard C file manipulation functions. The difference, of course, is that these functions cause the execution of various database processes as opposed to sequential file I/O. Note that when a multifunction-based API is used to access a database, it is very often called a *Host Language Interface (HLI)* because it is designed to integrate with a specified host language like C or COBOL.

Figure 12-1 shows an example of a multifunction-based API. When reviewing this example, note that each API function—in this case, `MathAdd()` and `MathSubtract()`—performs a single task: the first performs addition, while the second performs subtraction. In a "real-life" example, one function might initiate database access, one might read data, one might write data, and one might close database files (etc.).

```
double DoMathAdd(double, double);
double DoMathSubtract(double, double);


main()
{ double FirstNumber  = 2;
  double SecondNumber = 3;
  double Answer;

  Answer = DoMathAdd(FirstNumber, SecondNumber);
  printf("\n Add answer = %lf",Answer);

  Answer = DoMathSubtract(FirstNumber, SecondNumber);
  printf("\n Subtract answer = %lf",Answer);

}

double DoMathAdd(double First, double Second)
{ return(First + Second);
}

double DoMathSubtract(double First, double Second)
{ return(First - Second);
}
```

12-1 Multi-function API example.

Control-block-based APIs

A control-block-based API is characterized by the use of a *control block*, which is a C structure `struct` passed back and forth between your program and a single function contained in the vendor's .OBJ file. In essence, your program places data and instructions into the structure; then you call a specified API function contained within the APIs .OBJ file. The called function analyzes the passed data and instructions, performs the appropriate action, and replaces the data and instructions in the passed structure with execution and error information. This process is shown in Fig. 12-2.

When reviewing the above example, note that the structure field `DoMathBlock` `.Action` contains the action to be performed. Also note that, unlike the multifunction APIs, the function `DoMath()` is always called regardless of the action to be performed.

Protocol conversion protocols

Some APIs have the purpose of converting from one API format to another. As an example, note that the graphical interface of an Apple Macintosh computer is very similar to the display of an IBM-PC computer running Microsoft's Windows 3.0 product. Under the covers, however, the C functions used to program these interfaces is extremely different. Therefore, if a software company wants to market the same application in both the IBM and Macintosh marketplace, the company has two choices. First, the company can write the user interface part of the application twice. Alternately, the company can write the application's user interface once, using an intermediate product with the ability to interface with both graphical environments.

See Fig. 12-3 for a diagram of this process.

```
struct DoMathBlockTemplate
{ char Action;
  double FirstNumber;
  double SecondNumber;
  double Answer;
  int MessageCode;
  char MessageText[50];
} DoMathBlock;

main()
{

  DoMathBlock.FirstNumber  = 2;
  DoMathBlock.SecondNumber = 3;
  DoMathBlock.Action       = 'A';   /* A is for Add, S for Subtract */

  DoMath();
  if(DoMathBlock.MessageCode == 0)
    printf("\n The answer is %lf \n ",DoMathBlock.Answer);
  else
  { printf("\n Block returned with error message");
    printf("\n    Error Code = %d", DoMathBlock.MessageCode);
    printf("\n    Error Text = %s", DoMathBlock.MessageText);
  }
}

int DoMath()
{
  if(DoMathBlock.Action == 'A')
  { DoMathBlock.Answer = DoMathBlock.FirstNumber +
DoMathBlock.SecondNumber;
    DoMathBlock.MessageCode = 0;
    strcpy(DoMathBlock.MessageText,"Add procedure successful");
    return(0);
  }

  if(DoMathBlock.Action == 'S')
  { DoMathBlock.Answer = DoMathBlock.FirstNumber -
DoMathBlock.SecondNumber;
    DoMathBlock.MessageCode = 0;
    strcpy(DoMathBlock.MessageText,"Subtract procedure successful");
    return(0);
  }

  DoMathBlock.MessageCode = 100;
  strcpy(DoMathBlock.MessageText,"ERROR: Invalid action code");
  return(100);
}
```

12-2   Control block API example.

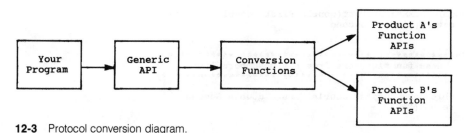

12-3   Protocol conversion diagram.

Figure 12-4 is an example of an API that performs protocol conversion using the multifunction API example presented in Fig. 12-1. When reviewing this example, assume that two math libraries exist, one being called DoMath (as in Fig. 12-1) and one being called DoNumbers. The code in Fig. 12-4 executes the appropriate function based on the value of the global variable LibraryType. If LibraryType is equal to LIBRARY _DOMATH, then the functions associated with the DoMath library are executed. If LibraryType is equal to LIBRARY__DONUMBERS, then the functions associated with the DoNumbers library are executed.

```c
#define LIBRARY_DOMATH      1
#define LIBRARY_DONUMBERS   2

double DoMathAdd(double, double);
double DoMathSubtract(double, double);

double DoNumbersAdd(double, double);
double DoNumbersSubtract(double, double);

main()
{ double FirstNumber  = 2;
  double SecondNumber = 3;
  double Answer;
  int    LibraryType;

  LibraryType = LIBRARY_DOMATH;

  if(LibraryType == LIBRARY_DOMATH)
  { Answer = DoMathAdd(FirstNumber, SecondNumber);
    printf("\n Add answer = %lf",Answer);

    Answer = DoMathSubtract(FirstNumber, SecondNumber);
    printf("\n Subtract answer = %lf",Answer);
  }

  if(LibraryType == LIBRARY_DONUMBERS)
  { Answer = DoNumbersAdd(FirstNumber, SecondNumber);
    printf("\n Add answer = %lf",Answer);

    Answer = DoNumbersSubtract(FirstNumber, SecondNumber);
    printf("\n Subtract answer = %lf",Answer);
  }

}
/***********************************************/
/* These functions are from the DoMAth library */
/***********************************************/

double DoMathAdd(double First, double Second)
{ return(First + Second);
}

double DoMathSubtract(double First, double Second)
{ return(First - Second);
}

/*************************************************/
/* These functions are from the DoNumbers library */
/*************************************************/

double DoNumbersAdd(double First, double Second)
{ return(First + Second);
}

double DoNumbersSubtract(double First, double Second)
{ return(First - Second);
}
```

12-4 Protocol conversion example.

13

C++ enhancements

When trying to conceptualize what C++ is, you must consider two things. First, remember that C++ is a superset of C. Therefore, any programs written in C should be able to be compiled with a C++ compiler. Second, C++ provides C programmers with the ability to write object-oriented programs, employ data streams, and maximize the maintainability and modularization of created software. This chapter will discuss these C++ enhancements.

When learning C++, four basic hurdles must be overcome. First, new terms must be learned and conceptualized. Second, the programmer must change his/her thinking from the traditional programming headset to an object-oriented approach. Third, C++ requires the use of new language verbs. Finally, the programmer must be able integrate the first three hurdles into working software. To this end, this chapter has been designed to assist you in these four basic areas.

C++ terms

This section presents technical jargon associated with object-oriented programming.

Objects and classes

An *object* is a self-contained unit having both data and the logic to maintain that data. In English, this means that when programming in a non-object-oriented language, you first define your data and then write functions to maintain and manipulate that data. With this approach, the programmer must ensure that the defined data (e.g., a push-down list) is only manipulated by specified push-down list functions. In essence, normal programming involves only two marginally related things—namely, data and functions. In OOP, the data and the functions manipulating that data are bound together into a single unit called an object.

Furthermore, the C++ verb that defines an object is *class*. Conceptually, a class is the definition of an object. Conversely, an object is an instance of a specified class. Again, using the push-down list example, the definition of the push-down list data structure coupled with the definition of functions that can be used to manipulate the structure is a class. Each piece of data contained in the structure is a class instance, also known as an object.

Figure 13-1 shows a sample class definition statement.

```
class PhoneBook {

  Private:
    char Name[30];
    char Number[15];

  public:
    int AddNAme(char *, char *);
    int DeleteName(char *, char *);

};
```

13-1 Example class definition.

Member functions

As mentioned already, a class contains data as well as the functions used to maintain that data. A *member function* is a function contained within a class definition. In essence, a member function does not stand by itself as does a standard C function but is defined specifically to be used within the context of its parent class. For example, if the function PopStack() is defined as a member function of the Pushstack class, then it should only be used when performing actions against that class.

Derived classes, base classes, and class inheritance

When defining a class (or more correctly, when defining objects through the creation of classes), you may include a class as part of the definition. For example, suppose you are defining objects to build a dictionary. First you describe the class "Definition," which includes a word and a number of meanings. Then you define the class "Dictionary," which includes many instances of the Definition class. Within this example, Dictionary is a derived class of Definition. Furthermore, the Definition class is the base class of the Dictionary class. Because the Definition class is part of the Dictionary class, the Dictionary class does not have to worry about the process of storing definitions; it simply passes the definition to the Definition class for processing.

Encapsulation

As previously discussed, the C++ keyword class is used to couple data with the functions that manipulate it. This process of joining data and functions is called *encapsulation*. Encapsulation is something that all good programmers have always tried to do; C++ provided a mechanism to facilitate it.

Inline functions

An *inline function* is somewhat like a C #define macro (see Chapter 11) except that it acts exactly like a function in regard to scope, type checking, and other function attributes. It offers you the advantages of a function without the overhead incurred when that function is called.

Mechanically, the code associated with an inline function is physically placed at each location where it is called. Although it helps you by not executing the overhead associated with calling a function, it can increase the size of your program if it is too big and called too often. As the general rule of thumb, if a function is called often, you must trade off the execution efficiencies of not placing another function on the stack against the increase in program size by physically placing the function at many places in your executable. Generally speaking, if the function takes up less space then the code needed to call that function, you are all set.

An example of an inline function is shown in Fig. 13-2.

```
inline double TimesTwo(double x) { return x * 2; }
```

13-2 Example inline function definition.

Public and private class members

When explaining encapsulation, I implied that only the functions contained within a class would be able to access that data within that class. The definition of what data and functions can be accessed from outside the class is managed by the keyboards "public" and "private." If a data element or function is *public*, then it can be accessed from functions outside the class. If data or functions are defined as *private*, they can only be accessed by functions defined within the class. By default, class data and functions are private.

Constructors and destructors

The creation and destruction (release of memory) of objects often requires some general housekeeping activities like allocating memory and setting specified constants. To facilitate these activities, C++ allows you to define constructors and destructors. A *constructor* is a member function called automatically when a class is first initialized, while a *destructor* is a member function called automatically when an object goes out of scope.

A constructor function is defined by creating a member function within the class definition with the same name as the class, while a destructor function is defined by creating a member function also with the same name as the class but prefixed with a tilde. Figure 13-3 illustrates a class definition including a constructor and a destructor.

```
class PhoneBook {

  Private:
    char Name[30];
    char Number[15];

  public:
    PhoneBook();
    PhoneBook();
    int AddNAme(char *, char *);
    int DeleteName(char *, char *);

};
```

13-3 Example class definition.

Friend functions and friend classes

Sometimes it makes programming sense to allow a specified function or the member function of a specified class to access the private members of class. This is done by specifying which functions and/or class can access the class from the outside, as shown in Fig. 13-4.

```
class Example {

  Private
    char a_string[10];

  public
    friend void Someclass::Afunction(int x);

      .   .   .
      .   .   .
};
```

13-4 Example of a "friend" function definition.

Function overloading

Function overloading allows you to have many functions with the same name, each responding to a specified data type. For example, if you wanted to write a function that converts feet to inches, you would declare the function like this:

```
int FeetToInches(int feet)
```

This definition (and, of course, its associated function) would work well converting integer values but would be useless in the conversion of floating point values. Therefore, you would be forced to write three functions with different names, all supporting different data types:

```
int     IntFeetToInches(int feet)
float   FloatFeetToInches(float feet)
double  DoubleFeetToInches(double feet)
```

Rather then being forced to follow this multiple naming convention, C++ allows you to give all the above functions the same name shown here:

```
int     FeetToInches(int feet)
float   FeetToInches(float feet)
double  FeetToInches(double feet)
```

Given the above scenario, C++ will decide which function should be called based on the data type of the parameter being passed.

C++ provides yet another overloading capability: it can overload C operators such as plus and minus sign. In fact, C++ can overload any C operator. The classic example of operator overloading, however, is allowing the + operator to add (or more specifically concatenate) string values.

Default function arguments

C++ also provides the facilities to define default values for function arguments. In standard C, the number of parameters passed to a function must exactly match the number of parameters that the function expects to receive. In Fig. 13-5, for example, the function is passed three parameters received into variables x, y, and z.

```
main()
{ int a, b, c;

  a = 1;
  b = 2;
  c = 3;
  TestFunc(a,b,c);
}

int TestFunc(x, y, z)
{ int x,y,z;
  // function logic
}
```

13-5 First function calling example.

In standard C, if the number of passed parameters does not match the number of function arguments, data is not correctly removed from the stack and your program will (or should) crash. In C++, functions may be passed less then the required number of variables by specifying default values for the missing parameters. Additionally, when this defaulting occurs, C++ manages adjusts the stack to keep it intact. The process used to define parameter defaults is shown in Fig. 13-6.

```
main()
{ int a, b;

  a = 1;
  b = 2;
  c = TestFunc(a,b);
}

int TestFunc(x, y, z=4)
{ int x,y,z;
  // function logic
}
```

13-6 First function calling example.

When reviewing Fig. 13-6, note that main() passes TestFunc() only two of the required three parameters. Given this scenario, the values of variables a and b are placed in function parameter variables x and y. Additionally, because z was not passed a value, it is given the default value assigned in the functions parameter definition list: z = 4.

Streams

A *data stream* is a facility by which data can be moved in and out of your program. The three most commonly used stream types are CIN, COUT, and CERR. CIN allows you to pass data from the keyboard (or, more correctly, "standard in") into your program. COUT allows you to pass data from your program to the screen—or more specifically, "standard out." CERR passes data to the screen via standard error that cannot be trapped through the conventional PC-DOS redirection techniques. Figure 13-7 illustrates how streams can be used within your programs.

When reviewing Fig. 13-7, note the use of the << and >> symbols. When used in this context, the << symbol is called the "put to" operator and is used to send data on its right to the stream on the left. The >> operator, called the "get from" operator, is used to get data from the specified stream and place its value within the variable on the right of the operator.

```
#include <iostream.h>

main()
{
  char name[20];
  char address[30];
  char city[30];
  char state[3];
  char zip[10];

  cout << "Enter name: ";
  cin >> name;

  cout << "Enter address: ";
  cin >> address;

  cout << "Enter city: ";
  cin >> city;

  cout << "Enter state: ";
  cin >> state;

  cout << "Enter zipcode: ";
  cin >> zip;

  cout << "\nName     : " << name;
  cout << "\nLocation : " << address;
  cout << "\n          " << city << ", " << state << "  " << zip;
```

13-7 Using streams example.

C++ keywords and operators

This section describes the various C++ keywords not generally considered to be part of the standard C verb set.

new   Facilitates the allocation of memory and can be considered a form of the malloc() function.

delete   Deallocates previously allocated memory and can be considered a form of the free() function. Generally speaking, you will find this verb used within a class's destructor function.

class   Used to define the structure of an object.

public   A modifier within the class keyword that specifies the class member functions and data that can be accessed from outside the class.

private	A modifier of the class keyword that specifies which member functions and data elements within the class cannot be accessed from outside the class. Note that member functions and data elements are private by default.
//	Specifies that the remainder of the line (until the carriage return character is found) is a comment.
const	Represents "constant" and defines constant values. It is used in a manner similar to the #define preprocessor command.
::	Used to inform the compiler that the function being defined is a member of a specific class. It is called the *scope resolution operator*.
inline	Used to specify the function being defined in an inline function.

Part Two
A C Language Reference

14
Language operators

Name	+ *(Addition operator)*
Function	Adds two numerically defined variables or constants.

Example setup	int a,b,c;
	a = 1;
	b = 2;

Examples

c = a + b;	Result—c is set to 5
c = a + 5;	Result—c is set to 6
c = 5 + b;	Result—c is set to 7
c = power(a+b);	Result—c is set to the power of 3(a + b)

Rules

The values being added must be numeric variables, constants, or numeric returns from user- or compiler-defined functions.

Valid values must be placed on both the left and right side of the addition operator as shown in the example.

When variables of different storage types (e.g., int, double, float, etc.) are added, the data is converted to the highest ranking operand as illustrated in Appendix B.

When addition is used in conjunction with other arithmetic operators, C follows the specific rules of precedence outlined in Appendix A.

| **Name** | — | *(Subtraction operator)* |

Function   Subtracts the value of one numerically defined variable or constant from another.

Example setup
```
int a,b,c;
a = 7;
b = 2;
```

Examples

`c = a - b;`	Result—c is set to 5
`c = a - 5;`	Result—c is set to 2
`c = 5 - b;`	Result—c is set to 3
`c = power(a-b);`	Result—c is set to the power of 5 (a - b)

Rules   The values being subtracted must be numeric variables, constants, or numeric returns from user- or compiler-defined functions.

Valid values must be placed on both the left and right side of the subtraction operator as shown in the example.

When variables of different storage types (e.g., `int`, `double`, `float`, etc.) are subtracted, the data is converted to the highest ranking operand as illustrated in Appendix B.

When subtraction is used in conjunction with other arithmetic operators, C follows the specific rules of precedence outlined in Appendix A.

Name	✳ *(Multiplication operator)*
Function	Multiplies two numerically defined variables or constants.

Example setup
```
int a,b,c;
a = 3;
b = 2;
```

Examples

`c = a * b;`	Result—c is set to 6
`c = a * 4;`	Result—c is set to 12
`c = 6 * b;`	Result—c is set to 12
`c = power(a*b);`	Result—c is set to the power of 6 (a * b)

Rules

The values being multiplied must be numeric variables, constants, or numeric returns from user- or compiler-defined functions.

Valid values must be placed on both the left and right side of the multiplication operator as shown in the example.

When variables of different storage types (e.g., int, double, float, etc.) are multiplied, the data is converted to the highest ranking operand as illustrated in Appendix B.

When multiplication is used in conjunction with other arithmetic operators, C follows the specific rules of precedence outlined in Appendix A.

Name	/ *(Division operator)*

Function	Divides the value of one numerically defined variable or constant into another.

Example setup

```
int a,b,c;
a = 2;
b = 6;
```

Examples

c = a / b;	Result—c is set to 3
c = a / 4;	Result—c is set to 2
c = 12 / b;	Result—c is set to 2
c = power (a/b);	Result—c is set to the power of 3 (a / b)

Rules

The values being divided must be numeric variables, constants, or numeric returns from user- or compiler-defined functions.

Valid values must be placed on both the left and right side of the division operator as shown in the example.

When variables of different storage types (e.g., int, double, float, etc.) are divided, the data is converted to the highest ranking operand as illustrated in Appendix B.

When division is used in conjunction with other arithmetic operators, C follows the specific rules of precedence outlined in Appendix A.

%

Name	*% (Remainder operator)*
Function	Calculates the remainder that would be caused by the division of two integer variables or constants.

Example setup
```
int a,b,c;
a = 2;
b = 5;
```

Examples

```
c = a % b;        Result—c is set to 1
c = a % 4;        Result—c is set to 0
c = 12 % b;       Result—c is set to 2
c = power(a%b);   Result—c is set to the power of 1 (a % b)
```

Rules

The values being divided must be numeric variables, integer constants, or numeric returns from user- or compiler-defined functions.

Valid values must be placed on both the left and right side of the remainder operator as shown in the example.

When variables of different storage types (e.g., int, double, float, etc.) are divided, the data is converted to the highest ranking operand as illustrated in Appendix B.

The remainder may only be placed into a variable defined as an integer. Hence, compilation errors might occur or erroneous results might be produced if the recipient of the % operation is a double or floating point variable.

| Name | ++ *(Incremental operator)* |

Function   Adds 1 to a specified numerically defined variable. This operator is generally used to increment counters.

Example setup   `int a,b,c`

Examples

| `a = 5;` | a is first set to 5 |
| `a++;` | a is incremented by 1, giving a a value of 6 |

| `a = 3;` | a is set to a value of 3 |
| `++a;` | a is incremented by 1, giving a a value of 4 |

| `a = 3;` | a is set to 3 |
| `b = ++a;` | b is set to the value of 4 (3 + 1) |

Note that in the third example, a is incremented by 1 before b is set to the value of a. This was done because the ++ operator was placed before the variables being incremented. If the ++ was after the a variable, b would have been given a value of 3 as shown here:

| `a = 3;` | a is set to 3 |
| `b = a++;` | b is set to 3, the value of a, before it was incremented by 1 |

Note that in this example, b was set to the value of a before the ++ operator incremented a by 1. This was done because the ++ was placed after the a variable, thus stating that a should be incremented after the equation has been completed.

Rules   The variable being incremented must be defined as a pointer or a numeric variable.

The ++ operator may be placed before or after the variable being incremented. If the ++ is before the variable, then the variable is incremented before the equation of function containing it is executed. If the ++ is placed after the variable, then the variable is incremented after the equation or function is executed.

When the ++ operator is used in conjunction with other operators, C follows the specific rules of precedence described in Appendix A.

Name	– – *(Decremental operator)*
Function	Subtracts 1 from the specified numerically defined variable. This operator is generally used to decrement counters.
Example setup	int a,b,c
Examples	a = 5; a is first set to 5 a – –; a is decremented by 1, giving a a value of 4

a = 3;	a is set to a value of 3
– – a;	a is decremented by 1, giving a a value of 2

a = 3;	a is set to 3
b = – – a;	b is set to the value of 2 (3 – 1)

Note that in the third example, a is decremented by 1 before b is set to the value of a. This was done because the – – operator was placed before the variables being decremented. If the – – was after the a variable, b would have been given a value of 3 as shown here:

a = 3;	a is set to 3
b = a – –;	b is set to 3, the value of a, before it was decremented by 1

Note that, in this example, b was set to the value of a before the – – operator decremented a by 1. This occurred because the – – was placed after the a variable, thus stating that a should be decremented by 1 after the equation has been completed.

Rules

The variable being decremented must be defined as a pointer or a numeric variable.

The – – operator may be placed before or after variable being decremented. If the – – is before the variable, then the variable is decremented before the equation of function containing it is executed. If the – – is placed after the variable, then the variable is decremented after the equation or function is performed.

When the – – operator is used in conjunction with other operators, C follows the specific rules of precedence described in Appendix A.

Name	= *(Assignment operator)*
Function	Sets a variable to a specified value. Note that this single equal sign operator cannot be used to test for equality; the equality operator is composed of two equal signs (i.e., " = = ").
Example setup	`int a,b;`
Example	`a = 5;` a is set to a value of 5 `b = a;` b is set to the value of a—namely, 5
Rules	The assignment operator goes from right to left. In other words, the value on the left side of the equal sign is set to the value of the variable, function, or constant on the right side of operator. Constants and functions may not be placed on the left side of the equal sign because they cannot logically be assigned a value. When assignments are made from one variable type to another, the data will be automatically converted to the format of the variable receiving the data. Therefore, given the following formula:

```
int a;
float b = 4.1;
float c = 3.0;
a = b + c;
```

a will be given a value of 7 and the .1 will be truncated.

+=

Name	+ = *(Addition assignment operator)*

Function Shorthand for adding the value of a variable or constant to another variable. The statement a + = 5 would thus be a shortcut for the statement a = a + 5. Basically, this shortcut operation is easier to write and generates more efficient machine code once compiled.

Example setup `int a,b;`

Examples

`a = 5;`	a is set to a value of 5
`a + = 3;`	3 is added to a, giving a a value of 8
`a = 5;`	a is set to a value of 5
`b = 2;`	b is set to a value of 2
`a + = b;`	b (2) is added to a (5), making a equal to 7

Rules The value on the right side of the + = is added to the value of the variable on the left.

Constants and functions may not be placed on the left side of the + = operator because they cannot logically be assigned a value.

The right side of the operator may contain constants, functions, or numerically defined variables.

The variable on the right side of the operator cannot be a pointer.

Name	– = *(Subtraction assignment operator)*

Function Shorthand for subtracting the value of a variable or constant from another variable. The statement a – = 5 would thus be a shortcut for the statement a = a – 5. Basically, this shortcut operation is easier to write and generates more efficient machine code once compiled.

Example setup int a,b;

Examples

a = 5 ;   a is set to a value of 5
a – = 3 ;   3 is added to a, making a equal to 2

a = 5 ;   a is set to a value of 5
b = 2 ;   b is set to a value of 2
a – = b ;   b (2) is subtracted from a (5), making a equal to 3

Rules The value on the right side of the – = is subtracted from the value of the variable on the left.

Constants and functions may not be placed on the left side of the – = operator because they cannot logically be assigned a value.

The right side of the operator may contain constants, functions, or numerically defined variables.

The variable on the right side of the operator cannot be a pointer.

* =

Name   * =   *(Multiplication assignment operator)*

Function   Shorthand for multiplying the value of a variable or constant by another variable. The statement a * = 5 would thus be a shortcut for the statement a = a * 5. Basically, this shortcut is easier to write and generates more efficient machine code once compiled.

Example setup   int a,b;

Examples

a = 5;   a is set to a value of 5
a * = 3;   3 is added to a, making a equal to 15

a = 5;   a is set to a value of 5
b = 2;   b is set to a value of 2
a * = b;   b (2) is multiplied by a (5), making a equal to 10

Rules   The value on the right side of the * = is multiplied by the value of the variable on the left, placing the product in the left side variable.

Constants and functions may not be placed on the left side of the * = operator because they cannot logically be assigned a value.

The right side of the operator may contain constants, functions, or numerically defined variables.

The variable on the right side of the operator cannot be a pointer.

Name	/ = *(Division assignment operator)*

Function　Shorthand for dividing the value of a variable or constant into another variable. The statement a / = 5 would thus be a shortcut for the statement a = a / 5. Basically, this shorthand is easier to write and generates more efficient machine code once compiled.

Example setup
```
int a,b;
float c;
```

Examples

a = 5;　　a is set to a value of 5
a / = 3;　　3 is divided by a, making a equal to 2[1]

a = 5;　　a is set to a value of 5
a / = 3;　　3 is divided to a, making a equal to 2.5

c = 5;　　c is set to a value of 5
b = 2;　　b is set to a value of 2
c / = b;　　b (2) is divided by c (5), making c equal to 2.5

Rules　The value on the right side of the / = is divided into the value of the variable on the left.

Constants and functions may not be placed on the left side of the / = operator because they cannot logically be assigned a value.

The right side of the operator may contain constants, functions, or numerically defined variables.

The variable on the right side of the operator cannot be a pointer.

---

[1]Remember, a is an integer; thus, the remainder of .5 is truncated.

%=

Name	%= *(Remainder assignment operator)*

Function Shorthand for calculating the remainder caused by the division of two integer-defined variables or constants. The statement a %= 5 would thus be a shortcut for the statement a = a % 5. Basically, this shortcut is easier to write and generates more efficient machine code once compiled.

Example setup `int a,b;`

Examples

a = 5;	a is set to a value of 5
a %= 3;	3 is divided into a, giving a a remainder value of 2
a = 5;	a is set to a value of 5
b = 2;	b is set to a value of 2
a %= b;	b (2) is divided into a (5), giving a a remainder value of 1

Rules The value on the right side of the %= is divided by the value of the variable on the left, placing the remainder from the division in the left side variable.

Constants and functions may not be placed on the left side of the %= operator because they cannot logically be assigned a value.

The right side of the operator may contain constants, functions, or numerically defined variables.

The variable on the right side of the operator cannot be a pointer.

Name	＊ *(Indirection operator)*
Function	When a ＊ is placed as the prefix of a variable (e.g., `*a_variable`), the combined expression refers to the memory location at which the variable is stored. For example, given this statement,

`int a_variable = 15;`

The value of `a_variable` is 15; however, the expression `*a_variable` refers to the memory location in which the value 15 is stored.

Example setup	`int *a_variable b_variable;` `a_variable = 10;`
Example	`b_variable = *a_variable;`
Rules	This operator may only be used with pointer variables.

The ＊ must be on the left side of the pointer variable being indirected.

An indirected pointer variable can be used like any regular variable.

&

Name	& *(Address operator)*

Function   Provides a means of obtaining the memory location of a specified variable. For example, if you want to obtain the location of variable a_variable, you can do so by referencing the variable as &a_variable. This operator is primarily used to pass the address of a variable to a pointer.

Example setup
```
int a_variable, *b_pointer;
a_variable = 5;
```

Example
```
b_variable = &a_variable;
```

Here, the address of variable a_variable is being placed in the integer pointer b_pointer.

Rules   The & operator can only be used to reference the address of variables because only variables have memory addresses. Therefore, because constants, functions, and mathematical formulas are not variables, it would not be logical to try to reference their location. If such a reference is attempted anyway, an error will occur during compilation.

The & character must be on the left side and adjacent to the variable being referenced. For example, &a_variable is valid but & a_variable and a_variable& are not.

Name   [] *(Array operator)*

Function   The [] operator indicates that the variable being suffixed is an array. Note
that this operator is used when defining the size of a character string
because C treats a character string like a single dimensional array. For
example, `char a_variable[11];` states that `a_variable` is a
character string of length 10 plus a one-character null terminator. Additionally, note that the character string definition is the most common use
of arrays, but not their only use.

Example   `char an_array[15];`

Rules   The [] characters must immediately follow the variable being suffixed.

All character strings are interpreted as one-dimensional arrays.

A static array can be initialized in the following manner:

`static int a_variable[] = {1,2,3,4,5};`

When using the above array assignment option, the compiler will automatically calculate the size of the array by counting the listing array values.

Name   *(Structure identification operator)*

Function   Associates a variable with its defined structure.

Example setup
```
struct name
   { char last[21];
     char first[21];
     char middle_initial[2];
   }
```

Example
```
strcpy(name.last, "Bloom");
strcpy(name.first, "Eric");
strcpy(name.middle_initial,"P");
```

The `strcpy` function used in this example stands for "string copy" and is used to assign the name values to the various structure components.

Rules   No spaces may be present between the structure name, the period, and the variable name.

The structure/variable relationship must be explicitly defined as shown here in the `struct` and cannot be created on the fly.

`name.first` and `(&name)->first` are equivalent expressions.

Name   – >   *(Structure identification operator)*

Function   Associates a variable with its defined structure.

Example setup
```
struct name
  { char last[21];
    char first[21];
    char middle_initial[2];
  }
```

Example
```
strcpy(name->last, "Bloom");
strcpy(name->first, "Eric");
strcpy(name->middle_initial,"P");
```

The `strcpy` statement used here stands for "string copy" and assigns the name values to the various structure components.

Rules   No spaces may be present between the structure name, the – >, and the variable name.

The structure/variable relationship must be explicitly defined as shown and cannot be created on the fly.

`name.first` and `(&name)->first` are equivalent expressions.

&&

Name	&& *(Logical AND operator)*
Function	Specifies the AND requirement within an i f statement or other testing area.
Example setup	int a,b,c,d;
Examples	if (a = = b && c = = d) if (a = = b && a = = c && a = = d)

The first example shown here states that a must equal b and c must equal d to make the i f statement true.

Rules   The && characters must be side by side with no spaces or other characters between them.

The operators & and && are not the same; & is a bitwise operator and serves a similar but very different function.

There must be a comparative expression on both the left and right of the && operator.

Name	¦¦ *(Logical OR operator)*
Function	Specifies the OR requirement within an i f statement or other testing area.
Example setup	int a,b,c,d;

Examples	if (a == b¦¦c == d)
	
	if (a == b¦¦a == c¦¦a == d)
	
	The first example shown here states that a must equal b or c must equal d to make the i f statement true.

Rules	The ¦¦ characters must be side by side with no spaces or other characters between them. The operators ¦ and ¦¦ are not the same; ¦ is a bitwise operator and serves a similar but very different function. There must be a comparative expression on both the left and right of the ¦¦ operator.

<

Name	< *(Less-than operator)*

Function   Compares the value of two expressions. Upon making this comparison, a non-zero is generated if the first operator is less than the second. If not, a zero value is produced. As shown next, when incorporated within an if statement, a non-zero value is construed as true and a zero value is construed as false.

Example setup   int a,b;

Example

a = 1;	a is set to 1
b = 2;	b is set to 2
if (a < b)	The equation a < b yields a non-zero value; hence, the if expression is true.

a = 2;	a is set to 2
b = 1;	b is set to 1
if (a < b)	The equation a < b yields a zero value; hence, the if expression is false.

Rules   There must be an expression on both the left and right of the > operator.

The two variables being compared should be of the same data type. If not, inconsistent results might occur.

Name	> *(Greater-than operator)*
Function	Compares the value of two expressions. Upon making this comparison, a non-zero is generated if the first operator is greater than the second. If not, a zero value is produced. As shown next, when incorporated within an i f statement, a non-zero value is construed as true and a zero value is construed as false.
Example setup	int a,b;

Example

a = 1;	a is set to 1
b = 2;	b is set to 2
if (a > b)	The equation a > b yields a zero value; hence, the i f expression is false.

a = 2;	a is set to 2
b = 1;	b is set to 1
if (a > b)	The equation a > b yields a non-zero value; hence, the i f expression is true.

Rules

There must be an expression on both the left and right of the > operator.

The two variables being compared should be of the same data type. If not, inconsistent results might occur.

$<=$

Name	$<=$ *(Less-than or equal-to operator)*

Function
Compares the value of two expressions. Upon making this comparison, a non-zero is generated if the first operator is less than or equal to the second. If not, a zero value is produced. As shown next, when incorporated within an if statement, a non-zero value is construed as true and a zero value is construed as false.

Example setup   int a,b;

Example

a = 1;	a is set to 1
b = 1;	b is set to 1
if (a <= b)	The equation a <= b yields a non-zero value; hence, the if expression is true.

a = 1;	a is set to 1
b = 2;	b is set to 2
if (a <= b)	The equation a <= b yields a non-zero value; hence, the if expression is true.

a = 2;	a is set to 2
b = 1;	b is set to 1
if (a <= b)	The equation a <= b yields a zero value; hence, the if expression is false.

Rules
There must be an expression on both the left and right of the $<=$ operator.

The two variables being compared should be of the same data type. If not, inconsistent results might occur.

The operator must be written as $<=$; the format $=<$ is invalid and will generate a syntax error during compilation.

| Name | > = *(Greater-than or equal-to operator)* |

Function Compares the value of two expressions. Upon making this comparison, a non-zero is generated if the first operator is greater than or equal to the second. If not, a zero value is produced. As shown next, when incorporated within an if statement, a non-zero value is construed as true and a zero value is construed as false.

Example setup int a,b;

Example

a = 1;   a is set to 1
b = 1;   b is set to 1
if (a > = b) The equation a > = b yields a non-zero value; hence, the if expression is true.

a = 1;   a is set to 1
b = 2;   b is set to 2
if (a > = b) The equation a > = b yields a zero value; hence, the if expression is false.

a = 2;   a is set to 2
b = 1;   b is set to 1
if (a > = b) The equation a > = b yields a non-zero value; hence, the if expression is true.

Rules There must be an expression on both the left and right of the > = operator.

The two variables being compared should be of the same data type. If not, inconsistent results might occur.

The operator must be written as > = ; the format = > is invalid and will generate a syntax error during compilation.

Name	= = *(Equal-to operator)*

Function   Compares the value of two expressions. Upon making this comparison, a non-zero is generated if the first operator is equal to the second. If not, a zero value is produced. As shown next, when incorporated within an i f statement, a non-zero value is construed as true and a zero value is construed as false.

Example setup   int a, b;

Example

a = 1 ;   a is set to 1
b = 1 ;   b is set to 1
if (a = = b)   The equation a = = b yields a non-zero value; hence, the i f expression is true.

a = 1 ;   a is set to 1
b = 2 ;   b is set to 2
if (a = = b)   The equation a = = b yields a zero value; hence, the i f expression is false.

a = 2 ;   a is set to 2
b = 1 ;   b is set to 1
if (a = = b)   The equation a = = b yields a zero value; hence, the i f expression is false.

Rules   There must be an expression on both the left and right of the = = operator.

The two variables being compared should be of the same data type. If not, inconsistent results might occur.

The = = and = operators perform totally different functions. The = = operator tests for equality between two values, while the = operator sets the variable on the left of the operator equal to the value of the variable, function, or constant on the right.

Name	! = *(Not-equal-to operator)*

Function   Compares the value of two expressions. Upon making this comparison, a non-zero is generated if the first operator is not equal to the second. If equal, a zero value is produced. As shown next, when ! = is incorporated within an i f statement, a non-zero value is construed as true and a zero value is construed as false.

Example setup   int a,b;

Example

a = 1;   a is set to 1
b = 1;   b is set to 1
if (a != b)   The equation a != b yields a zero value; hence, the if expression is false.

a = 1;   a is set to 1
b = 2;   b is set to 2
if (a != b)   The equation a != b yields a non-zero value; hence, the if expression is true.

a = 2;   a is set to 2
b = 1;   b is set to 1
if (a != b)   The equation a != b yields a non-zero value; hence, the if expression is true.

Rules   There must be an expression on both the left and right of the ! = operator.

The two variables being compared should be of the same data type. If not, inconsistent results might occur.

The ! = , = , and ! operators perform totally different functions. The ! = operator tests for non-equality between two values. The = operator sets the variable on the left of the operator equal to the value of the variable, function, or constant on the right. Lastly, the ! operator deals with the logical negative of a value.

?:

Name   ?:   *(Equation operator)*

Function   Resembles the if/else statement. If the first value or condition pro-
                  duces a non-zero value (i.e., "true"), then the second value is used. If
                  the first value yields a zero value (i.e., "false"), then the third value is
                  used.

Example setup int a,b,c,d,e;

Examples   a = 1;   a is set to 1
                  b = 2;   b is set to 2
                  c = 3;   c is set to 3
                  d = 4;   d is set to 4
                  e = (a= =b)?c:d   e will be set to 4, the value of d, because a and
                                      b are not equal. Hence, the expression
                                      (a= =b) yields a zero value.

Examples   a = 1;   a is set to 1
                  b = 2;   b is set to 2
                  c = 3;   c is set to 3
                  d = 4;   d is set to 4
                  e = a?c:d   e will be set to 3, the value of c because a has a
                                      non-zero value.

Rules   The leftmost operand is calculated first. Then, the second or third (but
                  never both) operand is calculated next, based on the outcome of the
                  first.

                  The first operand may be a variable, expression, or function. Note,
                  however, that if a constant is placed in the first position, the same result
                  would always be chosen, thus negating the non-chosen option.

&

Name	& *(Bitwise AND operator)*
Function	Used to AND two bit fields based on the Boolean principles shown here in the rules section.

Example setup

```
int a;
int b;
int c;
a = 1;
b = 2;
```

Example

```
c = a & b
```

Rules

Bitwise operations may only be performed on variables defined as integers—namely, `int`, `long`, `unsigned`, and `short`.

The AND operation is performed using the following rules:

Bit 1	Bit 2	Outcome
1	1	1
1	0	0
0	1	0
0	0	0

When this operator is used in conjunction with other operators, C follows the specific rules of precedence outlined in Appendix A.

Name	(Bitwise inclusive OR operator)
Function	Used to inclusive OR two bit fields based on the Boolean principles shown here in the rules section.

Example setup

```
int a;
int b;
int c;
a = 1;
b = 2;
```

Example

```
c = a|b
```

Rules

Bitwise operations may only be performed on variables defined as integers—namely, `int`, `long`, `unsigned`, and `short`.

The `inclusive` OR operation is performed using the following rules:

Bit 1	Bit 2	Outcome
1	1	1
1	0	1
0	1	1
0	0	0

When this operator is used in conjunction with other operators, C follows the specific rules of precedence outlined in Appendix A.

Name	∧ *(Bitwise exclusive OR operator)*
Function	Used to exclusive OR two bit fields based on the Boolean principles shown here in the rules section.

Example setup	`int a;`
	`int b;`
	`int c;`
	`a = 1;`
	`b = 2;`

Example	`c = a ∧ b`
Rules	Bitwise operations may only be performed on variables defined as integers—namely, `int`, `long`, `unsigned`, and `short`.

The exclusive OR operation is performed using the following rules:

Bit 1	Bit 2	Outcome
1	1	0
1	0	1
0	1	1
0	0	0

When this operator is used in conjunction with other operators, C follows the specific rules of precedence outlined in Appendix A.

Name	~ *(Bitwise ones complement operator)*
Function	Used to change all the 1 values to 0 and all the 0 values to 1, thus flip-flopping the bit values.

Example setup	`int a;`
	`int b;`
	`a = 1;`

Example	`b = a`
Rules	Bitwise operations may only be performed on variables defined as integers—namely, `int`, `long`, `unsigned`, and `short`.

The one's complement operation is performed using the following rules:

Bit 1	Outcome
1	0
0	1

When this operator is used in conjunction with other operators, C follows the specific rules of precedence outlined in Appendix A.

Name	`<<` *(Bitwise shift left operator)*

Function   Used to shift the bits contained within a variable or bit field a specified number of places to the left.

Example setup

```
int a;
int b;
int c;
a = 1;
b = 2;
```

Examples

c = a << b shifts bits in a 2 places and places the result in c

c = a << 3 shifts bits in a 3 places to the left and places the result in c

Rules

Bitwise operations may only be performed on variables defined as integers—namely, `int`, `long`, `unsigned`, and `short`.

The bits shifted out the left side of the variable are lost.

The spaces left vacant by the bit shifting are zero-filled.

When this operator is used in conjunction with other operators, C follows the specific rules of precedence outlined in Appendix A.

Name	>> *(Bitwise shift right operator)*
Function	Used to shift the bits contained within a variable or bit field a specified number of places to the right.

Example setup

```
int a;
int b;
int c;
a = 1;
b = 2;
```

Examples

c = a << b shifts bits in a 2 places and places the result in c

c = a << 3 shifts bits in a 3 places to the left and places the result in c

Rules

Bitwise operations may only be performed on variables defined as integers—namely, int, long, unsigned, and short.

The bits shifted out the right side of the variable are lost.

The spaces left vacant by the bit shifting are zero-filled.

When this operator is used in conjunction with other operators, C follows the specific rules of precedence outlined in Appendix A.

Name	&= *(Unary bitwise AND operator)*

Function   Used to AND two bit fields based on the Boolean principles shown next in the rules section and place the generated value in the variable on the left side of the operator.

Example setup
```
int a;
int b;
a = 1;
b = 2;
```

Example   b &= a

Rules   Bitwise operations may only be performed on variables defined as integers—namely, int, long, unsigned, and short.

The AND operation is performed using the following rules:

Bit 1	Bit 2	Outcome
1	1	1
1	0	0
0	1	0
0	0	0

When this operator is used in conjunction with other operators, C follows the specific rules of precedence outlined in Appendix A.

Name	$|=$ *(Unary bitwise inclusive OR operator)*

Function Used to inclusive OR two bit fields based on the Boolean principles shown here in the rules section and place the generated value in the variable on the left side of the operator.

Example setup
```
int a;
int b;
a = 1;
b = 2;
```

Example a |= b

Rules Bitwise operations may only be performed on variables defined as integers—namely, `int`, `long`, `unsigned`, and `short`.

The inclusive OR operation is performed using the following rules:

Bit 1	Bit 2	Outcome
1	1	1
1	0	1
0	1	1
0	0	0

When this operator is used in conjunction with other operators, C follows the specific rules of precedence outlined in Appendix A.

Name	^ = *(Unary bitwise exclusive OR operator)*

Function   Used to exclusive OR two bit fields based on the Boolean principles shown here in the rules section and place the generated value in the variable on the left side of the operator.

Example setup
```
int a;
int b;
a = 1;
b = 2;
```

Example   a^ = b

Rules   Bitwise operations may only be performed on variables defined as integers—namely, int, long, unsigned, and short.

The exclusive OR operation is performed using the following rules:

Bit 1	Bit 2	Outcome
1	1	0
1	0	1
0	1	1
0	0	0

When this operator is used in conjunction with other operators, C follows the specific rules of precedence outlined in Appendix A.

<< =

Name	<< = *(Unary bitwise shift left operator)*
Function	Used to shift the bits contained within a variable or bit field a specified number of places to the left and place the outcome in the variable on the left side of the operator.

Example setup	int a;
	int b;
	a = 1;
	b = 2;

Examples	a << = b shifts bits in a 2 places and places the result in a a << = 3 shifts bits in a 3 places to the left and places the result in a
Rules	Bitwise operations may only be performed on variables defined as integers—namely, int, long, unsigned, and short. The bits shifted out the left side of the variable are lost. The spaces left vacant by the bit shifting are zero-filled. When this operator is used in conjunction with other operators, C follows the specific rules of precedence outlined in Appendix A.

Name	>> = *(Unary bitwise shift right operator)*

Function   Used to shift the bits contained within a variable or bit field a specified number of places to the right and place the outcome in the variable on the left side of the operator.

Example setup
```
int a;
int b;
a = 1;
b = 2;
```

Examples   a >> = b   shifts bits in a 2 places and places the result in a

a >> = 3   shifts bits in a 3 places to the right and places the result in a

Rules   Bitwise operations may only be performed on variables defined as integers—namely, int, long, unsigned, and short.

The bits shifted out the right side of the variable are lost.

The spaces left vacant by the bit shifting are zero-filled.

When this operator is used in conjunction with other operators, C follows the specific rules of precedence outlined in Appendix A.

15
Storage classes and data types

auto

Name	auto
Type	Storage Class definition
Syntax	auto *variable-type variable-name;* auto *variable-type variable-name, variable-name ... ;*
Function	Defines a variable as automatic storage class. This means that C will not reserve space for the specified variable at the beginning of the program's execution but will dynamically allocate memory space at the time the function containing the element is called.
Examples	auto char a_variable[10]; auto int b_variable, c_variable, d_variable;
Rules	All locally defined variables default to automatic class unless expressly defined to be otherwise (extern, regester, static, or typedef).
	All data types can be defined as automatic.
	Prior to initialization, the value contained within automatic variables should be considered garbage (i.e., some unknown set of numbers or characters).
	Automatic variables are local to the function in which they are defined.
	A variable may only be defined as one storage class.

char

Name   char *(Character definition)*

Type   Data definition

Syntax   char *variable-name;*
char *variable-name, variable-name* ... ;
storage-class char *variable-name;*
storage-class char *variable-name, variable-name* ... ;

Function   States that the listed variables will contain a single ASCII character.

Example   char a_variable;
char a_variable, b_variable;
auto char a_variable;
extern char a_variable, b_variable, c_variable;

Rules   Character variables may be set to a particular value by placing that value in single quotes like this:

char a_variable;
a_variable = 'x';

Character variables may be set to non-printing character values (null, escape, line feed, etc.) by placing a backslash and the octal ASCII equivalent of that character in single quotes:

char a_variable;
a_variable = '\33';

Octal 33 is escape key ASCII equivalent.

Strings of characters may be defined by suffixing the defined variable with an array operator. For example, this statement defines a character string (array) of 21 characters:

char last_name[21];

Note that last_name would have a maximum length of 20 characters; the last character would be a null terminator, indicating the end of the character string.

double

Name	double *(Double floating point)*
Type	Data definition

Syntax	`double variable-name;`
	`double variable-name, variable-name . . . ;`
	`storage-class double variable-name;`
	`storage-class double variable-name, variable-name . . . ;`

Function	Declares that the listed variables are to be double precision floating point data types.

Example	`double a_variable;`
	`double a_variable, b_variable;`
	`auto double a_variable;`
	`extern double a_variable, b_variable, c_variable;`

Rules	Double precision floating point variables are two storage locations long (2 bytes), thus allowing for much larger and more precise values. Rounding errors might occur when moving double precision variables to other numerically defined data types. `double` and `long float` are equivalent expressions.

Name extern

Type Storage Class definition

Syntax extern *variable-type variable-name;*
extern *variable-type variable-name, variable-name ... ;*

Function Defines a variable as external storage class.

Examples extern char a_variable[10];
extern int b_variable, c_variable, d_variable;

FILE

Name	FILE
Type	Data definition
Syntax	FILE variable-name; FILE variable-name, variable-name ... ;
Function	Used exclusively to define the fopen() function and the variables needed to open, reference, and close data files.
Example	FILE *input_file, *fopen( );
Rules	The stdio.h leader file must be referenced in order to use the FILE data type. This file is the standard input/output header and is accessed by placing the following line at the beginning of your program: #include <stdio.h> The word FILE is almost always printed in uppercase. The particular rules surrounding the FILE statement tend to vary from compiler to compiler. FILE serves as a nice documentation method for stating which variables are file-related.

float

Name	float
Type	Data definition
Syntax	float *variable-name;* float *variable-name, variable-name* ... ; *storage-class* float *variable-name;* *storage-class* float *variable-name, variable-name* ... ;
Function	Declares that the listed variables are to be floating point data types.
Example	float a_variable; float a_variable, b_variable; auto float a_variable; extern float a_variable, b_variable, c_variable;
Rules	Floating point numbers are generally from 6 to 8 digits long and may be expressed in both conventional and exponential notation. Rounding errors might occur when moving float point variables to other numerically defined data types. double and long float are equivalent expressions.

int

Name	int
Type	Data definition
Syntax	int *variable-name;* int *variable-name, variable-name* ... ; *storage-class* int *variable-name;* *storage-class* int *variable-name, variable-name* ... ;
Function	Defines the listed variables as integer data types.
Example	int a_variable; int a_variable, b_variable; auto int a_variable; extern int a_variable, b_variable, c_variable;
Rules	Integer numbers may contain values ranging from -32767 through 32767. Integer type variables may only contain whole numbers. The decimal portion of a number will be truncated when moved to an integer data type variable. The valid range of numbers that can be placed in an integer field can be expanded by declaring it as long or unsigned.

Name   long

Type   Data definition

Syntax   long *variable-name*;
long *variable-name, variable-name* ... ;
long *variable-type variable-name*;
long *variable-type variable-name, variable-name* ... ;
storage-class long *variable-name*;
storage-class long *variable-name, variable-name* ... ;
storage-class long *variable-type variable-name*;
storage-class long *variable-type variable-name,*
  variable-name ... ;

Function   Defines variables to be twice as long as the normal specified data type (a type of double precision).

Example   long a_variable;
long a_variable, b_variable;
auto long a_variable;
extern long a_variable, b_variable, c_variable;

Rules   A long float is the same as a double.

If the word long is present with no specified data type, then the variable's data type is assumed to be integer.

A long integer may contain values ranging from −2,147,483,647 through 2,147,483,647.

The decimal portion of a number will be truncated when moved to an integer data type variable.

register

Name	`register`
Type	Storage Class definition
Syntax	`register` *variable-type variable-name;* `register` *variable-type variable-name, variable-name* `. . . ;`
Function	Are stored in the CPU's register list, thus speeding up calculations performed on that variable.
Examples	`register char a_variable[10];` `register int b_variable, c_variable, d_variable;`
Rules	If the CPU does not have room to store the register variable, then it is automatically converted to `auto` class.
	Structures, unions, and arrays cannot be defined as `register` class variables.
	The address of a `register` class variable cannot be obtained by the & address variable.
	A variable may only be defined as one storage class.

Name   short

Type   Data definition

Syntax   short *variable-name;*
short *variable-name, variable-name ... ;*
short *variable-type variable-name;*
short *variable-type variable-name, variable-name ... ;*
storage-class short *variable-name;*
storage-class short *variable-name, variable-name ... ;*
storage-class short *variable-type variable-name;*
storage-class short *variable-type variable-name,*
 variable-name ... ;

Function Defines variables to be a short integer data type.

Example   short a_variable;
short int a_variable;
short a_variable, b_variable;
auto short a_variable;
extern short a_variable, b_variable, c_variable;

Rules   The word "short" stands for short integer.

If the word short is present with no specified data type, then the variable's data type is assumed to be integer.

A short integer is stored in half the space of a regular integer. Thus, it requires less memory space but consequently can only hold smaller numbers.

Many IBM-PC compilers store a short integer in the same manner as a regular integer (i.e., in a full word) because, in a 16-bit machine, an 8-bit integer only allows for very small numbers. Because of this constraint, short is much more useful on a 32-bit machine.

Some compilers allow short data types other than integer, but this is not a standard C feature.

If your compiler stores short integers in a full 16-bit word, you can overcome this constraint by using bit fields as discussed in Chapter 11.

static

Name   `static`

Type   Storage Class definition

Syntax   `static` *variable-type variable-name;*
`static` *variable-type variable-name, variable-name ...*
`;`

Function   Used to allocate a variable's memory space prior to, or at the very beginning of, program execution and instructs the compiler to retain that space through the entire execution of the program.

Examples   `static char a_variable[] = "Hi, I'm a static";`
`static int b_variable = 5;`

Rules   The value placed within a static variable can be changed during program execution.

Static variables remain in memory throughout the entire execution of the program, thus permanently taking up storage space.

Static variables are generally placed in a special data area and thus do not use space within the program stack.

Static variables are assigned their initial values either during compilation or at the very beginning of program execution.

Variables may only be defined as one storage class.

If a static variable is defined within a function, that variable is not re-initialized each time the function is called. Therefore, if the function modifies the value of a static variable, that modified value will be present in the variable if the function is called a second time.

Name   `struct`

Type   Storage Class definition

Syntax
```
struct struct_name { member-list } ;
struct struct_name { member-list } a_variable;
struct struct_name a_variable;
struct struct_name a_variable, b_variable;
```

Function   Groups together variables under a common structure name.

Examples
```
struct name {
    char last[10];
    char first[10];
    char middle[10];
    };

struct name employee;
struct name name {
    char last[10];
    char first[10];
    char middle[10];
    } employee;
```

Rules   As shown here, the member-list is the set of the variable declarations included within the structure template.

The semicolon following the member-list's closing bracket is required.

A structure declaration is not allocated space in memory until it becomes associated with a structure variable. The association may be defined in one of two ways: you can define a structure template (as in the first example) followed by a structure variable assignment (like the second example), or you can incorporate the variable name into the original structure definition (like the third example).

typedef

Name   `typedef`

Type   Data definition

Syntax   `typedef `*`variable-type variable-name`*`;`

Function   `typedef` is used to define your own data definition types.

Example   `typedef long unsigned int lui;`
                         `lui a_variable;`

Rules   All characters after the word `typedef` and before the last word are considered to be part of the type definition being defined. For example,

            `typedef long unsigned int lui;`

            `typedef` is the statement name, `long unsigned int` is the definition being defined, and `lui` is the new data definition name.

Name   `union`

Type   Storage Class definition

Syntax   `union union_name { member-list } ;`
`union union_name { member-list } a_variable;`

Function   Allows you to store various data types within a single memory location.

Example
```
union all_types {
  char a_character;
  int an_integer;
  double a_double;
  };
```

Rules   Memory space is reserved based on the largest union data type. In the example shown here, the union would require two bytes to memory storage because of the `a_double` floating point variable.

A semicolon must be placed after the member list closing bracket.

unsigned

Name   unsigned

Type   Data definition

Syntax
```
unsigned variable-name;
unsigned variable-name, variable-name ... ;
unsigned variable-type variable-name;
unsigned variable-type variable-name, variable-name
... ;
storage-class unsigned variable-name;
storage-class unsigned variable-name, variable-name
... ;
storage-class unsigned variable-type variable-name;
storage-class unsigned variable-type variable-name,
variable-name ... ;
```

Function   Defines variables to be an unsigned integer data type.

Example
```
unsigned a_variable;
unsigned int a_variable;
unsigned a_variable, b_variable;
auto unsigned a_variable;
extern unsigned a_variable, b_variable, c_variable;
```

Rules   The word unsigned stands for unsigned integer.

An unsigned integer may contain values ranging from 0 to 65,635.

Unsigned integer variables may only contain positive values (or zero). When a negative number is moved to an unsigned variable, unpredictable results might occur.

16
Compiler directives

/* */

Name   /* */   *(Comment)*

Syntax   /* The comment is placed here */

Function   Instructs the compiler to ignore the text placed between the beginning and ending comment symbol indicators.

Examples   Comments are generally formatted in the following ways:

```
j + + ; /* on same line as a statement */

/* Outlining a group of comment lines by
 * placing asterisks at the beginning of
 * each commented line.
 */

/*
   Just using the beginning and ending
   indicators with no additional asterisk
   blocking.
*/

/ ******************************************
 * Outlining the comments within a four-sided  *
 * asterisk box.                               *
 ******************************************/

/* Outlining each line of the comments */
/* with its own beginning and ending    */
/* comment indicators                   */
```

Rules   A comment must begin with a slash, followed by an asterisk—"/*".

A comment statement must be terminated with an asterisk followed by a slash—"*/".

A good way to remember the comment syntax is to keep in mind that the asterisk is always on the inside of the comment.

#asm

Name	#asm *(Assembly language beginning indicator)*
Function	Informs the compiler that the lines of code written after it are assembly language and not C.
Syntax	#asm
	. . .
	#endasm
Example	#asm
	;
	;assembly language goes here
	;
	#endasm
Rules	Compiler directives are not followed by semicolons.
	The #endasm directive must be placed after the last assembly language statement and before the next C statement.
	The #asm and #endasm are not implemented on all C compilers.
	Many compilers require the # to be in the first column.
	The C compiler invokes a preprocessor that scans the source code in search of compiler directives. This preprocessor creates a temporary source code file that both reflects the compiler directive and is used as the compiler's input file.

#define

Name   #define   *(Define expression)*

Function   Instructs the C compiler to replace all occurrences of a specified key word with an associated character string.

Syntax   #define *defined-word expression*

Examples   #define BELL printf("%c",'\007');

#define isblank(x) ((x == '') ? 1 : 0)

#define TRUE 1

#define FALSE 0

#define EOF −1

Rules   Compiler directives are not followed by an ending semicolon.

As shown in the first #define example, a single word may be used to represent an entire statement.

As shown in the second #define example, the #define directive can be used to define small function-like procedures, which are called *macros*.

Define macros have an advantage over functions: during precompilation, the macro is actually placed within the source code at all the locations where the key word is found. Therefore, executing the macro does not require the overhead associated with a function—namely, placing data and program pointers in the push-down stack.

As shown in the last three #define examples, the #define directive can be used to set a variable equal to a specific value. In the case of TRUE and FALSE, given the values of 1 and 0 respectively, these words are much more self-documenting than 0 and 1.

General industry conventions dictate that define macros are written in lowercase and that simple word replacements (TRUE, FALSE, EOF, etc.) are in uppercase. Note that this is not a compiler requirement but just a standard programming practice.

When a define macro is passed a variable, as shown in the second #define example, the variable passed to the macro is placed within that macro during the precompilation process. For example, given the macro

#define square(x) (x * x)

as called by

square(a_value);

the precompiler would place the equivalent of (a_value * a_value) in the source code.

#else

Name #else

Function Used to provide the #if, #indef, and #ifndef directives with an if-then-else capability.

Syntax #else statement or statements

Example
```
#ifdef TESTRUN
  printf("This is a test run");
#else
  printf("This is not a test run");
#endif
```

Rules Compiler directives are not followed by an ending semicolon.

The #else directive may only be used within the #if, #ifdef, and #ifndef directives.

The #else directive is optional and should only be used when it will contain compilable statements.

The #else directive does not replace #endif; the #endif is still required and must be placed after the #else directive and its associated statements.

#endasm

Name	#endasm *(End assembly language section)*
Function	Used to inform the compiler that the assembly language statement section has ended and that the statements following are written in C.
Syntax	#endasm

Example

```
#asm
  ;
  ; assembly language source code
  ;
#endasm
```

Rules

Compiler directives are not followed by an ending semicolon.

The #endasm directive may only be used in conjunction with #asm.

All statements placed between #asm and #asmasm are assumed to be assembly language source code.

#endif

Name	#endif *(End if)*
Function	Used to signify the end of an #if, #ifdef, or #ifndef directive.
Syntax	#endif

Example	#if TESTRUN
	  printf("This is a test");
	#endif

Rules	Compiler directives are not followed by an ending semicolon.

Compiler directives are not followed by an ending semicolon.

This #endif directive may only be used in conjunction with #if, #ifdef, and #ifndef.

#endif is a required part of the three if directives mentioned in the function description. Note that if the #endif is not present (assuming a syntax error is not produced), then your entire program will be considered part of the if directive.

The #endif directive will only signify the completion of the innermost if. Thus, when nesting #if/-def/-ndef directives, you must have an associated #endif for each #if/-def/-ndef.

#if

Name	#if
Function	Provides the ability to compile or not compile sections of the source C code based on the value of a specified expression.
Syntax	#if
Examples	

```
#if TESTRUN
  printf("This is a test");
#else
  printf("this is not a test");
#endif

#if TESTRUN
  printf("This is a test");
#endif
```

Rules Compiler directives are not followed by an ending semicolon.

This directive can only interpret numerically defined constants. Note that the preprocessor is part of the compilation process; therefore, runtime values have not yet been defined.

All statements between the #if and the #endif are considered to be part of the #if directive. Hence, if the #endif is inadvertently left out, then your entire program from the #if forward will be compiled based on the outcome of that #if condition.

#if has an optional #else modifier.

When evaluating #if expressions, a zero is considered false and a non-zero is considered true.

#ifdef

Name   #ifdef   *(If defined)*

Function   Instructs the precompiler to conditionally compile statements (or review additional directives) based on whether a specified identifier has been defined using #define.

Syntax   #ifdef *expression-name statements* #endif
#ifdef *expression-name statements*
#else *statements* #endif

Examples #ifdef TESTRUN
#define TESTFLAG 1
printf("This is a test");
#else
#define TESTFLAG 0
printf("This is not a test");
#endif

#ifdef TESTRUN
printf("This is a test");
#endif

Rules   Compiler directives are not followed by an ending semicolon.

All statements between the #ifdef and the #endif are considered to be part of the #ifdef directive. Hence, if the #endif is inadvertently left out, then your entire program from the #ifdef forward will be compiled based on the outcome of that #ifdef condition.

#ifdef has an optional #else modifier.

This directive is true if the identifier being tested has previously been defined.

#ifdef is false if the identifier being tested has not been previously defined.

The #ifdef directive may be nested with other #ifdef's, #if, or #ifndef.

#ifndef

Name	#ifndef *(If not defined)*

Function   Instructs the precompiler to conditionally compile statements (or review additional directives) if a specified identifier has not been defined using #define.

Syntax   #ifndef *expression-name statements* #endif
#ifndef *expression-name statements*
 #else *statements* #endif

Examples

```
#ifndef TESTRUN
  #define TESTFLAG 0
 printf("This is not a test");
#else
 #define TESTFLAG
 printf("This is a test");
#endif

#ifndef TRUE
 #define TRUE 1
 #define FALSE 0
#endif
```

Rules   Compiler directives are not followed by an ending semicolon.

All statements between the #ifndef and the #endif are considered to be part of the #ifndef directive. Hence, if the #endif is inadvertently left out, then your entire program from the #ifndef forward will be compiled based on the outcome of that #ifndef condition.

#ifndef has an optional #else modifier.

This directive is true if the identifier being tested has not previously been defined.

#ifndef is false if the identifier being tested has been previously defined.

The #ifndef directive may be nested with other #ifndef's, #if, or #ifndef.

#include

Name   `#include`   *(Include this source file)*

Function   Instructs the compiler to insert the source code contained within a specified file into the program being compiled.

Syntax   `#include < filename.ext >`

Examples   `#include < stdio.h >`

             `#include < math.h >`

Rules   Compiler directives are not followed by an ending semicolon.

The main use of this directive is to load header files into the source code prior to compilation.

Header files are generally used to establish define macros and word constants (TRUE, FALSE, EOF, etc.).

The file being included into the program must contain valid C source code.

It is valid to nest `#include` statements. In other words, an `#include` directive can be placed in a file that was itself included.

When nesting `#include` statements, be sure not to cause an endless looping condition.

#undef

Name   #undef   *(Undefine a defined word or macro)*

Function   Used to undefine a word or define macro that has previously been defined using the #define directive.

Syntax   #undef *defined-word*
#undef *defined-macro*

Example   #define TRUE

. . .

#undef TRUE

Rules   Compiler directives are not followed by an ending semicolon.

In the previous example, the word TRUE was assigned a value of 1. That word then became unassigned by executing the #undef command.

17
Common C statements
and functions

abs( )

Name	abs() *(Absolute value)*
Library/header	math.h
Purpose	Receives an integer value and returns the absolute value of that integer.
Syntax	ret_value = abs(int_value);
Variables	ret_value *(integer)* contains the integer's absolute value as returned by the function.
	int_value *(integer)* contains the value being passed to the function.
Example setup	int ret_value; int int_value;

Examples	int_value = 10;
	ret_value = abs(int_value);
	printf("\nFirst example = %d",ret_value);

	int_value = -5;
	ret_value = abs(int_value);
	printf("\nSecond example = %d",ret_value);

Example output	First example = 10 Second example = 5
Rules	The math.h header file must be included using the #include compiler directive.
	The variable being passed to the function, as well as the variable receiving the function's return value, must be defined using the int data type.

acos( )

Name	acos() *(Arc cosine)*
Library/header	math.h
Purpose	Receives a variable defined as a double and returns its corresponding arc cosine value.
Syntax	ret_value = acos(double_value);
Variables	ret_value *(double)* will contain the returned value of the acos function.
	double_value *(double)* contains the value being passed to the function.
Example setup	double ret_value; double double_value;

Examples	double_value = 10;
	ret_value = acos(double_value);
	printf("\nFirst example = %f",ret_value);
	
	double_value = -5;
	ret_value = acos(double_value);
	printf("\nSecond example = %f",ret_value);

Rules	The math.h header file must be included using the #include compiler directive.
	The variable being passed to the function, as well as the variable receiving the function's return value, must be defined using the double data type.

asin( )

Name	asin() *(Arc sine)*
Library/header	math.h
Purpose	Receives a variable defined as a double and returns its corresponding arc sine value.
Syntax	ret_value = asin(double_value);
Variables	ret_value *(double)* will contain the returned value of the asin function.
	double-value *(double)* contains the value being passed to the function.

Example setup

```
double ret_value;
double double_value;
```

Examples

```
double_value = 10;
ret_value = asin(double_value);
printf("\n First example = %f", ret_value);

double_value = -5;
ret_value = asin(double_value);
printf("\n Second example = %f", ret_value);
```

Example output

```
First example = 10
Second Example = 5
```

Rules

The math.h header file must be included using the #include compiler directive.

The variable being passed to the function, as well as the variable receiving the function's return value, must be defined using the double data type.

atan( )

Name	atan() *(Arc tangent)*
Library/header	math.h
Purpose	Receives a variable defined as a double and returns its corresponding arc tangent value.
Syntax	ret_value = atan(double_value);
Variables	ret_value (*double*) variable will contain the returned value of the atan function.
	double-value (*double*) contains the value being passed to the function.
Example setup	double ret_value; double double_value;

Examples	double_value = 10;
	ret_value = atan(double_value);
	printf("\n First example = %f", ret_value);
	
	double_value = −5;
	ret_value = atan(double_value);
	printf("\n Second example = %f", ret_value);

Example output	First example = 10 Second example = 5
Rules	The math.h header file must be included using the #include compile directive.
	The variable being passed to the function, as well as the variable receiving the function's return value, must be defined using the double data type.

atof( )

Name	`atof()` *(ASCII to floating point)*
Library/header	math.h
Purpose	Receives a number in ASCII string format and converts it into a double precision floating point number (double).
Syntax	`ret_value = atof(string_pointer);`
Variables	`ret_value` *(double precision floating point)* receives the numeric value returned by the `atof` function.
	`string_pointer` *(string pointer)* contains the address of the string to be converted.

Examples setup	`char a_string[] = "150";`
	`char b_string[] = "-150.25";`
	`char c_string[] = "1.234e-6";`
	`double a_number;`
	`double b_number;`
	`double c_number;`

Example	`a_number = atof(a_string);`
	`b_number = atof(b_string);`
	`c_number = atof(c_string);`

Rules	The math.h header file must be included using the `#include` compiler directive.
	The `string_pointer` being passed to the function is usually the name of the character array containing the number to be converted without the array bracket notation [ ]. Note that when a character array is used without the array bracket notation, this unsuffixed array name is a pointer containing the address of the memory location in which the first array element resides.
	The variable to receive the function's return code must be defined as a `double`.
	The string being passed to the function must contain a valid numeric representation. This representation may include the numbers 0 through 9, a period, or exponential notation (i.e., "E" or "e" with a plus or minus sign and an appropriate numeric value).

Name	atoi() *(ASCII to integer)*
Library/header	math.h
Purpose	Receives a number in ASCII string format and converts it into an integer value.
Syntax	ret_value = atoi(string_pointer);
Variables	ret_value *(integer)* receives the numeric value returned by the atoi function.
	string_pointer *(string pointer)* contains the address of the string to be converted.

Examples setup

```
char a_string[] = "150";
char b_string[] = "-150";
int a_number;
int b_number;
```

Example

```
a_number = atoi(a_string);
b_number = atoi(b_string);
```

Rules

The math.h header file must be included using the #include compiler directive.

The string_pointer being passed to the function is actually the name of the character array containing the number to be converted without the array bracket notation [ ]. Note that when a character array is used without the array bracket notation, this unsuffixed array name is a pointer containing the address of the memory location in which the first array element resides.

The variable to receive the functions return code must be defined as an int.

The string being passed to the function must contain a valid numeric integer representation, which may include the numbers 0 through 9 and a minus sign if the value is negative.

atol( )

Name	atol() *(ASCII to long integer)*
Library/header	math.h
Purpose	Receives a number in ASCII string format and converts it into a long integer value.
Syntax	ret_value = atol(string_pointer);
Variables	ret_value *(long integer)* receives the numeric value returned by the atol function.
	string_pointer *(string pointer)* contains the address of the string to be converted.

Examples setup

```
char a_string[] = "150";
char b_string[] = "-150";
long a_number;
long int b_number;
```

Example

```
a_number = atol(a_string);
b_number = atol(b_string);
```

Rules

The math.h header file must be included using the #include compiler directive.

The string_pointer being passed to the function is usually the name of the character array containing the number to be converted without the array bracket notation [ ]. Note that when a character array is used without the array bracket notation, this unsuffixed array name is a pointer containing the address of the memory location in which the first array element resides.

The variable to receive the functions return code must be defined as a long int or long.

The string being passed to the function must contain a valid numeric integer representation, which may include the numbers 0 through 9.

If the long data type key word is used without any additional clarification, the variable being defined is considered to be a long integer.

calloc( )

Name calloc() *(Character allocation)*

Purpose Used to allocate a specified amount of contiguous CPU memory.

Syntax c_pointer = calloc(no_of_units,unit_size);

Variables c_pointer *(character pointer)* contains the address of the first allocated memory location.

no_of_units *(integer)* is the number of data units you want to allocate.

unit_size *(integer)* is the actual memory size in bytes of the data type, structure, or union being allocated space.

Examples
```
char *c_pointer;
char c_variable;
c_pointer = calloc ( 250, sizeof(c_variable);

char *c_pointer;
struct name {
    char last[10];
    char first[10];
    char middle[10];
};
struct name *n_pointer;
n_pointer = ( struct *)calloc(10,sizeof(struct name);
```

Rules The calloc function returns the address of the first allocated memory location. This address must be saved to use as the base address for accessing the allocated memory.

The cfree and free functions use the memory address returned by calloc to free space originally reserved by calloc.

calloc returns a null value if the function cannot allocate the requested amount of space.

General industry standards suggest that the calloc size parameter should be stated using the sizeof function as shown in the examples.

This function always allocated contiguous memory space. Therefore, the reserved memory area can be accessed through arrays or pointer arithmetic.

Many compilers require that when allocating memory space, non-char data types—such as integers, structures, and union—that the returned calloc value should be cast into the appropriate pointer type. An example of this casting is shown in the second example earlier.

calloc( )

The calloc function resembles the malloc function, with the main distinction being that calloc can allocate memory for structures of varying date types while malloc generally requires that all allocated space be of one data type.

Name	ceil() *(Ceiling of a number)*
Library/header	math.h
Purpose	Receives double-precision value and returns its ceiling value.
Syntax	ret_value = ceil(double_value);
Variables	ret_value *(double precision)* will contain the parameter's ceiling value returned by the function.
	double_value *(double)* contains the value being passed to the function.

Example setup

```
double ret_value;
double double_value;
```

Examples

```
double_value = 10;
ret_value = abs(double_value);
printf("\nFirst example = %f",ret_value);

double_value = 25;
ret_value = ceil(double_value);
printf("\nSecond example = %f",ret_value);
```

Rules

The math.h header file must be included using the #include compiler directive.

The variable being passed to the function, as well as the variable receiving the function's return value, must be defined using the double data type.

cfree( ) and free( )

Name   cfree() and free()   *[Free (deallocate) allocated memory]*

Purpose   The cfree and free functions are used to release memory space previously allocated through the use of calloc, malloc, or realloc.

Syntax   ret_code = cfree(character_pointer);

Variables   ret_code (*integer*) generally will be given a value of 0 if cfree executes successfully and a −1 if it does not.

c_pointer (*character pointer*) is returned from a memory allocation function and contains the address of the first allocated memory location.

Example
```
int ret_code;
char *c_pointer;
char c_variable;
c_pointer = calloc(250,sizeof(c_variable);
   . . .
ret_code = cfree(c_pointer);
```

Rules   The syntax, examples, and rules shown for cfree also apply to free if it exists on your particular compiler.

The pointer passed to cfree must be the address returned by a calloc, malloc, or realloc function call.

Generally, a 0 will be returned if the function is executed correctly; otherwise, a −1 is returned to signal an error.

If the calloc, malloc, or realloc pointer was cast to be a non-character pointer, it must be recast back to a character when passed to cfree.

clearerr( ) and clreer( )

Name	clearerr() and clreer() *(Clear error)*
Library/header	stdio.h
Purpose	Used to clear the appropriate file error flag.
Syntax	clearerr(file_pointer);
Variables	file_pointer (*file pointer*) is returned from an fopen function.

Example	FILE *f_pointer;
	f_pointer = fopen("data.dat","r");
	. . .
	clearerr(f_pointer);

Rules	The syntax, examples, and rules shown for clearerr also apply to clreer if it exists on your particular compiler.

When a file error occurs, the file's error flag is activated. From this time forward, an end of file message will be returned from file I/O functions that attempt to access that file until the error is cleared by calling clearerr.

The file pointer must be associated with an open data file.

cos( )

Name	cos() *(Cosine)*
Library/header	math.h
Purpose	Receives a variable defined as a double and returns its corresponding arc cosine value.
Syntax	ret_value = cos(double_value);
Variables	ret_value *(double)* will contain the returned value of the cos function.
	double_value *(double)* contains the value being passed to the function.

Example setup

```
double ret_value;
double double_value;
```

Examples

```
double_value = 10;
ret_value = cos(double_value);
printf("\n First example = %f",ret_value);

double_value = -5;
ret_value = cos(double_value);
printf("\n Second example = %f",ret_value);
```

Rules

The math.h header file must be included using the #include compiler directive.

The variable being passed to the function, as well as the variable receiving the function's return value, must be defined using the double data type.

cosh( )

Name	cosh() *(Cosine hyperbolic)*
Library/header	math.h
Purpose	Receives a variable defined as a double and returns its corresponding arc cosine value.
Syntax	ret_value = cosh(double_value);
Variables	ret_value *(double)* will contain the returned value of the cosh function.
	double_value *(double)* contains the value being passed to the function.
Example setup	double ret_value; double double_value;

Examples	double_value = 10;
	ret_value = cosh(double_value);
	printf("\n First example = %f", ret_value);
	
	double_value = -5;
	ret_value = cosh(double_value);
	printf("\n Second example = %f", ret_value);

Rules	The math.h header file must be included using the #include compiler directive.
	The variable being passed to the function, as well as the variable receiving the function's return value, must be defined using the double data type.

do

Name	do
Purpose	Used (with while) to repeat the execution of a selected group of statements based on the test criteria within the while statement.
Syntax	do *statement or statement block* while (*test-expression*);
Variables	*Statement* is a single C instruction or statement block that can be repeated by placing it between the key words do and while.
	Statement block is a group of one or more C statements contained within block control brackets {}.
	Test-expression is the criteria used to test if looping should be continued or if the do statement should be exited.

Example
```
int x = 0;
do
  printf("\nLets count to 5 : %d", x++);
while ( x < 5 );

char answer[2];
do
  { printf("\nEnter Y for yes or N for no: ");
    gets(answer);
  } while (answer[0] != 'Y' && answer[0] != 'N');
```

Rules

The statement or statement block within the do loop is always executed at least once.

The while condition is evaluated after each execution of the statement or statement block.

The statements will continue to execute until the while *test-expression* returns a zero value.

The semicolon after the while *test-expression* is required.

exit( )

Name   exit()

Purpose   Terminates execution of the current program, closes all open files, and purges all existing buffers.

Syntax   exit;
              exit(integer_value or integer_constant);

Variables The integer value or constant return value may be passed from the program being terminated to a host program or _main function.

Example   exit;

              exit(0);
                or
              exit(1);

              int ecode;
              ecode = 1;
              exit(ecode);

Rules   Some compilers require a return code parameter, while others assume a return of 0 if no parameter value is found.

exp( )

Name	exp() *(Exponential value)*
Library/header	math.h
Purpose	Receives a variable defined as a double and returns its corresponding exponential value.
Syntax	ret_value = exp(double_value);
Variables	ret_value *(double)* will contain the returned value of the exp function. double-value *(double)* contains the value being passed to the function.
Example setup	double ret_value; double double_value;

Examples	double_value = 10;
	ret_value = exp(double_value);
	printf("\n First example = %f", ret_value);
	
	double_value = −5;
	ret_value = exp(double_value);
	printf("\n Second example = %f", ret_value);

Rules	The math.h header file must be included using the #include compiler directive. The variable being passed to the function, as well as the variable receiving the function's return value, must be defined using the double data type.

fabs( )

Name	fabs() *(Floating point absolute value)*
Library/header	math.h
Purpose	Receives a variable defined as a double and returns its corresponding absolute value.
Syntax	ret_value = fabs(double_value);
Variables	ret_value (*double*) will contain the returned value of the fabs function.
	double-value (*double*) contains the value being passed to the function.
Example setup	double ret_value; double double_value;

Examples	double_value = 10;
	ret_value = fabs(double_value);
	printf("\n First example = %f", ret_value);

	double_value = −5;
	ret_value = fabs(double_value);
	printf("\n Second example = %f", ret_value);

Rules	The math.h header file must be included using the #include compiler directive.
	The variable being passed to the function, as well as the variable receiving the function's return value, must be defined using the double data type.

fclose( )

Name	fclose() *(File close)*
Library/header	stdio.h
Purpose	Used to close data files that has previously been opened using the fopen function.
Syntax	ret_value = fclose(f_pointer);
Variables	ret_value *(integer)* will contain the returned value of the fclose function.
	f_pointer *(file pointer)* points to an open data file. This variable must have obtained its pointer value from the return of the file open function fopen.

Example

```
FILE *f_pointer;
int ret_code;
f_pointer = (fopen("data.dat","r");
    . . .
ret_code = fclose(f_pointer);
```

Rules

In most compilers, a 0 is returned if the file was successfully closed and a −1 if an error was detected during the attempt to close.

The stdio.h header file must be included in the program using the #include compiler directive.

When called, the fclose function will delete the file attributes from the file access table, flush the buffers, and free up the file's associated pointers for reuse.

Upon program termination, all open files will automatically be closed by the system. However, it is good programming practice and strongly suggested that you use fclose to close all open files prior to program termination.

When checking to see if the fclose function worked correctly, look for a non-zero. Some compilers use 1 and others use −1 to signal success.

Name	feof() *(File / End of file)*
Library/header	stdio.h
Purpose	Used to test if an input file has been completely read or if data still remains to be processed.
Syntax	ret_value = feof(f_pointer);
Variables	ret_value (*integer*) will contain the returned value of the feof function.
	f_pointer (*file pointer*) points to an open data file. This variable must have obtained its pointer value from the return of the file open function fopen.

Examples	FILE *f_pointer;
	int ret_code;
	f_pointer = (fopen("data.dat","r");
	  . . .
	ret_code = feof(f_pointer);

Rules	In most compilers, a 1 is returned if the file is out of data and a 0 is returned if data still remains to be read.
	The stdio.h header file must be included in the program using the #include compiler directive.
	The file pointer must be a valid file pointer associated with an open file.

ferror( )

Name	ferror() *(File error status)*
Library/header	stdio.h
Purpose	Used to return the current error status of a specified file.
Syntax	ret_value = ferror(f_pointer);

Variables

ret_value *(integer)* will contain the returned value of the ferror function.

f_pointer *(file pointer)* is a pointer to an open data file. This variable must have obtained its pointer value from the return of the file open function fopen.

Example

```
FILE *f_pointer;
int ret_code;
f_pointer = (fopen("data.dat","r");
   . . .
ret_code = ferror(f_pointer);
```

Rules

In most compilers, a non-zero is returned if the file contains an error and a 0 is returned if no error has yet been detected.

The stdio.h header file must be included in the program using the #include compiler directive.

The file pointer must be a valid file pointer associated with an open file.

fflush( )

Name	f f l u s h ( ) *(File—Flush buffer)*
Library/header	stdio.h
Purpose	Causes the data contained within the file buffer to be written to disk.
Syntax	f f l u s h (f__po i n t e r) ;
Variables	f__po i n t e r *(file pointer)* points to an open data file. This variable must have obtained its pointer value from the return of the file open function f open.

Example

```
FILE *f_pointer;
int ret_code;
f_pointer = (fopen("data.dat","r");
   . . .
ret_code = fflush(f_pointer);
```

Rules

The stdio.h header file must be included in the program using the # i nc l ude compiler directive.

The file pointer must be a valid file pointer associated with an open file.

This function may only be used on files opened for output.

fgetc( )

Name	fgetc() *(File—Get character)*
Library/header	stdio.h
Purpose	Used to retrieve a single character from a specified data file.
Syntax	int_variable = fgetc(f_pointer);
Variables	int_variable *(integer)*, defined as int, will be given the return value of the fgetc function. This return will be the ASCII value of the character read from the file or a −1 if an end of file or error condition is found.
	f_pointer (*file pointer*) points to an open data file. This variable must have obtained its pointer value from the return of the file open function fopen.

Example

```
FILE *f_pointer;
int ret_code;
f_pointer = (fopen("data.dat","r");
   . . .
int_variable = fgetc(f_pointer);
```

Rules

The stdio.h header file must be included in the program using the #include compiler directive.

The file pointer must be a valid file pointer associated with an open file.

fgets is a function. Its define macro equivalent is the getc function.

fgets( )

Name	fgets() *(File—Get ASCII string)*
Library/header	stdio.h
Purpose	Reads an ASCII character string from a specified data file.
Syntax	s_pointer = fgets(b_pointer,no_of_char,f_pointer);

Variables

s_pointer (*character pointer*) will give the return value of the fgets function. This return will be the memory address of the first character read from the file or a NULL if an end of file or error condition is found.

b_pointer (*character pointer*) contains the address in which the retrieved string should be placed.

no_of_char (*integer variable or constant*) contains the number of characters to be read from the file.

f_pointer (*file pointer*) points to an open data file. This variable must have obtained its pointer value from the return of the file open function fopen.

Examples

```
FILE *f_pointer;
int no_of_char = 10;
char *s_pointer, *b_pointer;
f_pointer = (fopen("data.dat","r");
   . . .
s_pointer = fgets(b_pointer,no_of_char,f_pointer);
```

Rules

The stdio.h header file must be included in the program using the #include compiler directive.

The file pointer must be a valid file pointer associated with an open file opened with read access privileges.

fgets reads the file until it finds a new line indicator or one character less then the specified number of bytes (or characters) to be read. This last byte is reserved for a null terminator (\ 0).

Caution: Some compilers will read the file until it finds a new line indicator and will truncate all characters placed after the number specified in the fgets second parameter; thus, data may be lost.

floor( )

Name	floor() *(Floor of a number)*
Library/header	math.h
Purpose	Receives double-precision value and returns its floor value.
Syntax	ret_value = floor(double_value);
Variables	ret_value (*double precision*) will contain the parameter's floor value returned by the function. double_value (*double*) contains the value being passed to the function.
Example setup	double ret_value; double double_value;

Examples	double_value = 10;
	ret_value = abs(double_value);
	printf("\n First example = %f", ret_value);
	
	double_value = 25;
	ret_value = floor(double_value);
	printf("\n Second example = %f", ret_value);

Rules	The math.h header file must be included using the #include compiler directive. The variable being passed to the function, as well as the variable receiving the function's return value, must be defined using the double data type.

fopen( )

Name	`fopen()` *(File open)*
Library/header	stdio.h
Purpose	Opens a data file for access and establishes the appropriate file buffers.
Syntax	`file_pointer = fopen(filename,mode);`
Variables	`file_pointer` (*file pointer*) will contain the address of related file information. This pointer address must be saved because it is referenced by all file-related functions.
	`filename` (*string variable pointer or string constant*) contains the file's directory name as shown when using the DOS DIR function.
	mode specifies the file type and the access privileges that should established.

Examples	`FILE *f_pointer;`
	`char *file_name, *file_mode;`
	`f_pointer = (fopen("data.dat","r");`

Rules	The stdio.h header file must be included in the program using the `#include` compiler directive.
	A file must be opened before it may be accessed by any other function.
	Files can be opened in many modes (read, write, read binary, etc.). Refer to your particular compiler documentation for a list of all possible mode options.
	Most compilers return a null pointer value if the file did not open properly.

for

Name   for   *(For statement)*

Purpose   Facilitates the reiteration of source code based on a while condition and an incremental counter.

Syntax
```
for (initialization; while-test; increment)
    statement or statement block
```

Examples
```
int count;
for ( x=0; x<5; count++ )
printf("\ncount is : %d",count);

int count;
for ( x=0; x<5; count++ )
  { printf("\nThis is the first statement");
    printf("\nThis is the second statement");
  }
```

Rules   The initialization section is the first expression performed when the for statement is executed.

If more than one value must be initialized, the following techniques can be used:
```
x=1;
for ( y=0; x<5; x++ )
for ( x=1,y=2; x<5; x++ )
for ( x=y=0; x<5; x++ )
```

The for statement is executed in the following order:

1. Initialization.
2. Evaluation of while test condition.
3. Statement or statement block presentation.
4. Incrementation.

The initialization section, while section, and incrementing section are mandatory. However, if any of these sections are not logically required in your particular application, you can signify that section with a blank statement. A blank statement is just a semicolon with no statement before it. In the following example, no initialization was needed (note the stand alone semicolon):
```
for ( ; x<10; x++ )
```

Caution: If the while expression is placeheld with just a semicolon, then an endless loop condition is created that must be exited with a break statement, goto, or other means.

fprintf( )

Name	fprintf() *(File—Print function)*
Library/header	stdio.h
Purpose	Used to print formatted data to a specified data file.
Syntax	printf(f_pointer, format_control, arguments);

Variables   f_pointer (*file pointer*) points to an open data file. This variable must have obtained its pointer value from the return of the file open function fopen.

format_control (*string*) explains the output format.

arguments is a list of the variables to be printed.

Example setup
```
int i_variable;
char c_variable[] = {"hello there"};
FILE *f_pointer;
char f_control[] = {"integer is %d, text is %s");
```

Example
```
f_pointer = fopen("data.dat","w");
. . .
fprintf(f_pointer,f_control,i_variable,c_variable);
. . .
fprintf(f_pointer,"\nThe int value =
  %d",i_variable);
```

Rules   The fprintf file pointer must be associated with a data file opened in output mode.

The print types listed in the format control must identically match the printing argument list.

Each variable has a coinciding print type identifier. For example, %d is integer, %s is character string, and %lf is long float (double). Refer to your compiler documentation for a complete list of these identifiers. Note, however, that these identifiers are all prefixed with a percent sign %.

fputc( )

Name   fputc() *(File—Put character)*

Library/header   stdio.h

Purpose   Used to write a single character from a specified data file.

Syntax   ret_code = fputc(character,f_pointer);

Variables   ret_code *(integer)* will contain the return value of the fputc function. This return will be the ASCII value of the character written to the file or a −1 if an error condition is found.

character *(character variable or constant)* contains the character to be printed in the file.

f_pointer *(file pointer)* points to an open data file. This variable must have obtained its pointer value from the return of the file open function fopen.

Example
```
FILE *f_pointer;
int ret_code;
char c_variable;
f_pointer = (fopen("data.dat","r");
    . . .
c_variable = 'x';
ret_code = fputc(c_variable,f_pointer);
    . . .
ret_code = fputc('x',f_pointer);
```

Rules   The stdio.h header file must be included in the program using the #include compiler directive.

The file pointer must be a valid file pointer associated with a file open in output mode.

fputc is a function. Its define macro equivalent is the putc function.

fputs( )

Name	fputs() *(File—Put ASCII string)*
Library/header	stdio.h
Purpose	Writes an ASCII character string to a specified data file.
Syntax	fputs(s_pointer,f_pointer);

Variables   s_pointer (*character pointer*) contains the address of the character string to be written to the file.

f_pointer (*file pointer*) points to an open data file. This variable must have obtained its pointer value from the return of the file open function fopen.

Example
```
FILE *f_pointer;
char *s_pointer;
f_pointer = (fopen("data.dat","w");
   . . .
fputs(s_pointer,f_pointer);
```

Rules   The stdio.h header file must be included in the program using the #include compiler directive.

The file pointer must be a valid file pointer associated with an open file opened with write-access privileges.

fputs writes to the file until it encounters a null terminator ($\backslash$0) in the string being printed.

fread( )

Name	fread() *(File read)*
Library/header	stdio.h
Purpose	Used to read blocks of data from the file and place them in the memory buffer for further use.
Syntax	ret_code = fread(b_pointer,b_size, no_of_blocks,file_pointer);

Variables

ret_code *(integer)* receives the function return code stating the actual number of blocks retrieved.

b_pointer *(integer)* contains the starting point of the first file block to be read.

no_of_blocks *(integer variable/constant)* specifies the number of blocks to be read.

b_size *(integer variable/constant)* specifies the size of the data blocks being read.

f_pointer *(file pointer)* points to an open data file. This variable must have obtained its pointer value from the return of the file open function fopen.

Example

```
FILE *f_pointer;
char *b_pointer
int ret_code, b_number, b_size;
f_pointer = (fopen("data.dat","r");
    . . .
b_number = 50;
b_size = 512;
ret_code = fread(b_pointer,b_size,
            b_number,f_pointer);
```

Rules

The stdio.h header file must be included in the program using the #include compiler directive.

The file pointer must be a valid file pointer associated with an open file opened with read-access privileges.

Be careful not to overflow your file input buffer.

The function returns the actual number of blocks read. Therefore, a return of 0 or null might signify a file error or an end of file condition.

fscanf( )

Name	fscanf() *(File read)*
Library/header	stdio.h
Purpose	Used to read data from a data file, convert it to the appropriate data type, and place it into the specified variables.
Syntax	fscanf(f_pointer, conversion_mask, arguments)
Variables	f_pointer *(file pointer)* points to an open data file. This variable must have obtained its pointer value from the return of the file open function fopen.

conversion_mask *(string)* explains the format of the data being input.

arguments is a list of pointers to the variables that will be receiving the data. |
| **Example setup** | int i_variable;
char c_variable[];
FILE *f_pointer; |
| **Example** | fscanf(f_pointer,"%4d%6s",i_variable,c_variable); |
| **Rules** | The fscanf file pointer must be associated with a data file opened in input mode.

The data types listed in the conversion mask must identically match the argument list.

Each variable has a coinciding data type identifier. For example, %d is integer, %s is character string, and %lf is long float (double). Refer to your compiler documentation for a complete list of these identifiers. Note, however, that these identifiers are all prefixed with a percent sign %. |

fseek( )

Name	`fseek()` *(File—Seek to specified file location)*
Library/header	stdio.h
Purpose	Used to move the file pointer's current position.
Syntax	`ret_code = fseek(file_pointer,offset,mode);`
Variables	`ret_code` *(integer)* receives the function return code.

`f_pointer` *(file pointer)* points to an open data file. This variable must have obtained its pointer value from the return of the file open function `fopen`.

`offset` *(long integer)* specifies where the current file pointer should be placed, based on the current position and the mode specified in the third parameter.

`mode` states from where the function should start seeking the current file position. The possible modes—0, 1, and 2—are explained here within the Rules section.

| **Example** | ```
FILE *f_pointer;
long int offset;
int ret_code, mode;
f_pointer = (fopen("data.dat","r");
    . . .
ret_code = fseek(f_pointer,1l,0);
    . . .
mode = 1;
offset = 10;
ret_code = fseek(f_pointer,offset,mode);
``` |

Rules

The stdio.h header file must be included in the program using the `#include` compiler directive.

The file pointer must be a valid file pointer associated with an open file.

Do not try to seek before the beginning or after the end of the file; otherwise, unexpected results might occur.

The function might return either the new pointer position or a zero if successful. Refer to your compiler documentation for clarification.

If the seek was unsuccessful, a -1 will be returned.

Remember that the `offset` parameter is a long integer. Therefore, if you use an integer, it must be defined as `long int`. If you are using a numeric constant, it must be specified as a long by placing a lower-case "l" after the number (e.g., "50l").
```

The three seek modes are as follows:

1 Start seeking from the beginning of the file.
2 Start seeking at the current file position.
3 Start seeking from the end of the file.

ftell( )

Name	ftell() *(File—Tell current file pointer position)*
Library/header	stdio.h
Purpose	Returns the current access position of the data file being referenced.
Syntax	ret_code = ftell(file_pointer);
Variables	ret_code *(integer)* receives the function return code.
	f_pointer *(file pointer)* points to an open data file. This variable must have obtained its pointer value from the return of the file open function fopen.

Example	FILE *f_pointer;
	long int ret_code;
	f_pointer = (fopen("data.dat","r");
	  . . .
	ret_code = ftell(f_pointer);

Rules	The stdio.h header file must be included in the program using the #include compiler directive.
	The file pointer must be a valid file pointer associated with an open file.
	The value returned by the ftell function is the current position being referenced within the file. This value is the actual number of bytes from the beginning of the file.
	In most compilers, a −1 is returned if the function call was unsuccessful.
	The variable receiving the functions return code must be defined as a long integer data type (long int).

fwrite( )

Name	fwrite() *(File write)*
Library/header	stdio.h
Purpose	Used to write blocks of data from the memory buffer to the file.
Syntax	ret_code = fwrite(b_pointer,b_size,no_of_blocks, file_pointer);

Variables

ret_code *(integer)* receives the function return code stating the actual number of blocks written.

b_pointer *(integer)* contains the starting point of the first file block to be written.

no_of_blocks *(integer variable/constant)* specifies the number of blocks to be written.

b_size *(integer variable/constant)* specifies the size of the data blocks being written.

f_pointer *(file pointer)* points to an open data file. This variable must have obtained its pointer value from the return of the file open function fopen.

Example

```
FILE *f_pointer;
char *b_pointer
int ret_code, b_number, b_size;
f_pointer = (fopen("data.dat","w");
    . . .
b_number = 50;
b_size = 512;
ret_code = fwrite(b_pointer,b_size,
            b_number,f_pointer);
```

Rules

The stdio.h header file must be included in the program using the #include compiler directive.

The file pointer must be a valid file pointer associated with a file opened with write-access privileges.

The buffer value must be a valid memory location.

The return code should be checked to assure that the correct number of blocks are written to disk. Note that fwrite returns the actual number of blocks that were written. Therefore, if the number of blocks returned is different from the number specified in the third parameter, then an error might have occurred. If an error is suspected, execute ferror or feer to determine actual file status.

getc( )

Name	getc() *(Get character)*
Library/header	stdio.h
Purpose	Used to return a character from a specified data file.
Syntax	ret_code = getc(file_pointer);
Variables	ret_code *(integer)* receives the function return code, which is either the octal value of the retrieved character or a -1 if an error or end of file condition arose.

f_pointer (file pointer) points to an open data file. This variable must have obtained its pointer value from the return of the file open function fopen.

Example
```
FILE *f_pointer;
int ret_code;
f_pointer = (fopen("data.dat","r");
    . . .
ret_code = getc(f_pointer);
printf("\n Character is a %c",ret_code);
```

Rules

The stdio.h header file must be included in the program using the #include compiler directive.

The file pointer must be a valid file pointer associated with a file opened with read-access privileges.

In many compilers, the single character retrieval procedures are implemented as define macros and not functions. This can be done because these procedures are actually getting a character from the input buffer and not from the file directly.

getch( )

Name getch() *(Get character from the console)*

Library/header stdio.h

Purpose Used to return a single character from the keyboard.

Syntax ret_code = getch();

Variables ret_code *(integer)* receives the function return code, which is either the octal value of the retrieved character or a −1 if an error or end of file condition arose.

Example
```
int ret_code;
ret_code = getch(f_pointer);
putch(ret_code);
```

Rules The stdio.h header file must be included in the program using the #include compiler directive.

This function does not echo the input character to the screen—the input character can be echoed using the putch function.

getchar( )

Name   `getchar()` *(Get character)*

Library/header   stdio.h

Purpose   Used to return a character from the keyboard.

Syntax   `ret_code = getchar();`

Variables   `ret_code` *(integer)* receives the function return code, which is either the octal value of the retrieved character or a -1 if an error occurs.

Example
```
int ret_code;
ret_code = getchar(f_pointer);
printf("\n Character is a %c",ret_code);
```

Rules   The stdio.h header file must be included in the program using the #include compiler directive.

In many compilers, the single character retrieved procedures are implemented as define macros and not functions. This can be done because these procedures are actually getting a character from the input buffer and not from the file directly.

Because getch returns a character from the input buffer, it must wait until the input buffer contains data. In many cases, data is only moved to the buffer when the return key is entered, thus delaying when getchar can receive its data. Note that getch retrieves a character directly from the console and therefore does not have to wait for the return key.

Name   goto

Purpose   Transfers program control from the current line to a specified label identifier elsewhere within the function.

Syntax   goto label-name;

Variables   label-name is a user-defined line identifier ending with a colon.

Example
```
int x;
    . . .
if ( x = = 1 ) goto alabel;
    . . .
alabel:
```

Rules   The label name must follow standard C naming conventions.

The label being referenced must be within the same function as the goto.

To adhere to standard structured programming techniques, the goto statement should be used with care.

The goto is best used to exit from single and nested loops in search of specific data.

if

Name if

Purpose Facilitates procedural branching based on specified test criteria.

Syntax
```
if (test-condition)
   statement or statement block

if (test-condition)
   statement or statement block
else
   statement or statement block
```

Examples
```
int x;
if ( x == 1 )
printf("\n x has a value or one");

int x;
if ( x ==1 )
{ printf("\n x has a value of one");
  printf("\n this is line two of the block");
}
else
  printf("\n x does not have a value of 1");
```

Rules The else condition is optional and should only be used when needed.

A value of zero in an if test-condition denotes false, while a non-zero value is considered to be true.

As shown here, statements should be properly indented to assist in program readability.

isalnum( )

Name   `isalnum()` *(Is this character alphanumeric?)*

Library/header ctype.h

Purpose   Checks to see whether or not a character is a valid alphanumeric value.

Syntax   `ret_value = isalnum(char_value);`

Variables   `ret_value` (*integer*) will contain the function's return value. This value will be a 0 if the passed character is not alphanumeric and a non-zero if it is within the alphanumeric character set.

       `char_value` (*character*) contains the character being tested by the `isalnum` function.

Examples
```
char char_value;
int ret_value;
  . . .
ret_value = isalnum(char_value);
```

Rules   On some compilers, this procedure is implemented as a define macro and not a function.

       The ctype.h header file must be included using the `#include` compiler directive.

       On some compilers, these procedures are defined as functions within the C runtime libraries and as macros within the ctype.h header file. Therefore, if you include the ctype.h header file, you access the macros; and if you do not include the ctype.h header file, then you call the functions. Refer to your compiler documentation for clarification.

       Some compilers return a 1 if the tested character meets the test requirements, while other compilers return the octal value of the tested character. In both cases, however, a 0 is considered false and a non-zero is considered true.

isalpha( )

Name   isalpha() *(Is this character a valid alpha character?)*

Library/header ctype.h

Purpose   Checks to see whether or not a character is a valid alpha value.

Syntax   ret_value = isalpha(char_value);

Variables   ret_value *(integer)* variable will contain the function's return value. This value will be a 0 if the passed character is not an alpha and a non-zero if it is within the alpha character set.

char_value *(character)* variable contains the character being tested by the isalpha function.

Example
```
char char_value;
int ret_value;
    . . .
ret_value = isalpha(char_value);
```

Rules   On some compilers, this procedure is implemented as a define macro and not a function.

The ctype.h header file must be included using the #include compiler directive.

On some compilers, these procedures are defined as functions within the C runtime libraries and as macros within the ctype.h header file. Therefore, if you include the ctype.h header file, you access the macros; and if you do not include the ctype.h header file, then you call the functions. Refer to your compiler documentation for clarification.

Some compilers return a 1 if the tested character meets the test requirements, while other compilers return the octal value of the tested character. In both cases, however, a 0 is considered false and a non-zero is considered true.

isascii( )

Name	isascii ( ) *(Is this character a valid ASCII character?)*
Library/header	ctype.h
Purpose	Checks to see whether or not a character is a valid ASCII value.
Syntax	ret_value = isascii(char_value);
Variables	ret_value *(integer)* variable will contain the functions return value. This value will be a 0 if the passed character is not an ASCII and a non-zero if it is within the ASCII character set. char_value *(character)* contains the character being tested by the isascii function.
Example	char char_value; int ret_value; . . . ret_value = isascii(char_value);
Rules	On some compilers, this procedure is implemented as a define macro and not a function. The ctype.h header file must be included using the #include compiler directive. On some compilers, these procedures are defined as functions within the C runtime libraries and as macros within the ctype.h header file. Therefore, if you include the "ctype.h" header file, you access the macros; and if you do not include the ctype.h header file, then you call the functions. Refer to your compiler documentation for clarification. Some compilers return a 1 if the tested character meets the test requirements, while other compilers return the octal value of the tested character. In both cases, however, a 0 is considered false and a non-zero is considered true.

iscntrl( )

Name	iscntrl() *(Is this character a control character?)*
Library/header	ctype.h
Purpose	Checks to see whether or not a character is a valid control value.
Syntax	ret_value = iscntrl(char_value);

Variables   ret_value *(integer)* will contain the function's return value. This value will be a 0 if the passed character is not a control and a non-zero if it is within the control character set.

char_value *(character)* contains the character being tested by the iscntrl function.

Example
```
char char_value;
int ret_value;
 . . .
ret_value = iscntrl(char_value);
```

Rules   On some compilers, this procedure is implemented as a define macro and not a function.

The ctype.h header file must be included using the #include compiler directive.

On some compilers, these procedures are defined as functions within the C runtime libraries and as macros within the ctype.h header file. Therefore, if you include the ctype.h header file, you access the macros; and if you do not include the ctype.h header file, then you call the functions. Refer to your compiler documentation for clarification.

Some compilers return a 1 if the tested character meets the test requirements, while other compilers return the octal value of the tested character. In both cases, however, a 0 is considered false and a non-zero is considered true.

isdigit( )

Name   isdigit()   *(Is this character a numeric character?)*

Library/header   ctype.h

Purpose   Checks to see whether or not a character is a valid numeric value.

Syntax   ret_value = isdigit(char_value);

Variables   ret_value *(integer)* will contain the function's return value, which will be a 0 if the passed character is not a numeric and a non-zero if it is within the numeric character set.

char_value *(character)* contains the character being tested by the isdigit function.

Example
```
char char_value;
int ret_value;
   . . .
ret_value = isdigit(char_value);
```

Rules   On some compilers, this procedure is implemented as a define macro and not a function.

The ctype.h header file must be included using the #include compiler directive.

On some compilers, these procedures are defined as functions within the C runtime libraries and as macros within the ctype.h header file. Therefore, if you include the ctype.h header file, you access the macros; and if you do not include the ctype.h header file, then you call the functions. Refer to your compiler documentation for clarification.

Some compilers return a 1 if the tested character meets the test requirements, while other compilers return the octal value of the tested character. In both cases, however, a 0 is considered false and a non-zero is considered true.

islower( )

Name	`islower()` *(Is this character lowercase?)*
Library/header	ctype.h
Purpose	Checks to see whether or not a character is a valid lowercase value.
Syntax	`ret_value = islower(char_value);`

Variables   `ret_value` (*integer*) will contain the function's return value, which will be a 0 if the passed character is not lowercase and a non-zero if it is within the lowercase character set.

`char_value` (*character*) contains the character being tested by the `islower` function.

Examples
```
char char_value;
int ret_value;
    . . .
ret_value = islower(char_value);
```

Rules   On some compilers, this procedure is implemented as a define macro and not a function.

The ctype.h header file must be included using the `#include` compiler directive.

On some compilers, these procedures are defined as functions within the C runtime libraries and as macros within the ctype.h header file. Therefore, if you include the ctype.h header file, you access the macros; and if you do not include the ctype.h header file, then you call the functions. Refer to your compiler documentation for clarification.

Some compilers return a 1 if the tested character meets the test requirements, while other compilers return the octal value of the tested character. In both cases, however, a 0 is considered false and a non-zero is considered true.

isprint( )

Name	isprint() *(Is the character printable?)*
Library/header	ctype.h
Purpose	Checks to see whether or not a character is a valid printable value.
Syntax	ret_value = isprint(char_value);
Variables	ret_value *(integer)* will contain the function's return value, which will be a 0 if the passed character is not printable and a non-zero if it is within the printable character set. char_value *(character)* contains the character being tested by the isprint function.
Example	char char_value; int ret_value; . . . ret_value = isprint(char_value);
Rules	On some compilers, this procedure is implemented as a define macro and not a function. The ctype.h header file must be included using the #include compiler directive. On some compilers, these procedures are defined as functions within the C runtime libraries and as macros within the ctype.h header file. Therefore, if you include the ctype.h header file, you access the macros; and if you do not include the ctype.h header file, then you call the functions. Refer to your compiler documentation for clarification. Some compilers return a 1 if the tested character meets the test requirements, while other compilers return the octal value of the tested character. In both cases, however, a 0 is considered false and a non-zero is considered true.

ispunct( )

Name	ispunct() *(Is this character a punctuation character?)*
Library/header	ctype.h
Purpose	Checks to see whether or not a character is a valid punctuation value.
Syntax	ret_value = ispunct(char_value);
Variables	ret_value *(integer)* will contain the function's return value, which will be a 0 if the passed character is not a punctuation character and a non-zero if it is within the punctuation character set.
	char_value *(character)* contains the character being tested by the ispunct function.

Example

```
char char_value;
int ret_value;
    . . .
ret_value = ispunct(char_value);
```

Rules

On some compilers, this procedure is implemented as a define macro and not a function.

The ctype.h header file must be included using the #include compiler directive.

On some compilers, these procedures are defined as functions within the C runtime libraries and as macros within the ctype.h header file. Therefore, if you include the ctype.h header file, you access the macros; and if you do not include the ctype.h header file, then you call the functions. Refer to your compiler documentation for clarification.

Some compilers return a 1 if the tested character meets the test requirements, while other compilers return the octal value of the tested character. In both cases, however, a 0 is considered false and a non-zero is considered true.

isspace( )

Name	isspace() *(Is this character a white space character?)*
Library/header	ctype.h
Purpose	Checks to see whether or not a character is a valid white space value.
Syntax	ret_value = isspace(char_value);
Variables	ret_value *(integer)* will contain the function's return value, which will be a 0 if the passed character is not a white space character and a non-zero if it is within the white space character set.
	char_value *(character)* contains the character being tested by the isspace function.
Example	char char_value; int ret_value; . . . ret_value = isspace(char_value);
Rules	On some compilers, this procedure is implemented as a define macro and not a function.
	The ctype.h header file must be included using the #include compiler directive.
	On some compilers, these procedures are defined as functions within the C runtime libraries and as macros within the ctype.h header file. Therefore, if you include the ctype.h header file, you access the macros; and if you do not include the ctype.h header file, then you call the functions. Refer to your compiler documentation for clarification.
	Some compilers return a 1 if the tested character meets the test requirements, while other compilers return the octal value of the tested character. In both cases, however, a 0 is considered false and a non-zero is considered true.

isupper( )

Name	isupper() *(Is this character uppercase?)*
Library/header	ctype.h
Purpose	Checks to see whether or not a character is a valid uppercase value.
Syntax	ret_value = isupper(char_value);
Variables	ret_value *(integer)* will contain the function's return value, which will be a 0 if the passed character is not uppercase and a non-zero if it is within the uppercase character set.
	char_value *(character)* contains the character being tested by the isupper function.

Example

```
char char_value;
int ret_value;
    . . .
ret_value = isupper(char_value);
```

Rules

On some compilers, this procedure is implemented as a define macro and not a function.

The ctype.h header file must be included using the #include compiler directive.

On some compilers, these procedures are defined as functions within the C runtime libraries and as macros within the ctype.h header file. Therefore, if you include the ctype.h header file, you access the macros; and if you do not include the ctype.h header file, then you call the functions. Refer to your compiler documentation for clarification.

Some compilers return a 1 if the tested character meets the test requirements, while other compilers return the octal value of the tested character. In both cases, however, a 0 is considered false and a non-zero is considered true.

itoa( )

Name	itoa() *(Integer to ASCII conversion)*
Library/header	string.h
Purpose	Used to convert an integer number to its ASCII character string equivalent.
Syntax	itoa(int_value,char_pointer);
Variables	int_value (*integer*) contains the number to be converted to a character string.
	char_pointer (*character pointer*) states where in memory the converted number should be placed.

Example

```
int i_variable;
char *c_pointer;
    . . .
itoa(i_variable,c_pointer);
```

Rules

The character pointer must be associated with an area large enough to accommodate the converted integer number.

The character pointer may be either a defined character pointer associated with a character string or a character string name without the array brackets.

malloc( )

Name   `malloc()`   *(Character allocation)*

Purpose   Used to allocate a specified amount of contiguous CPU memory.

Syntax   `c_pointer = malloc(no_of_units,unit_size);`

Variables   `c_pointer` *(character pointer)* will contain the address of the first allocated memory location.

`no_of_units` is the number of data units you want to allocate.

`unit_size` is the actual memory size in bytes of the data type, structure, or union being allocated space.

Examples
```
char *c_pointer;
char c_variable;
c_pointer = malloc ( 250, sizeof(c_variable);

char *c_pointer;
struct name {
  char last[10];
  char first[10];
  char middle[10];
};
struct name *n_pointer;
n_pointer = ( struct *)malloc(10,
            sizeof(struct name);
```

Rules   The `malloc` function returns the address of the first allocated memory location. This address must be saved to use as the base address for accessing the allocated memory.

The `cfree` and `free` functions use the memory address returned by `malloc` to free space originally reserved by `malloc`.

A null value is returned by `malloc` if the function cannot allocate the requested amount of space.

General industry standards suggest that the `malloc` size parameter should be stated using the `sizeof` function as shown in the examples.

This function always allocated contiguous memory space. Therefore, the reserved memory area can be acceded through arrays or pointer arithmetic.

Many compilers require that when allocating memory space, non-`char` data types—such as integers, structures and union—that the returned `malloc` value should be cast into the appropriate pointer type. An example of this casting is shown in the second example.

The malloc function resembles the calloc function, the main distinction being that calloc can allocate memory for structures of varying date types while malloc generally requires that all allocated space be of one data type.

printf( )

Name	`printf()` *(Print function)*
Library/header	stdio.h
Purpose	Used to print formatted data to the screen or other specified output.
Syntax	`printf(format_control, arguments);`
Variables	`format_control` *(string)* explains the output format.
	`arguments` is a list of the variables to be printed.

Example setup	`int i_variable;`
	`char c_variable[] = {"hello there"};`
	`char f_control[] = {"integer is %d, text is %s");`

Example	`printf(i_variable,c_variable);`
	`. . .`
	`printf("\nThe int value = %d", i_variable);`

Rules	The print types listed in the format control must match exactly the printing argument list.
	Each variable has a coinciding print type identifier. For example, %d is integer, %s is character string, and %lf is long float (double). Refer to your compiler documentation for a complete list of these identifiers. Note, however, that these identifiers are all prefixed with a percent sign %.

putc( )

Name   `putc()` *(Put character)*

Library/header   stdio.h

Purpose   Used to write a character from a specified data file.

Syntax   `ret_code = putc(file_pointer);`

Variables   `ret_code` *(integer)* receives the function return code, which is either the octal value of the written character or a -1 if an error condition was encountered.

               `f_pointer` *(file pointer)* points to an open data file. This variable must have obtained its pointer value from the return of the file open function `fopen`.

Example
```
FILE *f_pointer;
int ret_code;
f_pointer = (fopen("data.dat","w");
 . . .
ret_code = putc(f_pointer);
```

Rules   The stdio.h header file must be included in the program through use of the `#include` compiler directive.

               The file pointer must be a valid file pointer associated with a file opened with write-access privileges.

               In many compilers, the single character write procedures are implemented as define macros and not functions. This can be done because these procedures are actually putting characters into the output buffer and not into the file directly.

putch( )

Name	putch() *(Put character to the screen)*
Library/header	stdio.h
Purpose	Used to send a single character to the screen.
Syntax	putch(int_value);
Variables	int_value *(integer)* contains the octal value of the character to be printed on the screen.

Example	int int_value;
	int_value = getch();
	putch(int_value);

Rules	The stdio.h header file must be included in the program through use of the #include compiler directive.
	This function is very commonly used in conjunction with getch, which reads a character directly from the keyboard without printing it on the screen.

putchar( )

Name   putchar()   *(Put character)*

Library/header   stdio.h

Purpose   Used to place a character in the output screen buffer (for file stdout—the screen output file area).

Syntax   ret_code = putchar(char_variable);

Variables   ret_code *(integer)* receives the function return code, which is either the octal value of the retrieved character or a -1 if an error occurs.

Example

```
int ret_code;
char c_variable;
ret_code = putchar(c_variable);
```

Rules   The stdio.h header file must be included in the program through use of the #include compiler directive.

In many compilers, the single character write procedures are implemented as define macros and not functions. This can be done because these procedures are actually putting characters in the output buffer and not directly into the file.

Because putch writes a character into the output buffer, data is not immediately written to the file, thus delaying the actual writing to the file.

rand( )

Name   `rand()`   *(Random number generation)*

Purpose   Generates a somewhat random number.

Syntax   `ret_value = rand();`

Variables   `ret_value` *(integer)* will contain the returned random number.

Example
```
int ret_value;
ret_value = rand();
printf("\n Random number = %d", ret_value);
```

Rules   The `rand` function generates a somewhat random number because the default random seed is always 1. Therefore, the same random numbers are always generated.

The `srand` function can be used to change the random number seed and generate a different set of random numbers.

For truly random numbers, use the `srand` function to set the random seed based on the PC clock's hours, minutes, seconds, and hundreths of seconds.

realloc( )

Name   realloc()   *(Character reallocation)*

Purpose   Reallocates specified amount of contiguous CPU memory.

Syntax   c_pointer = realloc(no_of_units,unit_size);

Variables   c_pointer *(character pointer)* will contain the address of the first allocated memory location.

no_of_units *(integer)* is the number of data units you want to allocate.

unit_size *(integer)* is the actual memory size in bytes of the data type, structure, or union being allocated space.

Examples
```
char *c_pointer;
char c_variable;
c_pointer = realloc (250, sizeof(c_variable));

char *c_pointer;
struct name {
  char last[10];
  char first[10];
  char middle[10];
};
struct name *n_pointer;
n_pointer = ( struct *)
                realloc(10,sizeof(struct name);
```

Rules   The realloc function returns the address of the first allocated memory location. This address must be saved to use as the base address for accessing the allocated memory.

The cfree and free functions use the memory address returned by realloc to free space originally reserved by realloc.

A null value is returned by realloc if the function cannot allocate the requested amount of space.

General industry standards suggest that the realloc size parameter should be stated using the sizeof function as shown in the examples.

This function always allocated contiguous memory space. Therefore, the reserved memory area can be accessed through arrays or pointer arithmetic.

Many compilers require that when allocating memory space, non-char data types—such as integers, structures, and union—that the returned realloc value should be cast into the appropriate pointer type. An example of this casting is shown back in the second example.

The realloc function is very similar to the calloc and malloc functions, except that this function is used to reallocate space previously allocated. For example, if you originally allocated memory for 50 integers and now require room for 75 integers, you would reallocate the 50 memory locations into 75 memory locations. By using realloc to reserve the additional 25 memory spaces, you are guaranteed that all 75 integers are stored in contiguous memory space. If you just allocated 25 new spaces using calloc or malloc, there would be no guarantee that all 75 memory locations would be contiguous. In fact, if they were contiguous, it would be by mere chance and not convention.

remove( )

Name remove() *(Remove a file from disk)*

Library/header stdio.h

Purpose Deletes a file from disk.

Syntax ret_code = remove(file_name);

Variables ret_code *(integer)* will contain the function's return code, which will be a 0 if the deletion was successful and a −1 if an error occurred.

file_name is the name of the file to be deleted.

Examples
```
int ret_code;
ret_code = remove("data.dat");

int ret_code;
char file_name[12];
strcpy(file_name,"data.dat");
ret_code = remove(file_name);
```

Rules If your compiler does not support the remove function, this task can easily be performed using the system function.

As shown in the examples, the file to be deleted is specified by using either a constant character string or a character string containing the filename.

The filename being specified for deletion must contain valid DOS filename.

rename( )

Name	rename( ) *(Rename a disk file)*
Library/header	stdio.h
Purpose	Renames a disk file.
Syntax	ret_code = rename(old_name,new_name);
Variables	ret_code *(integer)* will contain the function's return code, which will be a 0 if the rename was successful and a −1 if an error occurred.
	old_name is the name of the data file as it currently resides on disk.
	new_name is the data file's new name.
Examples	int ret_code; ret_code = rename("data.old","data.new");

	int ret_code;
	char old_name[12];
	char new_name[12];
	strcpy(old_name,"data.old");
	srecpy(new_name,"data.new");
	ret_code = rename(file_name);

Rules	If your compiler does not support the rename function, this task can easily be performed using the system function.
	As shown in the examples, the file to be deleted can be specified using either a constant character string or a character string containing the filename.
	The filename being specified for deletion must be a valid DOS filename.

rewind( )

Name rewind() *(File—Rewind data file)*

Library/header stdio.h

Purpose Moves the current file pointer to the beginning of the file.

Syntax rewind(f_pointer);

Variables f_pointer (*file pointer*) points to an open data file. This variable must have obtained its pointer value from the return of the file open function fopen.

Example
```
FILE *f_pointer;
f_pointer = (fopen("data.dat","r");
  . . .
rewind(f_pointer);
```

Rules The stdio.h header file must be included in the program through use of the #include compiler directive.

The file pointer must be a valid file pointer associated with an open file.

If your compiler does not support the rewind function, then the following fseek function will perform the same function:

ret_code = fseek(f_pointer,0l,0);

scanf( )

Name	scanf() *(Scan function)*
Library/header	stdio.h
Purpose	Reads data from a standard input, converts it to the appropriate data type, and places it into the specified variables.
Syntax	scanf(conversion_mask, arguments);
Variables	conversion_mask *(string)* explains the format of the data being input.
	arguments is a list of pointers to the variables that will be receiving the data.
Example setup	int i_variable; char c_variable[];
Example	scanf("%4d%6s", i_variable, c_variable);
Rules	The data types listed in the conversion mask must identically match the argument list.
	Each variable has a coinciding data type identifier. For example, %d is integer, %s is character string, and %lf is long float (double). Refer to your compiler documentation for a complete list of these identifiers. Note, however, that these identifiers are all prefixed with a percent sign %.

sin( )

Name	sin() *(sine)*
Library/header	math.h
Purpose	Receives a variable defined as a double and returns its corresponding sine value.
Syntax	ret_value = sin(double_value);
Variables	ret_value *(double)* will contain the returned value of the sin function.
	double_value *(double)* contains the value being passed to the function.
Example setup	double ret_value; double double_value;

Examples	double_value = 10;
	ret_value = sin(double_value);
	printf("\n First example = %d", ret_value);
	
	double_value = −5;
	ret_value = sin(double_value);
	printf("\n Second example = %d", ret_value);

Rules	The math.h header file must be included using the #include compiler directive.
	The variable being passed to the function, as well as the variable receiving the function's return value, must be defined using the double data type.

sinh( )

Name	`sinh()` *(Sin hyperbolic)*
Library/header	math.h
Purpose	Receives a variable defined as a `double` and returns its corresponding sine hyperbolic value.
Syntax	`ret_value = sinh(double_value);`
Variables	`ret_value` *(double)* will contain the returned value of the `sinh` function.
	`double_value` *(double)* contains the value being passed to the function.
Example setup	`double ret_value;` `double double_value;`

Examples	`double_value = 10;`
	`ret_value = sinh(double_value);`
	`printf("\nFirst example = %d",ret_value);`

	`double_value = -5;`
	`ret_value = sinh(double_value);`
	`printf("\nSecond example = %d",ret_value);`

Rules	The math.h header file must be included using the `#include` compiler directive.
	The variable being passed to the function, as well as the variable receiving the function's return value, must be defined using the `double` data type.

sprintf( )

Name	`sprintf()` *(String print function)*
Library/header	stdio.h
Purpose	Places formatted data to a specified memory location.
Syntax	`sprintf(s_pointer, format_control, arguments);`

Variables `s_pointer` *(string pointer)* specifies where in memory the formatted string should be placed.

`format_control` *(string)* explains the output format.

`arguments` is a list of the variables to be printed.

Example setup
```
int i_variable;
char *c_pointer;
char c_variable[] = {"hello there"};
char f_control[] = {"integer is %d, text is %s");
```

Example
```
printf(c_pointer,f_control,i_variable,
c_variable); . . .
printf(c_pointer,"\nThe int value = %d",
       i_variable);
```

Rules The string character pointer must point to a valid memory location with the appropriate amount of memory locations reserved for the output string.

The print types listed in the format control must identically match the printing argument list.

Each variable has a coinciding print type identifier. For example, %d is integer, %s is character string, and %lf is long float (double). Refer to your compiler documentation for a complete list of these identifiers. Note, however, that these identifiers are all prefixed with a percent sign %.

srand( )

Name   srand()   *(Random number seed)*

Purpose   Provides the ability to change the seed number used in the random number generation process.

Syntax   srand(int_variable);

Variables int_variable *(unsigned integer)* will become the seed used in future random number generation.

Example   unsigned int int_variable = 50;
              srand(int_variable);

Rules   The srand function generally has no return code.

              The function's input parameter must be defined as an unsigned integer—unsigned int.

              srand can be called at any time to change the random seed.

              To assist in generating true random numbers, you might want to use the PC clock time as the seed.

sscanf( )

Name	sscanf() *(String scan function)*
Library/header	stdio.h
Purpose	Converts data in memory from a character string data type to another specified data type.
Syntax	scanf(memory_pointer,conversion_mask, argument);
Variables	memory_string *(pointer)* contains the first memory address of the character string to be converted.
	conversion_mask *(string)* explains the data type of the variables receiving the converted data.
	arguments is a list pointers to the variables that will be receiving the converted data.
Example setup	int i_variable; char c_variable[]; char old_string[];
Example	scanf(old_string,"%4d%6s",i_variable, c_variable);
Rules	The data types listed in the conversion mask must identically match the argument list.
	Each variable has a coinciding data type identifier. For example, %d is integer, %s is character string, and %lf is long float (double). Refer to your compiler documentation for a complete list of these identifiers. Note, however, that these identifiers are all prefixed with a percent sign %.

strcat( )

Name	strcat() *(String concatenation)*
Library/header	string.h
Purpose	Adds one string to the end of another string, thus concatenating the two values.
Syntax	ret_code = strcat(to_pointer,from_pointer);

Variables

ret_code *(character pointer)* receives the function's return value, which be a character pointer to the string receiving the additional data.

to_pointer *(character pointer)* contains the address of the string receiving the new data.

from_pointer *(character pointer)* contains the address of the string to be added to the first parameter.

Example

```
char *ret_code;
char to_pointer[20] = {"hello "};
char from_pointer[] = {"there"};
ret_code = strcat(to_pointer,from_pointer);
```

Rules

The two passed parameters must be character pointers defined as char * or as the unsubscripted name of a string array. Remember, the default pointer to char to_pointer[20] is the word to_pointer with no subscript brackets.

The string receiving the concatenated data must be large enough to contain that data. Otherwise, the function will write over the next memory locations, thus destroying whatever is in them.

The return pointer contains the address of the string receiving the concatenated data.

strcmp( )

Name	`strcmp()` *(String comparison)*
Library/header	string.h
Purpose	Compares the value of two strings.
Syntax	`ret_code=strcmp(first_pointer,second_pointer);`

Variables

`ret_code` receives the function's return code. (Valid codes are presented in the Rules section.)

`first_pointer` (*character pointer*) contains the address of the first string being compared.

`second_pointer` (*character pointer*) contains the address of the second string to be compared.

Example

```
char *ret_code;
char *f_pointer;
char *s_pointer;
ret_code = strcmp(f_pointer,s_pointer);
```

Rules

The two passed parameters must be character pointers defined as `char *` or as the unsubscripted name of a string array. Remember, the default pointer to `char to_pointer[20]` is the word `to_pointer` with no subscript brackets.

The integer value returned by the function will fall into one of the following three categories:

Equal to 0	Strings are equal
Less than 0	First string is less than second
Greater than 0	First string is greater than second

The return code variable must be defined as an integer—`int`.

strcpy( )

Name	strcpy() *(String copy)*
Library/header	string.h
Purpose	Copies the value of one string to another string.
Syntax	ret_code = strcpy(to_pointer, from_pointer);

Variables

ret_code (*character pointer*) receives the function's return value, which will be a character pointer to the string receiving the data.

to_pointer (*character pointer*) contains the address of the string receiving the new data.

from_pointer (*character pointer*) contains the address of the string to be copied to the first parameter.

Example

```
char *ret_code;
char to_pointer[10];
char from_pointer[] = {"there"};
ret_code = strcpy(to_pointer, from_pointer);
```

Rules

The two passed parameters must be character pointers defined as char * or as the unsubscripted name of a string array. Remember, the default pointer to char to_pointer[10] is the word to_pointer with no subscript brackets.

The string receiving the concatenated data must be large enough to contain that data. Otherwise, the function will write over the next memory locations, thus destroying whatever is in them.

The return pointer contains the address of the string receiving the new data.

strlen( )

Name	`strlen()` *(String length)*
Library/header	string.h
Purpose	Measures the length of a string.
Syntax	`ret_code = strlen(char_pointer,);`

`ret_code` *(integer)* receives the function's return value, which will be an integer value stating the length of the string in characters. |
| **Variables** | `c_pointer` *(character pointer)* contains the address of the string being measured. |
| **Example** | `char *ret_code;`
`char c_pointer[] = {"I am 23 characters long"};`
`ret_code = strlen(c_pointer);` |
| **Rules** | The passed parameter must be character pointers defined as `char *` or as the unsubscripted name of a string array. Remember, the default pointer to `char c_pointer[]` is the word `c_pointer` with no subscript brackets.

The return code must be defined as an integer.

The null terminator `\0` at the end of the string is not included as part of its length. |

strncat( )

Name	strncat() *(String concatenation to a specified length)*
Library/header	string.h
Purpose	Adds a specified number of characters from one string to the end of another string, thus concatenating the two values.
Syntax	ret_code = strncat(to_pointer,from_pointer,max);
Variables	ret_code (*character pointer*) receives the function's return value, which will be a character pointer to the string receiving the additional data.
	to_pointer (*character pointer*) contains the address of the string receiving the new data.
	from_pointer (*character pointer*) contains the address of the string to be added to the first parameter.
	max (*integer variable/constant*) specifies the maximum number of characters to be concatenated.

Example

```
char *ret_code;
int max = 10;
char to_pointer[20] = {"hello "};
char from_pointer[] = {"there"};
ret_code = strncat(to_pointer,from_pointer,max);
   . . .
ret_code = strncat(to_pointer,from_pointer,7);
```

Rules

The two passed parameters must be character pointers defined as char * or as the unsubscripted name of a string array. Remember, the default pointer to char to_pointer[20] is the word to_poin ter with no subscript brackets.

The string receiving the concatenated data must be large enough to contain that data. Otherwise, the function will write over the next memory locations, thus destroying whatever is in them.

The return pointer contains the address of the string receiving the concatenated data.

The max parameter specifies the maximum number of characters that can be moved, not the exact amount. Therefore, if max has a value of 10 and the string being concatenated only has 6 characters, then only 6 characters are moved.

strncmp( )

Name   strncmp()   *(String comparison for a specified number of characters)*

Library/header   string.h

Purpose   Compares the value of a specified number of characters within two strings.

Syntax   ret_code = strncmp(f_pointer,s_pointer,length);

Variables   ret_code receives the function's return code. (Valid return codes are presented in the Rules section.)

f_pointer (*character pointer*) contains the address of the first string being compared.

s_pointer (*character pointer*) contains the address of the second string to be compared.

length (*integer*) specifies the number of characters within the two strings that should be compared.

Example
```
char *ret_code;
char *f_pointer;
char *s_pointer;
int length = 10;
ret_code = strncmp(f_pointer,s_pointer,length);
 . . .
ret_code = strncmp(f_pointer,s_pointer,8);
```

Rules   The two passed parameters must be character pointers defined as char * or as the unsubscripted name of a string array. Remember, the default pointer to char to_pointer[20] is the word to_pointer with no subscript brackets.

The integer value returned by the function will fall into one of the following three categories:

Equal to 0	Strings are equal
Less than 0	First string is less than second
Greater than 0	First string is greater than second

The return code variable must be defined as an integer—int.

The length parameter must be defined as an integer and specifies the maximum number of characters to be compared.

strncpy( )

Name	strncpy() *(String copy a specified number of characters)*
Library/header	string.h
Purpose	Copies a specified number of characters from one string to another string.
Syntax	ret_code = strncpy(to_pointer,from_pointer,max);
Variables	ret_code *(character pointer)* receives the function's return value, which will be a character pointer to the string receiving the data.
	to_pointer *(character pointer)* contains the address of the string receiving the new data.
	from_pointer *(character pointer)* contains the address of the string to be copied to the first parameter.
	max *(integer variable/constant)* specifies the maximum number of characters to be copied.

Example

```
char *ret_code;
int max = 10;
char to_pointer[10];
char from_pointer[] = {"hello"};
ret_code = strncpy(to_pointer,from_pointer,max);
. . .
ret_code = strncpy(to_pointer,from_pointer,7);
```

Rules

The two passed parameters must be character pointers defined as char * or as the unsubscripted name of a string array. Remember, the default pointer to char to_pointer[10] is the word to_pointer with no subscript brackets.

The string receiving the data must be large enough to contain that data. Otherwise, the function will write over the next memory locations, thus destroying whatever is in them.

The return pointer contains the address of the string to receive the copied data.

The max parameter specifies the maximum number of characters that can be moved, not the exact amount. Therefore, if max has a value of 10 and the string being copied only has 6 characters, then only 6 characters are moved.

switch( )

Name   switch()

Purpose   Executes selected statements based on specified selection criteria.

Syntax

```
switch (test-criteria)
  { case test-character:
    statement or statements
  case test-character:
    statement or statements

    . . .

  default:
    statement or statements
```

Example

```
char c_variable;
c_variable = 'y';

switch (c_variable)
  { case 'x':
    printf("\n c_variable has a value of x");
    break;
  case 'y':
    printf("\n c_variable has a value of y");
    break;
  case 'z':
    printf("\n c_variable has a value of z");
    break;
  default:
    printf("\n c_variable in not x, y, or z );
    break;
  }
```

Rules   The test-character being evaluated within the case statement must be an integer or a character data type.

Within a switch statement, no two case statements should contain the same test-character test value.

The default: label is not required to be the last switch option. However, general industry conventions suggest that it should always be used and placed last.

C does not guarantee that the case statements will be evaluated in the order specified within the source code. They may be reordered if you are using an optimizing compiler. Therefore, if the order of evaluation is important, turn optimization off with the appropriate compilation command or use consecutive if/else statements instead of switch.

switch( )

The `default:` label shown in the example has special meaning to the `switch` statement; it instructs the `switch` statement to execute the statements after that label if no `case` statement conditions are met.

The `break` statement should be used to signify the end of the statements associated with a `case` statement. Refer to the example for clarification.

tolower( )

Name tolower( ) *(Convert character to lowercase)*

Library/header ctype.h

Purpose Converts the specified alphabetic character to lowercase.

Syntax tolower(char_value);

Variables char_value (*character*) contains the character being converted by tolower.

Examples
```
char char_value;
char_value = 'X';
   . . .
tolower(char_value);
```

Rules On some compilers, this procedure is implemented as a define macro and not a function.

The ctype.h header file must be included through use of the #include compiler directive.

On some compilers, these procedures are defined as functions within the C runtime libraries and as macros within the ctype.h header file. Therefore, if you include the ctype.h header file, you access the macros; and if you do not include the ctype.h header file, then you call the functions. Refer to your compiler documentation for clarification.

A conversion will only occur if the character received by the function is an uppercase alphabetic. All other characters—including lowercase alphas, numerics, white space, punctuation, and control bytes—will be returned unchanged.

toupper( )

Name	`toupper()` *(Convert character to uppercase)*
Library/header	ctype.h
Purpose	Converts the specified alphabetic character to uppercase.
Syntax	`toupper(char_value);`
Variables	`char_value` (*character*) contains the character being converted by `toupper`.

Examples	`char char_value;`
	`char_value = 'X';`
	`    . . .`
	`toupper(char_value);`

Rules

On some compilers, this procedure is implemented as a define macro and not a function.

The ctype.h header file must be included through use of the `#include` compiler directive.

On some compilers, these procedures are defined as functions within the C runtime libraries and as macros within the ctype.h header file. Therefore, if you include the ctype.h header file, you access the macros; and if you do not include the ctype.h header file, then you call the functions. Refer to your compiler documentation for clarification.

A conversion will only occur if the character received by the function is an uppercase alphabetic. All other characters—including uppercase alphas, numerics, white space, punctuation, and control bytes—will be returned unchanged.

ungetc( )

Name	`ungetc()` *(Unget a character from a file)*
Library/header	stdio.h
Purpose	Returns to the file the last character read from that file, allowing it to be read again later.
Syntax	`ret_code = ungetc(char_variable, f_pointer);`
Variables	`ret_code` *(integer)* will given the `ungetc` function's return value, which will be the ASCII value of the character returned to the file or a -1 if an error condition occurred.

`char_variable` *(character)* contains the character to be returned to the file.

`f_pointer` *(file pointer)* points to an open data file. This variable must have obtained its pointer value from the return of the file open function `fopen`. |
| **Examples** | ```
FILE *f_pointer;
int ret_code;
c_variable;
f_pointer = (fopen("data.dat","r");
   . . .
c_variable = getc(f_pointer);
int_variable = ungetc(f_pointer);
``` |
| **Rules** | The stdio.h header file must be included in the program through use of the `#include` compiler directive.

The file pointer must be a valid file pointer associated with an open file.

The character returned to the file must be the last character retrieved from that file. |
```

unlink( )

Name	unlink() *(Unlink a file from disk)*
Library/header	stdio.h
Purpose	Deletes a file from disk.
Syntax	ret_code = unlink(file_name);

Variables   ret_code (*integer*) will contain the function's return code, which will be a 0 if the deletion was successful and a −1 if an error occurred.

file_name names the file to be deleted.

Examples
```
int ret_code;
ret_code = unlink("data.dat");

int ret_code;
char file_name[12];
strcpy(file_name,"data.dat");
ret_code = unlink(file_name);
```

Rules   If your compiler does not support the unlink function, this task can easily be performed using the system function.

As shown in the examples, the file to be deleted may be specified using either a constant character string or a character string containing the filename.

The filename being specified for deletion must be a valid DOS filename.

The remove function is an equivalent function.

Name   while

Purpose   Repeats the execution of a selected group of statements based on test criteria within the while statement.

Syntax   while (*test-expression*)
   statement or statement block

Variables *statement* is a single C instruction repeated by placing it after the key while.

statement block is a group of one or more C statements contained within block control brackets {}, all of which will repeat execution while the while test criteria is met.

test-expression is the criteria used to test if looping should be continued.

Examples
```
int x = 0;
while ( x < 5 );
printf("\nLets count to 5 : %d", x++);

char answer[2];
answer[0] = 'N';
while (answer[0] != 'Y' && answer[0] != 'N');
  { printf("\nEnter Y for yes or N for no: ");
  gets(answer);
  }
```

Rules   The statement or statement block within the while loop will only be executed if the while test criteria is met (unlike the do statement, where they are always executed at least once).

The while condition is evaluated before each execution of the statement or statement block.

The statements will continue to execute until the while test-expression returns a zero value.

_exit( )

Name	_exit()
Purpose	Terminates program execution without closing any open data files or purging any input/output buffers.
Syntax	_exit(int_variable);
Variables	int_variable (*integer*) contains the value to be passed back to the calling program, should one exist.

Examples	int int_variable = 1;
	_exit(int_variable);
	
	_exit(1);

Rules	Returning a value of zero generally implies a normal program termination. A return code of other than zero generally indicates an abnormal termination. The return value may be expressed as either the value of an integer variable or as a numeric constant.

18
C++ operators

//

Name	// *(Comment)*

Syntax   Two consecutive backslashes anywhere on a line specifies that the remainder of that line (until a carriage return is found) is a comment.

Purpose   Instructs the compiler to ignore the text placed after the // characters.

Examples   Comments are generally formatted in the following way:

j + +; // on same line as a statement

Rules   The // characters must be side by side with no characters or spaces between them.

Name	new *(Allocate new memory)*
Syntax	*name-pointer* = new name[*name-initializer*]
Purpose	Allocates memory in a manner similar to the standard malloc( ) library function.

Examples

```
int *int_pointer = new int[100];
if (!int_pointer)
{ error("ran out of memory");
  exit(1);
}
```

Rules

new returns a null if the specified amount of memory cannot be allocated.

Memory allocated by new will reside in memory until the program ends or until the delete verb is used to de-allocate the memory.

delete

Name   delete   *(Deallocate allocate memory)*

Syntax   delete *name-pointer*

Purpose   Deallocates previously allocated memory in a manner similar to the standard free( ) library function. This verb is often found within a class's destructor function.

Examples
```
int *int_pointer = new int[100];
if (!int_pointer)
{ error("ran out of memory");
  exit(1);
}
      . . .
      . . .
      . . .
    delete int_pointer;
```

Rules   The pointer placed after the word delete must contain the value (returned by new) that you want to deallocate.

Name   class   *(Define structure of an object)*

Syntax   class ([private:]*member-list*)
                      ([public: }*member-list*);

Purpose   Defines the structure of an object.

Example
```
class example-class {
 private:
  double a_variable;
  double a_private_function();
 public:
  int an_int;
  double a_public_function();
  friend a_friend_function();
};
```

Rules   Like the struct statement, this statement does not allocate memory but simply defines the class's structure.

The word "private" is optional.

The key word "friend" allows functions not defined outside the class to access data defined within the class.

Data and functions define after the keyword "private" can only be accessed from within the class.

Data and functions defined after the keyword "public" can be accessed by functions defined outside of the class.

A *constructor* is a member function automatically called when a class is first initialized. It is defined by creating within the class definition a name function with the same name as the class.

A *destructor* is a member function automatically called when an object goes out of scope. It is defined by creating a member function that also has the same name as the class but is prefixed with a tilde ~.

const

Name	const *(Constant variable)*
Syntax	const *variable-type variable-name;*
Purpose	Is a storage class like static and register. It informs the compiler that the variable being defined should be treated like a constant.
Examples	const double a__double; const int a__int, b__int;
Rules	A const type variable's value cannot be modified.

Name   : :   *(scope resolution operator)*

Syntax   *class-name::variable-or-function-name*

Purpose   Informs the compiler that the function or variable being referenced is the member of a specified class.

Examples   ```
class Xyz {
  int func( );
};

int Xyz::( ) { /* function text goes here */ }
```

**Rules**   There cannot be any spaces on either side of the scope operator.

The class and variable being defined must exist.
```

inline

Name	inline *(Inline keyword)*
Syntax	inline *function-return-type function-definition*;

Purpose   Imitates a C #define macro (see Chapter 11), except that it acts exactly like a function in regard to scope, type checking, and other function attributes. It gives you the advantages of a function without the overhead incured when calling that function.

Mechanically, the code associated with an inline function is physically placed at each location where called. As said, when called, the inline function does not execute the overhead associated with calling a function. Unfortunately, it can increase the size of your program if it is too large or called too often. Generally, if a function is called often, you must decide between the execution efficiency of not placing another function on the stack versus the growth in program size due to the physical placement of the function many times throughout your executable. Generally speaking, if the function takes up less space than the code needed to call it, you are all set.

Examples   inline double square(double x) {return(x * x); }

Rules   When compiled, functions defined in this manner are physically placed in the location where used.

Name $<<$ *(Put to)*

Syntax   `cout << value-to-be-output`

Purpose   Is called a *stream operator* and is used to pass a specified string value to an output buffer.

Examples `cout << "HelloWorld";`

```
char a_string[10];
strcpy(a_string,"hello");
   cout << a_string << " " << "world";
```

Rules   The values being passed to cout via the $<<$ operator must be null terminated strings.

>>

Name	>> *(Get from)*
Syntax	`cin >> value-to-get-input`
Purpose	Is called a *stream operator* and is used to get a string value from an input buffer.
Examples	`cout << "Hello World";`

	`char a_string[10];`
	`strcpy(a_string,"hello");`
	`cout << a_string << " " << "world";`

Rules	The values being passed to cout via the << operator must be null terminated strings.

Part Three
A C Toolbox Library

19

Printer output functions

Printer output functions header file

#ifndef HEAD19

#define HEAD19 1

```
void comp_off(void);      // compression off
void comp_on(void);       // compression on
void ds_off(void);        // double strike off
void ds_on(void);         // double strike on
void emph_off(void);      // emphasis off
void emph_on(void);       // emphasis on
void expl_off(void);      // single expand mode off
void expl_on(void);       // single expand mode on
void exp_off(void);       // expand mode off
void exp_on(void);        // expand mode on
void ital_off(void);      // italics off
void ital_on(void);       // italics on
void prop_off(void);      // proportional mode off
void prop_on(void);       // proportional mode on
void reset(void);         // reset printer
void sub_off(void);       // subscript mode off
void sub_on(void);        // subscript mode on
void super_off(void);     // superscript mode off
void super_on(void);      // superscript mode on
void under_off(void);     // underline mode off
void under_on(void);      // underline mode on
```

#endif

#include <stdio.h>
#include "head33.h"

Special note These functions are designed to work only on EPSON FX printers. If you are using a printer made by another manufacturer, you might have to send different control strings to the printer. If this is the case, you only must change the `fprintf( )` file print line function.

If you will be using many of these special calls in conjunction with report printing, it might be to your advantage to open the printer as a file once at the beginning of your report and close it after all your printing is complete. If you take this plan of action, comment out the file calls used in this function.

Name　　comp__off　*(Compression off)*

Description　Instructs the printer to turn compressed mode off. This function works in conjunction with comp__on ( ), which causes all characters to be printed in compressed format. The compressed type font allows 132-column reports to be printed on 80-column paper.

Variables　string is the string (octal 22) sent to the screen to instruct the printer to enter compressed print format.

　　prn__file (*file pointer*) is used to open, define, and close the file.

Example　comp__off( );

Rules　The function is not passed any variables and is called to negate the comp__on( ) function.

```
void comp__off(void)
{ FILE *prn__file;
  prn__file = fopen("prn","w");
  fprintf(prn__file,"%c",'\022');
  fclose(prn__file);
}
```

Name   comp_on   *(Compression on)*

Description   Instructs the printer to turn compressed mode on. This function works in conjunction with comp_off( ), which turns compression mode off. Compression mode prints using a smaller font allowing 132 column reports to be printed on 80 column paper.

Variables   string is the string (octal 17) sent to the screen to instruct the printer to enter compressed print format.

prn_file (*file pointer*) is used to open, define, and close the file.

Example   comp_on( );

Rules   The function is not passed any variables and is called to initiate compression mode.

```
void comp_on(void)
{ FILE *prn_file;
  prn_file = fopen("prn","w");
  fprintf(prn_file,"%c",'\017');
  fclose(prn_file);
}
```

ds_off

Name   ds_off   *(Turn double strike off)*

Description   Instructs the printer to turn double strike mode off. This function works in conjunction with ds_on( ), which causes all characters to be printed twice (overstrike) and thus produces a much darker copy because it actually prints the same character twice in the same place.

Variables   string is a string of ESCAPE (octal 33) followed by the ASCII string "H" sent to the screen to instruct the printer to enter double strike mode.

prn_file (*file pointer*) is used to open, define and close the file.

Example   ds_off( );

Rules   The function is not passed any variables and is called to negate the ds_on( ) function.

```
void ds_off(void)
{ FILE *prn_file;
  prn_file = fopen("prn","w");
  fprintf(prn_file,"%cH",'\033');
  fclose(prn_file);
}
```

ds_on

Name ds_on *(Double strike on)*

Description Instructs the printer to turn double strike mode on. This function works in conjunction with ds_off ( ), which turns double strike mode off. Double strike mode prints each character twice, making the printed output much darker.

Variables string is the string ESCAPE (octal 33) followed by the string "G" sent to the screen to instruct the printer to enter double strike mode.

prn_file (*file pointer*) is used to open, define, and close the file.

Example ds_on ( );

Rules The function is not passed any variables and is called to initiate double strike mode.

```
void ds_on(void)
{ FILE *prn_file;
  prn_file = fopen("prn","w");
  fprintf(prn_file,"%cG",'\033');
  fclose(prn_file);
}
```

emph_off

Name   emph_off   *(Turn emphasis off)*

Description Instructs the printer to turn emphasis mode off. This function works in conjunction with emph_on( ), which causes all characters to be printed twice—the second strike being slightly to the right of the first. This double striking produces a wider and darker copy because it actually prints the same character twice.

Variables   string is a string of ESCAPE (octal 33) followed by the ASCII string "F" sent to the screen to instruct the printer to exit emphasis mode.

             prn_file (*file pointer*) is used to open, define, and close the file.

Example   emph_off( );

Rules   The function is not passed any variables and is called to negate the emph_on( ) function.

```
void emph_off(void)
{ FILE *prn_file;
  prn_file = fopen("prn","w");
  fprintf(prn_file,"%cF",'\033');
  fclose(prn_file);
}
```

emph_on

Name   emph_on   *(Turn emphasis on)*

Description   Instructs the printer to turn emphasis mode on. This function, which works in conjunction with emph_off( ), causes all characters to be printed twice, the second strike being slightly to the right of the first. This double striking produces a wider and darker copy because it actually prints the same character twice.

Variables   string is a string of ESCAPE (octal 33) followed by the ASCII string "E" is sent to the screen to instruct the printer to enter emphasis mode.

prn_file (*file pointer*) is used to open, define, and close the file.

Example   emph_on( );

Rules   The function is not passed any variables and is called to turn emphasis mode on.

```
void emph_on(void)
{ FILE *prn_file;
  prn_file = fopen("prn","w");
  fprintf(prn_file,"%cE",'\033');
  fclose(prn_file);
}
```

expl_off

Name   expl_off   *(Single line expanded mode off)*

Description   Instructs the printer to turn single line expanded mode off. This function works in conjunction with expl_on( ), which causes all characters to be printed in expanded format. This larger type font prints letters twice as wide as regular printed characters.

Variables   string is the string (octal 24) is sent to the screen to instruct the printer to exit single line expanded print format.

prn_file (*file pointer*) is used to open, define, and close the file.

Example   expl_off( );

Rules   The function is not passed any variables and is called to negate the expl_on( ) function.

```
void expl_off(void)
{ FILE *prn_file;
 prn_file = fopen("prn","w");
 fprintf(prn_file,"%c",'\024');
 fclose(prn_file);
}
```

exp1_on

Name   expl_on   *(Single line expanded mode on)*

Description   Instructs the printer to turn single line expanded mode on. This function, which works in conjunction with expl_off( ), causes all characters to be printed in expanded format. This larger type font prints letters twice as wide as regular printed characters.

Variables   string is the string (octal 16) sent to the screen to instruct the printer to enter single line expanded print format.

prn_file (*file pointer*) is used to open, define, and close the file.

Example   expl_on( );

Rules   The function is not passed any variables and is called to turn single line expanded mode on.

```
void expl_on(void)
{ FILE *prn_file;
  prn_file = fopen("prn","w");
  fprintf(prn_file,"%c",'\016');
  fclose(prn_file);
}
```

exp_off

Name   exp_off   *(Expanded mode off)*

Description   Instructs the printer to turn expanded mode off. This function works in conjunction with exp_on( ), which causes all characters to be printed in expanded format. This larger type font prints letters twice as wide as regular printed characters.

Variables   string is the string ESCAPE (octal 33) followed by the ASCII characters "W0" sent to the screen to instruct the printer to exit expanded print format.

prn_file (*file pointer*) is used to open, define, and close the file.

Example   exp_off( );

Rules   The function is not passed any variables and is called to negate the exp_on( ) function.

```
void exp_off(void)
{ FILE *prn_file;
  prn_file = fopen("prn","w");
  fprintf(prn_file,"%cW0",'\033');
  fclose(prn_file);
}
```

exp_on

Name   exp_on   *(Expanded mode on)*

Description Instructs the printer to turn expanded mode on. This function, which works
in conjunction with exp_off( ), causes all characters to be printed in
expanded format. This larger type font prints letters twice as wide as regular printed characters.

Variables   string is the string ESCAPE (octal 33) followed by the ASCII characters
"W1" sent to the screen to instruct the printer to enter expanded print format.

prn_file (*file pointer*) is used to open, define, and close the file.

Example   exp_on( );

Rules   The function is not passed any variables and is called to turn expanded
mode on.

```
void exp_on(void)
{ FILE *prn_file;
  prn_file = fopen("prn","w");
  fprintf(prn_file,"%cW1",'\033');
  fclose(prn_file);
}
```

Name ital_off *(Italics mode off)*

Description Instructs the printer to turn italics mode off. This function works in conjunction with ital_on( ), which causes all characters to be printed in italics format. This fancy font type prints letters at a slight right angle.

Variables string is the string ESCAPE (octal 33) followed by the ASCII character "5" sent to the screen to instruct the printer to exit italics print format.

prn_file (*file pointer*) is used to open, define, and close the file.

Example ital_off( );

Rules The function is not passed any variables and is called to negate the ital_on( ) function.

```
void ital_off(void)
{ FILE *prn_file;
 prn_file = fopen("prn","w");
 fprintf(prn_file,"%c5",'\033');
 fclose(prn_file);
}
```

ital_on

Name   `ital_on`   *(Italics mode on)*

Description   Instructs the printer to turn italics mode off. This function, which works in conjunction with `ital_off( )`, causes all characters to be printed in italics format. This fancy font type prints letters at a slight right angle.

Variables   `string` is the string ESCAPE (octal 33) followed by the ASCII characters "4" sent to the screen to instruct the printer to exit italics print format.

     `prn_file` (*file pointer*) is used to open, define, and close the file.

Example   `ital_on( );`

Rules   The function is not passed any variables and is called to turn italics mode on.

```
void ital_on(void)
{ FILE *prn_file;
  prn_file = fopen("prn","w");
  fprintf(prn_file,"%c4",'\033');
  fclose(prn_file);
}
```

Name   prop_off   *(Proportional mode off)*

Description   Instructs the printer to turn proportional mode off. This function works in conjunction with prop_on( ), which causes all characters to be printed in proportional format. With proportional printing, the letters are printed close together, the exact spacing based on the size of the letters being printed.

Variables   string is the string ESCAPE (octal 33) followed by the ASCII characters "p0" sent to the screen to instruct the printer to exit proportional print format.

prn_file (*file pointer*) is used to open, define, and close the file.

Example   prop_off( );

Rules   The function is not passed any variables and is called to negate the prop_on( ) function.

```
void prop_off(void)
{ FILE *prn_file;
  prn_file = fopen("prn","w");
  fprintf(prn_file,"%cp0",'\033');
  fclose(prn_file);
}
```

prop_on

Name   prop_on   *(Proportional mode on)*

Description Instructs the printer to turn proportional mode on. This function, which works in conjunction with prop_off( ), causes all characters to be printed in proportional format. With proportional printing, the letters are printed close together, with the exact spacing based on the size of the letters being printed.

Variables string is the string ESCAPE (octal 33) followed by the ASCII characters "p1" is sent to the screen to instruct the printer to exit proportional print format.

prn_file (*file pointer*) is used to open, define, and close the file.

Example prop_on( );

Rules   The function is not passed any variables and is called to enter proportional mode.

```
void prop_on(void)
{ FILE *prn_file;
  prn_file = fopen("prn","w");
  fprintf(prn_file,"%cp1",'\033');
  fclose(prn_file);
}
```

reset

Name   reset   *(Reset printer)*

Description Instructs the printer to cancel all programmed settings and return to the settings that were in place when the printer was first turned on. These settings will be a combination of the manufacturers defaults and the position of the printer dip switches.

Variables   string is the string ESCAPE (octal 33) followed by the ASCII character "@" is sent to the screen to instruct the printer to reset settings.

prn_file (*file pointer*) is used to open, define, and close the file.

Example   reset( );

Rules   The function is not passed any variables and is called to reset the printer.

```
void reset(void)
{ FILE *prn_file;
  prn_file = fopen("prn","w");
  fprintf(prn_file,"%c@",'\033');
  fclose(prn_file);
}
```

sub_off

Name   sub_off   *(Subscript mode off)*

Description Instructs the printer to turn subscript mode off. This function works in conjunction with sub_on( ), which causes all characters to be printed in subscript format. This type font prints letters in a footnote type fashion, being lower and shorter than the regular printed characters.

Variables string is the string ESCAPE (octal 33) followed by the ASCII characters "T" is sent to the screen to tell the printer to exit subscript print format.

prn_file (*file pointer*) is used to open, define, and close the file.

Example   sub_off( );

Rules   The function is not passed any variables and is called to negate the sub_on( ) function.

```
void sub_off(void)
{ FILE *prn_file;
  prn_file = fopen("prn","w");
  fprintf(prn_file,"%cT",'\033');
  fclose(prn_file);
}
```

Name   sub_on   *(Subscript mode on)*

Description   Instructs the printer to turn subscript mode on. This function, which works in conjunction with sub_off( ), causes all characters to be printed in subscript format. This type font prints letters in a footnote type fashion, being lower and shorter than the regular printed characters.

Variables   string is the string ESCAPE (octal 33) followed by the ASCII characters "S1" is sent to the screen to tell the printer to exit subscript print format.

prn_file (*file pointer*) is used to open, define, and close the file.

Example   sub_on( );

Rules   The function is not passed any variables and is called to enter subscript mode.

```
void sub_on(void)
{ FILE *prn_file;
  prn_file = fopen("prn","w");
  fprintf(prn_file,"%cS1",'\033');
  fclose(prn_file);
}
```

super_off

Name   `super_off` *(Superscript mode off)*

Description   Instructs the printer to turn superscript mode off. This function works in conjunction with `super_on( )`, which causes all characters to be printed in superscript format. This type font prints letters in a footnote-type fashion, being lower and shorter than the regular printed characters.

Variables   `string` is the string ESCAPE (octal 33) followed by the ASCII character "T" sent to the screen to tell the printer to exit superscript print format.

    `prn_file` (*file pointer*) is used to open, define, and close the file.

Example   `super_off( );`

Rules   The function is not passed any variables and is called to negate the `super_on( )` function.

```
void super_off(void)
{ FILE *prn_file;
  prn_file = fopen("prn","w");
  fprintf(prn_file,"%cT",'\033');
  fclose(prn_file);
}
```

Name   super_on   *(Superscript mode on)*

Description   Instructs the printer to turn superscript mode on. This function, which works in conjunction with super_off( ), causes all characters to be printed in superscript format. This type font prints letters in a footnote type fashion, being higher and shorter than the regular printed characters.

Variables   string is the string ESCAPE (octal 33) followed by the ASCII characters "S0" sent to the screen to tell the printer to exit superscript print format.

prn_file (*file pointer*) is used to open, define, and close the file.

Example   super_on( );

Rules   The function is not passed any variables and is called to enter superscript mode.

```
void super_on(void)
{ FILE *prn_file;
 prn_file = fopen("prn","w");
 fprintf(prn_file,"%cS0",'\033');
 fclose(prn_file);
}
```

under_off

Name   under_off   *(Underline mode off)*

Description   Instructs the printer to turn underline mode off. This function works in conjunction with under_on( ), which causes all characters to be printed with an underline.

Variables   string is the string ESCAPE (octal 33) followed by the ASCII characters "-0" is sent to the screen to tell the printer to exit underline print format.

prn_file (*file pointer*) is used to open, define, and close the file.

Example   under_off( );

Rules   The function is not passed any variables and is called to negate the under_on( ) function.

```
void under_off(void)
{ FILE *prn_file;
  prn_file = fopen("prn","w");
  fprintf(prn_file,"%c-0",'\033');
  fclose(prn_file);
}
```

Name   under_on   *(Underline mode on)*

Description   Instructs the printer to turn underline mode off. This function, which works in conjunction with under_off( ), causes all characters to be printed with an underline.

Variables   string is the string ESCAPE (octal 33) followed by the ASCII characters "-1" sent to the screen to instruct the printer to exit underline print format.

prn_file (*file pointer*) is used to open, define, and close the file.

Example   under_on( );

Rules   The function is not passed any variables and is called to turn on underline mode.

```
void under_on(void)
{ FILE *prn_file;
  prn_file = fopen("prn","w");
  fprintf(prn_file,"%c-1",'\033');
  fclose(prn_file);
}
```

20
String functions

String manipulation header file

```
#ifndef HEAD20

#define HEAD20 1

void    str_convert(char *);        // convert upper- and lowercase
int     str_count(char *, char);    // count string size
void    str_delete(char *, int, int); // string characters delete
int     str_lindex(char *, char);   // string left index
void    str_lower(char *);          // convert to lowercase
void    str_lpad(char *, int);      // string left space pad
int     str_rindex(char *, char);   // string right index
void    str_rpad(char *, int);      // string right space pad
void    str_swap(char *, char *);   // string swap
void    str_upper(char *);          // convert to uppercase
#endif

#include <string.h>
#include <iostream.h>
#include <alloc.h>
#include <process.h>
```

Name   `str_convert`   *(String)*

Description   Converts lowercase alpha characters to uppercase and uppercase characters to lowercase.

Variables   `string` (*character pointer*) points to the string being modified.

Example
```
strcpy(str,"ABC");
str_convert(str); /* Returns the string abc */

strcpy(str,"abC");
str_convert(str); /* Returns the string ABc */
```

Rules   The function must be passed a character pointer containing the address of the character string to be converted.

This function does not use a return value. Therefore, it may be defined as a void.

```
void str_convert(char *string)
{
  int count;
  count = 0;
  while ( string[count] != '\0' )
    { if ( string[count] >= 'A' && string[count] <= 'Z' )
      string[count] = string[count] + 'a' - 'A';
      else
        if ( string[count] >= 'a' && string[count] <= 'z' )
          string[count] = string[count] - 'a' + 'A';
      count++;
    }
}
```

str_count

Name str_count

Description Counts the number of times a specified character is contained within a specified string.

Syntax str_count(string, sub_character)

Variables string (*character pointer*) points to the string being analyzed.

sub_character (*char*) is a single character.

Example
```
output = str_count("abcd",'a');  /* Returns a 1 */
output = str_count("ababa",'a'); /* Returns a 3 */
```

Rules The function must be passed a character pointer followed by a single char.

```
int str_count(char *string, char sub_character)
{
 int count, index;
 count = index = 0;
 while ( string[count] != '\0' )
   { if ( string[count++] == sub_character ) index++;
   }
 return(index);

}
```

Name   str_lindex

Description   Returns an integer value indicating the first location of the specified substring within the string being analyzed.

Syntax   str_lindex(string,sub_string)

Variables   string (*character pointer*) points to the string being analyzed.

sub_string (*character pointer*) points to the substring being searched.

Example   output = str_lindex("abcdefg","cd"); Returns a 3

Rules   The function must be passed two character pointers.

```
int str_lindex(char *string, char sub_string)
{
  int index;
  index = 0;
  while ( string[index] != '\0' && string[index] != sub-
_string)
    ++index;
  return(index);
}
```

str_delete

Name str_delete

Description Deletes a specified number of characters from within a character string as specified by the second and third characters.

Syntax str_delete(string, start_no, no_char)

Variables string (*character pointer*) points to the string being modified.

start_no is the location of the first character to be deleted.

no_char is the number of characters to be deleted.

Example
```
str_delete("abcdefg",3,1); /* Returns abdefg */
str_delete("abcdefg",2,5); /* Returns ag */
```

Rules The second and third characters must be defined as int's.

The start_no value plus the no_char value cannot be greater than the length of the string being modified.

```
void str_delete(char *string, int start, int no_char)
{
  int index1, index2;
  index1 = index2 = 0;
  index2 = start + no_char;
  for ( index1 = start; string[index1] = string[index2];
index1 + + )
    index2 + + ;
}
```

str_lower

Name str_lower(string)

Description Converts uppercase alpha characters to lowercase.

Syntax str_lower(string)

Variables string (*character pointer*) points to the string being modified.

Example
```
strcpy(str,"ABC");
str_convert(str); /*Returns the string abc */

strcpy(str,"abC");
str_convert(str); /*Returns the string abc */
```

Rules The function must be passed a character pointer containing the address of the character string to be converted.

This function does not use a return value and thus may be defined as a void.

```
void str_lower(char *string)
{
  int count;
  count = 0;
  while ( string[count] != '\0' )
    { if ( string[count] > = 'A' && string[count] < = 'Z' )
        string[count] = string[count] + 'a' - 'A';
      count + + ;
    }
}
```

str_lpad

Name	str__lpad
Description	Places a specified number of spaces at the beginning of the passed character string.
Syntax	str__lpad(string, no_char)
Variables	string (*character pointer*) points to the string being modified.
	no_char (*integer*) is the number of spaces to be placed in the string.
Example	str__lpad("ab",2); /* Returns " ab" */
	str__lpad("ab",5); /* Returns " ab" */
Rules	The passed character pointer must be allocated enough memory to contain the added space characters.

```
void str__lpad(char *string, int no_char)
{
 char *temp;
 int count;
 count = 0;
 temp = (char *)malloc(strlen(string)+1+no_char);
 if(temp == NULL)
 { cout << "Error in function str__lpad, could not
   malloc space";
   exit(1);
}
 strcpy(temp,"");
 for ( count = 0; count < no_char; count++)
  strcat(temp," ");
 strcat(temp,string);
 strcpy(string,temp);
}
```

Name   str_rindex

Description Returns an integer value indicating the last location of the specified sub-string within the string being analyzed.

Syntax   str_rindex(string)

Variables   string (*character pointer*) points to the string being analyzed.

sub_string (*character pointer*) points to the substring being searched.

Example   output = str_lindex("abcdefgcd","cd"); Returns an 8

Rules   The function must be passed two character pointers.

```
int str_rindex(char *string, char sub_string)
{
  int index1, index2;
  index1 = index2 = 0;
  while ( string[index1]!= '\0')
   { if ( string[index1] == sub_string ) index2 =
index1;
     ++index1;
   }
return(index2);
}
```

str_rpad

Name   str_rpad

Description Places a specified number of spaces at the end of the passed character string.

Syntax   str_rpad(string,no_char)

Variables string (*character pointer*) points to the string being modified.

           no_char (*integer*) is the number of spaces to be placed in the string.

Example   str_lpad("ab",2); /*Returns "ab " */
           str_lpad("ab",5); /*Returns "ab " */

Rules   The passed character pointer must be allocated enough memory to contain the added space characters.

```
void str_rpad(char *string, int no_char)
{
 int count;
 count = 0;
 for ( count = 0; count < no_char; count++)
  strcat(string," ");
}
```

Name   `str_swap`

Description   Exchanges the contents of two character variables.

Syntax   `str_swap(string1, string2)`

Variables   `string1` is the first character string to be swapped.

              `string2` is the second character string to be swapped.

Example

```
strcpy(a_string,"AAAAA");
strcpy(b_string,"BBBBB");
str_swap(a_string,b_string);

/*Returns: a_string = BBBBB
           b_string = AAAAA */
```

Rules   The strings being swapped must both have enough allocated memory to contain each other's value.

```
void str_swap(char *string1, char *string2)
{
 char *temp;
 temp = (char *)malloc(strlen(string1)+1);
 if(temp == NULL)
 { cout << "Error in function str_swap, cannot malloc
enough memory";
   exit(1);
 }
 strcpy(temp,string1);
 strcpy(string1,string2);
 strcpy(string2,temp);
}
```

str_upper

Name   str_upper

Description   Converts lowercase alpha characters to uppercase.

Syntax   str_upper(string)

Variables   string (*character pointer*) points to the string being modified.

Example
```
strcpy(str,"abc");
str_convert(str); /* Returns the string ABC */

strcpy(str,"abC");
str_convert(str); /* Returns the string ABC */
```

Rules   The function must be passed a character pointer containing the address of the character string to be converted.

This function does not use a return value. Therefore, it may be defined as a void.

```
void str_upper(char *string)
{ int count;
  count = 0;
  while ( string[count] != '\0' )
    { if ( string[count] >= 'a' && string[count] <= 'z' )
      string[count] = string[count] + 'A' - 'a';
      count + + ;
    }
}
```

21
Data input functions (C++)

Data input header file

```
#ifndef HEAD21

#define HEAD21 1

// locate with prompt - string
void get_loc_prompt(int, int, char *, char *);

// locate with prompt - double
double get_loc_prompt(int, int, char *, double);

// locate with prompt - long
long get_loc_prompt(int, int, char *, long );

// locate with prompt for response
void lpr_g_response(int, int, char * );

// locate with prompt for yes or no
void lpr_g_yes_no(int, int, int, int, char *,
                  char *, char *);

// locate with prompt - integer
int get_loc_prompt(int, int, char *, int );

// locate - string
void get_loc(int, int, char *);

// locate - double
double get_loc(int, int, double );

// locate for response
void l_g_response(int, int);

// locate for yes or no
void l_g_yes_no(int, int, int, int, char *, char *);
```

```
// locate - integer
int get_loc(int, int, int );

// prompt - string
void get_prompt(char *, char *);

// prompt - double
double get_prompt(char *, double );

// prompt for response
void pr_g_response(char *);

// prompt for yes or no
void pr_g_yes_no(char *, char *, char *);

// prompt - integer
int get_prompt(char *, int );

#endif

#include <stdlib.h>
#include <conio.h>
#include <stdio.h>
```

get_loc_prompt

Name get_loc_prompt *(ASCII character strings)*

Description Facilitates the input of ASCII character strings. Additionally, prior to the actual input, the cursor is placed at a specified screen location and a prompt is displayed.

Syntax get_loc_prompt(x, y, string, outstring)

Variables string *(character string)* is the vehicle used to receive the prompt displayed on the screen.

x defines the horizontal row on which the cursor will be placed. Consider x to be the "x" part of an "x, y" axis.

y defines the vertical column on which the cursor will be placed. Consider y to be the "y" part of an "x, y" axis.

outstring *(character string)* contains the ASCII character string input by the user.

Examples
```
char ascii_value[10];
lpr_char(10,5,"Enter employee name : ",ascii_value);
```

Rules Any ASCII characters can be entered.

The x value must be between 1 and 24.

The y value must be between 1 and 80.

```
void get_loc_prompt(int x, int y, char *string,
                    char *out_string)

{ gotoxy(y,x);
printf("%s",string);
gets(out_string);
}
```

get_loc_prompt

Name   get_loc_prompt   *(Double floating point numbers)*

Description   Facilitates the input of double floating point numbers. Additionally, prior to the actual input, the cursor is placed at a specified screen location and a prompt is displayed.

Syntax
```
get_loc_prompt(int x, int y, char *string,
               double out_num)
```

Variables   string *(character string)* is the vehicle used to receive the prompt displayed on the screen.

x defines the horizontal row on which the cursor will be placed. Consider x to be the "x" part of an "x, y" axis.

y defines the vertical column on which the cursor will be placed. Consider y to be the "y" part of an "x, y" axis.

out_num is the value to be returned.

Examples
```
double output, lpr_double( );
output = lpr_double(10,5,"Enter employee name : ");
```

Rules   Non-numeric values are ignored; thus, the value 12z3 is converted as 123.

The negative sign may be at either the beginning or ending of the input number.

The function name lpr_double must be defined as a double floating point number within the calling function.

The x value must be between 1 and 24.

The y value must be between 1 and 80.

```
double get_loc_prompt(int x, int y, char *string,
                      double out_num)
{
 char in_num[15];
 printf("%c[%d;%dH",'\33',x,y);
 printf("%s",string);
 gets(in_num);
 out_num = atof(in_num);
 return(out_num);
}
```

get_loc_prompt

Name get_loc_prompt *(Integer numbers)*

Description Facilitates the input of integer numbers. Additionally, prior to the actual input, the cursor is placed at a specified screen location and a prompt is displayed.

Syntax get_loc_prompt(int x, int y, char *string, int)

Variables string *(character string)* receives the prompt displayed on the screen.

x defines the horizontal row on which the cursor will be placed. Consider x to be the "x" part of an "x, y" axis.

y defines the vertical column on which the cursor will be placed. Consider y to be the "y" part of an "x, y" axis.

Examples
```
int output, lpr_integer;
output = lpr_integer(10,5,"Enter employee name : ");
```

Rules Non-numeric values are ignored; thus, the value 12z3 is converted as 123.

The negative sign may be at either the beginning or ending of the input number.

The function name lpr_integer may be optionally defined as an integer number within the calling function.

The x value must be between 1 and 24.

The y value must be between 1 and 80.

Decimal points are ignored.

```
int get_loc_prompt(int x, int y, char *string,
                   int out_num)
{
 char in_num[15];
 gotoxy(y,x);
 printf("%s",string);
 gets(in_num);
 out_num = atoi(in_num);
 return(out_num);
}
```

get_loc_prompt

Name   `get_loc_prompt` *(Long integers)*

Description   Facilitates the input of long integers. Additionally, prior to the actual input, the cursor is placed at a specified screen location and a prompt is displayed.

Syntax
```
get_loc_prompt(int x, int y, char *string,
               long *out_num)
```

Variables   `string` *(character string)* receives the prompt displayed on the screen.

x defines the horizontal row on which the cursor will be placed. Consider x to be the "x" part of an "x, y" axis.

y defines the vertical column on which the cursor will be placed. Consider y to be the "y" part of an "x, y" axis.

Examples
```
long output, lpr_long( ), a_long;
output = lpr_long(10,5,"Enter  employee  name  :
",a_long);
```

Rules   Non-numeric values are ignored; thus, the value 12z3 is converted as 123.

The negative sign may be at either the beginning or ending of the input number.

The function name `lpr_long` must be defined as a long integer number within the calling function.

The x value must be between 1 and 24.

The y value must be between 1 and 80.

```
long get_loc_prompt(int x, int y, char *string,
                    long out_num)
{
char in_num[25];
gotoxy(y,x);
printf("%s",string);
gets(in_num);
out_num = atol(in_num);
return(out_num);
}
```

lpr_g_response

Name   lpr__g__response

Description Facilitates the input of a keyboard response. Additionally, prior to the actual input, the cursor is placed at a specified screen location and a prompt is displayed.

Syntax   lpr__g__response(int x, int y, char *string)

Variables string (*character string*) receives the prompt displayed on the screen.

x defines the horizontal row on which the cursor will be placed. Consider x to be the "x" part of an "x, y" axis.

y defines the vertical column on which the cursor will be placed. Consider y to be the "y" part of an "x, y" axis.

Example   lpr__g__response(10,5,"Hit any key to continue : ");

Rules   The value input is ignored.

The function returns control to the calling module as soon as any keyboard character is pressed.

The x value must be between 1 and 24.

The y value must be between 1 and 80.

```
void lpr__g__response(int x, int y, char *string)
{
 char out__string;
 gotoxy(y,x);
 printf("%s",string);
 getch( );
}
```

lpr_g_yes_no

Name   lpr_g_yes_no

Description   Facilitates the input of a "y" or "n" value. Additionally, prior to the actual input, the cursor is placed at a specified screen location and a prompt is displayed. Also, if an invalid response is entered, an error message is displayed at a user-defined screen location.

Syntax   lpr_g_yes_no(x, y, x_error, y_error, string,
                e_string, out_string)

Variables   string (*character string*) receives the prompt displayed on the screen.

x defines the horizontal row on which the cursor will be placed. Consider x to be the "x" part of an "x, y" axis.

y defines the vertical column on which the cursor will be placed. Consider y to be the "y" part of an "x, y" axis.

x_error defines the horizontal row at which the error message is displayed. Consider x to be the "x" part of an "x, y" axis.

y defines the vertical column at which the error message is displayed. Consider y to be the "y" part of an "x, y" axis.

e_string passes the error message that will be displayed if an invalid response is entered.

out_string contains the yes or no response returned to the calling function.

Examples   char reply[2];
lpr_g_yes_no(5,5,25,5,"Enter Y or N",
            "ERROR, reenter",out_string);

Rules   The reply must be "y", "n", "Y", or "N."

The x and x_error values must be between 1 and 24.

The y and y_error values must be between 1 and 80.

```
void lpr_g_yes_no(int x, int y, int x_error,
                  int y_error, char *string,
    char *e_string, char *out_string)
{ do
    { gotoxy(y,x);
   printf("%s",string);
   gets(out_string);
   if ( *out_string!= 'n' && *out_string!= 'N' &&
      *out_string!= 'y' && *out_string!= 'Y' )
      { gotoxy(y_error,x_error);
```

```
        printf("%s",e_string);
            }
    } while ( *out_string != 'n' && *out_string != 'N' &&
            *out_string != 'y' && *out_string != 'Y' );

}
```

get_loc

Name	`get_loc` *(ASCII character strings)*

Description   Facilitates the input of ASCII character strings. Additionally, prior to the actual input, the cursor is placed at a specified screen location.

Syntax   `get_loc(int x, int y, char *out_string)`

Variables   x defines the horizontal row on which the cursor will be placed. Consider x to be the "x" part of an "x, y" axis.

y defines the vertical column on which the cursor will be placed. Consider y to be the "y" part of an "x, y" axis.

`out_string` *(character string)* contains the ASCII character string input by the user.

Examples
```
char ascii_value[10];
l_char(10,5,ascii_value);
```

Rules   Any ASCII characters can be entered.

The x value must be between 1 and 24.

The y value must be between 1 and 80.

```
void get_loc(int x, int y, char *out_string)
{
 gotoxy(y,x);
 gets(out_string);
}
```

get_loc

Name get_loc *(Double floating point numbers)*

Description Facilitates the input of double floating point numbers. Additionally, prior to the actual input, the cursor is placed at a specified screen location.

Syntax get_loc(int x, int y, double *out_num)

Variables x defines the horizontal row on which the cursor will be placed. Consider x to be the "x" part of an "x, y" axis.

y defines the vertical column on which the cursor will be placed. Consider y to be the "y" part of an "x, y" axis.

Examples
```
double output, l_double( );
output = l_double(10,5);
```

Rules Non-numeric values are ignored; thus, the value 12z3 is converted as 123.

The negative sign may be at either the beginning or ending of the input number.

The function name l_double must be defined as a double floating point number within the calling function.

The x value must be between 1 and 24.

The y value must be between 1 and 80.

```
double get_loc(int x, int y, double out_num)
{
 char in_num[15];
 gotoxy(y,x);
 gets(in_num);
 out_num = atof(in_num);
 return(out_num);
}
```

get_loc

Name   `get_loc`   *(Integer numbers)*

Description Facilitates the input of integer numbers. Additionally, prior to the actual input, the cursor is placed at a specified screen location.

Syntax   `get_loc(int x, int y, int *out_num)`

Variables x defines the horizontal row on which the cursor will be placed. Consider x to be the "x" part of an "x, y" axis.

y defines the vertical column on which the cursor will be placed. Consider y to be the "y" part of an "x, y" axis.

Examples
```
int output, I_integer;
output = I_integer(10,5);
```

Rules   Non-numeric values are ignored; thus, the value 12z3 is converted as 123.

The negative sign may be at either the beginning or ending of the input number.

The function name `I_integer` may be optionally defined as an integer number within the calling function.

The x value must be between 1 and 24.

The y value must be between 1 and 80.

Decimal points are ignored.

```
int get_loc(int x, int y, int out_num)
{
 char in_num[15];
 gotoxy(y,x);
 gets(in_num);
 out_num = atoi(in_num);
 return(out_num);
}
```

l_g_response

Name l__g__response

Description Facilitates the input of a keyboard response. Additionally, prior to the actual input, the cursor is placed at a specified screen location.

Syntax l__g__response(int x, int y)

Variables x defines the horizontal row on which the cursor will be placed. Consider x to be the "x" part of an "x, y" axis.

y defines the vertical column on which the cursor will be placed. Consider y to be the "y" part of an "x, y" axis.

Example l__g__response(10,5);

Rules The value input is ignored.

The function returns control to the calling module as soon as any keyboard character is pressed.

The x value must be between 1 and 24.

The y value must be between 1 and 80.

```
void l__g__response(int x, int y)
{
 gotoxy(y,x);
 getch( );
}
```

l_g_yes_no

Name	l_g_yes_no
Description	Facilitates the input of a "y" or "n" value. Additionally, prior to the actual input, the cursor is placed at a specified screen location and a prompt is displayed. Also, if an invalid response is entered, an error message is displayed.
Syntax	l_g_yes_no(x, y, x_error, y_error, e_string, out_string)
Variables	x defines the horizontal row on which the cursor will be placed. Consider x to be the "x" part of an "x, y" axis.
	y defines the vertical column on which the cursor will be placed. Consider y to be the "y" part of an "x, y" axis.
	x_error defines the horizontal row at which the error message is displayed. Consider x to be the "x" part of an "x, y" axis.
	y defines the vertical column at which the error message is displayed. Consider y to be the "y" part of an "x, y" axis.
	e_string passes the error message that will be displayed if an invalid response is entered.
	out_string contains the yes or no response returned to the calling function.
Examples	char reply[2]; l_g_yes_no(5,5,25,5,"ERROR, reenter", out_string);
Rules	The reply must be "y", "n", "Y", or "N."
	The x and x_error values must be between 1 and 24.
	The y and y_error values must be between 1 and 80.

```
void l_g_yes_no(int x, int y, int x_error,
                int y_error, char *e_string,
    char *out_string)
{ do
  { gotoxy(y,x);
    gets(out_string);
    if ( *out_string != 'n' && *out_string != 'N' &&
        *out_string != 'y' && *out_string != 'Y' )
        { gotoxy(y_error,x_error);
    printf("%s",e_string);
      }
    } while ( *out_string != 'n' && *out_string != 'N' &&
            *out_string != 'y' && *out_string != 'Y' );
}
```

get_prompt

Name   `get_prompt`   *(ASCII character strings)*

Description   Facilitates the input of ASCII character strings. Additionally, prior to the actual input, a specified prompt is displayed.

Syntax   `get_prompt(string, outstring)`

Variables   `string` *(character string)* receives the prompt displayed on the screen.

                 `outstring` contains the ASCII character string input by the user.

Examples
```
char ascii_value[10];
pr_char("Enter employee name : ",ascii_value);
```

Rules   Any ASCII characters can be entered.

```
void get_prompt(char *string, char *out_string)
{ printf("%s",string);
  gets(out_string);
}
```

get_prompt

Name   get_prompt   *(Double floating point numbers)*

Description Facilitates the input of double floating point numbers. Additionally, prior to the actual input, a specified prompt is displayed.

Syntax   get_prompt(char *string, double *out_num)

Variables   string *(character string)* receives the prompt displayed on the screen.

Examples
```
double output, pr_double( );
output = lpr_double("Enter employee name : ");
```

Rules   Non-numeric values are ignored; thus, the value 12z3 is converted as 123.

The negative sign may be at either the beginning or ending of the input number.

The function name pr_double must be defined as a double floating point number within the calling function.

```
double get_prompt(char *string, double out_num)
{
 char in_num[15];
 printf("%s",string);
 gets(in_num);
 out_num = atof(in_num);
 return(out_num);
}
```

get_prompt

Name   `get_prompt`   *(Integer numbers)*

Description   Facilitates the input of integer numbers. Additionally, prior to the actual input, a specified prompt is displayed.

Syntax   `get_prompt(string)`

Variables   `string` *(character string)* receives the prompt displayed on the screen.

Examples
```
int output, pr_integer;
output = pr_integer("Enter employee name : ");
```

Rules   Non-numeric values are ignored; thus, the value 12z3 is converted as 123.

The negative sign may be at either the beginning or ending of the input number.

The function name `pr_integer` may be optionally defined as an integer number within the calling function.

Decimal points are ignored.

```
get_prompt(char *string, int out_num)
{
 char in_num[15];
 printf("%s",string);
 gets(in_num);
 out_num = atoi(in_num);
 return(out_num);
}
```

pr_g_response

Name   `pr__g__response`

Description Facilitates the input of a keyboard response. Additionally, prior to the actual input, a specified prompt is displayed.

Syntax   `pr__g__response(char *string)`

Variables   `string` (*character string*) receives the prompt displayed on the screen.

Example   `pr__g__response("Hit any key to continue : ");`

Rules   The value input is ignored.

The function returns control to the calling module as soon as any keyboard character is pressed.

```
void pr__g__response(char *string)
{ char *out__string;
 printf("%s",string);
 getch( );
}
```

pr_g_yes_no

Name   pr_g_yes_no

Description Facilitates the input of a "y" or "n" value. Additionally, prior to the actual input, a specified prompt is displayed. Also, if an invalid response is entered, an error message is displayed.

Syntax   pr_g_yes_no(string, e_string, out_string)

Variables string (*character string*) receives the prompt displayed on the screen.

e_string passes the error message that will be displayed if an invalid response is entered.

out_string contains the yes or no response returned to the calling function.

Examples
```
char reply[2];
pr_g_yes_no("Enter  Y  or  N","ERROR,  reenter",out
_string);
```

Rules   The reply must be "y", "n", "Y", or "N."

```
void pr_g_yes_no(char *string, char *e_string,
                    char *out_string)
{
 do
   { printf("%s",string);
     gets(out_string);
     if ( *out_string!= 'n' && *out_string!= 'N' &&
         *out_string!= 'y' && *out_string!= 'Y' )
         { printf("\n%s",e_string);
         }
   } while ( *out_string!= 'n' && *out_string!= 'N' &&
           *out_string!= 'y' && *out_string!= 'Y' );

}
```

22

Array manipulation functions (C++)

Array manipulation header file

```
#ifndef HEAD22

#define HEAD22 1

double calc_ave(double *, int);
int calc_ave(int *, int);

int is_found(double *, int, double);
int is_found(int *, int, int);

double get_max(double *, int);
int get_max(int *, int);

double get_mean(double *, int);
int get_mean(int *, int);

double get_min(double *, int);
int get_min(int *, int);

int do_search(double *, int, double);
int do_search(int *, int, int);

double calc_sum(double *, int);
int calc_sum(int *, int);

#endif
```

calc_ave

Name   calc_ave   *(Double pointer)*

Description   Receives both an array starting location and the number of elements in that array and then calculates a numeric average of its contents.

Syntax   calc_ave(start,size)

Variables   start *(double pointer)* specifies the memory address of the first array element.

size *(integer)* specifies the number of array members.

Example   ave = ad_ave(d_array,50)

Rules   The calling program must define the function ad_ave() and the function's return value as a double. ad_ave() may be defined globally by use of the head25.h header file.

The size parameter denoting the number of elements contained within the array must be defined as an integer.

Calling Ex.

```
double a_array[50];
double out_average;
int a_size;
double ad_ave();

a_size = 50;
out_average = ad_ave(a_array,a_size);
```

Routine

```
double calc_ave(double *start, int size)
{
  int count;
  double sum = 0;

  double average = 0;
  for ( count=0; count < size; count++ )
    { sum += (*start++);
    }
    average = sum / count;
    return(average);
}
```

calc_ave

Name   calc_ave   *(Integer pointer)*

Description   Receives both an array starting location and the number of elements in that array and then calculates a numeric average of its contents.

Syntax   calc_ave(start,size)

Variables   start *(integer pointer)* specifies the memory address of the first array element.

size *(integer)* specifies the number of array members.

Example   ave = ai__ave(d__array,50)

Rules   The calling program must define the function ai__ave() and the function's return value as a integer. ai__ave() may be defined globally by use of the head25.h header file.

The size parameter denoting the number of elements contained within the array must be defined as an integer.

Calling Ex.
```
int a__array[50];5
  int out__average;
  int a__size;
  int ai__ave();

  a__size = 50;
  out__average = ai__ave(a__array,a__size);
```

Routine
```
calc__ave(int *start, int size)
{
  int count;
  int sum = 0;
  int average = 0;
  for ( count=0; count < size; count++ )
    { sum += (*start++);
    }
  average = sum/count;
  return(average);
}
```

Name   is_found

Description   Receives an array starting location, the number of elements in that array, and the appropriate search value, and then returns the number of times that the value appears in the array.

Syntax   is_found(start,size,value)

Variables   start (*double pointer*) specifies the memory address of the first array element.

size (*integer*) specifies the number of array members.

value contains the value to be searched for within the array.

Example   ave = ad_found(d_array,50,20.01)

Rules   This function must be passed a variable defined as a pointer to a double. However, the calling program must define the function ad_found() and the function's return value as an integer. ad_found() may be defined globally by use of the head25.h header file.

The size parameter denoting the number of elements contained within the array must be defined as an integer.

The value parameter must be defined as a double.

Calling Ex.
```
double a_array[50];
 double d_value;
 int output;
 int a_size;
 int ad_found();

 a_size = 50;
 d_value = 25.1;
 output = ad_found(a_array,a_size);
```

Routine
```
is_found(double *start,int size, double value)
{
  int count;
  int found = 0;
  for ( count=0; count < size; count++ )
    { if ( (*start++) == value ) found++;
    }
  return(found);
}
```

is_found

Name	is_found

Description   Receives an array starting location, the number of elements in that array, and the appropriate search value, and then returns the number of times that the value appears in the array.

Syntax   is_found(start,size,value)

Variables   start (*integer pointer*) specifies the memory address of the first array element.

size (*integer*) specifies the number of array members.

value contains the value to be searched for within the array.

Example   ave = ai_found(d_array,50,20)

Rules   This function must be passed a variable defined as a pointer to an int. Additionally, the calling program must define the function ai_found() and the function's return value as an integer. ai_found() may be defined globally by use of the head25.h header file.

The size parameter denoting the number of elements contained within the array must be defined as an integer.

The value parameter must be defined as an int.

Calling Ex.
```
int a_array[50];
  int d_value;
  int output;
  int a_size;
  int ai_found();

  a_size = 50;
  d_value = 25.1;
  output = ai_found(a_array,a_size);
```

Routine
```
is_found(int *start, int size, int value)
{
  int count;
  int found = 0;
  for ( count=0; count < size; count++ )
    { if ( (*start++) == value ) found++;
    }
    return(found);
}
```

get_max

Name	get_max *(Double)*
Description	Receives both an array starting location and the number of elements in that array and then returns the largest value contained within that array.
Syntax	get_max(start,size)
Variables	start *(double pointer)* specifies the memory address of the first array element.
	size *(integer)* specifies the number of array members.
Example	maximum = ad_max(d_array,50)
Rules	The calling program must define the function ad_max() and the function's return value as a double. ad_max() may be defined globally by use of the head25.h header file.
	The size parameter denoting the number of elements contained within the array must be defined as an integer.

Calling Ex.

```
double a_array[50];
  double output;
  int a_size;
  double ad_max();

  a_size = 50;
  output = ad_max(a_array,a_size);
```

Routine

```
double get_max(double *start, int size)
{
  int count;
  double max_value;
  max_value = (*start);
  for ( count=0; count < size; count++ )
    { if ( (*start) > max_value ) max_value = (*start);
      start++;
    }
  return(max_value);
}
```

get_max

Name	get_max *(Integer)*
Description	Receives both an array starting location and the number of elements in that array and then returns the largest value contained within that array.
Syntax	get_max(start,size)
Variables	start *(integer pointer)* specifies the memory address of the first array element.
	size *(integer)* specifies the number of array members.
Example	maximum = ai_max(d_array,50)
Rules	The calling program must define the function ai_max() and the function's return value as a integer. ai_max() may be defined globally by use of the head25.h header file.
	The size parameter denoting the number of elements contained within the array must be defined as an integer.

Calling Ex.

```
int a_array[50];
int output;
int a_size;
int ai_max();

a_size = 50;
output = ai_max(a_array,a_size);
```

Routine

```
get_max(int *start, int size)
{
  int count;
  int max_value;
  max_value = (*start);
  for ( count=0; count < size; count++ )
   { if ( (*start) > max_value ) max_value = (*start);
     start++;
   }
 return(max_value);
}
```

get_mean

Name	get_mean *(Double)*
Description	Receives both an array starting location and the number of elements in that array and then calculates a numeric mean of its contents.
Syntax	get_mean(start,size)
Variables	start *(double pointer)* specifies the memory address of the first array element.
	size *(integer)* number specifies the number of array members.
Example	mean = ad_mean(d_array,50)
Rules	This function must be passed a variable defined as a pointer to a double. Additionally, the calling program must define the function ad_mean() and the function's return value as a double.
	The size parameter denoting the number of elements contained within the array must be defined as an integer.
Calling Ex.	double a_array[50];

```
    double output;
    int a_size;
    double ad_mean();

    a_size = 50;
    output = ad_mean(a_array,a_size);
```

Routine

```
double get_mean(double *start, int size)
{
  int count;
  double max_value, min_value, mean_value;
  max_value = (*start);
  min_value = (*start);
  for ( count=0; count < size; count++ )
    { if ( (*start) > max_value ) max_value = (*start);
      if ( (*start) < min_value ) min_value = (*start);
      start++;
    }
  mean_value = ( max_value + min_value ) / 2;
  return(mean_value);
}
```

get_mean

Name	get_mean *(Integer)*
Description	Receives both an array starting location and the number of elements in that array and then calculates a numeric mean of its contents.
Syntax	get_mean(start,size)
Variables	start *(integer pointer)* specifies the memory address of the first array element. size *(integer)* specifies the number of array members.
Example	ave = ai_mean(d_array,50)
Rules	The calling program must define the function ai_mean() and the function's return value as an integer. ai_mean() may be defined globally by use of the head25.h header file. The size parameter denoting the number of elements contained within the array must be defined as an integer.

Calling Ex.

```
int a_array[50];
  int output;
  int a_size;
  int ai_mean();

  a_size = 50;
  output = ai_mean(a_array,a_size);
```

Routine

```
get_mean(int *start, int size)
{
  int count;
  int max_value, min_value, mean_value;
  max_value = (*start);
  min_value = (*start);
  for ( count=0; count < size; count++ )
    { if ( (*start) > max_value ) max_value = (*start);
      if ( (*start) < min_value ) min_value = (*start);
      start++;
    }
  mean_value = ( max_value + min_value ) / 2;
  return(mean_value);
}
```

get_min

Name	`get_min` *(Double)*
Description	Receives both an array starting location and the number of elements in that array and then returns the minimum array value.
Syntax	`get_min(start,size)`
Variables	`start` *(pointer double)* specifies the memory address of the first array element.
	`size` *(integer)* specifies the number of array members.
Example	`minimum = ad_min(d_array,50)`
Rules	The calling program must define the function `ad_min()` and the function's return value as a double. `ad_min()` may be defined globally by use of the head25.h header file.
	The size parameter denoting the number of elements contained within the array must be defined as an integer.
| **Calling Ex.** | ```
double a_array[50];
double output;

int a_size;
double ad_min();

a_size = 50;
output = ad_min(a_array,a_size);
``` |
| **Routine** | ```
double get_min(double *start, int size)
{
  int count;
  double min_value;
  min_value = (*start);
  for ( count=0; count < size; count++ )
    { if ( (*start) < min_value ) min_value = (*start);
      start++;
    }
  return(min_value);
}
``` |

get_min

Name	get_min
Description	Receives both an array starting location and the number of elements in that array and then returns the smallest value contained within that array.
Syntax	get_min(start,size)
Variables	start (*integer pointer*) specifies the memory address of the first array element.
	size (*integer*) specifies the number of array members.
Example	minimum = ai_min(d_array,50)
Rules	The calling program must define the function ai_min() and the function's return value as an integer. ai_min() may be defined globally by use of the head25.h header file.
	The size parameter denoting the number of elements contained within the array must be defined as an integer.

Calling Ex.
```
int a_array[50];
  int output;
  int a_size;
  int ai_min();

  a_size = 50;
  output = ai_min(a_array,a_size);
```

Routine
```
get_min(int *start, int size)
{
  int count;
  int min_value;
  min_value = (*start);
  for ( count=0; count < size; count++ )
    { if ( (*start) < min_value ) min_value = (*start);
      start++;
    }
  return(min_value);
}
```

do_search

Name do_search *(Double)*

Description Receives an array starting location, the number of elements in that array, and the appropriate search value, and then returns the location of the first occurrence of that value.

Syntax do_search(start,size,value)

Variables start *(double pointer)* specifies the memory address of the first array element.

size *(integer)* specifies the number of array members.

value contains the value to be searched for within the array.

Example location = ad_search(d_array,50,20.0l)

Rules The function must be passed a variable defined as a pointer to a double. However, the calling program must define the function ad_search() and the function's return value as an integer. ad_search() may be defined globally by use of the head25.h header file.

The size parameter denoting the number of elements contained within the array must be defined as an integer.

The value parameter must be defined as a double.

Calling Ex.
```
double a_array[50];
  double d_value;
  int a_size, output;
  int ad_search();

  a_size = 50;
  d_value = 25.1;
  output = ad_search(a_array,a_size);
```

Routine
```
do_search(double *start, int size, double value)
{
  int count;
  int location = -1;
  for ( count=0; count < size; count++ )
    { if ( (*start++) == value )
      { location = count;
        break;
      }
    }
  return(location);
}
```

do_search

Name	do_search *(Integer)*
Description	Receives an array starting location, the number of elements in that array, and the appropriate search value, and then returns the location of the first occurrence of that value.
Syntax	do_search(start,size,value)
Variables	start *(integer pointer)* specifies the memory address of the first array element.
	size *(integer)* specifies the number of array members.
	value contains the value to be searched for within the array.
Example	location = ai_search(d_array,50,20)
Rules	The function must be passed a variable defined as a pointer to an int. However, the calling program must define the function ai_search() and the function's return value as an integer. ai_search() may be defined globally by use of the head25.h header file.
	The size parameter denoting the number of elements contained within the array must be defined as an integer.
	The value parameter must be defined as an int.
Calling Ex.	`int a_array[50];`

```
int a_array[50];
 int d_value;
 int a_size, output;
 int ai_search();

 a_size = 50;
 d_value = 25;
 output = ai_search(a_array,a_size);
```

Routine

```
do_search(int *start, int size, int value)
{
  int count;
  int location = -1;
  for ( count=0; count < size; count++ )
    { if ( (*start++) == value )
      { location = count;
        break;
      }
    }
  return(location);
}
```

calc_sum

Name   calc_sum(start,size)   *(Double)*

Description   Receives both an array starting location and the number of elements in that array, and then calculates the sum of its contents.

Syntax   calc_sum(start,size)

Variables   start *(double pointer)* specifies the memory address of the first array element.

size *(integer)* specifies the number of array members.

Example   sum = ad_sum(d_array,50)

Rules   This function must be passed a variable defined as a pointer to a double. Additionally, the calling program must define the function ad_sum() and the function's return value as a double. ad_sum() may be defined globally by use of the head25.h header file.

The size parameter denoting the number of elements contained within the array must be defined as an integer.

Calling Ex.
```
double a_array[50];
  double output;
  int a_size;
  double ad_sum();

  a_size = 50;
  output = ad_sum(a_array,a_size);
```

Routine
```
double calc_sum(double *start, int size)
{
  int count;
  double sum = 0;
  for ( count=0; count < size; count++ )
    { sum += (*start++);
}
  return(sum);
}
```

calc_sum

Name   calc_sum   *(Integer)*

Description   Receives both an array starting location and the number of elements in that array and then calculates the sum of its contents.

Syntax   calc_sum(start,size)

Variables   start *(integer pointer)* specifies the memory address of the first array element.

             size *(integer)* specifies the number of array members.

Example   sum = ai_sum(d_array,50)

Rules   The calling program must define the function ai_sum() and the function's return value as an int. ai_sum() may be defined globally by use of the head25.h header file.

             The size parameter denoting the number of elements contained within the array must be defined as an integer.

Calling Ex.
```
int a_array[50];
  int output;
  int a_size;
  int ai_sum();

  a_size = 50;
  output = ai_sum(a_array,a_size);
```

Routine
```
calc_sum(int *start, int size)
{
  int count;
  int sum = 0;
  for ( count=0; count < size; count++)
    { sum += (*start++);
    }
  return(sum);
}
```

23

Measurement conversion functions

Measurement conversion header file

```
#ifndef HEAD23

#define HEAD23 1

double cmet_feet(double);        // centimeters to feet
double cmet_inch(double);        // centimeters to inches
double feet_cmet(double);        // feet to centimeters
double gal_liter(double);        // gallons to liters
double gram_ounce(double);       // grams to ounces
double inch_cmet(double);        // inches to centimeters
double inch_met(double);         // inches to meters
double kgram_ounce(double);      // kilograms to ounces
double kgram_pound(double);      // kilograms to pounds
double kmet_mile(double);        // kilometers to miles
double liter_gal(double);        // liters to gallons
double liter_quart(double);      // liters to quarts
double met_inch(double);         // meters to inches
double met_yards(double);        // meters to yards
double mile_kmet(double);        // miles to kilometers
double ounce_gram(double);       // ounces to grams
double ounce_kgram(double);      // ounces to kilograms
double pound_kgram(double);      // pounds to kilograms
double quart_liter(double);      // quarts to liters
double yards_met(double);        // yards to meters

#endif
```

cmet_feet

Name	cmet_feet
Description	Converts centimeters to feet.
Syntax	cmet_feet(cmet)
Variables	cmet is the input parameter and contains the number of centimeters to be converted.
	feet is the function's return value and contains the number of feet corresponding to the centimeter value in cmet.
Example	output = cmet_feet(5) /* Returns value .164 */ output = cmet_feet(10) /* Returns value .328 */
Rules	This function must be passed a variable defined as a double. Additionally, the calling program must define the function cmet_feet( ) and the function's return value as a double.

Calling ex.	double input;
	  double output;
	  double cmet_feet( );
	
	  input = 15;
	  output = cmet_feet(input);

Routine	double cmet_feet(double cmet)
	{
	 double feet;
	 feet = cmet * .0328;
	 return(feet);
	}

Name   `cmet_inch`

Description   Converts centimeters to inches.

Syntax   `cmet_inch(cmet)`

Variables   `cmet` is the input parameter and contains the number of centimeters to be converted.

                 `inch` is the function's return value and contains the number of inches corresponding to the centimeter value in `cmet`.

Example
```
output = cmet_inch(5)    /* Returns value 1.97 */
output = cmet_inch(10)   /* Returns value 3.94 */
```

Rules   This function must be passed a variable defined as a `double`. Additionally, the calling program must define the function `cmet_inch( )` and the function's return value as a double.

Calling ex.
```
double input;
 double output;
 double cmet_inch( );

 input = 15;
 output = cmet_inch(input);
```

Routine
```
double cmet_inch(double cmet)
{
 double inch;
 inch = cmet * .394;
 return(inch);
}
```

feet_cmet

Name   feet_cmet

Description   Converts feet to centimeters.

Syntax   feet_cmet(feet)

Variables   feet is the input parameter and contains the number of feet to be converted.

cmet is the function's return value and contains the number of centimeters corresponding to the feet value in feet.

Example
```
output = feet_cmet(5)    /* Returns value 152.4 */
output = feet_cmet(10)   /* Returns value 304.8 */
```

Rules   This function must be passed a variable defined as a double. Additionally, the calling program must define the function feet_cmet( ) and the function's return value as a double.

Calling ex.
```
double input;
 double output;
 double feet_cmet( );

 input = 15;
 output = feet_cmet(input);
```

Routine
```
double feet_cmet(double feet)
{
 double cmet;
 cmet = feet * 30.48;
 return(cmet);
}
```

Name   gal_liter

Description   Converts gallons to liters.

Syntax   gal_liter(gal)

Variables   gal is the input parameter and contains the number of gallons to be converted.

liter is the function's return value and contains the number of centimeters corresponding to the liters value in gal.

Example   output = gal_liter(5)   /* Returns value 18.925 */
output = gal_liter(10) /* Returns value 37.85 */

Rules   This function must be passed a variable defined as a double. Additionally, the calling program must define the function gal_liter( ) and
the function's return value as a double.

Calling ex.
```
double input;
 double output;
 double gal_liter( );

 input = 15;
 output = gal_liter(input);
```

Routine
```
double gal_liter(double gal)
{
 double liter;
 liter = gal * 3.785;
 return(liter);
}
```

gram_ounce

Name   gram_ounce

Description Converts grams to ounces.

Syntax   gram_ounce(gram)

Variables   gram is the input parameter and contains the number of grams to be converted.

ounce is the function's return value and contains the number of ounces corresponding to the value in gram.

Example
```
output = gram_ounce(5)   /* Returns value .175 */
output = gram_ounce(10)  /* Returns value .35  */
```

Rules   This function must be passed a variable defined as a double. Additionally, the calling program must define the function gram_ounce( ) and the function's return value as a double.

Calling ex.
```
double input;
  double output;
  double gram_ounce( );

  input = 15;
  output = gram_ounce(input);
```

Routine
```
double gram_ounce(double gram)
{
  double ounce;
  ounce = gram * .035;
  return(ounce);
}
```

Name inch_cmet

Description Converts inches to centimeters.

Syntax inch_cmet(inch)

Variables inch is the input parameter and contains the number of inch to be converted.

cmet is the function's return value and contains the number of centimeters corresponding to the value in inch.

Example
```
output = inch_cmet(5)   /* Returns value 12.7 */
output = inch_cmet(10) /* Returns value 25.4 */
```

Rules This function must be passed a variable defined as a double. Additionally, the calling program must define the function inch_cmet( ) and the function's return value as a double.

Calling ex.
```
double input;
 double output;
 double inch_cmet( );

 input = 15;
 output = inch_cmet(input);
```

Routine
```
double inch_cmet(double inch)
{
 double cmet;
 cmet = inch * 2.54;
 return(cmet);
}
```

inch_met

Name   inch_met

Description   Converts inches to meters.

Syntax   inch_met(inch)

Variables   inch is the input parameter and contains the number of inch to be converted.

met is the function's return value and contains the number of centimeters corresponding to the value in inch.

Example
```
output = inch_met(5)   /* Returns value .127 */
output = inch_met(10)  /* Returns value .254 */
```

Rules   This function must be passed a variable defined as a double. Additionally, the calling program must define the function inch_met( ) and the function's return value as a double.

Calling ex.
```
double input;
double output;
double inch_met( );

input = 15;
output = inch_met(input);
```

Routine
```
double inch_met(double inch)
{
double met;
met = inch / 39.37;
return(met);
}
```

Name   `kgram_ounce`

Description   Converts kilograms to ounces.

Syntax   `kgram_ounce(kgram)`

Variables   `kgram` is the input parameter and contains the number of kilograms to be converted.

    `ounce` is the function's return value and contains the number of ounces corresponding to the value in `kgram`.

Example
```
output = kgram_ounce(5)   /* Returns value 176.36 */
output = kgram_ounce(10)  /* Returns value 352.72 */
```

Rules   This function must be passed a variable defined as a `double`. Additionally, the calling program must define the function `kgram_ounce( )` and the function's return value as a double.

Calling ex.
```
double input;
 double output;
 double kgram_ounce( );

 input = 15;
 output = kgram_ounce(input);
```

Routine
```
double kgram_ounce(double kgram)
{
 double ounce;
 ounce = kgram * 35.272;
 return(ounce);
}
```

kgram_pound

Name	kgram_pound
Description	Converts kilograms to pounds.
Syntax	kgram_pound(kgram)
Variables	kgram is the input parameter and contains the number of kilograms to be converted.
	pound is the function's return value and contains the number of pounds corresponding to the value in kgram.

Example

```
output = kgram_pound(5)   /* Returns value 11.025 */
output = kgram_pound(10)  /* Returns value 22.05  */
```

Rules

This function must be passed a variable defined as a double. Additionally, the calling program must define the function kgram_pound( ) and the function's return value as a double.

Calling ex.

```
double input;
 double output;
 double kgram_pound( );

 input = 15;
 output = kgram_pound(input);
```

Routine

```
double kgram_pound(double kgram)
{
 double pound;
 pound = kgram * 2.205;
 return(pound);
}
```

kmet_mile

Name   kmet_mile

Description   Converts kilometers to miles.

Syntax   kmet_mile(kmet)

Variables   kmet is the input parameter and contains the number of kilometers to be converted.

mile is the function's return value and contains the number of miles corresponding to the value in kmet.

Example
```
output = kmet_mile(5)   /* Returns value 3.105 */
output = kmet_mile(10)  /* Returns value 6.21  */
```

Rules   This function must be passed a variable defined as a double. Additionally, the calling program must define the function kmet_mile( ) and the function's return value as a double.

Calling ex.
```
double input;
 double output;
 double kmet_mile( );

 input = 15;
 output = kmet_mile(input);
```

Routine
```
double kmet_mile(double kmet)
{
 double mile;
 mile = kmet * .621;
 return(mile);
}
```

liter_gal

Name	liter__gal
Description	Converts liters to gallons.
Syntax	liter__gal(liter)
Variables	liter is the input parameter and contains the number of liters to be converted.
	gal is the function's return value and contains the number of gallons corresponding to the value in liter.

Example

```
output = liter__gal(5)   /* Returns value 1.32 */
output = liter__gal(10) /* Returns value 2.64 */
```

Rules

This function must be passed a variable defined as a double. Additionally, the calling program must define the function liter__gal( ) and the function's return value as a double.

Calling ex.

```
double input;
 double output;
 double liter__gal( );

 input = 15;
 output = liter__gal(input);
```

Routine

```
double liter__gal(double liter)
{
 double gal;
 gal = liter * .264;
 return(gal);
}
```

liter_quart

Name liter_quart(liter)

Description Converts liters to quarts.

Syntax liter_quart(liter)

Variables liter is the input parameter and contains the number of liters to be converted.

quart is the function's return value and contains the number of quarts corresponding to the value in liter.

Example
```
output = liter_quart(5)   /* Returns value 5.285 */
output = liter_quart(10)  /* Returns value 10.57 */
```

Rules This function must be passed a variable defined as a double. Additionally, the calling program must define the function liter_quart( ) and the function's return value as a double.

Calling ex.
```
double input;
  double output;
  double liter_quart( );

  input = 15;
  output = liter_quart(input);
```

Routine
```
double liter_quart(double liter)
{
  double quart;
  quart = liter * 1.057;
  return(quart);
}
```

met_inch

Name	met_inch
Description	Converts meters to inches.
Syntax	met_inch(met)

Variables   met is the input parameter and contains the number of meters to be converted.

inches is the function's return value and contains the number of inches corresponding to the value in met.

Example
```
output = met_inch(5)    /* Returns value 196.85 */
output = met_inch(10)  /* Returns value 393.7 */
```

Rules   This function must be passed a variable defined as a double. Additionally, the calling program must define the function met_inch( ) and the function's return value as a double.

Calling ex.
```
double input;
double output;
double met_inch( );

input = 15;
output = met_inch(input);
```

Routine
```
double met_inch(double met)
{
double inch;
inch = met * 39.37;
return(inch);
}
```

Name   met_yards

Description   Converts meters to yards.

Syntax   met_yards(yards)

Variables   met is the input parameter and contains the number of meters to be converted.

yards is the function's return value and contains the number of yards corresponding to the value in met.

Example
```
output = met_yards(5)    /* Returns value 5.465 */
output = met_yards(10)   /* Returns value 10.93 */
```

Rules   This function must be passed a variable defined as a double. Additionally, the calling program must define the function met_yards( ) and the function's return value as a double.

Calling ex.
```
double input;
 double output;
 double met_yards( );

 input = 15;
 output = met_yards(input);
```

Routine
```
double met_yards(double met)
{
double yards;
yards = met * 1.093;
return(yards);
}
```

mile_kmet

Name	mile__kmet
Description	Converts miles to kilometers.
Syntax	mile__kmet(mile)
Variables	mile is the input parameter and contains the number of miles to be converted.
	kmet is the function's return value and contains the number of kilometers corresponding to the value in mile.

Example

```
output = mile__kmet(5)   /* Returns value 8.045 */
output = mile__kmet(10) /* Returns value 16.09 */
```

Rules

This function must be passed a variable defined as a double. Additionally, the calling program must define the function mile__kmet( ) and the function's return value as a double.

Calling ex.

```
double input;
 double output;
 double mile__kmet( );

 input = 15;
 output = mile__kmet(input);
```

Routine

```
double mile__kmet(double mile)
{
 double kmet;
 kmet = mile * 1.609;
 return(kmet);
}
```

Name   `ounce_gram`

Description   Converts ounces to grams.

Syntax   `ounce_gram(ounce)`

Variables   `ounce` is the input parameter and contains the number of ounces to be converted.

gram is the function's return value and contains the number of grams corresponding to the value in `ounce`.

Example

```
output = ounce_gram(5)   /* Returns value 141.75 */
output = ounce_gram(10)  /* Returns value 283.50 */
```

Rules   This function must be passed a variable defined as a `double`. Additionally, the calling program must define the function `ounce_gram( )` and the function's return value as a double.

Calling ex.

```
double input;
 double output;
 double ounce_gram( );

 input = 15;
 output = ounce_gram(input);
```

Routine

```
double ounce_gram(double ounce)
{
 double gram;
 gram = ounce * 28.35;
 return(gram);
}
```

ounce_kgram

Name	ounce_kgram
Description	Converts ounces to kilograms.
Syntax	ounce_kgram(ounce)
Variables	ounce is the input parameter and contains the number of ounces to be converted.
	kgram is the function's return value and contains the number of kilograms corresponding to the value in ounce.

Example

```
output = ounce_kgram(5)   /*Returns value .14 */
output = ounce_kgram(10) /* Returns value .28 */
```

Rules

This function must be passed a variable defined as a double. Additionally, the calling program must define the function ounce_kgram( ) and the function's return value as a double.

Calling ex.

```
double input;
 double output;
 double ounce_kgram( );

 input = 15;
 output = ounce_kgram(input);
```

Routine

```
double ounce_kgram(double ounce)
{
 double kgram;
 kgram = ounce * .028;
 return(kgram);
}
```

pound_kgram

Name   pound_kgram

Description Converts pounds to kilograms.

Syntax   `pound_kgram(ounce)`

Variables   `pound` is the input parameter and contains the number of pounds to be converted.

`kgram` is the function's return value and contains the number of kilograms corresponding to the value in `pound`.

Example
```
output = pound_kgram(5)   /* Returns value 2.27 */
output = pound_kgram(10)  /* Returns value 4.54 */
```

Rules   This function must be passed a variable defined as a `double`. Additionally, the calling program must define the function `pound_kgram( )` and the function's return value as a double.

Calling ex.
```
double input;
 double output;
 double pound_kgram( );

 input = 15;
 output = pound_kgram(input);
```

Routine
```
double pound_kgram(double pound)
{
 double kgram;
 kgram = pound * .454;
 return(kgram);
}
```

quart_liter

Name   quart_liter

Description   Converts quarts to liters.

Syntax   quart_liter(quart)

Variables   quart is the input parameter and contains the number of quarts to be converted.

liter is the function's return value and contains the number of liters corresponding to the value in quart.

Example
```
output = quart_liter(5)   /* Returns value 4.73 */
output = quart_liter(10)  /* Returns value 9.46 */
```

Rules   This function must be passed a variable defined as a double. Additionally, the calling program must define the function quart_liter( ) and the function's return value as a double.

Calling ex.
```
double input;
double output;
double quart_liter( );

input = 15;
output = quart_liter(input);
```

Routine
```
double quart_liter(double quart)
{
double liter;
liter = quart * .946;
return(liter);
}
```

yards_met

Name   yards_met

Description   Converts yards to meters.

Syntax   yards_met(quart)

Variables   yards is the input parameter and contains the number of yards to be converted.

meter is the function's return value and contains the number of meter corresponding to the value in yards.

Example

```
output = yards_met(5)   /* Returns value 4.57 */
output = yards_met(10)  /* Returns value 9.14 */
```

Rules   This function must be passed a variable defined as a double. Additionally, the calling program must define the function yards_met( ) and the function's return value as a double.

Calling ex.

```
double input;
 double output;
 double yards_met( );

 input = 15;
 output = yards_met(input);
```

Routine

```
double yards_met(double yards)
{
 double met;
 met = yards * .914;
 return(met);
}
```

24
Date functions

Date function header file

```
#ifndef HEAD27

#define HEAD27 1
void date__1(char *, char *);          // MM/DD/YYYY to DD-MMM-YYYY
void date__2(char *, char *);          // MM/DD/YYYY to YYYYMMDD
void date__3(char *, char *);          // MM/DD/YYYY to DDMMMYYYY
long date__4(char *);                  // MM/DD/YYYY to Julian date

int date__5(char *);                   // MM/DD/YYYY to day in year
int date__6(char *);                   // MM/DD/YYYY to leap year test
int date__7(char *);                   // MM/DD/YYYY to day of the week
void date__8(char *, char *);          // MM/DD/YYYY to Day., Mon. DD,
                                       YYYY
void date__9(char *, char *);          // MM/DD/YYYY to Dayyyyyy,
                                       Monthhhhh DD, YYYY
long date__10(char *, char *);         // MM/DD/YYYY dates to
                                          inclusive days between
long date__11(char *, char *);         // MM/DD/YYYY dates to
                                          exclusive days between
void date__12(char *, char *, int);    // MM/DD/YYYY, no. of days for
                                       new date
void date__13(char *, char *);         // DD-MM-YYYY to MM/DD/YYYY
void date__14(char *, char *);         // DD-MM-YYYY to YYYYMMDD
void date__15(char *, char *);         // DD-MM-YYYY to DDMMMYYYY
long date__16(char *);                 // DD-MM-YYYY to Julian date
int date__17(char *);                  // DD-MM-YYYY to day in year
int date__18(char *);                  // DD-MM-YYYY for leap year
                                       test
int date__19(char *);                  // DD-MM-YYYY to day of the
                                       week
```

```
void date_20(char *, char *);        // DD-MM-YYYY to Day., Mon.
                                     DD, YYYY
void date_21(char *, char *);        // DD-MM-YYYY to Dayyyyyy,
                                     Monthhhhh DD, YYYY
long date_22(char *, char *);        // DD-MM-YYYY dates to
                                     inclusive days between
long date_23(char *, char *);        // DD-MM-YYYY dates to
                                     exclusive days between
void date_24(char *, char *, int);   // DD-MM-YYYY, no. of days for
                                     new date
void date_25(char *, char *);        // YYYYMMDD to DD-MM-YYYY
void date_26(char *, char *);        // YYYYMMDD to MM/DD/YYYY
void date_27(char *, char *);        // YYYYMMDD to DDMMMYYYY
long date_28(char *);                // YYYYMMDD to Julian date
int date_29(char *);                 // YYYYMMDD to day in year
int date_30(char *);                 // YYYYMMDD for leap year test
int date_31(char *);                 // YYYYMMDD to day of the week
void date_32(char *, char *);        // YYYYMMDD to Day., Mon. DD,
                                     YYYY
void date_33(char *, char *);        // YYYYMMDD to Dayyyyyy,
                                     Monthhhhh DD, YYYY
long date_34(char *, char *);        // YYYYMMDD dates to
                                     inclusive days between
long date_35(char *, char *);        // YYYYMMDD dates to
                                     exclusive days between
void date_36(char *, char *, int);   // YYYYMMDD, no. of days for
                                     new date
void date_37(char *, char *);        // DDMMMYYYY to MM/DD/YYYY
void date_38(char *, char *);        // DDMMMYYYY to YYYYMMDD
void date_39(char *, char *);        // DDMMMYYYY to DD-MMM-YYYY
long date_40(char *);                // DDMMMYYYY to Julian date
int date_41(char *);                 // DDMMMYYYY to day in year
int date_42(char *);                 // DDMMMYYYY for leap year
                                     test
int date_43(char *);                 // DDMMMYYYY to day of the
                                     week
void date_44(char *, char *);        // DDMMMYYYY to Day., Mon. DD,
                                     YYYY
void date_45(char *, char *);        // DDMMMYYYY to Dayyyyyy,
                                     Monthhhhh DD, YYYY
long date_46(char *, char *);        // DDMMMYYYY dates to
                                     inclusive days between
long date_47(char *, char *);        // DDMMMYYYY dates to
                                     exclusive days between
void date_48(char *, char *, int);   // DDMMMYYYY, no. of days for
                                     new date
```

```
void date_49(long, char *);        // Julian to MM/DD/YYYY
void date_50(long, char *);        // Julian to DD-MMM-YYYY
void date_51(long, char *);        // Julian to YYYYMMDD
void date_52(long, char *);        // Julian to DDMMMYYYY
int date_53(long);                 // Julian to day in year
int date_54(long);                 // Julian for leap year test
int date_55(long);                 // Julian to day of the week
void date_56(long, char *);        // Julian to Day., Mon. DD,
                                   YYYY
void date_57(long, char *);        // Julian to Dayyyyyy,
                                   Monthhhh DD, YYYY
long date_58(long, long);          // Julian dates to inclusive
                                   days between
long date_59(long, long);          // Julian dates to exclusive
                                   days between
long date_60(long, int);           // Julian, no. of days for new
                                   date

#endif

#include <string.h>

void date_49(long, char *);        // Julian to MM/DD/YYYY
int i_convert(char *);
```

date_1

Name   date__1

Description   Converts the date from a format of MM/DD/YYYY to a format of DD-MMM-YYYY. (For example, 11/29/1991 becomes 29-NOV-1991.)

Variables   d__in contains the date passed to the function for reformatting.

d__out contains the reformatted date field passed back to the calling module.

Rules   The date must be passed in the correct format or unexpected results might occur.

The reformatted date will be returned through the second parameter; therefore, no actual return code is used.

The field into which the reformatted date is returned must be large enough to hold the output character string.

On this and all other date functions, all four digits of the year field are required. For example, 1986 is valid but 86 is not.

Calling ex.
```
char in__date[] = {"12/05/1986"};
char out__date[12];
date__1(ind__date, out__date);
```

Routine
```
/ ***************************
*  0123456789a    0123456789 *
*  DD-MMM-YYYY  =  MM/DD/YYYY  *
***************************/
void date__1(char *d__in, char *d__out)
{
 int int__month;
 char months[37];
 *(d__out) = *(d__in+3);
 *(d__out+1) = *(d__in+4);
 *(d__out+2) = '-';
 *(d__out+3) = 'X';
 *(d__out+4) = 'X';
 *(d__out+5) = 'X';
 *(d__out+6) = '-';
 *(d__out+7) = *(d__in+6); *(d__out+8) = *(d__in+7);
 *(d__out+9) = *(d__in+8);
 *(d__out+10) = *(d__in+9);
 *(d__out+11) = '\0';
 strcpy(months,"JANFEBMARAPRMAYJUNJULAUGSEPOCTNOVDEC");
 int__month = *(d__in+1) - '0';
 if ((*d__in) == '1') int__month += 10;
 if ( int__month >= 1 && int__month <= 12 )
  { *(d__out+3) = *(months+((int__month-1)*3));
    *(d__out+4) = *(months+1+((int__month-1)*3));
    *(d__out+5) = *(months+2+((int__month-1)*3));
  }
}
```

date_2

Name   date_2

Description   Converts the date from a format of MM/DD/YYYY to a format of YYYY MMDD. (For example, 11/29/1991 becomes 19911129.)

Variables   d_in contains the date passed to the function for reformatting.

d_out contains the reformatted date field passed back to the calling module.

Rules   The date must be passed in the correct format or unexpected results might occur.

The reformatted date will be returned thought the second parameter; thus, no actual return code is used.

The field into which the reformatted date is returned must be large enough to hold the output character string.

On this and all other date functions, all four digits of the year field are required. For example, 1986 is valid but 86 is not.

Calling ex.
```
char in_date[] = {"12/05/1986"};
char out_date[12];
date_2(ind_date, out_date);
```

Routine
```
/ *************************
* 01234567    0123456789 *
* YYYYMMDD = MM/DD/YYYY   *
*************************/
void date_2(char *d_in, char *d_out)
{
 int int_month;
 char months[37];
 *(d_out) = *(d_in+6);
 *(d_out+1) = *(d_in+7);
 *(d_out+2) =  *(d_in+8);
 *(d_out+3) =  *(d_in+9);
 *(d_out+4) = *(d_in);
 *(d_out+5) = *(d_in+1);
 *(d_out+6) = *(d_in+3);
 *(d_out+7) = *(d_in+4); *(d_out+8) = '\0';
}
```

date_3

Name	date_3
Description	Converts the date from a format of MM/DD/YYYY to a format of DD MMMYYYY. (For example, 11/29/1991 becomes 29NOV1991.)
Variables	d_in contains the date passed to the function for reformatting.
	d_out contains the reformatted date field passed back to the calling module.
Rules	The date must be passed in the correct format or unexpected results might occur.
	The reformatted date will be returned through the second parameter; therefore, no actual return code is used.
	A field into which the reformatted date is returned must be large enough to hold the output character string.
	On this and all other date functions, all four digits of the year field are required. For example, 1986 is valid but 86 is not.

Calling ex.
```
char in_date[] = {"12/05/1986"};
char out_date[12];
date_3(ind_date, out_date);
```

Routine
```
/ *************************
* 012345678   0123456789 *
* DDMMMYYYY = MM/DD/YYYY  *
*************************/
void date_3(char *d_in, char *d_out)
{
  int int_month;
  char months[37];
  *(d_out) = *(d_in+3);
  *(d_out+1) = *(d_in+4);
  *(d_out+2) = 'X';
  *(d_out+3) = 'X';
  *(d_out+4) = 'X';
  *(d_out+5) = *(d_in+6);
  *(d_out+6) = *(d_in+7);
  *(d_out+7) = *(d_in+8); *(d_out+8) = *(d_in+9);
  *(d_out+9) = '\0';
  strcpy(months,"JANFEBMARAPRMAYJUNJULAUGSEPOCTNOVDEC");
  int_month = *(d_in+1) - '0';
  if ((*d_in) == '1') int_month += 10;
  if ( int_month >= 1 && int_month <= 12 )
  { *(d_out+2) = *(months+((int_month-1)*3));
    *(d_out+3) = *(months+1+((int_month-1)*3));
    *(d_out+4) = *(months+2+((int_month-1)*3));
  }
}
```

date_4

Name	date_4
Description	Converts the date from a format of MM/DD/YYYY to its julian equivalent.
Variables	d__in contains the date passed to the function for conversion to its julian date.
	julian (*long integer*) contains the numeric julian value returned to the calling function.
Rules	The date must be passed in the correct format or unexpected results might occur.
	The converted date will be returned via a long integer long int long __day. Therefore, the function must be defined as a long integer and the variable receiving the returned value must also be a long integer data type.
	On this and all other date functions, all four digits of the year field are required. For example, 1986 is valid but 86 is not.

Calling ex.

```
char in__date[] = {"12/05/1986"};
long int out julian;
long int date__4();
julian = date__4(in__date);
```

Routine

```
/ *******************
* 0123456789        *
* MM/DD/YYYY input  *
*******************/
long int date__4(char *d__in)
{
 int in__year, in__month, in__day;
 int cent, cent__y, month, year, out__day;
 long int long__day, temp__long;
 *(d__in+2) = '\0';
 *(d__in+5) = '\0';
 in__year  = i__convert(d__in+6);
 in__month = i__convert(d__in);
 in__day   = i__convert(d__in+3);

 if ( in__month > 2 )
  { month = in__month - 3;
    year = in__year;    }
 else
  { month = in__month + 9;
    year = in__year - 1;
  }
 temp__long = 146097;
 cent  = year / 100;
 cent__y = year - ( cent * 100 );
 long__day = temp__long * cent / 4;
 long__day = long__day + 1461.0 * cent__y / 4;
 long__day = long__day + ( 153 * month + 2 ) / 5;
 long__day = long__day + in__day;

 return(long__day);
}
```

date_5

Name   date_5

Description   Receives a date in the format MM/DD/YYYY and returns its daily position within the year. For example, February 5th would return as 36 because it is the 36th day of the year.

Variables   d_in contains the date passed to the function for conversion to its julian date.

out_day (*long integer*) contains the numeric value returned to the calling function.

Rules   The date must be passed in the correct format or unexpected results might occur.

The converted date will be returned via an integer int out_day. Therefore, the function must be defined as an integer and the variable receiving the returned value must also be an integer data type.

On this and all other date functions, all four digits of the year field are required. For example, 1986 is valid but 86 is not.

Calling ex.   char in_date[] = {"12/05/1986"};
int days;
int date_5();
days = date_5(in_date);

Routine

```
/ *****************
 * 0123456789       *
 * MM/DD/YYYY input *
 *****************/
int date_5(char *d_in)
{
 int in_year, in_month, in_day;
 int cent, cent_y, month, year, out_day, leap_year;
 long int long_day;
 *(d_in+2) = '\0';
 *(d_in+5) = '\0';
 in_year  = i_convert(d_in+6);
 in_month = i_convert(d_in);
 in_day   = i_convert(d_in+3);

 long_day = ( 3055.0 * ( in_month + 2 ) / 100 ) -91; out_day = long_day;

 if ( in_month > 2 )
  { leap_year = 0;
   if (( in_year % 4 )  == 0 ) leap_year = 1;
   if (( in_year % 100 ) == 0 ) leap_year = 0;
   if (( in_year % 400 ) == 0 ) leap_year = 1;
   out_day = out_day - 2 + leap_year;
  }
 out_day += in_day;
 return(out_day);}
}
```

date_6

Name	date_6

Description   Receives a date in the format MM/DD/YYYY, returning a 0 if the year is not a leap year and a 1 if it is.

Variables   d_in contains the date passed to the function for conversion to its julian date.

leap-year (*integer*) contains the numeric value returned to the calling function.

Rules   The date must be passed in the correct format or unexpected results might occur.

The converted date will be returned via an integer int leap_year. Therefore, the function must be defined as an integer and the variable receiving the returned value must also be an integer data type.

On this and all other date functions, all four digits of the year field are required. For example, 1986 is valid but 86 is not.

Calling ex.
```
char in_date[] = {"12/05/1986"};
int leap_year;
int date_6();
leap_year = date_6(in_date);
```

Routine
```
/ ******************
 * 0123456789       *
 * MM/DD/YYYY input  *
 ******************/
int date_6(char *d_in)
{
 int in_year;
 int leap_year;
 *(d_in+2) = '\0';
 *(d_in+5) = '\0';
 in_year  = i_convert(d_in+6);

 leap_year = 0;
 if (( in_year % 4 )  == 0 ) leap_year = 1;
 if (( in_year % 100 ) == 0 ) leap_year = 0;
 if (( in_year % 400 ) == 0 ) leap_year = 1;
 return(leap_year);
}
```

date_7

Name   date__7

Description   Receives a date in the format MM/DD/YYYY and returns its daily position within the week. For example, Dec. 5, 1986, fell on a Friday; thus, this function will return a 5. (In essence, 0=Sun, 1=Mon, 2=Tue, 3=Wed, 4=Thu, 5=Fri, and 6=Sat.)

Variables   d__in contains the date passed to the function for conversion to its julian date.

out__day (*integer*) contains the numeric value standing for the day of the week returned to the calling function.

Rules   The date must be passed in the correct format or unexpected results might occur.

The numeric value will be returned via an integer int out__day. Therefore, the function must be defined as an integer and the variable receiving the returned value must also be an integer data type.

On this and all other date functions, all four digits of the year field are required. For example, 1986 is valid but 86 is not.

Calling ex.
```
char in__date[] = {"12/05/1986"};
int day;
int date__7();
days = date__7(in__date);
```

Routine
```
/ ******************
* 0123456789        *
* MM/DD/YYYY input  *
******************/
int date__7(char *d__in)
{
 int in__year, in__month, in__day;
 int cent, cent__y, month, year, out__day;
 long int long__day;
 *(d__in+2) = '\0';
 *(d__in+5) = '\0';
 in__year  = i__convert(d__in+6);
 in__month = i__convert(d__in);
 in__day   = i__convert(d__in+3);
 if ( in__month > 2 )
  {month = in__month − 2;
   year = in__year;
  }
 else
  {month = in__month + 10;
   year = in__year − 1;
  }
 cent  = year / 100;
 cent__y = year − ( cent * 100 );
 long__day = ( 13 * month − 1 ) / 5;
 long__day = long__day + in__day + cent__y + ( cent__y/4 );
```

```
long_day = long_day + ( cent/4 ) - cent - cent + 77;
long_day = long_day - 7 * ( long_day / 7 );
out_day = long_day;

return(out_day);
}
```

Name   date_8

Description   Converts the date from a format of MM/DD/YYYY to a format of "Day. Mon. DD, YYYY". (For example, 11/29/1991 becomes "Fri. Nov. 29, 1991".)

Variables   d_in contains the date passed to the function for reformatting.

d_out contains the reformatted date field passed back to the calling module.

Rules   This function must be passed the pointer associated with a character field. This may be in the format of a defined character pointer or as the name of a character array with no array brackets.

The date must be passed in the correct format or unexpected results might occur.

The reformatted date will be returned by way of the second parameter; thus, no actual return code is used.

The field into which the reformatted date is returned must be large enough to hold the output character string.

On this and all other date functions, all four digits of the year field are required. For example, 1986 is valid but 86 is not.

Calling ex.
```
char in_date[] = {"12/05/1986"};
char out_date[30];
date_8(ind_date, out_date);
```

Routine
```
/ *********************************
*            11111              *
* 012345678901234567 0123456789 *
* Day, MMM. DD, YYYY = MM/DD/YYYY *
********************************/
void date_8(char *d_in, char *d_out)
{
 int int_month, int_day;
 char months[37];
 char days[22];
 *(d_out) = 'X';
 *(d_out+1) = 'X';
 *(d_out+2) = 'X';
 *(d_out+3) = '.';
 *(d_out+4) = ' ';
 *(d_out+5) = 'X'; *(d_out+6) = 'X';
 *(d_out+7) = 'X';
 *(d_out+8) = '.';
 *(d_out+9) = ' ';
 *(d_out+10) = *(d_in+3);
 *(d_out+11) = *(d_in+4);
 *(d_out+12) = ',';
 *(d_out+13) = ' ';
```

date_8

```
          *(d__out+14) = *(d__in+6);
          *(d__out+15) = *(d__in+7);
          *(d__out+16) = *(d__in+8);
          *(d__out+17) = *(d__in+9);
          *(d__out+18) = '\0';
          strcpy(months,"JanFebMarAprMayJunJulAugSepOctNovDec");
          int__month = *(d__in+1) - '0';
          if ((*d__in) == '1') int__month +=10;
          if ( int__month >= 1 && int__month <= 12 )
          { *(d__out+5) = *(months+((int__month-1)*3));
            *(d__out+6) = *(months+1+((int__month-1)*3));
            *(d__out+7) = *(months+2+((int__month-1)*3));
          }

          strcpy(days,"SunMonTueWedThuFriSat");
          int__day = date__7(d__in) + 1;
          if ((*d__in) == '1') int__day +=10;
          if ( int__day >= 1 && int__day <= 7 )
          { *(d__out) = *(days+((int__day-1)*3));
            *(d__out+1) = *(days+1+((int__day-1)*3));
            *(d__out+2) = *(days+2+((int__day-1)*3));
          }
}
```

date_9

Name	date_9
Description	Converts the date from a format of MM/DD/YYYY to a format of "Day-yyyy Monthhhhh DD, YYYY". (For example, 11/29/1991 becomes "Friday November 29, 1991".)
Variables	d_in contains the date passed to the function for reformatting.
	d_out contains the reformatted date field passed back to the calling module.
Rules	The date must be passed in the correct format or unexpected results might occur.
	The reformatted date will be returned through the second parameter; thus, no actual return code is used.
	The field into which the reformatted date is returned must be large enough to hold the output character string.
	On this and all other date functions, all four digits of the year field are required. For example, 1986 is valid but 86 is not.
Calling ex.	char in_date[] = {"12/05/1986"};
	char out_date[30];
	date_9(ind_date, out_date);

Routine

```
/************************************************
*             1                2               *
* 012345678901234567890123456 78 0123456789    *
* Dayyyyyy, Monthhhhh DD, YYYY = MM/DD/YYYY     *
************************************************/
void date_9(char *d_in, char *d_out)
{
 int int_month, int_day;
 char months[109];
 char days[64];
 *(d_out+9) = ',';
 *(d_out+10) = ' ';
 *(d_out+20) = ' ';
 *(d_out+21) = *(d_in+3);
 *(d_out+22) = *(d_in+4);
 *(d_out+23) = ','; *(d_out+24) = ' ';
 *(d_out+25) = *(d_in+6);
 *(d_out+26) = *(d_in+7);
 *(d_out+27) = *(d_in+8);
 *(d_out+28) = *(d_in+9);
 *(d_out+29) = '\0';
 strcpy(months,"January February March April May Jun");
 strcat(months,"July August September October November December");
 int_month = *(d_in+1) - '0';
 if ((*d_in) == '1') int_month += 10;
 if ( int_month >= 1 && int_month <= 12 )
  { *(d_out+11) = *(months+((int_month-1)*9)); }
```

date_9

```
        *(d__out+12) = *(months+1+((int__month-1)*9));
        *(d__out+13) = *(months+2+((int__month-1)*9));
        *(d__out+14) = *(months+3+((int__month-1)*9));
        *(d__out+15) = *(months+4+((int__month-1)*9));
        *(d__out+16) = *(months+5+((int__month-1)*9));
        *(d__out+17) = *(months+6+((int__month-1)*9));
        *(d__out+18) = *(months+7+((int__month-1)*9));
        *(d__out+19) = *(months+8+((int__month-1)*9));
    }

    strcpy(days,"Sunday Monday Tuesday Wednesday Thursday Friday");
    strcat(days,"Sunday ");
    int__day = date__7(d__in) + 1;
    if ( int__day >= 1 && int__day <= 7 )
    { *(d__out) = *(days+((int__day-1)*9));
        *(d__out+1) = *(days+1+((int__day-1)*9));
        *(d__out+2) = *(days+2+((int__day-1)*9));
        *(d__out+3) = *(days+3+((int__day-1)*9));
        *(d__out+4) = *(days+4+((int__day-1)*9));
        *(d__out+5) = *(days+5+((int__day-1)*9));
        *(d__out+6) = *(days+6+((int__day-1)*9));
        *(d__out+7) = *(days+7+((int__day-1)*9));
        *(d__out+8) = *(days+8+((int__day-1)*9));
    }
}
```

date_10

Name   date_10

Description   Calculates the number of days between two dates including the days passed in the format MM/DD/YYYY.

Variables   s_date contains the date from which to start counting.

                e_date contains the date at which to stop counting.

                no_days (*long integer*) will contain the number of days returned to the calling function.

Rules   This function must be passed the pointers associated with a character field. They may be in the format of defined character pointers or as the name of character arrays with no array brackets.

                The dates must be passed in the correct format or unexpected results might occur.

                On this and all other date functions, all four digits of the year field are required. For example, 1986 is valid but 86 is not.

                The calculated value will be returned via a long integer long int no_days. Therefore, the function must be defined as a long integer and the variable receiving the returned value must also be a long integer data type.

Calling ex.
```
char start_date[] = {"12/05/1986"};
char end_date[] = {"12/10/1986"};
long int days;
long int date_10();
days = date_10(start_date, end_date);
```

Routine
```
/ ******************
 * 0123456789       *
 * MM/DD/YYYY input  *
 ******************/
long int date_10(char *s_date, char *e_date)
{
 long int no_days;
 no_days = date_4(e_date) - date_4(s_date) + 1;
 return(no_days);
}
```

date_11

Name date__11

Description Calculates the number of days between two dates in the format MM/DD/ YYYY not including the days passed.

Variables s__date contains the date from which to start counting.

e__date contains the date at which to stop counting.

no__days (*long integer*) will contain the number of days returned to the calling function.

Rules This function must be passed the pointers associated with a character field. They may be in the format of defined character pointers or as the name of character arrays with no array brackets.

The dates must be passed in the correct format or unexpected results might occur.

On this and all other date functions, all four digits of the year field are required. For example, 1986 is valid but 86 is not.

The calculated value will be returned via a long integer long int no__days. Therefore, the function must be defined as a long integer and the variable receiving the returned value must also be a long integer data type.

Calling ex.
```
char start__date[] = {"12/05/1986"};
char end__date[] = {"12/10/1986"};
long int days;
long int date__11();
days = date__11(start__date, end__date);
```

Routine
```
/ *******************
 * 0123456789        *
 * MM/DD/YYYY input  *
 *******************/
long int date__11(char *s__date, char *e__date)
{
  long int no__days;
  no__days = date__4(e__date) - date__4(s__date) - 1;
  return(no__days);
}
```

Name   date__12

Description   Calculates what the date will be in a specified number of days, given the starting date in the format MM/DD/YYYY and the number of days to count.

Variables   d__in contains the starting date from which to start counting.

d__out contains the date reached after the appropriate number of days have been counted.

no__days (*integer*) contains the number of days that must be counted to reach the ending date.

Rules   The dates must be passed in the correct format or unexpected results might occur.

On this and all other date functions, all four digits of the year field are required. For example, 1986 is valid but 86 is not.

Calling ex.
```
char start__date[] = {"12/05/1986"};
char end__date[];
int days = 10;
date__12(in__date, out__date, days);
```

Routine
```
/ ******************
 * 0123456789       *
 * MM/DD/YYYY input  *
 ******************/
void date__12(char *d__in, char *d__out, int no__days)
{
 long int s__julian, e__julian;
 s__julian = date__4(d__in);
 e__julian = s__julian + no__days;
 date__49(e__julian,d__out);
}
```

date_13

Name   date__13

Description   Converts the date from a format of DD-MMM-YYYY to a format of MM/ DD/YYYY. (For example, 29-NOV-1991 becomes 11/29/1991.)

Variables   d__in contains the date passed to the function for reformatting.

d__out contains the reformatted date field passed back to the calling module.

Rules   The date must be passed in the correct format or unexpected results might occur.

The reformatted date will be returned through the second parameter; thus, no actual return code is used.

The field into which the reformatted date is returned must be large enough to hold the output character string.

On this and all other date functions, all four digits of the year field are required. For example, 1986 is valid but 86 is not.

Calling ex.
```
char in__date[] = {"12-DEC-1986"};
char out__date[12];
date__13(ind_date, out__date);
```

Routine
```
/ ***************************
 * 0123456789 01234567890     *
 * MM/DD/YYYY = DD-MMM-YYYY    *
 ***************************/
void date__13(char *d__in, char *d__out)
{
 int int__month;
 char months[37];
 *(d__out) = 'X';
 *(d__out+1) = 'X';
 *(d__out+2) = '/';
 *(d__out+3) = *(d__in);
 *(d__out+4) = *(d__in+1);
 *(d__out+5) = '/';
 *(d__out+6) = *(d__in+7);
 *(d__out+7) = *(d__in+8); *(d__out+8) = *(d__in+9);
 *(d__out+9) = *(d__in+10);
 *(d__out+10) = '\0';
 strcpy(months,"JANFEBMARAPRMAYJUNJULAUGSEPOCTNOVDEC");
 for(int__month=0; int__month < 37; int__month+=3 )
 { if ( *(d__in+3) == *(months+int__month) &&
   *(d__in+4) == *(months+int__month+1) &&
   *(d__in+5) == *(months+int__month+2)
   )
   { int__month = (int__month+3) / 3;
    *(d__out) = '0';
    if ( int__month >= 10 )
    { *(d__out) = '1';
      int__month -= 10;
    }
    *(d__out+1) = int__month + '0';
    break;
   }
 }
}
```

date_14

Name   date__14

Description Converts the date from a format of DD-MMM-YYYY to a format of YYYYMMDD. (For example, 29-NOV-1991 becomes 19911129.)

Variables   d__in contains the date passed to the function for reformatting.

d__out contains the reformatted date field passed back to the calling module.

Rules   The date must be passed in the correct format or unexpected results might occur.

The reformatted date will be returned through the second parameter; thus, no actual return code is used.

The field into which the reformatted date is returned must be large enough to hold the output character string.

On this and all other date functions, all four digits of the year field are required. For example, 1986 is valid but 86 is not.

Calling ex.
```
char in_date[] = {"12-DEC-1986"};
char out_date[12];
date_14(ind_date, out_date);
```

Routine
```
/ *************************
* 01234567 01234567890    *
* YYYYMMDD = DD-MMM-YYYY   *
*************************/
void date_14(char *d__in, char *d__out)
{
 int int_month;
 char months[37];
 *(d_out) = *(d__in+7);
 *(d_out+1) = *(d__in+8);
 *(d_out+2) = *(d__in+9);
 *(d_out+3) = *(d__in+10);
 *(d_out+4) = 'X';
 *(d_out+5) = 'X';
 *(d_out+6) = *(d__in);
 *(d_out+7) = *(d__in+1); *(d_out+8) = '\0';
 strcpy(months,"JANFEBMARAPRMAYJUNJULAUGSEPOCTNOVDEC");
 for(int_month=0; int_month < 37; int_month+=3 )<
 { if ( *(d__in+3) = = *(months+int_month) &&
       *(d__in+4) = = *(months+int_month+1) &&
       *(d__in+5) = = *(months+int_month+2)
   )
    { int_month = (int_month+3)/3;
     *(d_out+4) = '0';
     if ( int_month > = 10 )
      { *(d_out+4) = '1';
       int_month - = 10;
      }
     *(d_out+5) = int_month + '0';
     break;
    }
 }
}
```

date_15

Name	date__15
Description	Converts the date from a format of DD-MMM-YYYY to a format of DDMMMYYYY. (For example, 29-NOV-1991 becomes 29NOV1991.)
Variables	d__in contains the date passed to the function for reformatting.
	d__out contains the reformatted date field that is passed back to the calling module.
Rules	The date must be passed in the correct format or unexpected results might occur.
	The reformatted date will be returned through the second parameter; thus, no actual return code is used.
	The field into which the reformatted date is returned must be large enough to hold the output character string.
	On this and all other date functions, all four digits of the year field are required. For example, 1986 is valid but 86 is not valid.

Calling ex.
```
char in__date[] = {"12-DEC-1986"};
char out__date[12];
date__15(ind_date, out_date);
```

Routine
```
/ *************************
 * 012345678 01234567890   *
 * DDMMMYYYY = DD-MMM-YYYY  *
 *************************/
void date__15(char *d__in, char *d__out)
{
  int int__month;
  char months[37];
  *(d__out) = *(d__in);
  *(d__out+1) = *(d__in+1);
  *(d__out+2) = *(d__in+3);
  *(d__out+3) = *(d__in+4);
  *(d__out+4) = *(d__in+5);
  *(d__out+5) = *(d__in+7);
  *(d__out+6) = *(d__in+8);
  *(d__out+7) = *(d__in+9); *(d__out+8) = *(d__in+10);
  *(d__out+9) = '\0';
}

#include <string.h>

int i__convert(char *);
void date__50(long, char *); // Julian to DD-MMM-YYYY
```

Name date__16

Description Converts the date from a format of DD-MMM-YYYY to its julian equivalent.

Variables d__in contains the date passed to the function for conversion to its julian date.

     julian (*long integer*) contains the numeric julian value returned to the calling function.

Rules The date must be passed in the correct format or unexpected results might occur.

     The converted date will be returned via a long integer long int long __day. Therefore, the function must be defined as a long integer and the variable receiving the returned value must also be a long integer data type.

     On this and all other date functions, all four digits of the year field are required. For example, 1986 is valid but 86 is not.

Calling ex.
```
char in_date[] = {"05-DEC-1986"};
long int out julian;
long int date__16();
julian = date__16(in_date);
```

Routine
```
/ *********************
 * 0123456789         *
 * DD-MMM-YYYY input  *
 *********************/
long int date__16(char *d__in)
{
 int in__year, in__month, in__day;
 int cent, cent__y, month, year, out__day;
 long int long__day, temp__long;
 char months[37];
 *(d__in+2) = '\0';
 in__year = i__convert(d__in+7);
 in__day  = i__convert(d__in);
 strcpy(months,"JANFEBMARAPRMAYJUNJULAUGSEPOCTNOVDEC");
 for(in__month=0; in__month < 37; in__month+=3)
 { if ( *(d__in+3) == *(months+in__month) &&
        *(d__in+4) == *(months+in__month+1) &&
        *(d__in+5) == *(months+in__month+2) )
  { in__month = (in__month+3)/3;
   break;
  }
 }

 if ( in__month > 2 )
  {month = in__month − 3;
   year  = in__year;
  }
 else
  {month = in__month + 9;
   year = in__year − 1;
  }
```

date_16

```
        temp__long = 146097;
        cent  = year / 100;
        cent__y = year - ( cent * 100 );
        long__day = temp__long * cent / 4;
        long__day = long__day + 1461.0 * cent__y / 4;
        long__day = long__day + ( 153 * month + 2 ) / 5;
        long__day = long__day + in__day;

        return( long__day );
}
```

Name   date_17

Description Receives data in the format DD-MMM-YYYY and returns its daily position within the year. For example, February 5th returns a 36 because it is the 36th day of the year.

Variables   d_in contains the date passed to the function for conversion to its julian date.

out_day (*long integer*) contains the numeric value returned to the calling function.

Rules   The date must be passed in the correct format or unexpected results might occur.

The converted date will be returned via an integer int out_day. Therefore, the function must be defined as an integer and the variable receiving the returned value must also be an integer data type.

On this and all other date functions, all four digits of the year field are required. For example, 1986 is valid but 86 is not.

Calling ex.
```
char in_date[] = {"05-DEC-1986"};
int days;
int date_17();
days = date_17(in_date);
```

Routine
```
/ ********************
* 0123456789         *
* DD-MMM-YYYY input   *
********************/
int date_17(char *d_in)
{
 int in_year, in_month, in_day;
 int cent, cent_y, month, year, out_day, leap_year;
 long int long_day;
 char months[37];
 *(d_in+2) = '\0';
 in_year  = i_convert(d_in+7);
 in_day   = i_convert(d_in);
 strcpy(months,"JANFEBMARAPRMAYJUNJULAUGSEPOCTNOVDEC");
 for(in_month=0; in_month < 37; in_month+=3 )
 { if ( *(d_in+3) == *(months+in_month) && *(d_in+4) ==
*(months+in_month+1) &&
    *(d_in+5) == *(months+in_month+2)
    )
    { in_month = (in_month+3)/3;
    break;
    }
 }

 long_day = ( 3055.0 * ( in_month + 2 ) /100 ) -91;
 out_day = long_day;
```

```
      if ( in__month > 2 )
       { leap__year = 0;
         if (( in__year % 4 )  = = 0 ) leap__year = 1;
         if (( in__year % 100 ) = = 0 ) leap__year = 0;
         if (( in__year % 400 ) = = 0 ) leap__year = 1;
         out__day = out__day - 2 + leap__year;
       }
      out__day + = in__day;
      return(out__day);
    }
```

Name   `date__18`

Description   Receives date in the format DD-MMM-YYYY, returning a 0 if the year is not a leap year and a 1 if it is.

Variables   `d__in` contains the date passed to the function for conversion to its julian date.

`leap-year` (*integer*) contains the numeric value returned to the calling function.

Rules   The date must be passed in the correct format or unexpected results might occur.

The converted date will be returned via an integer `int leap__year`. Therefore, the function must be defined as an integer and the variable receiving the returned value must also be an integer data type.

On this and all other date functions, all four digits of the year field are required. For example, 1986 is valid but 86 is not.

Calling ex.
```
char in__date[] = {"05-DEC-1986"};
int leap__year;
int date__18();
leap__year = date__18(in__date);
```

Routine
```
/ *********************
* 0123456789         *
* DD-MMM-YYYY input  *
*********************/
int date__18(char *d__in)
{
 int in__year, in__month;
 int leap__year;
 char months[37];
 *(d__in+2) = '\0';
 *(d__in+5) = '\0';
 in__year = i__convert(d__in+7);
 strcpy(months,"JANFEBMARAPRMAYJUNJULAUGSEPOCTNOVDEC");
 for(in__month=0; in__month < 37; in__month+=3)
 { if ( *(d__in+3) == *(months+in__month) &&
       *(d__in+4) == *(months+in__month+1) &&
       *(d__in+5) == *(months+in__month+2) )
   { in__month = (in__month+3)/3;
   break;
   }
 }

 leap__year = 0;
 if (( in__year % 4 )  == 0 ) leap__year = 1;
 if (( in__year % 100 ) == 0 ) leap__year = 0;
 if (( in__year % 400 ) == 0 ) leap__year = 1;
 return(leap__year);
}
```

date_19

Name   date_19

Description   Receives date in the format DD-MMM-YYYY and returns its daily position within the week. For example, Dec. 5, 1986 fell on a Friday; therefore, this function will return a 5. (In essence, 0=Sun, 1=Mon, 2=Tue, 3=Wed, 4=Thu, 5=Fri, and 6=Sat.)

Variables   d_in contains the date passed to the function for conversion to its julian date.

out_day (*integer*) contains the numeric value standing for the day of the week returned to the calling function.

Rules   The date must be passed in the correct format or unexpected results might occur.

The numeric value will be returned via an integer int out_day. Therefore, the function must be defined as an integer and the variable receiving the returned value must also be an integer data type.

On this and all other date functions, all four digits of the year field are required. For example, 1986 is valid but 86 is not.

Calling ex.
```
char in_date[] = {"05-DEC-1096"};
int day;
int date_19();
days = date_19(in_date);
```

Routine
```
/ ********************
* 0123456789         *
* DD-MMM-YYYY input   *
*********************/
int date_19(char *d_in)
{
 int in_year, in_month, in_day;
 int cent, cent_y, month, year, out_day;
 long int long_day;
 char months[37];
 *(d_in+2) = '\0';
 in_year    = i_convert(d_in+7);
 strcpy(months,"JANFEBMARAPRMAYJUNJULAUGSEPOCTNOVDEC");
 for(in_month=0; in_month < 37; in_month+=3 )
   { if ( *(d_in+3) = = *(months+in_month) &&
          *(d_in+4) = = *(months+in_month+1) &&
          *(d_in+5) = = *(months+in_month+2)
          )
          { in_month = (in_month+3) /3;
            break;
          }
 }
 in_day   = i_convert(d_in);

 if ( in_month > 2 )
   { month = in_month - 2;
     year = in_year;
   }
```

```
    else
      { month = in__month + 10;
        year = in__year - 1;
      }
  cent  = year / 100;
  cent__y = year - ( cent * 100 );
  long__day = ( 13 * month - 1 ) / 5;
  long__day = long__day + in__day + cent__y + ( cent__y/4 );
  long__day = long__day + ( cent/4 ) - cent - cent + 77;
  long__day = long__day - 7 * ( long__day / 7 );
  out__day = long__day;

  return(out__day);
}
```

date_20

Name date__20

Description Converts the date from a format of DD-MMM-YYYY to a format of "Day. Mon. DD, YYYY". (For example, 29-NOV-1991 becomes "Fri. Nov. 29, 1991".)

Variables d__in contains the date passed to the function for reformatting.

d__out contains the reformatted date field passed back to the calling module.

Rules This function must be passed the pointer associated with a character field. This may be in the format of defined character pointer or as the name of a character array with no array brackets.

The date must be passed in the correct format or unexpected results might occur.

The reformatted date will be returned by way of the second parameter, therefore, no actual return code is used.

The field into which the reformatted date is returned, must be large enough to hold the output character string.

On this and all other date functions, all four digits of the year field are required. For example, 1986 is valid but 86 is not.

Calling ex.
```
char in__date[] = {"12-DEC-1986"};
char out__date[30];
date__20(ind__date, out__date);
```

Routine
```
/ **********************************
*              11111               *
* 012345678901234567 0123456789    *
* Day, MMM. DD, YYYY = DD-MMM-YYYY *
***********************************/
void date__20(char *d__in, char *d__out)
{
 int int__month, int__day;
 char months[37];
 char days[22];
 *(d__out) = 'X';
 *(d__out + 1) = 'X';
 *(d__out + 2) = 'X';
 *(d__out + 3) = '.';
 *(d__out + 4) = ' ';
 *(d__out + 5) = *(d__in + 3); *(d__out + 6) = *(d__in + 4);
 *(d__out + 7) = *(d__in + 5);
 *(d__out + 8) = '.';
 *(d__out + 9) = ' ';
 *(d__out + 10) = *(d__in);
 *(d__out + 11) = *(d__in + 1);
 *(d__out + 12) = ',';
 *(d__out + 13) = ' ';
 *(d__out + 14) = *(d__in + 7);
 *(d__out + 15) = *(d__in + 8);
```

```
*(d__out+16) = *(d__in+9);
*(d__out+17) = *(d__in+10);
*(d__out+18) = '\0';

strcpy(days,"SunMonTueWedThuFriSat");
int__day = date__19(d__in) + 1;
if ((*d__in) == '1') int__day += 10;
if ( int__day >= 1 && int__day <= 7 )
   { *(d__out) = *(days+((int__day-1)*3));
     *(d__out+1) = *(days+1+((int__day-1)*3));
     *(d__out+2) = *(days+2+((int__day-1)*3));
   }
}
```

date_21

Name	date__21
Description	Converts the date from a format of DD-MMM-YYYY to a format of Day-yyy, Monthhhhh DD, YYYY. (For example, 29-NOV-1991 becomes Friday, November 29, 1991.)
Variables	d__in contains the date passed to the function for reformatting.
	d__out contains the reformatted date field passed back to the calling module.
Rules	The date must be passed in the correct format or unexpected results might occur.
	The reformatted date will be returned through the second parameter; thus, no actual return code is used.
	The field into which the reformatted date is returned must be large enough to hold the output character string.
	On this and all other date functions, all four digits of the year field are required. For example, 1986 is valid but 86 is not.

Calling ex.	`char in__date[] = {"12-DEC-1986"};`
	`char out__date[30];`
	`date__21(ind__date, out__date);`

Routine	

```
/***********************************************
*              1         2                     *
* 0123456789012345678901234567  0123456789     *
* Dayyyyyyy, Monthhhhh DD, YYYY = DD-MMM-YYYY   *
***********************************************/
void date__21(char *d__in, char *d__out)
{
 int int__month, int__day;
 char months[109];
 char days[64];
 *(d__out+9) = ',';
 *(d__out+10) = ' ';
 *(d__out+20) = ' ';
 *(d__out+21) = *(d__in);
 *(d__out+22) = *(d__in+1);
 *(d__out+23) = ','; *(d__out+24) = ' ';
 *(d__out+25) = *(d__in+7);
 *(d__out+26) = *(d__in+8);
 *(d__out+27) = *(d__in+9);
 *(d__out+28) = *(d__in+10);
 *(d__out+29) = '\0';
 strcpy(months,"JANFEBMARAPRMAYJUNJULAUGSEPOCTNOVDEC");
 for(int__month=0; int__month < 37; int__month+=3)
  { if ( *(d__in+3) == *(months+int__month) &&<
        *(d__in+4) == *(months+int__month+1) &&
        *(d__in+5) == *(months+int__month+2)
       )
      { int__month = (int__month+3) /3;
```

```
            break;
        }
    }
strcpy(months,"January February March April May Jun");
strcat(months,"July August September October November December");
if ((*d__in) == '1') int__month +=10;
if ( int__month >= 1 && int__month <= 12 )
  { *(d__out+11) = *(months+((int__month-1)*9));
    *(d__out+12) = *(months+1+((int__month-1)*9));
    *(d__out+13) = *(months+2+((int__month-1)*9));
    *(d__out+14) = *(months+3+((int__month-1)*9));
    *(d__out+15) = *(months+4+((int__month-1)*9));
    *(d__out+16) = *(months+5+((int__month-1)*9));
    *(d__out+17) = *(months+6+((int__month-1)*9));
    *(d__out+18) = *(months+7+((int__month-1)*9));
    *(d__out+19) = *(months+8+((int__month-1)*9));
  }


strcpy(days,"Sunday Monday Tuesday Wednesday Thursday Friday");
strcat(days,"Saturday ");
int__day = date__19(d__in) + 1;
if ( int__day >= 1 && int__day <= 7 )
  { *(d__out) = *(days+((int__day-1)*9));
    *(d__out+1) = *(days+1+((int__day-1)*9));
    *(d__out+2) = *(days+2+((int__day-1)*9));
    *(d__out+3) = *(days+3+((int__day-1)*9));
    *(d__out+4) = *(days+4+((int__day-1)*9));
    *(d__out+5) = *(days+5+((int__day-1)*9));
    *(d__out+6) = *(days+6+((int__day-1)*9));
    *(d__out+7) = *(days+7+((int__day-1)*9));
    *(d__out+8) = *(days+8+((int__day-1)*9));
  }
}
```

date_22

Name	date__22
Description	Calculates the number of days between two dates including the days passed in the format DD-MMM-YYYY.
Variables	s__date contains the date from which to start counting.
	e__date contains the date at which to stop counting.
	no__days (*long integer*) will contain the number of days returned to the calling function.
Rules	The dates must be passed in the correct format or unexpected results might occur.
	On this and all other date functions, all four digits of the year field are required. For example, 1986 is valid but 86 is not.
	The calculated value will be returned via a long integer long int no__days. Therefore, the function must be defined as a long integer and the variable receiving the returned value must also be a long integer data type.

Calling ex.

```
char start_date[] = {"05-DEC-1986"};
char end_date[] = {"10-DEC-1986"};
long int days;
long int date_22();
days = date_22(start_date, end_date);
```

Routine

```
/ *********************
 * 0123456789a        *
 * DD-MMM-YYYY input  *
 *********************/
long int date_22(char *s_date, char *e_date)
{
 long int no_days;
 no_days = date_16(e_date) - date_16(s_date) + 1;
 return(no_days);
}
```

Name   date_23

Description   Calculates the number of days between two dates in the format DD-MMM-YYYY not including the days passed.

Variables   s_date contains the date from which to start counting.

e_date contains the date at which to stop counting.

no_days (*long integer*) will contain the number of days returned to the calling function.

Rules   The dates must be passed in the correct format or unexpected results might occur.

On this and all other date functions, all four digits of the year field are required. For example, 1986 is valid but 86 is not.

The calculated value will be returned via a long integer long int no_days. Therefore, the function must be defined as a long integer and the variable receiving the returned value must also be a long integer data type.

Calling ex.
```
char start_date[] = {"05-DEC-1986"};
char end_date[] = {"10-DEC-1986"};
long int days;
long int date_23();
days = date_23(start_date, end_date);
```

Routine
```
/ *********************
 * 0123456789a         *
 * DD-MMM-YYYY input   *
 *********************/
long int date_23(char *s_date, char *e_date)
{
  long int no_days;
  no_days = date_16(e_date) - date_16(s_date) - 1;
  return(no_days);
}
```

date_24

Name date__24

Description Calculates what the date will be in a specified number of days, given the starting date in the format DD-MMM-YYYY and the number of days to count.

Variables d__in contains the date from which to start counting.

d__out contains the date being searched for.

no__days (*integer*) contains the number of days that must be counted to calculate d__out.

Rules The dates must be passed in the correct format or unexpected results might occur.

On this and all other date functions, all four digits of the year field are required. For example, 1986 is valid but 86 is not.

Calling ex.
```
char start__date[] = {"05-DEC-1986"};
char end__date[];
int days = 10;
date__24(in__date, out__date, days);
```

Routine
```
/ *****************
 * 0123456789      *
 * MM/DD/YYYY input *
 *****************/
void date__24(char *d__in, char *d__out, int no__days)
{
 long int s__julian, e__julian;
 s__julian = date__16(d__in);
 e__julian = s__julian + no__days;
 date__50(e__julian,d__out);
}
```

date_25

Name	date_25

Description Converts the date from a format of YYYYMMDD to a format of DD-MMM-YYYY.

Variables d__in contains the date passed to the function for reformatting.

d__out contains the reformatted date field passed back to the calling module.

Rules The date must be passed in the correct format or unexpected results might occur.

The reformatted date will be returned through the second parameter; thus, no actual return code is used.

The field into which the reformatted date is returned must be large enough to hold the output character string.

On this and all other date functions, all four digits of the year field are required. For example, 1986 is valid but 86 is not.

Calling ex.
```
char in__date[] = {"19861205"};
char out__date[12];
date__25(ind_date, out_date);
```

Routine
```
/ ************************
 * 0123456789a 01234567   *
 * DD-MMM-YYYY = YYYYMMDD  *
 *************************/
void date__25(char *d__in, char *d__out)
{
 int int__month;
 char months[37];
 *(d__out) = *(d__in+6);
 *(d__out+1) = *(d__in+7);
 *(d__out+2) = '-';
 *(d__out+3) = 'X';
 *(d__out+4) = 'X';
 *(d__out+5) = 'X';
 *(d__out+6) = '-';
 *(d__out+7) = *(d__in); *(d__out+8) = *(d__in+1);
 *(d__out+9) = *(d__in+2);
 *(d__out+10) = *(d__in+3);
 *(d__out+11) = '\0';
 strcpy(months,"JANFEBMARAPRMAYJUNJULAUGSEPOCTNOVDEC");
 int__month = *(d__in+5) - '0';
 if ((*d__in+4) == '1') int__month +=10;
 if ( int__month >= 1 && int__month <= 12 )
   { *(d__out+3) = *(months+((int__month-1)*3));
     *(d__out+4) = *(months+1+((int__month-1)*3));
     *(d__out+5) = *(months+2+((int__month-1)*3));
   }
}
```

date_26

Name	date__26
Description	Converts the date from a format of YYYYMMDD to a format of MM/DD/YYYY. (For example, 19911129 becomes 11/29/1991.)
Variables	d__in contains the date passed to the function for reformatting. d__out contains the reformatted date field passed back to the calling module.
Rules	The date must be passed in the correct format or unexpected results might occur. The reformatted date will be returned through the second parameter; thus, no actual return code is used. The field into which the reformatted date is returned must be large enough to hold the output character string. On this and all other date functions, all four digits of the year field are required. For example, 1986 is valid but 86 is not.

Calling ex.	`char in__date[] = {"19861205"};`
	`char out__date[12];`
	`date__26(ind__date, out__date);`

Routine	

```
/ *************************
 * 0123456789 01234567    *
 * MM/DD/YYYY = YYYYMMDD   *
 *************************/
void date__26(char *d__in, char *d__out)
{
 int int__month;
 char months[37];
 *(d__out) = *(d__in+4);
 *(d__out+1) = *(d__in+5);
 *(d__out+2) = '/';
 *(d__out+3) = *(d__in+6);
 *(d__out+4) = *(d__in+7);
 *(d__out+5) = '/';
 *(d__out+6) = *(d__in);
 *(d__out+7) = *(d__in+1); *(d__out+8) = *(d__in+2);
 *(d__out+9) = *(d__in+3);
 *(d__out+10) = '\0';
}
```

date_27

Name   date_27

Description   Converts the date from a format of YYYYMMDD to a format of DDMM-MYYYY. (For example, 19911129 becomes 29NOV1991.)

Variables   d_in contains the date passed to the function for reformatting.

d_out contains the reformatted date field passed back to the calling module.

Rules   The date must be passed in the correct format or unexpected results might occur.

The reformatted date will be returned through the second parameter; thus, no actual return code is used.

The field into which the reformatted date is returned must be large enough to hold the output character string.

On this and all other date functions, all four digits of the year field are required. For example, 1986 is valid but 86 is not.

Calling ex.
```
char in_date[] = {"19861205"};
char out_date[12];
date_27(ind_date, out_date);
```

Routine
```
/ *************************
*  012345678   01234567  *
*  DDMMMYYYY = YYYYMMDD   *
*************************/
void date_27(char *d_in, char *d_out)
{
 int int_month;
 char months[37];
 *(d_out) = *(d_in+6);
 *(d_out+1) = *(d_in+7);
 *(d_out+2) = 'X';
 *(d_out+3) = 'X';
 *(d_out+4) = 'X';
 *(d_out+5) = *(d_in);
 *(d_out+6) = *(d_in+1);
 *(d_out+7) = *(d_in+2); *(d_out+8) = *(d_in+3);
 *(d_out+9) = '\0';
 strcpy(months,"JANFEBMARAPRMAYJUNJULAUGSEPOCTNOVDEC");
 int_month = *(d_in+5) - '0';
 if ((*d_in+4) == '1') int_month += 10;
 if ( int_month >= 1 && int_month <= 12 )
   *(d_out+2) = *(months+((int_month-1)*3));
   *(d_out+3) = *(months+1+((int_month-1)*3));
   *(d_out+4) = *(months+2+((int_month-1)*3));
   }
}
```

date_28

Name   date__28

Description   Converts the date from a format of YYYYMMDD to its julian equivalent.

Variables   d__in contains the date passed to the function for conversion to its julian date.

julian (*long integer*) contains the numeric julian value returned to the calling function.

Rules   The date must be passed in the correct format or unexpected results might occur.

The converted date will be returned via a long integer long int long __day. Therefore, the function must be defined as a long integer and the variable receiving the returned value must also be a long integer data type.

On this and all other date functions, all four digits of the year field are required. For example, 1986 is valid but 86 is not.

Calling ex.
```
char in__date[] = {"19861205"};
long int out julian;
long int date__128();
julian = date__28(in__date);
```

Routine
```
/ ******************
* 01234569         *
* YYYYMMDD input   *
******************/
long int date__28(char *d__in)
{
int in__year, in__month, in__day;
int cent, cent__y, month, year, out__day;
long int long__day, temp__long;
char temp[10];
strncpy(temp,d__in,4);
in__year = i__convert(temp);
strncpy(temp,d__in+4,2);
 in__month = i__convert(temp);
in__day = i__convert(d__in+6);

if ( in__month > 2 )
   {month = in__month - 3;   year = in__year;
   }
else
   {month = in__month + 9;
    year = in__year - 1;
   }
temp__long = 146097;
cent = year / 100;
cent__y = year - ( cent * 100 );
long__day = temp__long * cent / 4;
long__day = long__day + 1461.0 * cent__y / 4;
long__day = long__day + ( 153 * month + 2 ) / 5;
long__day = long__day + in__day;

return(long__day);
}
```

Name date__29

Description Receives a date in the format YYYYMMDD and returns its daily position within the year. For example, February 5th returns a value of 36 because it is the 36th day of the year.

Variables d__in contains the date passed to the function for conversion to its julian date.

out__day (*long integer*) contains the numeric value returned to the calling function.

Rules The date must be passed in the correct format or unexpected results might occur.

The converted date will be returned via an integer int out__day. Therefore, the function must be defined as an integer and the variable receiving the returned value must also be an integer data type.

On this and all other date functions, all four digits of the year field are required. For example, 1986 is valid but 86 is not.

Calling ex.
```
char in__date[] = {"19861205"};
int days;
int date__29();
days = date__29(in__date);
```

Routine
```
/ ******************
* 01234567         *
* YYYYMMDD input   *
*******************/
int date__29(char *d__in)
{
  int in__year, in__month, in__day;
  int cent, cent__y, month, year, out__day, leap__year;
  long int long__day;
  char temp[10];
  strncpy(temp,d__in,4);
  in__year  = i__convert(temp);
  strncpy(temp,d__in+4,2);
  in__month  = i__convert(temp);
  in__day   = i__convert(d__in+6);
  long__day = ( 3055.0 * ( in__month + 2 ) / 100 ) -91;
  out__day = long__day;

  if ( in__month > 2 )
    { leap__year = 0;
      if (( in__year % 4 )  = = 0 ) leap__year = 1;
      if (( in__year % 100 ) = = 0 ) leap__year = 0;
      if (( in__year % 400 ) = = 0 ) leap__year = 1;
      out__day = out__day – 2 + leap__year;
    }
  out__day += in__day;
  return(out__day);
}
```

date_30

Name   date__30

Description   Receives date in the format YYYYMMDD, returning a 0 if the year is not a leap year and a 1 if it is.

Variables   d__in contains the date passed to the function for conversion to its julian date.

leap__year (*integer*) contains the numeric value that is returned to the calling function.

Rules   The date must be passed in the correct format or unexpected results might occur.

The converted date will be returned via an integer int leap__year. Therefore, the function must be defined as an integer and the variable receiving the returned value must also be an integer data type.

On this and all other date functions, all four digits of the year field are required. For example, 1986 is valid but 86 is not.

Calling ex.
```
char in__date[] = {"19861205"};
int leap__year;
int date__30();
leap__year = date__30(in__date);
```

Routine
```
/ *****************
* 01234567        *
* YYYYMMDD input  *
*****************/
int date__30(char *d__in)
{
 int in__year;
 int leap__year;
 char temp[10];
 strncpy(temp,d__in,4);
 in__year = i__convert(temp);
 strncpy(temp,d__in+4,2);

 leap__year = 0;
 if (( in__year % 4 ) == 0 ) leap__year = 1;
 if (( in__year % 100 ) == 0 ) leap__year = 0;
 if (( in__year % 400 ) == 0 ) leap__year = 1;
 return(leap__year);
}

#include <string.h>

int i__convert(char *);
long date__28(char *);          // YYYYMMDD to Julian date
void date__51(long, char *);    // Julian to YYYYMMDD
```

Name   date__31

Description   Receives date in the format YYYYMMDD and returns its daily position within the week. For example, Dec. 5, 1986 fell on a Friday; thus, this function will return a 5. (In essence, 0=Sun, 1=Mon, 2=Tue, 3=Wed, 4=Thu, 5=Fri, 6=Sat.)

Variables   d__in contains the date that is passed to the function for conversion to its julian date.

out__day (*integer*) contains the numeric value standing for the day of the week returned to the calling function.

Rules   The date must be passed in the correct format or unexpected results might occur.

The numeric value will be returned via an integer int out__day. Therefore, the function must be defined as an integer and the variable receiving the returned value must also be an integer data type.

On this and all other date functions, all four digits of the year field are required. For example, 1986 is valid but 86 is not.

Calling ex.
```
char in__date[] = {"19861205"};
int day;
int date__31();
days = date__31(in__date);
```

Routine
```
/ *****************
* 0123456789        *
* YYYYMMDD input    *
*****************/
int date__31(char *d__in)
{
 int in__year, in__month, in__day;
 int cent, cent__y, month, year, out__day;
 long int long__day;
 char temp[10];
 strncpy(temp,d__in,4);
 in__year = i__convert(temp);
 strncpy(temp,d__in+4,2);
 in__month = i__convert(temp);
 in__day = i__convert(d__in+6);
 if ( in__month > 2 )
   {month = in__month – 2;
    year = in__year;
   }
 else
   {month = in__month + 10;
    year = in__year – 1;
   }
 cent  = year / 100;
 cent__y = year – ( cent * 100 );
 long__day = ( 13 *month – 1 ) / 5;
 long__day = long__day + in__day + cent__y + ( cent__y/4 );
```

date_31

```
        long__day = long__day + ( cent/4 ) − cent − cent + 77;
        long__day = long__day − 7 * ( long__day / 7 );
        out__day = long__day;

        return(out__day);
}
```

Name   date__32

Description   Converts the date from a format of YYYYMMDD to a format of Day. Mon. DD, YYYY. (For example, 19911129 becomes FRI, NOV. 29, 1991.)

Variables   d__in contains the date passed to the function for reformatting.

d__out contains the reformatted date field passed back to the calling module.

Rules   This function must be passed the pointer associated with a character field. This may be in the format of defined character pointer or as the name of a character array with no array brackets.

The date must be passed in the correct format or unexpected results might occur.

The reformatted date will be returned through the second parameter; thus, no actual return code is used.

The field into which the reformatted date is returned must be large enough to hold the output character string.

On this and all other date functions, all four digits of the year field are required. For example, 1986 is valid but 86 is not.

Calling ex.
```
char in__date[] = {"19861205"};
char out__date[30];
date__32(ind__date, out__date);
```

Routine
```
/ *********************************
*          1                     *
*  012345678901234567   01234567 *
*  Day, MMM. DD, YYYY = YYYYMMDD  *
*********************************/
void date__32(char *d__in, char *d__out)
{
 int int__month, int__day;
 char months[37];
 char days[22];
 *(d__out) = 'X';
 *(d__out + 1) = 'X';
 *(d__out + 2) = 'X';
 *(d__out + 3) = '.';
 *(d__out + 4) = ' ';
 *(d__out + 5) = 'X';
 *(d__out + 6) = 'X';
 *(d__out + 7) = 'X';
 *(d__out + 8) = '.';
 *(d__out + 9) = ' ';
 *(d__out + 10) = *(d__in + 6);
 *(d__out + 11) = *(d__in + 7);
 *(d__out + 12) = ',';
 *(d__out + 13) = ' ';
 *(d__out + 14) = *(d__in);
```

```
      *(d_out+15) = *(d_in+1);
      *(d_out+16) = *(d_in+2);
      *(d_out+17) = *(d_in+3);
      *(d_out+18) = '\0';
      strcpy(months,"JanFebMarAprMayJunJulAugSepOctNovDec");
      int_month = *(d_in+5) - '0';
      if ((*d_in+4) == '1') int_month +=10;
      if ( int_month >= 1 && int_month <= 12 )
         {*(d_out+5) = *(months+((int_month-1)*3));
          *(d_out+6) = *(months+1+((int_month-1)*3));
          *(d_out+7) = *(months+2+((int_month-1)*3));
         }

      strcpy(days,"SunMonTueWedThuFriSat");
      int_day = date_31(d_in) + 1;
      if ( int_day >= 1 && int_day <= 7 )
         {*(d_out) = *(days+((int_day-1)*3));
          *(d_out+1) = *(days+1+((int_day-1)*3));
          *(d_out+2) = *(days+2+((int_day-1)*3));
         }
}
```

date_33

Name   date_33

Description Converts the date from a format of YYYYMMDD to a format of Dayyyyy, Monthhhh DD, YYYY. (For example, 19911129 becomes Friday November 29, 1991.)

Variables   d_in contains the date passed to the function for reformatting.

d_out contains the reformatted date field passed back to the calling module.

Rules   This function must be passed the pointer associated with a character field. This may be in the format of defined character pointer or as the name of a character array with no array brackets.

The date must be passed in the correct format or unexpected results might occur.

The reformatted date will be returned through the second parameter; thus, no actual return code is used.

The field into which the reformatted date is returned must be large enough to hold the output character string.

On this and all other date functions, all four digits of the year field are required. For example, 1986 is valid but 86 is not.

Calling ex.
```
char in_date[] = {"19861205"};
char out_date[30];
date_33(ind_date, out_date);
```

Routine
```
/ *******************************************
*          1         2                      *
* 01234567890123456789012345678 0123456789  *
* Dayyyyyy, Monthhhhh DD, YYYY = YYYYMMD     *
********************************************/
void date_33(char *d_in, char *d_out)
{
 int int_month, int_day;
 char months[109];
 char days[64];
 *(d_out+9)  = ',';
 *(d_out+10) = ' ';
 *(d_out+20) = ' ';
 *(d_out+21) = *(d_in+6);
 *(d_out+22) = *(d_in+7);
 *(d_out+23) = ',';
 *(d_out+24) = ' ';
 *(d_out+25) = *(d_in);
 *(d_out+26) = *(d_in+1);
 *(d_out+27) = *(d_in+2);
 *(d_out+28) = *(d_in+3);
 *(d_out+29) = '\0';
 strcpy(months,"January February March April May Jun ");
 strcat(months,"July August September October November December");
```

```
int_month = *(d_in+5) - '0';
if ((*d_in+4) == '1') int_month += 10;
if ( int_month >= 1 && int_month <= 12 )
{ *(d_out+11) = *(months+((int_month-1)*9));
  *(d_out+12) = *(months+1+((int_month-1)*9));
  *(d_out+13) = *(months+2+((int_month-1)*9));
  *(d_out+14) = *(months+3+((int_month-1)*9));
  *(d_out+15) = *(months+4+((int_month-1)*9));
  *(d_out+16) = *(months+5+((int_month-1)*9));
  *(d_out+17) = *(months+6+((int_month-1)*9));
  *(d_out+18) = *(months+7+((int_month-1)*9));
  *(d_out+19) = *(months+8+((int_month-1)*9));
}

strcpy(days,"Sunday Monday Tuesday Wednesday Thursday Friday ");
strcat(days,"Sunday ");
int_day = date_31(d_in) + 1;
if ( int_day >= 1 && int_day <= 7 )
{ *(d_out) = *(days+((int_day-1)*9));
  *(d_out+1) = *(days+1+((int_day-1)*9));
  *(d_out+2) = *(days+2+((int_day-1)*9));
  *(d_out+3) = *(days+3+((int_day-1)*9));
  *(d_out+4) = *(days+4+((int_day-1)*9));
  *(d_out+5) = *(days+5+((int_day-1)*9));
  *(d_out+6) = *(days+6+((int_day-1)*9));
  *(d_out+7) = *(days+7+((int_day-1)*9));
  *(d_out+8) = *(days+8+((int_day-1)*9));
}
}
```

date_34

Name   date_34

Description   Calculates the number of days between two dates in the format YYYY MMDD including the days passed.

Variables   s_date contains the date from which to start counting.

e_date contains the date at which to stop counting.

no_days (*long integer*) will contain the number of days returned to the calling function.

Rules   The dates must be passed in the correct format or unexpected results might occur.

On this and all other date functions, all four digits of the year field are required. For example, 1986 is valid but 86 is not.

The calculated value will be returned via a long integer long int no_days. Therefore, the function must be defined as a long integer and the variable receiving the returned value must also be a long integer data type.

Calling ex.
```
char start_date[] = {"19861205"};
char end_date[] = {"19861210"};
long int days;
long int date_34( );
days = date_34(start_date, end_date);
```

Routine
```
/ ******************
 * 0123456789a      *
 * YYYYMMDD input    *
 ******************/
long int date_34(char *s_date, char *e_date)
{
  long int no_days;
  no_days = date_28(e_date) - date_28(s_date) + 1;
  return(no_days);
}
```

date_35

Name	date__35

Description Calculates the number of days between two dates in the format YYYY MMDD not including the days passed.

Variables s__date contains the date from which to start counting.

e__date contains the date at which to stop counting.

no__days (*long integer*) will contain the number of days returned to the calling function.

Rules The dates must be passed in the correct format or unexpected results might occur.

On this and all other date functions, all four digits of the year field are required. For example, 1986 is valid but 86 is not.

The calculated value will be returned via a long integer long int no__days. Therefore, the function must be defined as a long integer and the variable receiving the returned value must also be a long integer data type.

Calling ex.
```
char start_date[] = {"05-DEC-1986"};
char end_date[] = {"10-DEC-1986"};
long int days;
long int date__35( );
days = date__35(start_date, end_date);
```

Routine
```
/ ******************
 * 0123456789a     *
 * YYYYMMDD input   *
 ******************/
long int date__35(char *s__date, char *e__date)
{
 long int no__days;
 no__days = date__28(e__date) - date__28(s__date) - 1;
 return(no__days);
}
```

date_36

Name   date_36

Description Calculates what the date will be in a specified number of days, given the stating date in the format YYYYMMD) and the number of days to count.

Variables   d_in contains the date from which to start counting.

d_out contains the date at which to stop counting.

no_days (*integer*) contains the number of days that must be counted to calculate the ending date.

Rules   The dates must be passed in the correct format or unexpected results might occur.

On this and all other date functions, all four digits of the year field are required. For example, 1986 is valid but 86 is not.

Calling ex.
```
char start_date[] = {"19861205"};
char end_date[];
int days = 10;
date_36(in_date, out_date, days);
```

Routine
```
/ *****************
* 0123456789       *
* MM/DD/YYYY input *
******************/
void date_36(char *d_in, char *d_out, int no_days)
{
  long int s_julian, e_julian;
  s_julian = date_28(d_in);
  e_julian = s_julian + no_days;
  date_51(e_julian,d_out);
}
```

date_37

Name   date_37

Description   Converts the date from a format of DDMMMYYYY to a format of MM/DD/YYYY. (For example, 29NOV1991 becomes 11/29/1991.)

Variables   d_in contains the date passed to the function for reformatting.

d_out contains the reformatted date field passed back to the calling module.

Rules   The date must be passed in the correct format or unexpected results might occur.

The reformatted date will be returned through the second parameter; thus, no actual return code is used.

The field into which the reformatted date is returned must be large enough to hold the output character string.

On this and all other date functions, all four digits of the year field are required. For example, 1986 is valid but 86 is not.

Calling ex.
```
char in_date[] = {"DDMMMYYYY"};
char out_date[12];
date_37(ind_date, out_date);
```

Routine
```
/**************************
* 0123456789   012345678   *
* MM/DD/YYYY = DDMMMYYYY    *
**************************/
void date_37(char *d_in, char *d_out)
{
 int int_month;
 char months[37];
 *(d_out)    = 'X';
 *(d_out+1)  = 'X';
 *(d_out+2)  = '/';
 *(d_out+3)  = *(d_in);
 *(d_out+4)  = *(d_in+1);
 *(d_out+5)  = '/';
 *(d_out+6)  = *(d_in+5);
 *(d_out+7)  = *(d_in+6);
 *(d_out+8)  = *(d_in+7);
 *(d_out+9)  = *(d_in+8);
 *(d_ouC'); = '\0';
 strcpy(months,"JANFEBMARAPRMAYJUNJULAUGSEPOCTNOVDEC");
 for(int_month=0; int_month < 37; int_month+=3)
  { if ( *(d_in+2) == *(months+int_month) &&
         *(d_in+3) == *(months+int_month+1) &&
         *(d_in+4) == *(months+int_month+2)
   )
    { int_month = (int_month+3) /3;
     *(d_out) = '0';
     if ( int_month <= 10 )
     *(d_out) = '1';
      int_month -= 10;
      }
```

```
            *(d__out + 1) = int__month + '0';
              break;
      }
    }
  }
```

date_38

Name   date_38

Description Converts the date from a format of DDMMMYYYY to a format of YYYY MMDD. (For example, 29NOV1991 becomes 19911129.)

Variables d_in contains the date passed to the function for reformatting.

d_out contains the reformatted date field passed back to the calling module.

Rules   The date must be passed in the correct format or unexpected results might occur.

The reformatted date will be returned through the second parameter; thus, no actual return code is used.

The field into which the reformatted date is returned must be large enough to hold the output character string.

On this and all other date functions, all four digits of the year field are required. For example, 1986 is valid but 86 is not.

Calling ex.
```
char in_date[] = {"DDMMMYYYY"};
char out_date[12];
date_38(ind_date, out_date);
```

Routine
```
/ ************************
* 01234567   012345678    *
* YYYYMMDD = DDMMMYYYY    *
*************************/
void date_38(char *d_in, char *d_out)
{
 int int_month;
 char months[37];
 *(d_out)    = *(d_in+5);
 *(d_out+1) = *(d_in+6);
 *(d_out+2) = *(d_in+7);
 *(d_out+3) = *(d_in+8);
 *(d_out+4) = 'X';
 *(d_out+5) = 'X';
 *(d_out+6) = *(d_in);
 *(d_out+7) = *(d_in+1);
 *(d_out+8) = '\0';
 strcpy(months,"JANFEBMARAPRMAYJUNJULAUGSEPOCTNOVDEC");
 for(int_month=0; int_month < 37; int_month+=3)
   { if ( *(d_in+2) == *(months+int_month) &&
        *(d_in+3) == *(months+int_month+1) &&
        *(d_in+4) == *(months+int_month+2)
      )
     { int_month = (int_month+3) /3;
      *(d_out+4) = '0';
      if ( int_month >= 10 )
     { *(d_out+4) = '1';
       int_month -= 10;
     }
       *(d_out+5) = int_month + '0';
       break;
   }
  }
 }
```

date_39

Name   `date__39`

Description Converts the date from a format of DDMMMYYYY to a format of DD-MMM-YYYY. (For example, 29NOV1991 29-NOV-91.)

Variables   `d__in` contains the date passed to the function for reformatting.

`d__out` contains the reformatted date field passed back to the calling module.

Rules   The date must be passed in the correct format or unexpected results might occur.

The reformatted date will be returned through the second parameter; thus, no actual return code is used.

The field into which the reformatted date is returned must be large enough to hold the output character string.

With this and all other date functions, all four digits of the year field are required. For example, 1986 is valid but 86 is not.

Calling ex.
```
char in__date[] = {"DDMMMYYYY"};
char out__date[12];
date__39(ind__date, out__date);
```

Routine
```
/ ********************* *****
* 0123456789a - 0123456678 *
* DD-MMM-YYYY = DDMMMYYYY *
********************* ****:**/
void date__39(char *d__in, char *d__out)
{
int int__month;
char months[37];
*(d__out)    = *(d__in);
*(d__out+1)  = *(d__in+1);
*(d__out+2)  = '-';
*(d__out+3)  = *(d__in+2);
*(d__out+4)  = *(d__in+3);
*(d__out+5)  = *(d__in+4);
*(d__out+6)  = '-';
*(d__out+7)  = *(d__in+5);
*(d__out+8)  = *(d__in+6);
*(d__out+9)  = *(d__in+7);
*(d__out+10) = *(d__in+8);
*(d__out+11) = '\0';}
```

date_40

Name	date__40

Description Converts the date from a format of DDMMMYYYY to its julian equivalent.

Variables d__in contains the date passed to the function for conversion to its julian date.

julian (*long integer*) contains the numeric julian value returned to the calling function.

Rules The date must be passed in the correct format or unexpected results might occur.

The converted date will be returned via a long integer long int long __day. Therefore, the function must be defined as a long integer and the variable receiving the returned value must also be a long integer data type.

On this and all other date functions, all four digits of the year field are required. For example, 1986 is valid but 86 is not.

Calling ex.
```
char in__date[] = {"05DEC1986"};
long int out julian;
long int date__40( );
julian = date__40(in__date);
```

Routine
```
/ ******************
 * 0123456789       *
 * DDMMMYYYY input  *
 ******************/
long int date__40(char *d__in)
{
 int in__year, in__month, in__day;
 int cent, cent__y, month, year, out__day;
 long int long__day, temp__long;
 char months[37];
 char temp[3];
 strncpy(temp,d__in,2);
 in__day  = i__convert(temp);
 in__year = i__convert(d__in+5);
 strcpy(months,"JANFEBMARAPRMAYJUNJULAUGSEPOCTNOVDEC");
 for(in__month=0; in__month < 37; in__month+=3 )
  { if ( *(d__in+2) = = *(months+in__month) &&
      *(d__in+3) = = *(months+in__month+1) &&
      *(d__in+4) = = *(months+in__month+2)
     )
     { in__month = (in__month+3) /3;
        break;
     }
  }

 if ( in__month > 2 )
  {month = in__month - 3;
   year = in__year;
  }
```

```
        else
          { month = in_month + 9;
            year = in_year - 1;
          }
        temp_long = 146097;
        cent     = year / 100;
        cent_y = year - ( cent * 100 );
        long_day = temp_long * cent / 4;
        long_day = long_day + 1461.0 * cent_y / 4;
        long_day = long_day + ( 153 * month + 2 ) / 5;
        long_day = long_day + in_day;

        return( long_day );
}
```

date_41

Name   date_41

Description   Receives date in the format DDMMMYYYY and returns its daily position within the year. For example, February 5th returns a 36 because it is the 36th day of the year.

Variables   d_in contains the date passed to the function for conversion to its julian date.

            out_day (*long integer*) contains the numeric value returned to the calling function.

Rules   The date must be passed in the correct format or unexpected results might occur.

            The converted date will be returned via an integer int out_day. Therefore, the function must be defined as an integer and the variable receiving the returned value must also be an integer data type.

            On this and all other date functions, all four digits of the year field are required. For example, 1986 is valid but 86 is not.

Calling ex.
```
char in_date[] = {"05DEC1986"};
int days;
int date_41( );
days = date_41(in_date);
```

Routine
```
/ ******************
* 0123456789       *
* DDMMMYYYY input  *
******************/
int date_41(char *d_in)
{
 int in_year, in_month, in_day;
 int cent, cent_y, month, year, out_day, leap_year;
 long int long_day;
 char months[37];
 char temp[3];
 strncpy(temp,d_in,2);
 in_day  = i_convert(temp);
 in_year"); i_convert(d_in+5);
 strcpy(months,"JANFEBMARAPRMAYJUNJULAUGSEPOCTNOVDEC");
 for(in_month=0; in_month < 37; in_month+=3 )
  { if ( *(d_in+2) = = *(months+ in_month) &&
       *(d_in+3) = = *(months+ in_month+1) &&
       *(d_in+4) = = *(months+ in_month+2)
     { in_month = (in_month+3) / 3;
     )
       break;
     }
  }

 long_day = ( 3055.0 * ( in_month + 2 ) / 100 ) -91;
 out_day = long_day;
```

```
      if ( in_month > 2 )
       { leap_year = 0;
         if (( in_year % 4 ) = = 0 ) leap_year = 1;
         if (( in_year % 100 ) = = 0 ) leap_year = 0;
         if (( in_year % 400 ) = = 0 ) leap_year = 1;
         out_day = out_day --2 + leap_year;
       }
out_day += in_day;
return(out_day);
}
```

date_42

Name   date_42

Description Receives date in the format DDMMMYYYY, returning a 0 if the year is not a leap year and a 1 if it is.

Variables   d_in contains the date passed to the function for conversion to its julian date.

leap-year (*integer*) contains the numeric value returned to the calling function.

Rules   The date must be passed in the correct format or unexpected results might occur.

The converted date will be returned via an integer int leap_year. Therefore, the function must be defined as an integer and the variable receiving the returned value must also be an integer data type.

On this and all other date functions, all four digits of the year field are required. For example, 1986 is valid but 86 is not.

Calling ex.
```
char in_date[] = {"05DEC1986"};
int leap_year;
int date_42( );
leap_year = date_42(in_date);
```

Routine
```
/ *****************
* 0123456789      *
* DDMMMYYYY input  *
*****************/
int date_42(char *d_in)
{
 int in_year, in_month;
 int leap_year;
 char months[37];
 char temp[3];
 strncpy(temp,d_in,2);
 in_year"); i_convert(d_in+5);
 strcpy(months,"JANFEBMARAPRMAYJUNJULAUGSEPOCTNOVDEC");
  for(in_month=0; in_month < 37; in_month+=3 )
  { if ( *(d_in+2) = = *(months+in_month) &&
       *(d_in+3) = = *(months+in_month+1) &&
       *(d_in+4) = = *(months+in_month+2)
       )
      { in_month = (in_month+3) /3;
       break;
       }
   }

 leap_year = 0;
 if (( in_year % 4 )   = = 0 ) leap_year = 1;
 if (( in_year % 100 ) = = 0 ) leap_year = 0;
 if (( in_year % 400 ) = = 0 ) leap_year = 1;
 return(leap_year);
}
```

date_43

Name   date__43

Description   Receives date in the format DDMMMYYYY and returns its daily position within the week. For example, Dec. 5, 1986 fell on a Friday; therefore, this function will return a 5. (In essence, 0=Sun, 1=Mon, 2=Tue, 3=Wed, 4=Thu, 5=Fri, and 6=Sat.)

Variables   d__in contains the date passed to the function for conversion to its julian date.

                out__day (*integer*) contains the numeric value standing for the day of the week returned to the calling function.

Rules   The date must be passed in the correct format or unexpected results might occur.

                The numeric value will be returned via an integer int out__day. Therefore, the function must be defined as an integer and the variable receiving the returned value must also be an integer data type.

                On this and all other date functions, all four digits of the year field are required. For example, 1986 is valid but 86 is not.

Calling ex.
```
char in__date[] = {"05DEC1986"};
int day;
int date__43( );
days = date__43(in__date);
```

Routine
```
/ *****************
 * 0123456789      *
 * DDMMMYYYY input *
 ******************/
int date__43(char *d__in)
{
  int in__year, in__month, in__day;
  int cent, cent__y, month, year, out__day;
  long int long__day;
  char months[37];
  char temp[3];
  strncpy(temp,d__in,2);
  in__day  = i__convert(temp);
  in__year = i__convert(d__in+5);
  strcpy(months,"JANFEBMARAPRMAYJUNJULAUGSEPOCTNOVDEC");
  for(in__month=0; in__month < 37; in__month+=3)
    { if ( *(d__in+2) = = *(months+in__month) &&
           *(d__in+3) = = *(months+in__month+1) &&
           *(d__in+4) = = *(months+in__month+2)
          )
      { in__month = (in__month+3) /3;
         break;
         }
    }

  if ( in__month > 2 )
    {month = in__month --2;
     year  = in__year;
```

```
     }
   else
    {month = in__month + 10;
     year  = in__year --1;
    }
  cent    = year / 100;
  cent__y = year --( cent * 100 );
  long__day = ( 13 * month --1 ) / 5;
  long__day = long__day + in__day + cent__y + ( cent__y/4 );
  long__day = long__day + ( cent/4 ) --cent --cent + 77;
  long__day = long__day --7 * ( long__day / 7 );
  out__day = long__day;

  return(out__day);
}
```

Name   `date__44`

Description   Converts the date from a format of DDMMMYYYY to a format of Day, Mon. DD, YYYY. (For example, 29NOV1991 becomes Fri, NOV. 29, 1991.)

Variables   `d__in` contains the date passed to the function for reformatting.

                `d__out` contains the reformatted date field passed back to the calling module.

Rules   The date must be passed in the correct format or unexpected results might occur.

                The reformatted date will be returned through the second parameter; thus, no actual return code is used.

                The field into which the reformatted date is returned must be large enough to hold the output character string.

                On this and all other date functions, all four digits of the year field are required. For example, 1986 is valid but 86 is not.

Calling ex.

```
char in__date[] = {"DDMMMYYYY"};
char out__date[30];
date__44(ind__date, out__date);
```

Routine

```
/ *********************************
*               1               *
* 0123456789012345678           *
* Day, MMM. DD, YYYY = DDMMMYYYY *
*********************************/
void date__44(char *d__in, char *d__out)
{
 int int__month, int__day;
 char months[37];
 char days[22];
 *(d__out)      = 'X';
 *(d__out+1)   = 'X';
 *(d__out+2)   = 'X';
 *(d__out+3)   = '.';
 *(d__out+4)   = ' ';
 *(d__out+5)   = *(d__in+2);
 *(d__out+6)   = *(d__in+3);
 *(d__out+7)   = *(d__in+4);
 *(d__out+8)   = '.';
 *(d__out+9)   = ' ';
 *(d__out+10)  = *(d__in);
 *(d__out+11)  = *(d__in+1);
 *(d__out+12)  = ',';
 *(d__out+13)  = ' ';
 *(d__out+14)  = *(d__in+5);
 *(d__out+15)  = *(d__in+6);
 *(d__out+16)  = *(d__in+7);
 *(d__out+17)  = *(d__in+8);
 *(d__out+18)  = '\0';
```

```
        strcpy(days,"SunMonTueWedThuFriSat");
        int__day = date__43(d__in) + 1;
        if ( int__day >= 1 && int__day <= 7 )
        { *(d__out) = *(days+((int__day-1)*3));
          *(d__out+1) = *(days+1+((int__day-1)*3));
          *(d__out+2) = *(days+2+((int__day-1)*3));
        }
}
```

Name   date_45

Description   Converts the date from a format of DDMMMYYYY to a format of Day-yyyy, Monthhhhh DD, YYYY. (For example, 29NOV1991 becomes Friday, November 29, 1991.)

Variables   d_in contains the date passed to the function for reformatting.

d_out contains the reformatted date field passed back to the calling module.

Rules   The date must be passed in the correct format or unexpected results might occur.

The reformatted date will be returned through the second parameter; thus, no actual return code is used.

The field into which the reformatted date is returned must be large enough to hold the output character string.

On this and all other date functions, all four digits of the year field are required. For example, 1986 is valid but 86 is not.

Calling ex.
```
char in_date[] = {"DDMMMYYYY"};
char out_date[30];
date_45(ind_date, out_date);
```

Routine
```
/ *********************************************
*          1         2                        *
* 012345678901234567890123455678  012345678   *
* Dayyyyyyy, Monthhhhh DD, YYYY = DDMMMYYYY    *
**********************************************/
void date_45(char *d_in, char *d_out)
{
 int int_month, int_day;
 char months[109];
 char days[64];
 *(d_out+9)   = ',';
 *(d_out+10) = ' ';
 *(d_out+20) = ' ';
 *(d_out+21) = *(d_in);
 *(d_out+22) = *(d_in+1);
 *(d_out+23) = ',';
 *(d_out+24) = ' ';
 *(d_out+25) = *(d_in+5);
 *(d_out+26) = *(d_in+6);
 *(d_out+27) = *(d_in+7);
 *(d_out+28) = *(d_in+8);
 *(d_out+29) = '\0';
 strcpy(months,"JANFEBMARAPRMAYJUNJULAUGSEPOCTNOVDEC");
 for(int_month=0; int_month < 37; int_month+=3 )
  { if ( *(d_in+2) == *(months+int_month) &&
        *(d_in+3) == *(months+int_month+1) &&
        *(d_in+4) == *(months+int_month+2)
      )
```

```
        { int_month = (int_month+3)/3;
          break;
        }
    }
    strcpy(months,"January February March April May June ");
    strcat(months,"July August September October November December ");
      if ( int_month >= 1 && int_month >= 12 )
        { *(d_out+11) = *(months+((int_month-1)*9));
          *(d_out+12) = *(months+1+((int_month-1)*9));
          *(d_out+13) = *(months+2+((int_month-1)*9));
          *(d_out+14) = *(months+3+((int_month-1)*9));
          *(d_out+15) = *(months+4+((int_month-1)*9));
          *(d_out+16) = *(months+5+((int_month-1)*9));
          *(d_out+17) = *(months+6+((int_month-1)*9));
          *(d_out+18) = *(months+7+((int_month-1)*9));
          *(d_out+19) = *(months+8+((int_month-1)*9));
        }

    strcpy(days,"Sunday Monday Tuesday Wednesday Thursday Friday ");
    strcat(days,"Saturday ");
    int_day = date_43(d_in) + 1;
    if ( int_day >= 1 && int_day <= 7 )
        { *(d_out) = *(days+((int_day-1)*9));
          *(d_out+1) = *(days+1+((int_day-1)*9));
          *(d_out+2) = *(days+2+((int_day-1)*9));
          *(d_out+3) = *(days+3+((int_day-1)*9));
          *(d_out+4) = *(days+4+((int_day-1)*9));
          *(d_out+5) = *(days+5+((int_day-1)*9));
          *(d_out+6) = *(days+6+((int_day-1)*9));
          *(d_out+7) = *(days+7+((int_day-1)*9));
          *(d_out+8) = *(days+8+((int_day-1)*9));
        }
}

#include <string.h>

void i_to_a(int, char *);
long date_40(char *);       // DDMMMYYYY to Julian date
void date_52(long, char *); // Julian to DDMMMYYYY
```

Name   date_46

Description Calculates the number of days between two dates in the format DDMMM YYYY including the days passed.

Variables   s_date contains the date from which to start counting.

e_date contains the date at which to stop counting.

no_days (*long integer*) will contain the number of days returned to the calling function.

Rules   The dates must be passed in the correct format or unexpected results might occur.

On this and all other date functions, all four digits of the year field are required. For example, 1986 is valid but 86 is not.

The calculated value will be returned via a long integer long int no_days. Therefore, the function must be defined as a long integer and the variable receiving the returned value must also be a long integer data type.

Calling ex.
```
char start_date[] = {"05DEC1986"};
char end_date[] = {"10DEC1986"};
long int days;
long int date_46( );
days = date_46(start_date, end_date);
```

Routine
```
/ ******************
 * 0123456789a      *
 * DDMMMYYYY input  *
 ******************/
long int date_46(char *s_date, char *e_date)
{
  long int no_days;
  no_days = date_40(e_date) - date_40(s_date) + 1;
  return(no_days);
}
```

date_47

Name   date__47

Description   Calculates the number of days between two dates in the format DDMMM YYYY not including the days passed.

Variables   s__date contains the date from which to start counting.

              e__date contains the date at which to stop counting.

              no__days (*long integer*) will contain the number of days returned to the calling function.

Rules   The dates must be passed in the correct format or unexpected results might occur.

              On this and all other date functions, all four digits of the year field are required. For example, 1986 is valid but 86 is not.

              The calculated value will be returned via a long integer long int no__days. Therefore, the function must be defined as a long integer and the variable receiving the returned value must also be a long integer data type.

Calling ex.

```
char start_date[] = {"05DEC1986"};
char end_date[] = {"10DEC1986"};
long int days;
long int date_47( );
days = date_47(start_date, end_date);
```

Routine

```
/ ******************
 * 0123456789a      *
 * DDMMMYYYY input  *
 ******************/
long int date_47(char *s_date, char *e_date)
{
 long int no_days;
 no_days = date_40(e_date) - date_40(s_date) - 1;
 return(no_days);
}
```

Name   date__48

Description Calculates what the date will be in a specified number of days, given the starting date in the format YYYYMMDD and the number of days to count.

Variables   d__i n contains the date from which to start counting.

                  d__out contains the date at which to stop counting.

                  no__days (*integer*) contains the number of days that must be counted to calculate the ending date.

Rules   The dates must be passed in the correct format or unexpected results might occur.

                  On this and all other date functions, all four digits of the year field are required. For example, 1986 is valid but 86 is not.

Calling ex.
```
char start__date[] = {"05DEC1986"};
char end__date[];
int days = 10;
date__48(in__date, out__date, days);
```

Routine
```
/ ******************
* 0123456789        *
* MM/DD/YYYY input  *
******************/
void date__48(char *d__in, char *d__out, int no__days)
{
  long int s__julian, e__julian;
  s__julian = date__40(d__in);
  e__julian = s__julian + no__days;
  date__52(e__julian,d__out);
}
```

date_49

Name   date__49

Description Converts the date from a julian to a format of MM/DD/YYYY.

Variables   julian (*long integer*) contains the julian value to be transformed and placed in d__out.

d__out contains the reformatted date field passed back to the calling module.

Rules   The first parameter must be a long integer containing the julian date value to be analyzed.

The reformatted date will be returned through the second parameter; thus, no actual return code is used.

The field into which the reformatted date is returned must be large enough to hold the output character string.

On this and all other date functions, all four digits of the year field are required. For example, 1986 is valid but 86 is not.

Calling ex.
```
long int in__julian
char out__date[12];
date__49(in__julian, out__date);
```

Routine

```
/ ******************
 * 0123456789      *
 * MM/DD/YYYY output *
 ******************/
void date__49(long julian, char *d__out)
{
 long int out__year, out__month, out__day;
 long int long__day, temp__long, temp__julian;
 int year, month, day;
 char temp__char[5];
 *(d__out+2) = '/';
 *(d__out+5) = '/';
 *(d__out+10) = '\0';

 temp__long = 146097;
 temp__julian = julian; out__year = (4 * julian - 1) / temp__long;
 temp__julian = 4 * temp__julian - 1 - temp__long * out__year;
 out__day = temp__julian / 4;
 temp__julian = (4 * out__day + 3) / 1461;
 out__day = 4 * out__day + 3 - -1461 * temp__julian;
 out__day = (out__day + 4) / 4;
 out__month = (5 * out__day - -3) / 153;
 out__day = 5 * out__day - -3 - -153 * out__month;
 out__day = (out__day + 5) / 5;
 out__year = 100 * out__year + temp__julian;


 if (out__month < 10)
  { out__month = out__month + 3;
  }
```

```
      else
       { out__month = out__month - -9;
         out__year = out__year + 1;
       }

      year = out__year;
      month = out__month;
      day = out__day;

      i__to__a(year,temp__char);
             *(d__out + 6) = *(temp__char);
             *(d__out + 7) = *(temp__char+1);
             *(d__out + 8) = *(temp__char+2);
             *(d__out + 9) = *(temp__char+3);

      i__to__a(month,temp__char);
      if ( out__month < 10 )
         { *(d__out)      = '0';
           *(d__out + 1) = *(temp__char);
         }
      else
         { *(d__out)      = *(temp__char);
           *(d__out + 1) = *(temp__char+1);
         }

      i__to__a(day,temp__char);
      if ( out__day < 10 )
           *(d__out + 3) = '0';
           *(d__out + 4) = *(temp__char);
         }
      else
         { *(d__out + 3) = *(temp__char);
           *(d__out + 4) = *(temp__char+1);
         }
      }
```

date_50

Name   date_50

Description   Converts the date from a julian to a format of DD-MMM-YYYY.

Variables   julian (*long integer*) contains the julian value to be transformed and placed in d_out.

d_out contains the reformatted date field passed back to the calling module.

Rules   The first parameter must be a long integer containing the julian date value to be analyzed.

The reformatted date will be returned through the second parameter; thus, no actual return code is used.

The field into which the reformatted date is returned must be large enough to hold the output character string.

On this and all other date functions, all four digits of the year field are required. For example, 1986 is valid but 86 is not.

Calling ex.
```
long int in_julian
char out_date[12];
date_50(in_julian, out_date);
```

Routine

```
/ ********************
* 0123456789a        *
* DD-MMM-YYYY output *
********************/
void date_50(long julian, char *d_out)
{
 long int out_year, out_month, out_day;
 long int long_day, temp_long, temp_julian;
 int year, month, day;
 char temp_char[5];
 char months[37];
 *(d_out +2 ) = '-';
 *(d_out +6)  = '-';
 *(d_out +11) = '\0';

 temp_long = 146097; temp_julian = julian;
 out_year = (4 * julian - 1 ) / temp_long;
 temp_julian = 4 * temp_julian - 1 - temp_long * out_year;
 out_day = temp_julian / 4;
 temp_julian = ( 4 * out_day + 3 ) / 1461;
 out_day = 4 * out_day + 3 - 1461 * temp_julian;
 out_day = ( out_day + 4 ) / 4;
 out_month = ( 5 * out_day - 3 ) / 153;
 out_day = 5 * out_day - 3 - 153 k out_month;
 out_day = ( out_day + 5 ) / 5;
 out_year = 100 * out_year + temp_julian;

 if ( out_month < 10 )
 { out_month = out_month + 3;
```

```
    }
  else
   { out__month = out__month - 9;
     out__year = out__year + 1;
   }

  year = out__year;
  month = out__month;
  day = out__day;

  i__to__a(year,temp__char);
       *(d__out + 7)  = *(temp__char);
       *(d__out + 8)  = *(temp__char+1);
       *(d__out + 9)  = *(temp__char+2);
       *(d__out + 10) = *(temp__char+3);
  strcpy(months,"JANFEBMARAPRMAYJUNJULAUGSEPOCTNOVDEC");
  if ( month > = 1 && month < = 12 )
   { *(d__out+3) = *(months+((month-1)*3));
     *(d__out+4) = *(months+1+((month-1)*3));
     *(d__out+5) = *(months+2+((month-1)*3));
   }

  i__to__a(day,temp__char);
  if ( out__day < 10 )
   { *(d__out) = '0';
     *(d__out + 1) = *(temp__char);
   }
  else
   { *(d__out) = *(temp__char);
     *(d__out + 1) = *(temp__char+1);
   }

}
```

date_51

Name   date_51

Description Converts the date from a julian to a format of YYYYMMDD.

Variables   julian (*long integer*) contains the julian value to be transformed and placed in d__out.

d__out contains the reformatted date field passed back to the calling module.

Rules   The first parameter must be a long integer containing the julian date value to be analyzed.

The reformatted date will be returned through the second parameter; thus, no actual return code is used.

The field into which the reformatted date is returned must be large enough to hold the output character string.

On this and all other date functions, all four digits of the year field are required. For example, 1986 is valid but 86 is not.

Calling ex.
```
long int in__julian
char out__date[12];
date__51(in__julian, out__date);
```

Routine
```
/ ******************
* 01234567         *
* YYYYMMDD output   *
******************/
void date__51(long julian, char *d__out)
{
 long int out__year, out__month, out__day;
 long int long__day, temp__long, temp__julian;
 int year, month, day;
 char temp__char[5];
 *(d__out +8) = '\0';

 temp__long = 146097;
 temp__julian = julian;
 out__year = (4 * julian − 1 ) / temp__long;
 temp__julian = 4 * temp__julian − 1 − temp__long * out__year; out__day = temp
 __julian / 4;
 temp__julian = ( 4 * out__day + 3 ) / 1461;
 out__day = 4 * out__day + 3 − 1461 * temp__julian;
 out__day = ( out__day + 4 ) / 4;
 out__month = ( 5 * out__day − 3 ) / 153;
 out__day = 5 * out__day − 3 − 153 * out__month;
 out__day = ( out__day + 5 ) / 5;
 out__year = 100 * out__year + temp__julian;


 if ( out__month < 10 )
  { out__month = out__month + 3;
  }
```

```
   else
    { out_month = out_month - 9;
      out_year = out_year + 1;
    }

   year = out_year;
   month = out_month;
   day = out_day;

   i_to_a(year,temp_char);
      *(d_out) = *(temp_char);
      *(d_out + 1) = *(temp_char+1);
      *(d_out + 2) = *(temp_char+2);
      *(d_out + 3) = *(temp_char+3);

   i_to_a(month,temp_char);
   if ( out_month < 10 )
    { *(d_out + 4) = '0';
      *(d_out + 5) = *(temp_char);
    }
   else
    { *(d_out + 4) = *(temp_char);
      *(d_out + 5) = *(temp_char+1);
    }

   i_to_a(day,temp_char);
   if ( out_day < 10 )
    { *(d_out + 6) = '0';
      *(d_out + 7) = *(temp_char);
    }
   else
    { *(d_out + 6) = *(temp_char);
      *(d_out + 7) = *(temp_char+1);
    }
}
```

date_52

Name	date_52

Description Converts the date from a julian to a format of DDMMMYYYY.

Variables julian (*long integer*) contains the julian value to be transformed and placed in d_out.

d_out contains the reformatted date field passed back to the calling module.

Rules The first parameter must be a long integer containing the julian date value to be analyzed.

The reformatted date will be returned through the second parameter; thus, no actual return code is used.

The field into which the reformatted date is returned must be large enough to hold the output character string.

On this and all other date functions, all four digits of the year field are required. For example, 1986 is valid but 86 is not.

Calling ex.
```
long int in_julian
char out_date[12];
date_52(in_julian, out_date);
```

Routine
```
/ ******************
* 012345678        *
* DDMMMYYYY output *
******************/
void date_52(long julian, char *d_out)
{
 long int out_year, out_month, out_day;
 long int long_day, temp_long, temp_julian;
 int year, month, day;
 char temp_char[5];
 char months[37];
 *(d_out +9) = '\0';

 temp_long = 146097;
 temp_julian = julian;
 out_year = (4 * julian - 1) / temp_long; temp_julian = 4 * temp_julian - 1 -
 temp_long * out_year;
 out_day = temp_julian / 4;
 temp_julian = (4 * out_day + 3) / 1461;
 out_day = 4 * out_day + 3 - 1461 * temp_julian;
 out_day = (out_day + 4) / 4;
 out_month = (5 * out_day - 3) / 153;
 out_day = 5 * out_day - 3 - 153 * out_month;
 out_day = (out_day + 5) / 5;
 out_year = 100 * out_year + temp_julian;

 if (out_month < 10)
 { out_month = out_month + 3;
 }
```

```
    else
     { out__month = out__month - 9;
       out__year = out__year + 1;
     }

    year = out__year;
    month = out__month;
    day = out__day;

    i__to__a(year,temp__char);
       *(d__out + 5) = *(temp__char);
       *(d__out + 6) = *(temp__char+1);
       *(d__out + 7) = *(temp__char+2);
       *(d__out + 8) = *(temp__char+3);

    strcpy(months,"JANFEBMARAPRMAYJUNJULAUGSEPOCTNOVDEC");
     if ( month >= 1 && month <= 12 )
     { *(d__out+2) = *(months+((month-1)*3));
       *(d__out+3) = *(months+1+((month-1)*3));
       *(d__out+4) = (months+2+((month-1)*3));
     }

     i__to__a(day,temp__char);
     if ( out__day < 10 )
     { *(d__out)      = '0';
       *(d__out + 1) = *(temp__char);
     }
     else
     { *(d__out)      = *(temp__char);
       *(d__out + 1) = *(temp__char+1);
     }
}
```

date__53

Name	date__53
Description	Receives date in a julian format and returns its daily position within the year. For example, February 5th returns a 36 because it is the 36th day of the year.
Variables	julian (*long integer*) contains the julian value to be transformed and placed in d__out.
	out__day (*long integer*) contains the numeric value returned to the calling function.
Rules	The julian value which is passed to the function must be defined as a long integer long int.
	The converted date will be returned via an integer int out__day. Therefore, the function must be defined as an integer and the variable receiving the returned value must also be an integer data type.
	On this and all other date functions, all four digits of the year field are required. For example, 1986 is valid but 86 is not.
Calling ex.	long int julian = 725651;
	int days;
	int date__41();
	days = date__53(julian);

Routine

```
/ ***************
 *  julian input  *
 ***************/
int date__53(long julian)
{
  long int out__year, out__month, out__day;
  long int long__day, temp__long, temp__julian;
  int year, month, day, leap__year, no__days;
  char temp__char[5];
  char months[37];

  temp__long = 146097;
  temp__julian = julian;
  out__year = (4 * julian -1 ) / temp__long;
  temp__julian = 4 * temp__julian -1 - temp__long * out__year;
  out__day = temp__julian / 4;
  temp__julian = ( 4 * out__day + 3 ) / 1461;
  out__day = 4 * out__day + 3 -1461 * temp__julian;
  out__day = ( out__day + 4) / 4;
  out__month = ( 5 * out__day -3 ) / 153;
  out__day = 5 * out__day -3 -153 * out__month; out__day = ( out__day + 5 ) / 5;
  out__year = 100 * out__year + temp__julian;

  if ( out__month < 10 )
    { out__month = out__month + 3;
    }
```

```
else
  { out__month = out__month - 9;
    out__year = out__year + 1;
  }


year = out__year;
month = out__month;
day = out__day;


long__day = ( 3055.0 * ( month + 2 ) / 100 ) - 91;
no__days = long__day;


if ( month > 2 )
  { leap__year = 0;
    if (( year % 4 ) = = 0 ) leap__year = 1;
    if (( year % 100 ) = = 0 ) leap__year = 0;
    if (( year % 400 ) = = 0 ) leap__year = 1;
    no__days = no__days - 2 + leap__year;
  }
no__days + = day;
return(no__days);
}
```

date_54

Name   `date__54`

Description Receives date in julian format, returning a 0 if the year is not a leap year and a 1 if it is.

Variables   `julian` (*long integer*) contains the julian value to be transformed and placed in `d__out`.

              `leap__year` (*integer*) contains the numeric value returned to the calling function.

Rules   The julian value which is passed to the function must be defined as a long integer `long int`.

              The leap year indicator will be returned via an integer `int out__day`. Therefore, the function must be defined as an integer and the variable receiving the returned value must also be an integer data type.

              On this and all other date functions, all four digits of the year field are required. For example, 1986 is valid but 86 is not.

Calling ex.
```
long int julian = 725651;
int leapyear;
int date__54();
leapyear = date__54(julian);
```

Routine
```
/ **************
 * 012345678    *
 * julian input  *
 **************/
int date__54(long julian)
{
  long int out__year, out__month, out__day;
  long int long__day, temp__long, temp__julian;
  int year, month, day, leap__year;
  char temp__char[5];
  char months[37];


  temp__long = 146097;
  temp__julian = julian;
  out__year = (4 * julian -1 ) / temp__long;
  temp__julian = 4 * temp__julian -1 - temp__long * out__year;
  out__day = temp__julian / 4;
  temp__julian = ( 4 * out__day + 3 ) / 1461;
  out__day = 4 * out__day + 3 - 1461 * temp__julian;
  out__day = ( out__day + 4) / 4;
  out__month = ( 5 * out__day -3 ) / 153;
  out__day = 5 * out__day -3 - 153 * out__month; out__day = ( out__day + 5 ) / 5;
  out__year = 100 * out__year + temp__julian;

  if ( out__month < 10 )
    { out__month = out__month + 3;
    }
```

```
    else
      { out__month = out__month −9;
        out__year = out__year + 1;
      }

    year = out__year;

    leap__year = 0;
    if (( year % 4 ) = = 0 ) leap__year = 1;
    if (( year % 100 ) = = 0 ) leap__year = 0;
    if (( year % 400 ) = = 0 ) leap__year = 1;
    return(leap__year);
}
```

date_55

Name   date_55

Description   Receives date in julian format and returns its daily position within the week. For example, Dec. 5, 1986 fell on a Friday; thus, this function will return a 5. (In essence, 0=Sun, 1=Mon, 2=Tue, 3=Wed, 4=Thu, 5=Fri, and 6=Sat.)

Variables   julian (*long integer*) contains the julian value to be transformed and placed in d_out.

out_day (*integer*) contains the numeric value standing for the day of the week returned to the calling function.

Rules   The julian value which is passed to the function must be defined as a long integer long int.

The leap year indicator will be returned via an integer int out_day. Therefore, the function must be defined as an integer and the variable receiving the returned value must also be an integer data type.

On this and all other date functions, all four digits of the year field are required. For example, 1986 is valid but 86 is not.

Calling ex.   long int julian = 725651;
int day;
int date_55();
day = date_55(julian);

Routine

```
/ **************
 * 012345678    *
 * julian input  *
 **************/
int date_55(long julian)
{
  long int out_year, out_month, out_day;
  long int long_day, temp_long, temp_julian;
  int year, month, day, the_day, cent, cent_y;
  char temp_char[5];
  char months[37];


  temp_long = 146097;
  temp_julian = julian;
  out_year = (4 * julian - 1) / temp_long;

  temp_julian = 4 * temp_julian - 1 - temp_long * out_year;
  out_day = temp_julian / 4;
  temp_julian = (4 * out_day + 3) / 1461;
  out_day = 4 * out_day + 3 - 1461 * temp_julian;
  out_day = (out_day + 4) / 4; out_month = (5 * out_day - 3) / 153;
  out_day = 5 * out_day - 3 - 153 * out_month;
  out_day = (out_day + 5) / 5;
  out_year = 100 * out_year + temp_julian;
```

```
    year = out__year;
    month = out__month;
    day = out__day;


    if ( month < 10 )
      { month = month + 3;
      }
    else
      { month = month -9;
        year = year + 1;
      }


    if ( month > 2 )
      { month = month -2;
        year = year;
      }
    else
      { month = month + 10;
        year = year -1;
      }
    cent = year / 100;
    cent__y = year -( cent * 100 );
    long__day = ( 13 * month -1 ) / 5;
    long__day = long__day + day + cent__y + ( cent__y/4 );
    long__day = long__day + ( cent/4 ) -cent -cent + 77;
    long__day = long__day -7 * ( long__day / 7 );
    the__day = long__day;


    return(the__day);
}
```

date_56

Name   date__56

Description   Converts the date from a julian to a format of Day, MMM, DD, YYYY.

Variables   julian (*long integer*) contains the julian value to be transformed and placed in d__out.

d__out contains the reformatted date field passed back to the calling module.

Rules   The first parameter must be a long integer containing the julian date value to be analyzed.

The reformatted date will be returned through the second parameter; thus, no actual return code is used.

The field into which the reformatted date is returned must be large enough to hold the output character string.

On this and all other date functions, all four digits of the year field are required. For example, 1986 is valid but 86 is not.

Calling ex.
```
long int in__julian
char out__date[30];
date__56(in__julian, out__date);
```

Routine
```
/ *****************************
*              1             *
* 012345678901234567         *
* Day, MMM. DD, YYYY output  *
*****************************/
void date__56(long julian, char *d__out)
{
  long int out__year, out__month, out__day;
  long int long__day, temp__long, temp__julian;
  int year, month, day, temp__day;
  char temp__char[5];
  char months[37];
  char days[21];


  temp__long = 146097;
  temp__julian = julian; out__year = (4 * julian -1 ) / temp__long;
  temp__julian = 4 * temp__julian -1 - temp__long * out__year;
  out__day = temp__julian / 4;
  temp__julian = ( 4 * out__day + 3 ) / 1461;
  out__day = 4 * out__day + 3 - 1461 * temp__julian;
  out__day = ( out__day + 4) / 4;
  out__month = ( 5 * out__day -3 ) / 153;
  out__day = 5 * out__day -3 - 153 * out__month;
  out__day = ( out__day + 5 ) / 5;
  out__year = 100 * out__year + temp__julian;

  if ( out__month < 10 )
    { out__month = out__month + 3;
```

```
        }
    else
      { out__month = out__month -9;
        out__year = out__year + 1;
      }


    year = out__year;
    month = out__month;
    day = out__day;


    *(d__out + 3) = ',';
    *(d__out + 4) = ' ';
    *(d__out + 8) = '.';
    *(d__out + 9) = ' ';
    *(d__out + 12) = ',';
    *(d__out + 13) = ' ';
    *(d__out + 18) = '\0';


    i__to__a(year,temp__char);
        *(d__out + 14) = *(temp__char);
        *(d__out + 15) = *(temp__char + 1);
        *(d__out + 16) = *(temp__char + 2);
        *(d__out + 17) = *(temp__char + 3);

    strcpy(months,"JANFEBMARAPRMAYJUNJULAUGSEPOCTNOVDEC");
    if ( month >= 1 && month <= 12 )
      { *(d__out + 5) = *(months + ((month - 1)*3));
        *(d__out + 6) = *(months + 1 + ((month - 1)*3));
        *(d__out + 7) = *(months + 2 + ((month - 1)*3));
      }


    i__to__a(day,temp__char);
    if ( out__day < 10 )
      { *(d__out + 10) = '0';
        *(d__out + 11) = *(temp__char);
      }
    else
      { *(d__out + 10) = *(temp__char);
        *(d__out + 11) = *(temp__char + 1);
      }
    strcpy(days,"SunMonTueWedThuFriSat");
    temp__day = date__55(julian) + 1;
    if ( temp__day >= 1 && temp__day <= 7 )
      { *(d__out) = *(days + ((temp__day - 1)*3));
        *(d__out + 1) = *(days + 1 + ((temp__day - 1)*3));
        *(d__out + 2) = *(days + 2 + ((temp__day - 1)*3));
      }
}
```

date_57

Name	date_57
Description	Converts the date from a julian to a format of Dayyyyyy, Monthhhhh DD, YYYY.
Variables	julian (*long integer*) contains the julian value to be transformed and placed in d__out.
	d__out contains the reformatted date field passed back to the calling module.
Rules	The first parameter must be a long integer containing the julian date value to be analyzed.
	The reformatted date will be returned through the second parameter; thus, no actual return code is used.
	The field into which the reformatted date is returned must be large enough to hold the output character string.
	On this and all other date functions, all four digits of the year field are required. For example, 1986 is valid but 86 is not.
Calling ex.	long int in__julian char out__date[30]; date_57(in__julian, out__date);

Routine

```
/ *************************************
*          1         2           *
* 01234567890123456789012345678   *
* Dayyyyyyy, Monthhhhh DD, YYYY output   *
**************************************/
void date__57(long julian, char *d__out)
{
  long int out__year, out__month, out__day;
  long int long__day, temp__long, temp__julian;
  int year, month, day, temp__day;
  char temp__char[5];
  char months[109];
  char days[64];


  temp__long = 146097;
  temp__julian = julian; out__year = (4 * julian -1 ) / temp__long;
  temp__julian = 4 * temp__julian -1 - temp__long * out__year;
  out__day = temp__julian / 4;
  temp__julian = ( 4 * out__day + 3 ) / 1461;
  out__day = 4 * out__day + 3 - 1461 * temp__julian;
  out__day = ( out__day + 4) / 4;
  out__month = ( 5 * out__day -3 ) / 153;
  out__day = 5 * out__day -3 - 153 * out__month;
  out__day = ( out__day + 5 ) / 5;
  out__year = 100 * out__year + temp__julian;
```

```
if ( out_month < 10 )
  { out_month = out_month + 3;
  }
else
  { out_month = out_month -9;
    out_year = out_year + 1;
  }


year = out_year;
month = out_month;
day = out_day;


*(d_out+9) = ',';
*(d_out+10) = ' ';
*(d_out+20) = ' ';
*(d_out+23) = ',';
*(d_out+24) = ' ';
*(d_out+29) = '\0';


i_to_a(year,temp_char);
  *(d_out + 25) = *(temp_char);
  *(d_out + 26) = *(temp_char+1);
  *(d_out + 27) = *(temp_char+2);
  *(d_out + 28) = *(temp_char+3);


i_to_a(day,temp_char);
if ( out_day < 10 )
  { *(d_out + 21) = '0';
    *(d_out + 22) = *(temp_char);
  }
else
  { *(d_out + 21) = *(temp_char);
    *(d_out + 22) = *(temp_char+1);
  }
strcpy(months,"January February March April May  Jun ");
strcat(months,"July August SeptemberOctober November December ");
if ( month >= 1 && month <= 12 )
  { *(d_out+11) = *(months+((month-1)*9));
    *(d_out+12) = *(months+1+((month-1)*9));
    *(d_out+13) = *(months+2+((month-1)*9));
    *(d_out+14) = *(months+3+((month-1)*9));
    *(d_out+15) = *(months+4+((month-1)*9));
    *(d_out+16) = *(months+5+((month-1)*9));
    *(d_out+17) = *(months+6+((month-1)*9));
    *(d_out+18) = *(months+7+((month-1)*9));
    *(d_out+19) = *(months+8+((month-1)*9));
  }


strcpy(days,"Sunday Monday Tuesday WednesdayThursday Friday ");
strcat(days,"Saturday ");
temp_day = date_55(julian) + 1;
if ( temp_day >= 1 && temp_day <= 7 )
  { *(d_out) = *(days+((temp_day-1)*9));
    *(d_out+1) = *(days+1+((temp_day-1)*9));
    *(d_out+2) = *(days+2+((temp_day-1)*9));
    *(d_out+3) = *(days+3+((temp_day-1)*9));
    *(d_out+4) = *(days+4+((temp_day-1)*9));
    *(d_out+5) = *(days+5+((temp_day-1)*9));
```

```
        *(d__out+6) = *(days+6+((temp__day-1)*9));
        *(d__out+7) = *(days+7+((temp__day-1)*9));
        *(d__out+8) = *(days+8+((temp__day-1)*9));
    }

}
```

date_58

Name   date_58

Description   This function calculates the number of days between two dates in a julian format including the days passed.

Variables   s_julian (*long integer*) contains the julian date from which to start counting.

                e_julian (*long integer*) contains the julian date at which to stop counting.

                no_days (*long integer*) will contain the number of days returned to the calling function.

Rules   The julian values which are passed to the function must be defined as a long integers long int.

                The calculated value will be returned via an integer long int no_days. Therefore, the function must be defined as an integer and the variable receiving the returned value must also be an integer data type.

Calling ex.
```
long int start_julian = 725651;
long int end_julian = 725660;
long int no_days;
long int date_58();
no_days = date_58(start_julian, end_julian);
```

Routine
```
/ **************
* julian input  *
***************/
long int date_58(long s_julian, long e_julian)
{
  long int no_days;
  no_days = e_julian - s_julian + 1;

  return(no_days);
}
```

date_59

Name   date_59

Description   Calculates the number of days between two dates not including the days passed in a julian format.

Variables   s_julian (*long integer*) contains the julian date from which to start counting.

e_julian (*long integer*) contains the julian date at which to stop counting.

no_days (*long integer*) will contain the number of days returned to the calling function.

Rules   The julian values which are passed to the function must be defined as a long integers long int.

The calculated value will be returned via an integer long int no_days. Therefore, the function must be defined as an integer and the variable receiving the returned value must also be an integer data type.

Calling ex.
```
long int start_julian = 725651;
long int end_julian = 725660;
long int no_days;
long int date_59();
no_days = date_59(start_julian, end_julian);
```

Routine
```
/ **************
 * julian input  *
 ***************/
long int date_59(long s_julian, long e_julian)
{
  long int no_days;
  no_days = e_julian - s_julian - 1;

  return(no_days);
}
```

date_60

Name   date_60

Description   Calculates what the date will be in a specified number of days, given the starting date in the format YYYYMMDD and the number of days to count.

Variables   s_julian (*long integer*) contains the julian date from which to start counting.

e_julian (*long integer*) contains the julian date at which to stop counting.

no_days (*integer*) contains the number of days that must be counted to calculate the ending date.

Rules   The julian value that is passed to the function must be defined as a long integer long int.

The calculated julian date will be returned via an integer long int e_julian. Therefore, the function must be defined as an integer and the variable receiving the returned value must also be an integer data type.

Calling ex.
```
long int start_julian = 725651;
long int end_julian;
int no_days = 10;
long int date_60();
end_julian = date_60(start_julian, no_days);
```

Routine
```
/ **************
* julian input  *
***************/
long int date_60(long s_julian, int no_days)
{
  long int e_julian;
  e_julian = s_julian + no_days;

  return(e_julian);
}
```

i_convert

Name   i_convert(string)

Description   Converts a character string number into the actual numerical value and places it in an integer variable.

Variables   string receives the character string sent by the calling function.

count assists in loop control

sign is set to 1 at the onset of the function and is changed to -1 if a negative sign is encountered in the number. Just prior to returning, the numerical value is multiplied by sign. Thus, if a negative sign was encountered, the multiplication by -1 would make the returned value negative.

digit contains the individual character values to be converted.

Examples
```
char ascii_number[] = "123.45";
int output, f_convert();
output = i_convert(ascii_number);
```

Rules   Non-numeric values are ignored; thus, the value 12z3 is converted as 123.

The negative sign may be at either the beginning or ending of the input number.

The function name i_convert may optionally be defined as an integer within the calling function.

Decimal points are ignored.

Routine
```
i_convert(char *string)
{
  int count, sign, amount, digit;
  count = 0;
  sign = 1;
  while (string[count])
    if (string[count++] == '-') sign = -1;

  count = amount = 0;
  while ( string[count] )
    { if ( string[count] >= '0' && string[count] <= '9' )
        { digit = string[count] - '0';
          amount *= 10;  amount += digit;
        }
      count++;
    }
  amount *= sign;
  return(amount);
}
```

Name   i_to_a(in_number, out_number)

Description Converts an integer number to an ASCII character string.

Variables in_number (*integer*) is passed to the function to be converted into a string.

out_number (*character string*) contains the returned chracter string.

Examples char ascii_number[6];
int int_variable;
i_convert(int_variable, ascii_number);

Rules   The variable passed must be defined as an int.

Routine
```
void i_to_a(int in_number, char *out_number)
{
  int r, count, length;
  char work_number[10];

  for ( count = 0; in_number > 0; count + +)
    { r = ( in_number % 10 );
      *(work_number + count) = r + '0';
      in_number /= 10;
    }
    *(work_number + count) = '\0';

  length = strlen(work_number);
  for ( count = 0; count < length; count + + )
    *(out_number + length − count − 1 ) = *(work_number + count);
  *(out_number + length ) = '\0';
}
```

25
Mathematical functions

Mathematical functions header file

```
#ifndef HEAD25

#define HEAD25 1

long comdenom(long, long);
long primenum(long, long *);
long poly3(long *, long *);
long poly4(long *, long *);
long poly5(long *, long *);
long poly6(long *, long *);
long poly7(long *, long *);
long poly8(long *, long *);
long poly9(long *, long *);
long poly10(long *, long *);
void vmath1(long, long, long, long, long, long, long *, long *, long *);
void vmath2(long, long, long, long, long, long, long *, long *, long *);
void vmath3(long, long, long, long, long, long, long *, long *, long *);

#endif

#include "head25.h"
```

comdenom

Name   comdenom   (*Common denominator*)

Description   Returns the highest common denominator of two numbers.

Variables   num1 (*integer*) is the first number being calculated.

num2 (*integer*) is the second number being calculated.

Example   comdenom(10,15); /* Will return the value 5 */

Rules   Both parameters must be integers and greater than zero.

Calling ex.
```
int a = 10;
int b = 15;
int ret_value;
ret_value = comdenom(a,b);
```

Routine
```
long comdenom(long num1, long num2)
{
  long num3 = 1;

  if ( num1 < 0 ) num1 *= −1;
  if ( num2 < 0 ) num2 *= −1;

  while ( num3 != 0 )
  { num3 = num1 − num2 * ( num1 / num2 );
    num1 = num2;
    num2 = num3;
  }
  return(num1);

} /* end comdenom */
```

primenum

Name	primenum (*Prime numbers*)
Description	Breaks down the passed number into its root primes and places them in the primes array.
Variables	inval is the number being primed.
	primes is the array containing the prime numbers.
Example	primenum(12, primarray); /* Places the values 2, 2, and 3 in primearray */
Rules	The parameter must be an integer and greater than zero.
	The calling function must make primes large enough to hold all the generated prime numbers.

Calling ex.	int a = 12;
	int prime_values[20];
	primenum(a, prime_values);

Routine

```
long primenum( long inval, long *primes )
{
   long counter, tms, tmp;

   if ( inval < 0 ) inval *= -1;

   for( counter = 2; counter <= inval * inval; counter++ )
   { tms = 0;
     while ( inval % counter == 0 )
     { inval /= counter;
       tms++;
     }
     if ( tms != 0 )
       for (tmp = 1; tmp <= tms; tmp++ )
     *(primes++) = counter;
   }
   *(primes++) = 0;
   return(tms);
} /* end primenum() */
```

Name poly3 (*Area of a polygon with three sides*)

Description Calculates the area within a polygon after being passed the appropriate sets of X and Y coordinates.

Variables x refers to the X-axis coordinate.

y refers to the Y-axis coordinate.

Example poly3(x,y); /* Returns the area of the polygon */

Rules The parameters passed must create a polygon.

Review the Chapter 32 function call program for an understanding on how to call this function.

Routine

```
long poly3(long *x, long *y)
{
  long int area = 0;
  int counter;
  x[3] = x[0];
  y[3] = y[0];

  for ( counter=0; counter < 3; counter++ )
    area += ( x[counter] + x[counter+1] ) * ( y[counter] − y[counter+1] );


  if ( area < 0 ) area *= −1;
  area /= 2;
  return(area);
}
```

poly4

Name   poly4   (*Area of a polygon with four sides*)

Description   Calculates the area within a polygon after being passed the appropriate sets of X and Y coordinates.

Variables   x refers to the X-axis coordinate.

                  y refers to the Y-axis coordinate.

Example   poly4(x,y); /* Returns the area of the polygon */

Rules   The parameters passed must create a polygon.

                  Review the Chapter 32 function call program for an understanding on how to call this function.

Routine

```
long poly4(long *x, long *y)
{
  long int area = 0;
  int counter;
  x[4] = x[0];
  y[4] = y[0];

  for ( counter=0; counter < 4; counter++ )
    area += ( x[counter] + x[counter+1] ) * ( y[counter] - y[counter+1] );

  if ( area < 0 ) area *= -1;
  area /= 2;
  return(area);
}
```

Name   poly5   (*Area of a polygon with five sides*)

Description   Calculates the area within a polygon after being passed the appropriate sets of X and Y coordinates.

Variables   x refers to the X-axis coordinate.

y refers to the Y-axis coordinate.

Example   poly5(x,y); /* Returns the area of the polygon */

Rules   The parameters passed must create a polygon.

Review the Chapter 32 function call program for an understanding on how to call this function.

Routine
```
long poly5(long *x, long *y)
{
  long int area = 0;
  int counter;
  x[5] = x[0];
  y[5] = y[0];

  for ( counter=0; counter < 5; counter++ )
    area += ( x[counter] + x[counter+1] ) * ( y[counter] - y[counter+1] );

  if ( area < 0 ) area *= -1;
  area /= 2;
  return(area);
}
```

poly6

Name poly6 *(Area of a polygon with six sides)*

Description Calculates the area within a polygon after being passed the appropriate sets of X and Y coordinates.

Variables x refers to the X-axis coordinate.

y refers to the Y-axis coordinate.

Example poly6(x,y); /* Returns the area of the polygon */

Rules The parameters passed must create a polygon.

Review the Chapter 32 function call program for an understanding on how to call this function.

Routine

```
long poly6(long *x, long *y)
{
  long int area = 0;
  int counter;
  x[6] = x[0];
  y[6] = y[0];

  for ( counter=0; counter < 6; counter++ )
    area += ( x[counter] + x[counter+1] ) * ( y[counter] - y[counter+1] );

  if ( area < 0 ) area *= -1;
  area /= 2;
  return(area);
}
```

poly7

Name   poly7   (*Area of a polygon with seven sides*)

Description   Calculates the area within a polygon after being passed the appropriate sets of X and Y coordinates.

Variables   x refers to the X-axis coordinate.

y refers to the Y-axis coordinate.

Example   poly7(x,y); /* Returns the area of the polygon */

Rules   The parameters passed must create a polygon.

Review the Chapter 32 function call program for an understanding on how to call this function.

Routine
```
long poly7(long *x, long *y)
{
  long int area = 0;
  int counter;
  x[7] = x[0];
  y[7] = y[0];

  for ( counter=0; counter < 7; counter++ )
    area += ( x[counter] + x[counter+1] ) * ( y[counter] − y[counter+1] );

  if ( area < 0 ) area *= −1;
  area /= 2;
  return(area);
}
```

poly8

Name   poly8   (*Area of a polygon with eight sides*)

Description   Calculates the area within a polygon by being passed the appropriate sets of X and Y coordinates.

Variables   x refers to the X-axis coordinate.

y refers to the Y-axis coordinate.

Example   poly8(x,y); /* Returns the area of the polygon */

Rules   The parameters passed must create a polygon.

Review the Chapter 32 function call program for an understanding on how to call this function.

Routine

```
long poly8(long *x, long *y)
{
  long int area = 0;
  int counter;
  x[8] = x[0];
  y[8] = y[0];

  for ( counter=0; counter < 8; counter++ )
    area += ( x[counter] + x[counter+1] ) * ( y[counter] – y[counter+1] );

  if ( area < 0 ) area *= –1;
  area /= 2;
  return(area);
}
```

poly9

Name   poly9   (*Area of a polygon with nine sides*)

Description   Calculates the area within a polygon after being passed the appropriate sets of X and Y coordinates.

Variables   x refers to the X-axis coordinate.

y refers to the Y-axis coordinate.

Example   poly9(x,y); /* Returns the area of the polygon */

Rules   The parameters passed must create a polygon.

Review the Chapter 32 function call program for an understanding on how to call this function.

Routine
```
long poly9(long *x, long *y)
{
  long int area = 0;
  int counter;
  x[9] = x[0];
  y[9] = y[0];

  for ( counter=0; counter < 9; counter++ )
    area += ( x[counter] + x[counter+1] ) * ( y[counter] - y[counter+1] );

  if ( area < 0 ) area *= -1;
  area /= 2;
  return(area);
}
```

poly10

Name   poly10   (*Area of a polygon with ten sides*)

Description   Calculates the area within a polygon after being passed the appropriate sets of X and Y coordinates.

Variables   x refers to the X-axis coordinate.

                  y refers to the Y-axis coordinate.

Example   poly10(x,y); /* Returns the area of the polygon */

Rules   The parameters passed must create a polygon.

                  Review the Chapter 32 function call program for an understanding on how to call this function.

Routine

```
long poly10( long *x, long *y)
{
  long int area = 0;
  int counter;
  x[10] = x[0];
  y[10] = y[0];

  for ( counter=0; counter < 10; counter++ )
    area += ( x[counter] + x[counter+1] ) * ( y[counter] - y[counter+1] );

  if ( area < 0 ) area *= -1;
  area /= 2;
  return(area);
}
```

vmath1

Name   vmath1   (*Vector math—Addition*)

Description   Performs vector addition.

Variables   x1 and x2 (both *integer*) are the X values.

y1 and y2 (both *integer*) are the Y values.

z1 and z2 (both *integer*) are the Z values.

x, y, and z (all *integer*) are the funtion return values.

Example   vmath1(2,3,4,6,7,8,x,y,z); /* Will add 2, 3, and 4 to 6,
7, and 8 */
/* and then place the total
in x, y, and z. */

Rules   The parameters must be integer values.

Routine
```
void vmath1(long x1, long y1, long z1, long x2, long y2, long z2,
           long *x, long *y, long *z)
{
  *(x) = x1 + x2;
  *(y) = y1 + y2;
  *(z) = z1 + z2;
}
```

vmath2

Name   vmath2   (*Vector math—Subtraction*)

Description   Performs vector subtraction.

Variables   x1 and x2 (both *integer*) are the X values.

                y1 and y2 (both *integer*) are the Y values.

                z1 and z2 (both *integer*) are the Z values

                x, y, and z (all *integer*) are the funtion return values.

Example   vmath1(6,7,8,,2,3,4,x,y,z); /*Will subtract 2, 3, and
                              4 from 6, 7, and 8 */
                              /* and then place the dif
                              ference in x, y, and z. */

Rules   The parameters must be integer values.

Routine

```
void vmath2(long x1, long y1, long z1, long x2, long y2, long z2,
          long *x, long *y, long *z)
{
  *(x) = x1 - x2;
  *(y) = y1 - y2;
  *(z) = z1 - z2;
}
```

Name   vmath3   (*Vector math—Multiplication*)

Description   Performs vector multiplication.

Variables   x1 and x2 (both *integer*) are the X values.

y1 and y2 (both *integer*) are the Y values.

z1 and z2 (both *integer*) are the Z values.

x, y, and z (all *integer)* are the funtion return values.

Example   vmath3(2,3,4,6,7,8,x,y,z); /*Will multiply 2, 3, and 4
by 6, 7, and 8 */
/* and then place th total
in x, y, and z.*/

Rules   The parameters must be integer values.

Routine

```
void vmath3 (long x1, long y1, long z1, long x2, long y2, long z2,
            long *x, long *y, long *z)
{
  *(x) = x1 * x2;
  *(y) = y1 * y2;
  *(z) = z1 * z2;
}
```

26

Push-down stacks

Push-down stacks header file

```
#ifndef HEAD26

#define HEAD26 1

#define ISTACK_SIZE    10
static int istack[100];
static int istack_loc = 0;

#define DSTACK_SIZE    10
static double dstack[100];
static int dstack_loc = 0;
void      clear_i(void);        /* re-initialize the stack ( empty it ) */
int       push_i(int);          /* push a value into the stack */
int       pop_i(void);          /* pop a value out of the stack */
int       gettop_i(void);       /* get the top value in the stack */
int       empty_i(void);        /* test to see if the stack is empty */
int       full_i(void);         /* test to see if the stack is full */
int       getloc_i(int);        /* get value from a specified location
                                   in the stack */

int       getsize_i(void);      /* number of values in the stack */

void      clear_d(void);        /* re-initialize the stack ( empty it ) */
int       push_d(double);       /* push a value into the stack */
double    pop_d(void);          /* pop a value out of the stack */
double    gettop_d(void);       /* get the top value in the stack */
int       empty_d(void);        /* test to see if the stack is empty */
int       full_d(void);         /* test to see if the stack is full */
double    getloc_d(int);        /* get value from a specified location
                                   in the stack */
int       getsize_d(void);      /* number of values in the stack */
```

```
#endif

#include "head26.h"
#include <stdio.h>
```

push_i

Name   push_i   *(Push integer)*

Description   Pushed an integer onto the stack.

Variables   value is the value to be placed on the stack.

Example   push_i(a_val); /* Adds the value of a_val to the stack.

Rules   The stack can only hold the number of values specified by the variable ISTACK_SIZE defined in head33.h.

Calling ex.   int value, ret_value;
value = 5;
ret_value = push_i(value);

Routine

```
int push_i(value)
int value;
{ if ( istack_loc = = ISTACK_SIZE )
 { printf("ERROR: push_1() stack overflow \n");
   return(1);
 }
 istack[istack_loc + +] = value;
 return(0);
}
```

pop_i

Name   pop_i   *(Pop integer)*

Description   Pops an integer off the stack and returns the popped value.

Variables   None

Example   a_val = pop_i(); /* Pops the next value off the stack
                          and places its value in variable
                          a_val */.

Rules   The stack can only hold the number of values specified by the variable ISTACK_SIZE defined in head33.h.

Values are popped off the stack using the LIFO (*Last-In First-Out*) process.

Values can only be popped (taken off) the stack if they have been placed there. In other words, you cannot push more values than you pop.

Calling ex.
```
int value, ret_value, got_value;
value = 5;
ret_value = push_i(value);
got_value = pop_i();
```

Routine
```
int pop_i()
{ if ( istack_loc == 0 )
  { printf("ERROR: pop_i() stack empty, no value to pop");
    return(0);
  }
  return(istack[-istack_loc]);
}
```

gettop_i

Name   gettop_i   *(Get top stack value)*

Description   Returns the top integer value in the stack (i.e., the last value pushed into the stack) without removing that value from the stack.

Variables   None

Example
```
a_val = gettop_i(); /* Pops the next value of the stack
                        and places its value in varia
                        ble a_val */.
```

Rules   The stack can only hold the number of values specified by the variable ISTACK_SIZE defined in head33.h.

Values are popped off the stack using the LIFO (*Last-In First-Out*) process.

Values can only be popped (taken off) the stack if they have been placed there. In other words, you cannot push more values than you pop.

Calling ex.
```
int value, ret_value, got_value;
value = 5;
ret_value = push_i(value);
got_value = gettop_i();
```

Routine
```
int gettop_i()
{ if ( istack_loc == 0 )
  { printf("ERROR: pop_i() stack empty, no value to pop");
    return(0);
  }
  return(istack[istack_loc - 1]);
}
```

empty_i

Name   empty_i   *(Is the stack empty?)*

Description   Checks to see if the stack is empty.

Variables   None

Example   `ret_val = empty_i(); /* If the stack is empty, ret_val will have a value of 0. If the stack is not empty, ret_val will have a non-zero value. */`

Rules   The stack can only hold the number of values specified by the variable ISTACK_SIZE defined in head33.h.

Values can only be popped (taken off) the stack if they have been placed there. In other words, you cannot push more values than you pop.

Calling ex.
```
int ret_value;
ret_value = empty_i();
```

Routine
```
int empty_i()
{ return( ( istack_loc == 0 ) );
}
```

full_i

Name	full_i *(Is the stack full?)*

Description   Checks to see if the stack is full.

Variables   None

Example
```
ret_val = full_i(); /* If the stack is full, ret_val
                       will have a value of 0. If the
                       stack is not full, ret_val
                       will have a non-zero value. */
```

Rules   The stack can only hold the number of values specified by the variable ISTACK_SIZE defined in head33.h.

Values can only be popped (taken off) the stack if they have been placed there. In other words, you cannot push more values than you pop.

Calling ex.
```
int ret_value;
ret_value = full_i();
```

Routine
```
int full_i()
{ return( ( istack_loc = = ISTACK_SIZE ) );
}
```

Name   clear_i   *(Clears the stack)*

Description   Deletes the contents of the stack.

Variables   None

Example   clear_i(); /* The stack is now empty */

Rules   The stack can only hold the number of values specified by the variable ISTACK_SIZE defined in head33.h.

Values are popped off the stack using the LIFO (*Last-In First-Out*) process.

Values can only be popped (taken off) the stack if they have been placed there. In other words, you cannot push more values than you pop.

Calling ex.   clear_i();

Routine
```
void clear_i()
{ istack_loc = 0;
}
```

getloc_i

Name getloc_i *(Get value at specified stack location)*

Description Returns the value of a specified stack location.

Variables loc is the stack location to be returned.

Example
```
ret_value = getloc_i(a_val); /* Returns the value stored
                                at stack location a_val
                                and places it in ret_
                                value. */
```

Rules The stack can only hold the number of values specified by the variable ISTACK_SIZE defined in head33.h.

Calling ex.
```
int location, ret_value;
location = 5;
ret_value = getloc_i(location);
```

Routine
```
int getloc_i(loc)
int loc;
{ return istack[loc];
}
```

Name   getsize_i   *(Get the number of values in the stack)*

Description   Returns the number of values in the stack.

Variables   None

Example   ret_value = getsize_i(); /* Returns the number of values stored in the stack
and places it in ret_val-
ue. */

Rules   The stack can only hold the number of values specified by the variable ISTACK_SIZE defined in head33.h.

Calling ex.
```
int ret_value;
ret_value = getsize_i();
```

Routine
```
int getsize_i()
{ return(istack_loc);
}
```

push_d

Name   push_d   *(Push double)*

Description Pushed a double onto the stack.

Variables   value is the value to be placed on the stack.

Example   push_d(a_val); /* Adds the value of a_val to the stack. */

Rules   The stack can only hold the number of values specified by the variable ISTACK_SIZE defined in head33.h.

Calling ex.
```
int value, ret_value;
value = 5;
ret_value = push_d(value);
```

Routine
```
int push_d(value)
double value;
{ if (dstack_loc == DSTACK_SIZE)
  { printf("ERROR: push_d() stack overflow \n");
    return(1);
  }
  dstack[dstack_loc++] = value;
  return(0);
}
```

pop_d

Name pop_d *(Pop double)*

Description Pops a double of the stack and returns the popped value.

Variables None

Example
```
a_val = pop_d(); /* Pops the next value of the stack and
                    places its value in a_val. */.
```

Rules The stack can only hold the number of values specified by the variable ISTACK_SIZE defined in head33.h.

Values are popped off the stack using the LIFO (*Last-In First-Out*) process.

Values can only be popped (taken off) the stack if they have been placed there. In other words, you cannot push more values than you pop.

Calling ex.
```
int value, ret_value, got_value;
value = 5;
ret_value = push_d(value);
got_value = pop_d();
```

Routine
```
double pop_d()
{ if ( dstack_loc == 0 )
  { printf("ERROR: pop_d() stack empty, no value to pop");
   return(0.0);
  }
  return(dstack[-dstack_loc]);
}
```

gettop_d

Name   gettop_d   *(Get top stack value)*

Description   Returns the top double value in the stack (i.e., the last value pushed into the stack) without removing it from the stack.

Variables   None

Example   a_val = gettop_d(); /* Pops the next value of the stack
                          and places its value in a_val.
                          */

Rules   The stack can only hold the number of values specified by the variable ISTACK_SIZE defined in head33.h.

Values are popped off the stack using the LIFO (*Last-In First-Out*) process.

Values can only be popped (taken off) the stack if they have been placed there. In other words, you cannot push more values than you pop.

Calling ex.
```
int value, ret_value, got_value;
value = 5;
ret_value = push_d(value);
got_value = gettop_d();
```

Routine
```
double gettop_d()
{ if ( dstack_loc == 0 )
 { printf("ERROR: gettop_d() stack empty, no value to pop");
   return(0.0);
 }
 return(dstack[dstack_loc - 1]);
}
```

empty_d

Name   empty_d   *(Is the stack empty?)*

Description   Checks to see if the stack is empty.

Variables   None

Example
```
ret_val = empty_d(); /* If the stack is empty, ret_val
                        will have a value of 0. If the
                        stack is not empty, ret_val
                        will have a non-zero value. */
```

Rules   The stack can only hold the number of values specified by the variable ISTACK_SIZE defined in head33.h.

Values can only be popped (taken off) the stack if they have been placed there. In other words, you cannot push more values than you pop.

Calling ex.
```
int ret_value;
ret_value = empty_d();
```

Routine
```
int empty_d()
{ return( ( dstack_loc = = 0 ) );
}
```

full_d

Name	full_d *(Is the stack full?)*

Description   Checks to see if the stack is full.

Variables   None

Example

```
ret_val = full_d(); /* If the stack is full, ret_val
                       will have a value of 0. If the
                       stack is not full, ret_val
                       will have a non-zero value. */
```

Rules   The stack can only hold the number of values specified by the variable ISTACK_SIZE defined in head33.h.

Values can only be popped (taken off) the stack if they have been placed there. In other words, you cannot push more values than you pop.

Calling ex.
```
int ret_value;
ret_value = full_d();
```

Routine
```
int full_d()
{ return( ( dstack_loc == DSTACK_SIZE ) );
}
```

clear_d

Name   clear_d   *(Clears the stack)*

Description   Deletes the contents of the stack.

Variables   None

Example   clear_d(); /* The stack is now empty */

Rules   The stack can only hold the number of values specified by the variable ISTACK_SIZE defined in head33.h.

Values are popped off the stack using the LIFO (*Last-In First-Out*) process.

Values can only be popped (taken off) the stack if they have been placed there. In other words, you cannot push more values than you pop.

Calling ex.   clear_d();

Routine
```
void clear_d()
{ dstack_loc = 0;
}
```

getloc_d

Name   getloc_d   *(Get value at specified stack location)*

Description   Returns the value of a specified stack location.

Variables   loc is the stack location to be returned.

Example

```
ret_value = getloc_d(a_val); /*Returns the value stored
                               at stack location a_val
                               and places it in ret_
                               value. */
```

Rules   The stack can only hold the number of values specified by the variable ISTACK_SIZE defined in head33.h.

Calling ex.

```
int location, ret_value;
location = 5;
ret_value = getloc_d(location);
```

Routine

```
double getloc_d(loc)
int loc;
{ return dstack[loc];
}
```

getsize_d

Name   getsize_d   *(Get the number of values in the stack)*

Description   Returns the number of values in the stack.

Variables   None

Example
```
ret_value = getsize_d(); /* Returns the number of val-
                            ues stored in the stack
                            and places it in ret_val-
                            ue. */
```

Rules   The stack can only hold the number of values specified by the variable ISTACK_SIZE defined in head33.h.

Calling ex.
```
int ret_value;
ret_value = getsize_d();
```

Routine
```
int getsize_d()
{ return(dstack_loc);
}
```

27
Making boxes on the screen

Box header file

```
#ifndef HEAD27

#define HEAD27 1

void box_1(int, int, int, int);        // print box with single lines
void box_2(int, int, int, int);        // print box with double lines
void box_3(int, int, int, int);        // print box with wide lines

void box_1(int, int, int, int, char *);  // box with single lines and
                                         //   title

void box_2(int, int, int, int, char *);  // box with double lines and
                                         //   title

void box_3(int, int, int, int, char *);  // box with wide lines and
                                         //   title

#endif

#include "head27.h"
#include "head28.h"
#include <stdio.h>
#include <string.h>
#include <conio.h>
```

box_1

Name	box__1 *(Print box type 1 on the screen)*
Description	Instructs the PC to print a single line box on the screen. Note that the box's screen location and size are defined by input parameters.
Variables	x refers to the horizontal row on which the top line of the box will be placed. Consider this x to be the "x" part of an "x, y" axis.
	y refers to the vertical row on which the left line of the box will be placed. Consider this y to be the "y" part of an "x, y" axis.
	w refers to the width of the displayed box and is measured in horizontal print positions.
	h refers to the height of the displayed box and is measured in vertical print lines.
Example	box__1(4,5,6,7); /* Creates a single line box 6 rows wide, 7 lines high, and having a top left corner at screen location (4,5). */
Rules	The passed parameters must physically allow the desired box to fit on the screen. For example, on an 80-character screen, a box starting in column 60 cannot be 30 characters wide.
Caution	This function has been designed to work on standard IBM hardware and might not work appropriately on all IBM-compatibles.

Calling exs.	int x__axis, y__axis, wide, high;
	x__axis = 4;
	y__axis = 5;
	wide = 6;
	high = 7;
	box__1(x__axis, y__axis, wide, high);
	
	box__1(x__axis, y__axis, 5, 10);

Routine

```
void box__1(int x, int y, int w, int h)
{
  int w__count, h__count;

  locate(x,y);
  putch('\332');
  for ( w__count = 0; w__count < = w; ++w__count ) putch('\304');
  putch('\277');

  for ( h__count = 0; h__count < = h; ++h__count )
    { locate(x + h__count + 1, y );
      putch('\263');
      for ( w__count = 0; w__count < = w; ++w__count ) putch(' ');
      putch('\263');
    }
}
```

box_1

```
        locate(x + h + 1, y);
        putch('\300');
        for ( w__count = 0; w__count <= w; ++w__count ) putch('\304');
        putch('\331');

    }
```

box_2

Name   box_2   *(Print box type 2 on the screen)*

Description   Instructs the PC to print a double line box on the screen. Note that the box's screen location and size are defined by input parameters.

Variables   x refers to the horizontal row on which the top line of the box will be placed. Consider this x to be the "x" part of an "x, y" axis.

y refers to the vertical row on which the left line of the box will be placed. Consider this y to be the "y" part of an "x, y" axis.

w refers to the width of the displayed box and is measured in horizontal print positions.

h refers to the height of the displayed box and is measured in vertical print lines.

Example   box_2(4,5,6,7); /* Creates a double line box 6 rows wide, 7 lines high, and having a top left corner at screen location (4,5). */

Rules   The passed parameters must physically allow the desired box to fit on the screen. For example, on an 80-character screen, a box starting in column 60 cannot be 30 characters wide.

Caution   This function has been designed to work on standard IBM hardware and might not work appropriately on all IBM-compatibles.

Calling ex.
```
int x_axis, y_axis, wide, high;
x_axis = 4;
y_axis = 5;
wide = 6;
high = 7;
box_2(x_axis, y_axis, wide, high);

box_2(x_axis, y_axis, 5, 10);
```

Routine
```
void box_2(int x, int y, int w, int h)
{
  int w_count, h_count, ;

  locate(x,y);
  putch('\311');
  for ( w_count = 0; w_count <= w; ++w_count ) putch('\315');
  putch('\273');

  for ( h_count = 0; h_count <= h; ++h_count )
    { locate(x + h_count + 1, y );
      putch('\272');
```

box_2

```
        for ( w_count = 0; w_count < = w; ++w_count ) putch(' ');
        putch('\272');
    }


    locate(x + h + 1, y);
    putch('\310');
    for ( w_count = 0; w_count < = w; ++w_count ) putch('\315');
    putch('\274');


}
```

box_3

Name   box__3   *(Print box type 3 on the screen)*

Description   Instructs the PC to print a wide line box on the screen. Note that the box's screen location and size are defined by input parameters.

Variables   x refers to the horizontal row on which the top line of the box will be placed. Consider this x to be the "x" part of an "x, y" axis.

y refers to the vertical row on which the left line of the box will be placed. Consider this y to be the "y" part of an "x, y" axis.

w refers to the width of the displayed box and is measured in horizontal print positions.

h refers to the height of the displayed box and is measured in vertical print lines.

Example   box__3(4,5,6,7); /*Creates a wide line box 6 rows wide, 7 lines high, and having a top left corner at screen location (4,5). */

Rules   The passed parameters must physically allow the desired box to fit on the screen. For example, on an 80-character screen, a box starting in column 60 cannot be 30 characters wide.

Caution   This function has been designed to work on standard IBM hardware and might not work appropriately on all IBM-compatibles.

Calling ex.
```
int x__axis, y__axis, wide, high;
x__axis = 4;
y__axis = 5;
wide = 6;
high = 7;
box__3(x__axis, y__axis, wide, high);

box__3(x__axis, y__axis, 5, 10);
```

Routine
```
void box__3(int x, int y, int w, int h)
{
  int w__count, h__count;

  locate(x,y);
  putch('\333');
  for ( w__count = 0; w__count <= w; ++w__count ) putch('\333');
  putch('\333');

  for ( h__count = 0; h__count <= h; ++h__count )
   { locate(x + h__count + 1, y );
     putch('\333');
     for ( w__count = 0; w__count <= w; ++w__count ) putch(' ');
     putch('\333');
   }
```

box_3

```
        locate(x + h + 1, y);
        putch('\333');
        for ( w__count = 0; w__count < = w; ++w__count ) putch('\333');
        putch('\333');

}
```

box_4

Name   box__4   *(Print box type 4 on the screen with title)*

Description   Instructs the PC to print a single line box on the screen with a centered title. Note that its screen location and size are defined by input parameters.

Variables   x refers to the horizontal row on which the top line of the box will be placed. Consider this x to be the "x" part of an "x, y" axis.

y refers to the vertical row on which the left line of the box will be placed. Consider this y to be the "y" part of an "x, y" axis.

w refers to the width of the displayed box and is measured in horizontal print positions.

h refers to the height of the displayed box and is measured in vertical print lines.

t i t l e contains the title to be centered.

Example   box__1(4,5,6,7,"The Title"); /*Creates a single line box 6 rows wide, 7 lines high, and having its top left corner at screen location (4,5). */

Rules   The passed parameters must physically allow the desired box to fit on the screen. For example, on an 80-character screen, a box starting in column 60 cannot be 30 characters wide.

Caution   This function has been designed to work on standard IBM hardware and might not work appropriately on all IBM-compatibles.

Calling exs.
```
int x__axis, y__axis, wide, high;
char title[20]
x__axis = 4;
y__axis = 5;
strcat(title,"The box Title");
wide = 6;
high = 7;
box__4(x__axis, y__axis, wide, high, title);

box__4(x__axis, y__axis, 5, 10, title);
```

Routine
```
void box__4(int x, int y, int w, int h, char *title)
{
    int w__count, h__count;

    locate(x,y);
    putch('\332');
    for ( w__count = 0; w__count < = w; ++w__count ) putch('\304');
    putch('\277');
```

box_4

```
        for ( h__count = 0; h__count < = h; ++h__count )
          { locate(x + h__count + 1, y ) ;
            putch('\263') ;
            for ( w__count = 0; w__count < = w; ++w__count ) putch('') ;
            putch('\263') ;
          }

        locate(x + h + 1, y ) ;
        putch('\300') ;
        for ( w__count = 0; w__count < = w; ++w__count ) putch('\304') ;
        putch('\331') ;

        locate(x, y + ((w-strlen(title))/2 ) + 1) ;
        printf("%s",title) ;

    }
```

box_5

Name	box_5 *(Print box type 5 on the screen with title)*

Description   Instructs the PC to print a double line box on the screen with a centered title. Note that its screen location and size are defined by input parameters.

Variables   x refers to the horizontal row on which the top line of the box will be placed. Consider this x to be the "x" part of an "x, y" axis.

y refers to the vertical row on which the left line of the box will be placed. Consider this y to be the "y" part of an "x, y" axis.

w refers to the width of the displayed box and is measured in horizontal print positions.

h refers to the height of the displayed box and is measured in vertical print lines.

title contains the title to be centered.

Example
```
box_1(4,5,6,7,"The Title"); /* Creates a double line box
                             6 rows wide, 7 lines
                             high, and having its top
                             left corner at screen
                             location (4,5). */
```

Rules   The passed parameters must physically allow the desired box to fit on the screen. For example, on an 80-character screen, a box starting in column 60 cannot be 30 characters wide.

Caution   This function has been designed to work on standard IBM hardware and might not work appropriately on all IBM-compatibles.

Calling exs.
```
int x_axis, y_axis, wide, high;
char title[20]
x_axis = 4;
y_axis = 5;
strcat(title,"The box Title");
wide = 6;
high = 7;
box_5(x_axis, y_axis, wide, high, title);

box_5(x_axis, y_axis, 5, 10, title);
```

Routine
```
void box_5(int x, int y, int w, int h, char *title)
{
    int w_count, h_count;

    locate(x,y);
    putch('\311');
    for ( w_count = 0; w_count < = w; ++w_count ) putch('\315');
    putch('\273');
```

box_5

```
          for ( h__count = 0; h__count < = h; ++h__count )

          { locate(x + h__count + 1, y ) ;
            putch('\272') ;
            for ( w__count = 0; w__count < = w; ++w__count ) putch(' ') ;
            putch('\272') ;
          }

          locate(x + h + 1, y) ;
          putch('\310') ;
          for ( w__count = 0; w__count < = w; ++w__count ) putch('\315') ;
          putch('\274') ;


          locate(x, y + ((w-strlen(title))/2 ) + 1) ;
          printf("%s",title) ;


     }
```

box_6

Name box__6 *(Print box type 6 on the screen with title)*

Description Instructs the PC to print a wide line box on the screen with a centered title. Note that its screen location and size are defined by input parameters.

Variables x refers to the horizontal row on which the top line of the box will be placed. Consider this x to be the "x" part of an "x, y" axis.

y refers to the vertical row on which the left line of the box will be placed. Consider this y to be the "y" part of an "x, y" axis.

w refers to the width of the displayed box and is measured in horizontal print positions.

h refers to the height of the displayed box and is measured in vertical print lines.

title contains the title to be centered.

Example box__1(4,5,6,7,"The Title"); /* Creates a wide line box 6 rows wide, 7 lines high, and having its top left corner at screen location (4,5). */

Rules The passed parameters must physically allow the desired box to fit on the screen. For example, on an 80-character screen, a box starting in column 60 cannot be 30 characters wide.

Caution This function has been designed to work on standard IBM hardware and might not work appropriately on all IBM-compatibles.

Calling exs.
```
int x__axis, y__axis, wide, high;
char title[20]
x__axis = 4;
y__axis = 5;
strcat(title,"The box Title");
wide = 6;
high = 7;
box__6(x__axis, y__axis, wide, high, title);

box__6(x__axis, y__axis, 5, 10, title);
```

Routine
```
void box__6(int x, int y, int w, int h, char *title)
{
    int w__count, h__count;

    locate(x,y);
    putch('\333');
    for ( w__count = 0; w__count < = w; ++w__count ) putch('\333');
    putch('\333');
```

box_6

```
      for ( h__count = 0; h__count < = h; ++h__count )
        { locate(x + h__count + 1, y );
          putch('\333');
          for ( w__count = 0; w__count < = w; ++w__count ) putch(' ');
          putch('\333');
      }

      locate(x + h + 1, y);
      putch('\333');
      for ( w__count = 0; w__count < = w; ++w__count ) putch('\333');
      putch('\333');

      locate(x, y + ((w-strlen(title))/2 ) + 1);
      printf("%s",title);

    }
```

28

Making lines on the screen

Line header file

```
#ifndef HEAD28

#define HEAD28 1

void line1_east(int, int, int);      // single line going from left to
                                      right
void line1_west(int, int, int);      // single line going from right to
                                      left
void line1_north(int, int, int);     // single line going up
void line1_south(int, int, int);     // single line going down

void line1_ne(int, int);             // top right corner symbol
void line1_nw(int, int);             // top left corner symbol
void line1_se(int, int);             // bottom right corner symbol
void line1_sw(int, int);             // bottom left corner symbol

void line2_east(int, int, int);      // double line going from left to
                                      right
void line2_west(int, int, int);      // double line going from right to
                                      left
void line2_north(int, int, int);     // double line going up
void line2_south(int, int, int);     // double line going down

void line2_ne(int, int);             // top right corner symbol
void line2_nw(int, int);             // top left corner symbol
void line2_se(int, int);             // bottom right corner symbol
void line2_sw(int, int);             // bottom left corner symbol

void line3_east(int, int, int);      // wide line going from left to
                                      right
void line3_west(int, int, int);      // wide line going from right to
                                      left
void line3_north(int, int, int);     // wide line going up
void line3_south(int, int, int);     // wide line going down
```

```
void line3__ne(int, int);      // top right corner symbol
void line3__nw(int, int);      // top left corner symbol
void line3__se(int, int);      // bottom right corner symbol
void line3__sw(int, int);      // bottom left corner symbol

#endif

#include <stdio.h>
#include <conio.h>
#include "head28.h"
```

Name   l ine1_east   *(Print line on the screen)*

Description Instructs the PC to print a single line on the screen. Note that its screen location and length are defined by input parameters.

Variables x refers to the horizontal row where the line will be placed. Consider this x to be the "x" part of an "x, y" axis.

y refers to the vertical column where the line will be placed. Consider this y to be the "y" part of an "x, y" axis.

s refers to the length of the line being displayed.

Example
```
line1_east(4,5,6); /* Creates a single line 6 charac
                      ters long beginning at screen
                      location (4,5). */
```

Rules The parameters passed must physically allow the line being created to fit on the screen. For example, on an 80-character screen, a line starting in column 60 cannot be 30 characters long.

Caution This function has been designed to work on standard IBM hardware and might not work appropriately on all IBM-compatibles.

Calling ex.
```
int x_axis, y_axis, size;
x_axis = 4;
y_axis = 5;
size = 6;
line1_east(x_axis, y_axis, size);

line1_east(x_axis, y_axis, 10);
```

Routine
```
void line1_east(int x, int y, int s)
{
  int s_count;

  if ( x != 0 && y != 0 )
   locate(x,y);

  for ( s_count = 0; s_count <= s; ++s_count ) putch('\304');
}
```

line1_west

Name   line1_west   *(Print line on the screen)*

Description   Instructs the PC to print a single line on the screen. Note that its screen location and length are defined by input parameters.

Variables   x refers to the horizontal row where the line will be placed. Consider this x to be the "x" part of an "x, y" axis.

y refers to the vertical column where the line will be placed. Consider this y to be the "y" part of an "x, y" axis.

s refers to the length of the line being displayed.

Example   line1_west(4,5,6); /* Creates a single line 6 characters long beginning at screen location (4,5). */

Rules   The parameters passed must physically allow the line being created to fit on the screen. For example, on an 80-character screen, a line starting in column 60 cannot be 30 characters long.

Caution   This function has been designed to work on standard IBM hardware and might not work appropriately on all IBM-compatibles.

Calling ex.
```
int x_axis, y_axis, size;
x_axis = 4;
y_axis = 5;
size = 6;
line1_west(x_axis, y_axis, size);

line1_west(x_axis, y_axis, 10);
```

Routine
```
void line1_west(int x, int y, int s)
{
  int s_count;

  if ( x != 0 && y != 0 )
    locate(x,y);

  for ( s_count = 0; s_count <= s; ++s_count ) putch('\10');
  for ( s_count = 0; s_count <= s; ++s_count ) putch('\304');

}
```

line1_south

Name   line1_south   *(Print line on the screen)*

Description   Instructs the PC to print a single line on the screen. Note that its screen location and length are defined by input parameters.

Variables   x refers to the horizontal row where the line will be placed. Consider this x to be the "x" part of an "x, y" axis.

y refers to the vertical column where the line will be placed. Consider this y to be the "y" part of an "x, y" axis.

s refers to the length of the line being displayed.

Example   line1_south(4,5,6); /* Creates a single line 6 charac ters long beginning at screen location (4,5).*/

Rules   The parameters passed must physically allow the line being created to fit on the screen. For example, on an 80-character screen, a line starting in column 60 cannot be 30 characters long.

Caution   This function has been designed to work on standard IBM hardware and might not work appropriately on all IBM-compatibles.

Calling ex.
```
int x_axis, y_axis, size;
x_axis = 4;
y_axis = 5;
size = 6;
line1_south(x_axis, y_axis, size);

line1_south(x_axis, y_axis, 10);
```

Routine
```
void line1_south(int x, int y, int s)
{
  int s_count;

  if ( x != 0 && y != 0 )
   locate(x,y);

  for ( s_count = 0; s_count <= s; ++s_count )
  {  putch('\263');
     putch('\10');
     putch('\12');
  }

}
```

line1_north

Name	line1_north *(Print line on the screen)*
Description	Instructs the PC to print a single line on the screen. Note that its screen location and length are defined by input parameters.
Variables	x refers to the horizontal row where the line will be placed. Consider this x to be the "x" part of an "x, y" axis.
	y refers to the vertical column where the line will be placed. Consider this y to be the "y" part of an "x, y" axis.
	s refers to the length of the line being displayed.
Example	line1_north(4,5,6); /* Creates a single line 6 charac ters long beginning at screen location (4,5). */
Rules	The parameters passed must physically allow the line being created to fit on the screen. For example, on an 80-character screen, a line starting in column 60 cannot be 30 characters long.
Caution	This function has been designed to work on standard IBM hardware and might not work appropriately on all IBM-compatibles.

Calling ex.	int x_axis, y_axis, size;
	x_axis = 4;
	y_axis = 5;
	size = 6;
	line1_north(x_axis, y_axis, size);
	
	line1_north(x_axis, y_axis, 10);

Routine	

```
void line1_north(int x, int y, int s)
{
  int s_count;

  if ( x != 0 && y != 0 )
   locate(x,y-s+1);

  for ( s_count = 0; s_count <= s; ++s_count )
  {  putch('\263');
     putch('\10');
     putch('\12');
  }

}
```

line1_nw

Name	l ine1__nw *(Print the northwest corner of a box)*
Description	Instructs the PC to print a single line box corner on the screen. Note that its screen location is defined by input parameters.
Variables	x refers to the horizontal row where the line will be placed. Consider this x to be the "x" part of an "x, y" axis.
	y refers to the vertical column where the line will be placed. Consider this y to be the "y" part of an "x, y" axis.
	s refers to the length of the line being displayed.
Example	l ine1__nw(4,5,6); /*Creates a single line box corner at screen locat ion (4,5) . */
Rules	x must be between 1 and 24 and y must be between 1 and 80.
Caution	This function has been designed to work on standard IBM hardware and might not work appropriately on all IBM-compatibles.
Calling ex.	int x__axis, y__axis;

```
int x__axis, y__axis;
x__axis = 4;
y__axis = 5;
line1__nw(x__axis, y__axis);

line1__nw(5,9);
```

Routine

```
void line1__nw(int x, int y)
{
  int s__count;

  if ( x != 0 && y != 0 )
   locate(x,y);

   putch('\332');

}
```

line1_ne

Name   line1_ne   *(Print the northeast corner of a box)*

Description   Instructs the PC to print a single line box corner on the screen. Note that its screen location is defined by input parameters.

Variables   x refers to the horizontal row where the line will be placed. Consider this x to be the "x" part of an "x, y" axis.

y refers to the vertical column where the line will be placed. Consider this y to be the "y" part of an "x, y" axis.

s refers to the length of the line being displayed.

Example   line1_ne(4,5,6); /*Creates a single line box corner at screen location (4,5). */

Rules   x must be between 1 and 24 and y must be between 1 and 80.

Caution   This function has been designed to work on standard IBM hardware and might not work appropriately on all IBM-compatibles.

Calling ex.
```
int x_axis, y_axis;
x_axis = 4;
y_axis = 5;
line1_ne(x_axis, y_axis);

line1_ne(5,9);
```

Routine
```
void line1_ne(int x, int y)
{
  int s_count;

  if ( x != 0 && y != 0 )
    locate(x,y);

    putch('\277');
}
```

line1_sw

Name   line1_sw   *(Print the southwest corner of a box)*

Description   Instructs the PC to print a single line box corner on the screen. Note that its screen location is defined by input parameters.

Variables   x refers to the horizontal row where the line will be placed. Consider this x to be the "x" part of an "x, y" axis.

y refers to the vertical column where the line will be placed. Consider this y to be the "y" part of an "x, y" axis.

s refers to the length of the line being displayed.

Example   line1_sw(4,5,6); /*Creates a single line box corner at screen location (4,5). */

Rules   x must be between 1 and 24 and y must be between 1 and 80.

Caution   This function has been designed to work on standard IBM hardware and might not work appropriately on all IBM-compatibles.

Calling ex.
```
int x_axis, y_axis;
x_axis = 4;
y_axis = 5;
line1_sw(x_axis, y_axis);

line1_sw(5,9);
```

Routine
```
void line1_sw(int x, int y)
{
  int s_count;

  if ( x != 0 && y != 0 )
   locate(x,y);

    putch('\300');
}
```

line1_se

Name	line1_se *(Print the southeast corner of a box)*
Description	Instructs the PC to print a single line box corner on the screen. Note that its screen location is defined by input parameters.
Variables	x refers to the horizontal row where the line will be placed. Consider this x to be the "x" part of an "x, y" axis.
	y refers to the vertical column where the line will be placed. Consider this y to be the "y" part of an "x, y" axis.
	s refers to the length of the line being displayed.
Example	line1_se(4,5,6); /*Creates a single line box corner at screen location (4,5). */
Rules	x must be between 1 and 24 and y must be between 1 and 80.
Caution	This function has been designed to work on standard IBM hardware and might not work appropriately on all IBM-compatibles.

Calling ex.	int x_axis, y_axis;
	x_axis = 4;
	y_axis = 5;
	line1_se(x_axis, y_axis);
	
	line1_se(5,9);

Routine	void line1_se(int x, int y)
	{
	  int s_count;
	
	  if (x != 0 && y != 0)
	   locate(x,y);
	
	   putch('\331');
	}

line2_east

Name   line2__east *(Print line on the screen)*

Description   Instructs the PC to print a double line on the screen. Note that its screen location and length are defined by input parameters.

Variables   x refers to the horizontal row where the line will be placed. Consider this x to be the "x" part of an "x, y" axis.

y refers to the vertical column where the line will be placed. Consider this y to be the "y" part of an "x, y" axis.

s refers to the length of the line being displayed.

Example   line2__east(4,5,6); /* Creates a double line 6 charac ters long beginning at screen location (4,5). */

Rules   The passed parameters must physically allow the desired line to fit on the screen. For example, on an 80-character screen, a line starting in column 60 cannot be 30 characters long.

Caution   This function has been designed to work on standard IBM hardware and might not work appropriately on all IBM-compatibles.

Calling ex.
```
int x__axis, y__axis, size;
x__axis = 4;
y__axis = 5;
size = 6;
line2__east(x__axis, y__axis, size);

line2__east(x__axis, y__axis, 10);
```

Routine
```
void line2__east(int x, int y, int s)
{
  int s__count;

  if ( x != 0 && y != 0 )
    locate(x,y);

  for ( s__count = 0; s__count <= s; ++s__count ) putch('\315');
}
```

line2_west

Name	`line2_west` *(Print line on the screen)*
Description	Instructs the PC to print a double line on the screen. Note that its screen location and length are defined by input parameters.
Variables	x refers to the horizontal row where the line will be placed. Consider this x to be the "x" part of an "x, y" axis.
	y refers to the vertical column where the line will be placed. Consider this y to be the "y" part of an "x, y" axis.
	s refers to the length of the line being displayed.
Example	`line2_west(4,5,6);` `/* Creates a double line 6 charac ters long beginning at screen location (4,5). */`
Rules	The passed parameters must physically allow the desired line to fit on the screen. For example, on an 80-character screen, a line starting in column 60 cannot be 30 characters long.
Caution	This function has been designed to work on standard IBM hardware and might not work appropriately on all IBM-compatibles.

Calling ex.	`int x_axis, y_axis, size;`
	`x_axis = 4;`
	`y_axis = 5;`
	`size = 6;`
	`line2_west(x_axis, y_axis, size);`
	
	`line2_west(x_axis, y_axis, 10);`

Routine	`void line2_west(int x, int y, int s)`
	`{`
	  `int s_count;`
	
	  `if ( x != 0 && y != 0 )`
	   `locate(x,y);`
	
	  `for ( s_count = 0; s_count <= s; ++s_count ) putch('\10');`
	  `for ( s_count = 0; s_count <= s; ++s_count ) putch('\315');`
	
	`}`

Name   line2__south   *(Print line on the screen)*

Description   Instructs the PC to print a double line on the screen. Note that its screen location and length are defined by input parameters.

Variables   x refers to the horizontal row where the line will be placed. Consider this x to be the "x" part of an "x, y" axis.

y refers to the vertical column where the line will be placed. Consider this y to be the "y" part of an "x, y" axis.

s refers to the length of the line being displayed.

Example   line2__south(4,5,6); /* Creates a double line 6 charac ters long beginning at screen location (4,5). */

Rules   The passed parameters must physically allow the desired line to fit on the screen. For example, on an 80-character screen, a line starting in column 60 cannot be 30 characters long.

Caution   This function has been designed to work on standard IBM hardware and might not work appropriately on all IBM-compatibles.

Calling ex.
```
int x__axis, y__axis, size;
x__axis = 4;
y__axis = 5;
size = 6;
line2__south(x__axis, y__axis, size);

line2__south(x__axis, y__axis, 10);
```

Routine
```
void line2__south(int x, int y, int s)
{
  int s__count;

  if ( x != 0 && y != 0 )
   locate(x,y);

  for ( s__count = 0; s__count <= s; ++s__count )
  {  putch('\272');
     putch('\10');
     putch('\12');
  }

}
```

line2_north

Name   line2_north *(Print line on the screen)*

Description Instructs the PC to print a double line on the screen. Note that its screen location and length are defined by input parameters.

Variables x refers to the horizontal row where the line will be placed. Consider this x to be the "x" part of an "x, y" axis.

y refers to the vertical column where the line will be placed. Consider this y to be the "y" part of an "x, y" axis.

s refers to the length of the line being displayed.

Example line2_north(4,5,6); /* Creates a double line 6 charac ters long beginning at screen location (4,5). */

Rules The passed parameters must physically allow the desired line to fit on the screen. For example, on an 80-character screen, a line starting in column 60 cannot be 30 characters long.

Caution This function has been designed to work on standard IBM hardware and might not work appropriately on all IBM-compatibles.

Calling ex.
```
int x_axis, y_axis, size;
x_axis = 4;
y_axis = 5;
size = 6;
line2_north(x_axis, y_axis, size);

line2_north(x_axis, y_axis, 10);
```

Routine
```
void line2_north(int x, int y, int s)
{
 int s_count;

 if ( x != 0 && y != 0 )
  locate(x,y-s+1);

 for ( s_count = 0; s_count <= s; ++s_count )
 {  putch('\272');
    putch('\10');
    putch('\12');
 }

}
```

line2_nw

Name   line2_nw   *(Print the northwest corner of a box)*

Description   Instructs the PC to print a double line box corner on the screen. Note that its screen location is defined by input parameters.

Variables   x refers to the horizontal row where the corner will be placed. Consider this x to be the "x" part of an "x, y" axis.

y refers to the vertical column where the corner will be placed. Consider this y to be the "y" part of an "x, y" axis.

Example   line2_nw(4,5); /* Creates a double line box corner at screen location (4,5). */

Rules   x must be between 1 and 24 and y must be between 1 and 80.

Caution   This function has been designed to work on standard IBM hardware and might not work appropriately on all IBM-compatibles.

Calling ex.
```
int x_axis, y_axis;
x_axis = 4;
y_axis = 5;
line2_nw(x_axis, y_axis);

line2_nw(5,9);
```

Routine
```
void line2_nw(int x, int y)
{
  int s_count;

  if ( x != 0 && y != 0 )
   locate(x,y);

   putch('\311');

}
```

line2_ne

Name   line2_ne *(Print the northeast corner of a box)*

Description Instructs the PC to print a double line box corner on the screen. Note that its screen location is defined by input parameters.

Variables x refers to the horizontal row where the corner will be placed. Consider this x to be the "x" part of an "x, y" axis.

y refers to the vertical column where the corner will be placed. Consider this y to be the "y" part of an "x, y" axis.

Example   line2_ne(4,5); /* Creates a double line box corner at screen location (4,5). */

Rules   x must be between 1 and 24 and y must be between 1 and 80.

Caution   This function has been designed to work on standard IBM hardware and might not work appropriately on all IBM-compatibles.

Calling ex.
```
int x_axis, y_axis;
x_axis = 4;
y_axis = 5;
line2_ne(x_axis, y_axis);

line2_ne(5,9);
```

Routine
```
void line2_ne(int x, int y)
{
  int s_count;

  if ( x != 0 && y != 0 )
    locate(x,y);

    putch('\273');

}
```

Name line2_sw *(Print the southwest corner of a box)*

Description Instructs the PC to print a double line box corner on the screen. Note that its screen location is defined by input parameters.

Variables x refers to the horizontal row where the corner will be placed. Consider this x to be the "x" part of an "x, y" axis.

y refers to the vertical column where the corner will be placed. Consider this y to be the "y" part of an "x, y" axis.

Example line2_sw(4,5); /* Creates a double line box corner at screen location (4,5). */

Rules x must be between 1 and 24 and y must be between 1 and 80.

Caution This function has been designed to work on standard IBM hardware and might not work appropriately on all IBM-compatibles.

Calling ex.
```
int x_axis, y_axis;
x_axis = 4;
y_axis = 5;
line2_sw(x_axis, y_axis);

line2_sw(5,9);
```

Routine
```
void line2_sw(int x, int y)
{
  int s_count;

  if ( x != 0 && y != 0 )
    locate(x,y);

    putch('\310');
}
```

line2_se

Name   line2__se   *(Print the southeast corner of a box)*

Description   Instructs the PC to print a double line box corner on the screen. Note that its screen location is defined by input parameters.

Variables   x refers to the horizontal row where the corner will be placed. Consider this x to be the "x" part of an "x, y" axis.

y refers to the vertical column where the corner will be placed. Consider this y to be the "y" part of an "x, y" axis.

Example   line2__se(4,5); /* Creates a double line box corner at screen location (4,5). */

Rules   x must be between 1 and 24 and y must be between 1 and 80.

Caution   This function has been designed to work on standard IBM hardware and might not work appropriately on all IBM-compatibles.

Calling ex.
```
int x__axis, y__axis;
x__axis = 4;
y__axis = 5;
line2__se(x__axis, y__axis);

line2__se(5,9);
```

Routine
```
void line2__se(int x, int y)
{
 int s__count;

 if ( x != 0 && y != 0 )
  locate(x,y);

   putch('\274');
}
```

Name   line3_east   *(Print line on the screen)*

Description   Instructs the PC to print a wide line on the screen. Note that its screen location and length are defined by input parameters.

Variables   x refers to the horizontal row where the line will be placed. Consider this x to be the "x" part of an "x, y" axis.

y refers to the vertical column where the line will be placed. Consider this y to be the "y" part of an "x, y" axis.

s refers to the length of the line being displayed.

Example   line3_east(4,5,6); /* Creates a wide line 6 characters long beginning at screen loca tion (4,5). */

Rules   The passed parameters must physically allow the desired line to fit on the screen. For example, on an 80-character screen, a line starting in column 60 cannot be 30 characters long.

Caution   This function has been designed to work on standard IBM hardware and might not work appropriately on all IBM-compatibles.

Calling ex.
```
int x_axis, y_axis, size;
x_axis = 4;
y_axis = 5;
size = 6;
line3_east(x_axis, y_axis, size);

line3_east(x_axis, y_axis, 10);
```

Routine
```
void line3_east(int x, int y, int s)
{
  int s_count;

if ( x != 0 && y != 0 )
  locate(x,y);

for ( s_count = 0; s_count <= s; ++s_count ) putch('\333');
}
```

line3_west

Name	l i ne3_west *(Prints a line on the screen)*
Description	Instructs the PC to print a wide line on the screen. Note that its screen location and length are defined by input parameters.
Variables	x refers to the horizontal row where the line will be placed. Consider this x to be the "x" part of an "x, y" axis.
	y refers to the vertical column where the line will be placed. Consider this y to be the "y" part of an "x, y" axis.
	s refers to the length of the line being displayed.
Example	l i ne3_west(4,5,6); /*Creates a wide l i ne 6 characters l ong beginning at screen loca t i on (4,5). */
Rules	The passed parameters must physically allow the desired line to fit on the screen. For example, on an 80-character screen, a line starting in column 60 cannot be 30 characters long.
Caution	This function has been designed to work on standard IBM hardware and might not work appropriately on all IBM-compatibles.

Calling ex.	int x_axis, y_axis, size;
	x_axis = 4;
	y_axis = 5;
	size = 6;
	l i ne3_west(x_axis, y_axis, size);
	
	l i ne3_west(x_axis, y_axis, 10);

Routine	void l i ne3_west(int x, int y, int s)
	{
	  int s_count;
	  if (x != 0 && y != 0)
	   locate(x,y);
	
	  for (s_count = 0; s_count <= s; ++s_count) putch('\10');
	  for (s_count = 0; s_count <= s; ++s_count) putch('\333');
	
	}

line3_south

Name   line3_south   *(Print a line on the screen)*

Description   Instructs the PC to print a wide line on the screen. Note that its screen location and length are defined by input parameters.

Variables   x refers to the horizontal row where the line will be placed. Consider this x to be the "x" part of an "x, y" axis.

y refers to the vertical column where the line will be placed. Consider this y to be the "y" part of an "x, y" axis.

s refers to the length of the line being displayed.

Example   line3_south(4,5,6); /* Creates a wide line 6 characters long beginning at screen location (4,5). */

Rules   The passed parameters must physically allow the desired line to fit on the screen. For example, on an 80-character screen, a line starting in column 60 cannot be 30 characters long.

Caution   This function has been designed to work on standard IBM hardware and might not work appropriately on all IBM-compatibles.

Calling ex.
```
int x_axis, y_axis, size;
x_axis = 4;
y_axis = 5;
size = 6;
line3_south(x_axis, y_axis, size);

line3_south(x_axis, y_axis, 10);
```

Routine
```
void line3_south(int x, int y, int s)
{
  int s_count;

  if ( x != 0 && y != 0 )
   locate(x,y);

  for ( s_count = 0; s_count <= s; ++s_count )
  {  putch('\333');
     putch('\10');
     putch('\12');
  }

}
```

line3_north

Name	line3_north (*Print a line on the screen*)

Description   Instructs the PC to print a wide line on the screen. Note that its screen location and length are defined by input parameters.

Variables   x refers to the horizontal row where the line will be placed. Consider this x to be the "x" part of an "x, y" axis.

y refers to the vertical column where the line will be placed. Consider this y to be the "y" part of an "x, y" axis.

s refers to the length of the line being displayed.

Example
```
line3_north(4,5,6); /* Creates a wide line 6 charac-
                       ters long beginning at screen
                       location (4,5). */
```

Rules   The passed parameters must physically allow the desired line to fit on the screen. For example, on an 80-character screen, a line starting in column 60 cannot be 30 characters long.

Caution   This function has been designed to work on standard IBM hardware and might not work appropriately on all IBM-compatibles.

Calling ex.
```
int x_axis, y_axis, size;
x_axis = 4;
y_axis = 5;
size = 6;
line3_north(x_axis, y_axis, size);

line3_north(x_axis, y_axis, 10);
```

Routine
```
void line3_north(int x, int y, int s)
{
  int s_count;

  if ( x != 0 && y != 0 )
    locate(x,y-s+1);

  for ( s_count = 0; s_count <= s; ++s_count )
  {   putch('\333');
      putch('\10');
      putch('\12');
  }

}
```

Name	line3_nw *(Print the northwest corner of a box)*
Description	Instructs the PC to print a wide line box corner on the screen. Note that its screen location is defined by input parameters.
Variables	x refers to the horizontal row where the corner will be placed. Consider this x to be the "x" part of an "x, y" axis.
	y refers to the vertical column where the corner will be placed. Consider this y to be the "y" part of an "x, y" axis.
Example	line3_nw(4,5); /* Creates a wide line box corner at screen location (4,5). */
Rules	x must be between 1 and 24 and y must be between 1 and 80.
Caution	This function has been designed to work on standard IBM hardware and might not work appropriately on all IBM compatibles.

Calling ex.

```
int x_axis, y_axis;
x_axis = 4;
y_axis = 5;
line3_nw(x_axis, y_axis);

line3_nw(5,9);
```

Routine

```
void line3_nw(int x, int y)
{
  int s_count;

  if ( x != 0 && y != 0 )
    locate(x,y);

    putch('\333');

}
```

line3_ne

Name   line3_ne   *(Print the northeast corner of a box)*

Description   Instructs the PC to print a wide line box corner on the screen. Note that its screen location is defined by input parameters.

Variables   x refers to the horizontal row where the corner will be placed. Consider this x to be the "x" part of an "x, y" axis.

y refers to the vertical column where the corner will be placed. Consider this y to be the "y" part of an "x, y" axis.

Example   line3_ne(4,5); /* Creates a wide line box corner at
                    screen location (4,5). */

Rules   x must be between 1 and 24 and y must be between 1 and 80.

Caution   This function has been designed to work on standard IBM hardware and might not work appropriately on all IBM compatibles.

Calling ex.
```
int x_axis, y_axis;
x_axis = 4;
y_axis = 5;
line3_ne(x_axis, y_axis);

line3_ne(5,9);
```

Routine
```
void line3_ne(int x, int y)
{
  int s_count;

if ( x != 0 && y != 0 )
   locate(x,y);

    putch('\333');
}
```

line3_sw

Name	line3_sw *(Print the southwest corner of a box)*
Description	Instructs the PC to print a wide line box corner on the screen. Note that its screen location is defined by input parameters.
Variables	x refers to the horizontal row where the corner will be placed. Consider this x to be the "x" part of an "x, y" axis.
	y refers to the vertical column where the corner will be placed. Consider this y to be the "y" part of an "x, y" axis.
Example	line3_sw(4,5); /* Creates a wide line box corner at screen location (4,5). */
Rules	x must be between 1 and 24 and y must be between 1 and 80.
Caution	This function has been designed to work on standard IBM hardware and might not work appropriately on all IBM compatibles.

Calling ex.

```
int x_axis, y_axis;
x_axis = 4;
y_axis = 5;
line3_sw(x_axis, y_axis);

line3_sw(5,9);
```

Routine

```
void line3_sw(int x, int y)
{
 int s_count;

 if ( x != 0 && y != 0 )
  locate(x,y);

   putch('\333');
}
```

line3_se

Name   line3__se   *(Print the southeast corner of a box)*

Description Instructs the PC to print a wide line box corner on the screen. Note that its screen location is defined by input parameters.

Variables   x refers to the horizontal row where the corner will be placed. Consider this x to be the "x" part of an "x, y" axis.

                 y refers to the vertical column where the corner will be placed. Consider this y to be the "y" part of an "x, y" axis.

Example   line3__se(4,5); /* Creates a wide line box corner at screen location (4,5). */

Rules   x must be between 1 and 24 and y must be between 1 and 80.

Caution   This function has been designed to work on standard IBM hardware and might not work appropriately on all IBM compatibles.

Calling ex.
```
int x__axis, y__axis;
x__axis = 4;
y__axis = 5;
line3__se(x__axis, y__axis);

line3__se(5,9);
```

Routine
```
void line3__se(int x, int y)
{
  int s__count;

  if ( x != 0 && y != 0 )
    locate(x,y);

    putch('\333');
}
```

29
UNIX-like filtering programs

uxhead

Name   uxhead

Description   Lists the first 10 lines of your program.

Rules   This program can be used as either a stand-alone program or as a filter within a pipe.

This program outputs to the screen (standard out). To send the output to a file, use the " > " redirection character followed by the output filename.

Examples   uxhead 10 file1.dat > file2.dat

type file1.dat |uxhead 25 > file2.dat

Routine
```
#include <stdio.h>

void main(arg,argv)
int arg;
char *argv[ ];
{ char in__char;
  FILE *fopen( ), *f__pointer;
  int count, amount;

  amount = atoi(argv[1]);
  count = 1;

  if ( arg > 2 )
  { f__pointer = fopen(argv[2],"r");
  }
  else
  { f__pointer = stdin;
  }

  while ( ( in__char = getc(f__pointer) ) != -1 )
  { if ( in__char == '\12' )
      count + +;
    if ( count <= amount )
putchar(in__char);
  }
  fclose(f__pointer);
}
```

uxstrip

Name   uxstrip

Description Strips off characters not within the standard printed character set.

Rules   This program can be used as either a stand-alone program or as a filter within a pipe.

This program outputs to the screen (standard out). To send the output to a file, use the " > " redirection character followed by the output filename.

Examples   uxstrip file1.dat > file2.dat

type file1.dat¦uxstrip > file2.dat

Routine
```
#include <stdio.h>

main(arg,argv)
int arg;
char *argv[ ];
{ char in__char;
  FILE *fopen( ), *f__pointer;

  if ( arg > 1 )
  { f__pointer = fopen(argv[1],"r");
  }
  else
  { f__pointer = stdin;
  }

  while ( ( in__char = getc(f__pointer) ) != -1 )
  { if ((in__char >='' && in__char <= '}')¦in__char == '\11'¦
    in__char == '\12')
      putchar(in__char);
  }

  fclose(f__pointer);
}
```

uxprefix

Name   uxprefix

Description Places your specified value at the beginning of each printed line.

Rules   This program can be used as either a stand-alone program or as a filter within a pipe.

This program outputs to the screen (standard out). To send the output to a file, use the ">" redirection character followed by the output filename.

Examples   uxprefix theprefix file1.dat > file2.dat

type file1.dat｜uxprefix xyz > file2.dat

Routine
```
#include <stdio.h>

void main(arg,argv)
int arg;
char *argv[ ];
{ char in_char;
  FILE *fopen( ), *f_pointer;

  if ( arg > 2 )
  { f_pointer = fopen(argv[2],"r");
  }
  else
  { f_pointer = stdin;
  }

  printf("%s",argv[1]);
  while ( ( in_char = getc(f_pointer) ) != -1 )
  { putchar(in_char);
    if ( in_char == '\12' )
      printf("%s",argv[1]);
  }
  fclose(f_pointer);
}
```

uxtee

Name   uxtee

Description   Reads data from standard in and directs it to both a file and standard out.

Rules   This program can be used as either a stand-alone program or as a filter within a pipe.

Example   uxcat file1 file2|uxtee file3|sort > file4

Routine
```
#include <stdio.h>

main(arg,argv)
int arg;
char *argv[ ];
{ char in__char;
  FILE *fopen( ), *f__pointer;

  f__pointer = fopen(argv[1],"w");

  while ( ( in__char = getchar( ) )!= -1 )
  { putchar(in__char);
    fputc(in__char,f__pointer);
  }

  fclose(f__pointer);
}
```

uxcat

Name   uxcat

Description   Reads a file or group of files and directs them to standard out.

Rules   This program can be used as either a stand-alone program or as a filter within a pipe.

This program outputs to the screen (standard out). To send the output to a file, use the " > " redirection character followed by the output filename.

Examples
```
uxcat file1.dat
uxcat file1.dat file2.dat
uxcat file1.dat file2.dat|uxupper > file3.dat
```

Routine
```c
#include <stdio.h>

main(arg,argv)
int arg;
char *argv[ ];
{ char in__char;
  FILE *fopen( ), *f__pointer;
  int args;

  args = arg;

  while ( args > 0 )
  { f__pointer = fopen(argv[args],"r");

    while ( ( in__char = getc(f__pointer) ) != -1 )
    { putchar(in__char);
    }
    args-;
    fclose(f__pointer);
  }
}
```

uxlinesz

Name uxlinesz

Description Counts and outputs the number of characters in each line of the file or pipe stream.

Rules This program can be used as either a stand-alone program or as a filter within a pipe.

This program outputs to the screen (standard out). To send the output to a file, use the " > " redirection character followed by the output filename.

Examples
```
uxlinesz file1.dat
uxlinesz file1.dat > file2.dat
type file1.dat¦uxlinesz > file2.dat
```

Routine
```c
#include <stdio.h>

main(arg,argv)
int arg;
char *argv[ ];
{ char in__char;
  FILE *fopen( ), *f__pointer;
  long int count = 0;

  if ( arg > 1 )
  { f__pointer = fopen(argv[1],"r");
  }
  else
  { f__pointer = stdin;
  }

  while ( ( in__char = getc(f__pointer) ) != -1 )
  { if ( in__char != '\11' && in__char != '\12' ) count + + ;
    if ( in__char == '\12' )
    { printf("%ld\n",count);
      count = 0;
    }
  }
  fclose(f__pointer);
}
```

uxcountl

Name   uxcount l

Description Counts the number of lines in a given file or pipe stream.

Rules   This program can be used as either a stand-alone program or as a filter within a pipe.

This program outputs to the screen (standard out). To send the output to a file, use the " > " redirection character followed by the output filename.

Examples   uxcount l file1.dat
type file1.dat¦uxcount l > file2.dat

Routine
```
#include <stdio.h>

main(arg,argv)
int arg;
char *argv[ ];
{ char in__char;
  FILE *fopen( ), *f__pointer;
  long int count = 0;

  if ( arg > 1 )
  { f__pointer = fopen(argv[1],"r");
  }
  else
  { f__pointer = stdin;
  }

  while ( ( in__char = getc(f__pointer) ) != -1 )
  { if ( in__char == '\12') count++;
  }
  printf("%ld\n",count);
  fclose(f__pointer);
}
```

Name uxcountw

Description Counts the number of words in a given file or pipe stream.

Rules This program can be used as either a stand-alone program or as a filter within a pipe.

This program outputs to the screen (standard out). To send the output to a file, use the " > " redirection character followed by the output filename.

Examples
```
uxcountw file1.dat
type file1.dat|uxcountw > file2.dat
```

Routine
```c
#include <stdio.h>

main(arg,argv)
int arg;
char *argv[ ];
{ char in__char, last__char;
  FILE *fopen( ), *f__pointer;
  long int count = 0;

  if ( arg > 1 )
  { f__pointer = fopen(argv[1],"r");
  }
  else
  { f__pointer = stdin;
  }

  last__char = '';
  while ( ( in__char = getc(f__pointer) ) != -1 )
  { if (( last__char == ''|last__char == '\11'|last__char == '\12') &&
      ( in__char != '' && in__char != '\11' && in__char != '\12'))
      count + + ;
    last__char = in__char;
  }
  printf("%ld\n",count);
  fclose(f__pointer);
}
```

uxcountc

Name   uxcountc

Description   Counts the number of characters in a given file or pipe stream.

Rules   This program can be used as either a stand-alone program or as a filter within a pipe.

This program outputs to the screen (standard out). To send the output to a file, use the " > " redirection character followed by the output filename.

Examples
```
uxcountc file1.dat
type file1.dat|uxcountc > file2.dat
```

Routine
```c
#include <stdio.h>

main(arg,argv)
int arg;
char *argv[ ];
{ char in__char;
  FILE *fopen( ), *f__pointer;
  long int count = 0;
  if ( arg > 1 )
  { f__pointer = fopen(argv[1],"r");
  }
  else
  { f__pointer = stdin;
  }

  while ( ( in__char = getc(f__pointer) ) != -1 )
  { if ( in__char != '\11' && in__char != '\12') count++;
  }
  printf("%ld\n",count);
  fclose(f__pointer);
}
```

uxlower

Name   uxlower

Description   Converts all uppercase characters to lowercase. Non-letter or previously lowercase characters remain untouched.

Rules   This program can be used as either a stand-alone program or as a filter within a pipe.

This program outputs to the screen (standard out). To send the output to a file, use the " > " redirection character followed by the output filename.

Examples   uxlower file1.dat > file2.dat
type file1.dat¦uxlower > file2.dat

Routine

```
include <stdio.h>

main(arg,argv)
int arg;
char *argv[ ];
{ char in_char;
  FILE *fopen( ), *f_pointer;

  if ( arg > 1 )
  { f_pointer = fopen(argv[1],"r");
  }
  else
  { f_pointer = stdin;
  }

  while ( ( in_char = getc(f_pointer) ) != -1 )
  { if (in_char >='A' && in_char <= 'Z') in_char = 'a' - 'A' + in_char;
    putchar(in_char);
  }

  fclose(f_pointer);
}
```

uxdouble

Name   uxdouble

Description   Places a blank line, essentially double-spacing the data output.

Rules   This program can be used as either a stand-alone program or as a filter within a pipe.

This program outputs to the screen (standard out). To send the output to a file, use the ">" redirection character followed by the output filename.

Examples   uxdouble file1.dat > file2.dat
type file1.dat¦uxdouble > file2.dat

Routine

```
#include <stdio.h>

void main(arg,argv)
int arg;
char *argv[ ];
{ char in__char;
  FILE *fopen( ), *f__pointer;

  if ( arg > 1 )
  { f__pointer = fopen(argv[1],"r");
  }
  else
  { f__pointer = stdin;
  }

  while ( ( in__char = getc(f__pointer) ) != -1 )
  { if ( in__char == '\12' )
    putchar(in__char);
    putchar(in__char);
  }
  fclose(f__pointer);
}
```

Name   uxupper

Description   Converts all lowercase characters to uppercase. Non-letter or previously uppercase characters remain untouched.

Rules   This program can be used as either a stand-alone program or as a filter within a pipe.

This program outputs to the screen (standard out). To send the output to a file, use the " > " redirection character followed by the output filename.

Examples
```
uxupper file1.dat > file2.dat
type file1.dat|uxupper > file2.dat
```

Routine
```c
#include <stdio.h>

main(arg,argv)
int arg;
char *argv[ ];
{ char in__char;
  FILE *fopen( ), *f__pointer;

  if ( arg > 1 )
  { f__pointer = fopen(argv[1],"r");
  }
  else
  { f__pointer = stdin;
  }

  while ( ( in__char = getc(f__pointer) ) != -1 )
  { if (in__char >='a' && in__char <= 'z') in__char = 'A' - 'a' + in__char;
    putchar(in__char);
  }

  fclose(f__pointer);
}
```

uxcut

Name   uxcut

Description   Cuts a group of characters out of the middle of a file or pipe stream.

Rules   This program can be used as either a stand-alone program or as a filter within a pipe.

This program outputs to the screen (standard out). To send the output to a file, use the " > " redirection character followed by the output filename.

Examples   uxcut 5 10 file1.dat > file2.dat
type file1.dat¦uxcut 5 10 > file2.dat

Routine

```
#include <stdio.h>

voidmain(arg,argv)
int arg;
char *argv[ ];
{ char in__char;
  FILE *fopen( ), *f__pointer;
  int start, end, count;

  start = atoi(argv[1]);
  end = atoi(argv[2]);
  count = 0;

  if ( arg > 3 )
  { f__pointer = fopen(argv[3],"r");
  }
  else
  { f__pointer = stdin;
  }

  while ( ( in__char = getc(f__pointer) ) != -1 )
  { if ( in__char == '\12' )
    { count = -1;
  putchar(in__char);
    }
    count++;
    if ( count >= start && count <= end )
      putchar(in__char);
  }
  fclose(f__pointer);
}
```

uxpack

Name   uxpack

Description   Deletes blank lines, thus packing the file closer together.

Rules   This program can be used as either a stand-alone program or as a filter within a pipe.

This program outputs to the screen (standard out). To send the output to a file, use the " > " redirection character followed by the output filename.

Examples
```
uxpack file1.dat > file2.dat
type file1.dat|uxpack > file2.dat
```

Routine
```
#include <stdio.h>

void main(arg,argv)
int arg;
char *argv[ ];
{ char in_char, last_char;
  FILE *fopen( ), *f_pointer;

  if ( arg > 1 )
  { f_pointer = fopen(argv[1],"r");
  }
  else
  { f_pointer = stdin;
  }
  last_char = '\0';

  while ( ( in_char = getc(f_pointer) ) != -1 )
  { if ( in_char != '\12'|last_char != '\12' )
  putchar(in_char);
    last_char = in_char;
  }
  fclose(f_pointer);
}
```

uxsuffix

Name   uxsuffix

Description   Places a specified string at the end of each output line.

Rules   This program can be used as either a stand-alone program or as a filter within a pipe.

This program outputs to the screen (standard out). To send the output to a file, use the " > " redirection character followed by the output filename.

Examples

```
uxsuffix the suffix file1.dat > file2.dat
type file1.dat|uxsuffix xyz > file2.dat
```

Routine

```c
#include <stdio.h>

void main(arg,argv)
int arg;
char *argv[ ];
{ char in_char;
  FILE *fopen( ), *f_pointer;

  if ( arg > 2 )
  { f_pointer = fopen(argv[2],"r");
  }
  else
  { f_pointer = stdin;
  }

  while ( ( in_char = getc(f_pointer) ) != -1 )
  { if ( in_char == '\12')
      printf("%s",argv[1]);
    putchar(in_char);
  }
  printf("%s",argv[1]);
  fclose(f_pointer);
}
```

A
Operator precedence

The following operators are listed in order from highest precedence to lowest precedence:

```
->   [ ]     .

*    &    -    /    ++    !       (Unary)

*    /    %

+    -

>>   <<

<    >    <=    >=

==   !=

&

|
|

&&

||
||

?!

=    +=    -=    *=    /=    %=
```

B

Data type conversions

The following table describes how the different numerical data types are converted from one to the other:

Data type from	Data type to	Outcome
double	int	Truncates decimals
double	float	Rounds where needed
float	int	Truncates decimals
float	double	Zero fills
int	float	Zero fills
int	double	Zero fills

Index

#asm directive, 217
#define directive, 137-140, 218
#else directive, 143, 219
#endasm directive, 220
#endif directive, 221
#if directive, 142-143, 222
#ifdef directive, 142, 223
#ifndef directive, 142, 224
#include directive, 140-141, 225
#undef directive, 143, 226
% (remainder) operator, 36-37, 164
%= (remainder assignment) operator, 172
& (address) operator, 174
& (bitwise AND) operator, 125-127, 187
&& (logical AND) operator, 44-45, 178
&= (unary bitwise AND) operator, 193
* (indirection) operator, 173
* (multiplication) operator, 36-37, 162
*= (multiplication assignment) operator, 170
+ (addition) operator, 36-37, 160
++ (incremental) operator, 38, 165
+= (addition assignment) operator, 168
− (subtraction) operator, 36-37, 161
−− (decremental) operator, 38, 166
−= (subtraction assignment) operator, 169
−> (structure identification) operator, 177
. (structure identification) operator, 176
/ (division) operator, 36-37, 163
/* */ (comment) directive, 216
// (comment) operator, 155, 314
/= (division assignment) operator, 171

:: (scope resolution) operator, 155, 319
< (less-than) operator, 180
< < (bitwise shift left) operator, 191
< < (put to) operator, 321
< < operator, 125, 131-133
< < = (unary bitwise shift left) operator, 196
< = (less-than or equal to) operator, 182
= (assignment) operator, 167
= = (equal to) operator, 184
> (greater-than) operator, 181
> > = (greater-than or equal to) operator, 183
> > (bitwise shift right) operator, 192
> > (get from) operator, 322
> > operator, 125, 133-134
> > = (unary bitwise shift right) operator, 197
?: (equation) operator, 186
!= (not-equal to) operator, 185
[] (array) operator, 175
^ (bitwise exclusive OR) operator, 125, 128-130, 189
^= (unary bitwise exclusive OR) operator, 195
_exit() function, 312
| (bitwise inclusive OR) operator, 125, 127-128, 188
|= (unary bitwise inclusive OR) operator, 194
| (logical OR) operator, 44-45, 179
~ ~ (bitwise ones complement) operator, 125, 130-131, 190
. (structure identification), 176

A

abs( ) function, 228
acos( ) function, 229

Application Programming Interface (API)
  control-block-based, 146
  multifunction-based, 145-146
  protocol conversion protocols, 146-148
  using, 145-148
arithmetic operators, 35-39
  % (remainder), 36-37, 164
  * (multiplication), 36-37, 162
  + (addition), 36-37, 160
  ++ (incremental), 38, 165
  − (subtraction), 36-37, 161
  −− (decremental), 38, 166
  / (division), 36-37, 163
  increment/decrement expressions, 38
  standard expressions, 36-37
  unary expressions, 37
array manipulation functions, 378-392
  calc_ave, 379-380
  calc_sum, 391-392
  do_search, 389-390
  get_max, 383-384
  get_mean, 385-386
  get_min, 387-388
  header file, 378
  is_found, 381-382
arrays, 61-71
  character, 65-71
  numeric, 61-65
  passing to a function, 103-105
  pointers and, 88-92
  string (see character arrays)
  structures and, 79-80
  within structures, 82-83
  within structures containing arrays, 83-84
ASCII codes, function key, 122
asin( ) function, 230
atan( ) function, 231

atof( ) function, 232
atoi( ) function, 233
atol( ) function, 234
auto storage class, 200
automatic variables, 106-108

B

bit fields, 134-135
bits, 29
bitwise operators, 125-135
  & (AND), 125-127, 187
  &= (unary bitwise AND), 193
  << (shift left), 131-133, 191
  <<= (unary bitwise shift left), 196
  >> (shift right), 133-134, 192
  >>= (unary bitwise shift right), 197
  | (exclusive OR), 128-130, 189
  ^= (unary bitwise exclusive OR), 195
  | (inclusive OR), 127-128, 188
  |= (unary bitwise inclusive OR), 194
  ~ (ones complement), 130-131, 190
  bit fields, 134-135
boxes
  box_1, 539-540
  box_2, 541-542
  box_3, 543-544
  box_4, 545-546
  box_5, 547-548
  box_6, 549-550
  header file, 538
  making on the screen, 538-550
break statement, 55-56
byte, 29

C

C programming (see also programming; Turbo C++)
  designing a program, 3-19
  getting started, 21-25
  precompiler, 137-143
  Turbo C++ enhancements, 149-155
  using APIs, 145-148
calc_ave function, 379-380
calc_sum function, 391-392
calloc( ) function, 235-236
ceil( ) function, 237
cfree( ) function, 238
char data type, 34-35, 86-87, 201
character arrays, 65-71
character strings, 67-71
  calculating length, 67-68
  comparing string equality, 69-71
  copying, 71
class, 154, 317
clearerr( ) function, 239

clear_d, 535
clear_i, 527
clreer( ) function, 239
cmet_feet function, 394
cmet_inch function, 395
comdenom function, 507
commands (see also directives; functions; statements)
  conditional logic, 12
  file-handling, 117-120
  functional, 12
  pseudocode, 12
  repetition, 12
compiler directives (see directives)
comp_off function, 327
comp_on function, 328
conditional logic, 12, 41-48
conditional operator, 49-50
const, 155, 318
constants, 27
continue statement, 57
control statements, 41-59
  conditional logic, 41-48
  conditional operators, 49-50
  looping, 50-59
cos( ) function, 240
cosh( ) function, 241

D

data definitions
  % types, 23
  types of, 23, 29
data dictionaries, 6-7
data direction, 115-116
data input functions
  get_loc, 368-370
  get_loc_prompt, 361-364
  get_prompt, 373-375
  header file, 359-360
  lpr_g_yes_no, 366-367
  l_g_response, 371
  l_g_yes_no, 372
  pr_g_response, 365, 376
  pr_g_yes_no, 377
  Turbo C++, 359-377
data streams, 153-154
data types, 27-35, 199-214
  char, 34-35, 201
  conversions, 595
  double, 32, 202
  FILE, 204
  float, 30-31, 205
  identifiers, 110-111
  int, 29-30, 206
  long, 32-33, 207
  short, 33, 209
  typedef, 212
  unsigned, 34, 214
  variable name formats, 28-29
  variables, 29-35
date functions, 414-505

date_1, 417
date_2, 418
date_3, 419
date_4, 420
date_5, 421
date_6, 422
date_7, 423-424
date_8, 425-426
date_9, 427-428
date_10, 429
date_11, 430
date_12, 431
date_13, 432
date_14, 433
date_15, 434
date_16, 435-436
date_17, 437-438
date_18, 439
date_19, 440-441
date_20, 442-443
date_21, 444-445
date_22, 446
date_23, 447
date_24, 448
date_25, 449
date_26, 450
date_27, 451
date_28, 452
date_29, 453
date_30, 454
date_31, 455-456
date_32, 457-458
date_33, 459-460
date_34, 461
date_35, 462
date_36, 463
date_37, 464-465
date_38, 466
date_39, 467
date_40, 468-469
date_41, 470-471
date_42, 472
date_43, 473-474
date_44, 475-476
date_45, 477-478
date_46, 479
date_47, 480
date_48, 481
date_49, 482-483
date_50, 484-485
date_51, 486-487
date_52, 488-489
date_53, 490-491
date_54, 492-493
date_55, 494-495
date_56, 496-497
date_57, 498-500
date_58, 501
date_59, 502
date_60, 503
header file, 414-416

i_convert, 504
i_to_a, 505
decision tables, 8-9
decision trees, 7-8
delete, 154, 316
directives, 215-226
 /* */ (comment), 216
 #asm, 217
 #define, 218
 #define, 137-140
 #else, 143, 219
 #endasm, 220
 #endif, 221
 #if, 222
 #if, 142-143
 #ifdef, 142, 223
 #ifndef, 142, 224
 #include, 225
 #include, 140-141
 #undef, 143, 226
 conditional, 142-143
do statement, 242
do-while statement, 17-19, 52-53
DoMath( ) function, 146-148
double data type, 32, 202
do_search function, 389-390
ds_off function, 329
ds_on function, 330

E

emph_off function, 331
emph_on function, 332
empty_1, 525
empty_d, 533
encapsulation, 150
errors, 12-13
 logical, 12-13
 syntax, 12
escape sequence, 110
exit( ) function, 243
exp( ) function, 244
exp1_off function, 333
exp1_on function, 334
exp_off function, 335
exp_on function, 336
extern storage class, 203

F

fabs( ) function, 245
fclose( ) function, 120, 246
feet_cmet function, 396
feof( ) function, 247
ferror( ) function, 248
fflush( ) function, 249
fgetc( ) function, 119, 250
fgets( ) function, 117-118, 251
FILE data type, 204
filtering programs, 115-116
 uxcat, 582
 uxcountc, 586
 uxcountl, 584

uxcountw, 585
uxcut, 590
uxdouble, 588
uxhead, 578
uxlinesz, 583
uxlower, 587
uxpack, 591
uxprefix, 580
uxstrip, 579
uxsuffix, 592
uxtee, 581
uxupper, 589
UNIX-like, 577-592
float data type, 30-31, 205
floor( ) function, 252
flowcharts, 4-6
 sequential processing, 16
fopen( ) function, 117, 253
for statement, 53-54, 254
fprintf( ) function, 118-119, 255
fputc( ) function, 119, 256
fputs( ) function, 118, 257
fread( ) function, 258
free( ) function, 154, 238
fscanf( ) function, 118-119, 259
fseek( ) function, 260-261
ftell( ) function, 262
full_d, 534
full_i, 526
functional commands, 12
function keys, ASCII codes, 122
functions, 97-108, 227-312
 abs( ), 228
 acos( ), 229
 array manipulation, 378-392
 asin( ), 230
 atan( ), 231
 atof( ), 232
 atoi( ), 233
 atol( ), 234
 automatic/static variables, 106-108
 calling, 98-99
 calloc( ), 235-236
 ceil( ), 237
 cfree( ), 238
 clearerr( ), 239
 clreer( ), 239
 cos( ), 240
 cosh( ), 241
 data input, 359-377
 date, 414-505
 default arguments, 153
 DoMath( ), 146-148
 exit( ), 243
 exp( ), 244
 fabs( ), 245
 fclose( ), 120, 246
 feof( ), 247
 ferror( ), 248
 fflush( ), 249
 fgetc( ), 119, 250

fgets( ), 117-118, 251
floor( ), 252
fopen( ), 117, 253
fprintf( ), 118-119, 255
fputc( ), 119, 256
fputs( ), 118, 257
fread( ), 258
free( ), 154, 238
fscanf( ), 118-119, 259
fseek( ), 260-261
ftell( ), 262
fwrite( ), 263
getc( ), 264
getch( ), 115, 265
getchar( ), 266
global variables, 105-106
inline, 150-151
isalnum( ), 269
isalpha( ), 270
isascii( ), 271
iscntrl( ), 272
isdigit( ), 273
islower( ), 274
isprint( ), 275
ispunct( ), 276
isspace( ), 277
isupper( ), 278
itoa( ), 279
length( ), 104
main( ), 21, 97, 106
malloc( ), 154, 280
mathematical, 506-519
measurement conversion, 393-413
member, 150
overloading, 152
passing arrays, 103-105
passing parameters by value/
 address, 108
passing/receiving parameters, 99-
 101
printer output, 325-348
printf( ), 22-25, 30-31, 38, 62,
 97-99, 109-111, 282
putc( ), 283
putch( ), 113-114, 284
putchar( ), 285
rand( ), 286
realloc( ), 287
remove( ), 289
rename( ), 290
return values, 101-103
rewind( ), 291
scanf( ), 48, 111-113, 292
sin( ), 293
sinh( ), 294
sprintf( ), 295
square( ), 99-100, 103
srand( ), 296
sscanf( ), 297
strcat( ), 298
strcmp( ), 299

functions *cont.*
  strcpy( ), 300
  strien( ), 99
  string, 348-358
  strlen( ), 301
  strncat( ), 302
  strncmp( ), 303
  strncpy( ), 304
  switch( ), 305-306
  times( ), 100-101
  tolower( ), 307
  toupper( ), 308
  ungetc( ), 309
  unlink( ), 310
  _exit( ), 312
fwrite( ) function, 263

G

gal_liter function, 397
getc( ) function, 264
getch( ) function, 115, 265
getchar( ) function, 266
getloc_d, 536
getloc_i, 528
getsize_d, 537
getsize_i, 529
gettop_d, 532
gettop_i, 524
get_loc function, 368-370
get_loc_prompt function, 361-364
get_max function, 383-384
get_mean function, 385-386
get_min function, 387-388
get_prompt function, 373-375
global variables, 105-106
goto statement, 19, 57-59, 267
gram_ounce function, 398

H

header file, 140
Hierarchical Input Process Output (HIPO) charts, 9-11
Host Language Interface (HLI) (*see* API), 145

I

if statement, 42-47, 268
  multi-if conditions, 44-45
  nested, 45-46
  tandem, 46-47
If-Then-Else statement, 16-17, 49
inch_cmet function, 399
inch_met function, 400
inline, 155, 320
inline functions, 150-151
Input Process Output (IPO) charts, 10-11
input/output, 109-123
  data direction, 115-116
  file-handling commands, 117-120

IBM PC, 120-123
IBM PC formatting screen outputs, 120-121
IBM PC function key input, 122-123
IBM PC printer output, 121-122
  stdeer, 120
  stdin, 120
  stdout, 120
inputs, 3
int data type, 29-30, 206
isalnum( ) function, 269
isalpha( ) function, 270
isascii( ) function, 271
iscntrl( ) function, 272
isdigit( ) function, 273
islower( ) function, 274
isprint( ) function, 275
ispunct( ) function, 276
isspace( ) function, 277
isupper( ) function, 278
is_found function, 381-382
ital_off function, 337
ital_on function, 338
itoa( ) function, 279
i_convert function, 504
i_to_a function, 505

K

kgram_ounce function, 401
kgram_pound function, 402
kmet_mile function, 403

L

language operators, 159-197
  != (not-equal to), 185
  % (remainder), 36-37, 164
  %= (remainder assignment), 172
  & (address), 174
  & (bitwise AND), 125-127, 187
  && (logical AND), 44-45, 178
  &= (unary bitwise AND), 193
  * (indirection), 173
  * (multiplication), 36-37, 162
  *= (multiplication assignment), 170
  + (addition), 36-37, 160
  ++ (incremental), 38, 165
  += (addition assignment), 168
  - (subtraction), 36-37, 161
  -- (decremental), 38, 166
  -= (subtraction assignment), 169
  -> (structure identification), 177
  . (structure identification), 176
  / (division), 36-37, 163
  /= (division assignment), 171
  < (less-than), 180
  << (bitwise shift left), 191
  <<= (unary bitwise shift left), 196
  <= (less-than or equal to), 182
  = (assignment), 167
  == (equal to), 184

  > (greater-than), 181
  >= (greater-than or equal to), 183
  > (bitwise shift right), 192
  >= (unary bitwise shift right), 197
  ?: (equation), 186
  [] (array), 175
  ^ (bitwise exclusive OR), 125, 128-130, 189
  ^= (unary bitwise exclusive OR), 195
  |(bitwise inclusive OR), 125, 127-128, 188
  |= (unary bitwise inclusive OR), 194
  |(logical OR), 44-45, 179
  ~ (bitwise ones complement), 125, 130-131, 190
length( ) function, 104
lines
  header file, 551-552
  line1_east, 553
  line1_ne, 558
  line1_north, 556
  line1_nw, 557
  line1_se, 560
  line1_south, 555
  line1_sw, 559
  line1_west, 554
  line2_east, 561
  line2_ne, 566
  line2_north, 564
  line2_nw, 565
  line2_se, 568
  line2_south, 563
  line2_sw, 567
  line2_west, 562
  line3_east, 569
  line3_ne, 574
  line3_north, 572
  line3_nw, 573
  line3_se, 576
  line3_south, 571
  line3_sw, 575
  line3_west, 570
  making on the screen, 551-576
liter_gal function, 404
liter_quart function, 405
logical errors, 12-13
long data type, 32-33, 207
looping, 50-59
  associated statements, 55-57
  nested, 54-55
  statements, 51-54
l_g_response function, 371
l_g_yes_no function, 372
lpr_g_response function, 365
lpr_g_yes_no function, 366-367
Lvalues, 27-28

M

macros, 137

defining, 138-140
main( ) function, 21, 97, 106
malloc( ) function, 154, 280-281
mathematical functions, 506-519
  comdenom, 507
  header file, 506
  poly3, 509
  poly4, 510
  poly5, 511
  poly6, 512
  poly7, 513
  poly8, 514
  poly9, 515
  poly10, 516
  primenum, 508
  vmath1, 517
  vmath2, 518
  vmath3, 519
measurement conversion functions,
  393-413
  cmet_feet, 394
  cmet_inch, 395
  feet_cmet, 396
  gal_liter, 397
  gram_ounce, 398
  inch_cmet, 399
  inch_met, 400
  kgram_ounce, 401
  kgram_pound, 402
  kmet_mile, 403
  liter_gal, 404
  liter_quart, 405
  met_inch, 406
  met_yards, 407
  mile_kmet, 408
  ounce_gram, 409
  ounce_kgram, 410
  pound_kgram, 411
  quart_liter, 412
  yards_met, 413
member functions, 150
met_inch function, 406
met_yards function, 407
mile_kmet function, 408

N

nested loops, 54-55
new, 154, 315
numeric arrays, 61-65

O

object-oriented programming (OOP),
  149-154
operators, 35-39 (*see also* specific
  operator symbol)
  arithmetic (*see* arithmetic)
  bitwise (*see* bitwise operators)
  conditional, 49-50
  language, (*see* language operators)
  precedence of, 593
  Turbo C++, (*see* Turbo C++)

ounce_gram function, 409
ounce_kgram function, 410
outputs, 3

P

parallel testing, 13
parameters, 21
  passing by value/address, 108
  passing/receiving, 99-101
piping, 115-116
pointers, 85-95
  arithmetic, 90-92
  arrays and, 88-92
  structures and, 92-95
poly3 function, 509
poly4 function, 510
poly5 function, 511
poly6 function, 512
poly7 function, 513
poly8 function, 514
poly9 function, 515
poly10 function, 516
pop_d, 531
pop_i, 523
pound_kgram function, 411
precompiler, 137-143
  defining macros, 138-140
  directives, 137-143, 215-226
  replacing text, 137-138
primenum function, 508
print mask, 109
printer output functions, 325-348
  comp_off, 327
  comp_on, 328
  ds_off, 329
  ds_on, 330
  emph_off, 331
  emph_on, 332
  exp1_off, 333
  exp1_on, 334
  exp_off, 335
  exp_on, 336
  header file, 325-326
  ital_off, 337
  ital_on, 338
  prop_off, 339
  prop_on, 340
  reset, 341
  sub_off, 342
  sub_on, 343
  super_off, 344
  super_on, 345
  under_off, 346
  under_on, 347
printf( ) function, 22-25, 30-31,
  38, 62, 86, 97-99, 109, 282
prior testing, 13
private, 155
processes, 3
programming, 12-13 (*see also* C
  programming; Turbo C++)

object-oriented (OOP), 149-154
preliminary testing, 12-13
structured, 15-16
writing source code, 12
programs
  compilation process, 14-15
  conceptual overview, 16-19
  data dictionaries, 6-7
  decision tables, 8-9
  decision trees, 7-8
  designing, 3-19
  flowcharts, 4-6, 16
  functional design, 3-9
  implementing and maintaining, 13-
    15
  linkage process, 15
  precompilation, 15
  preliminary testing, 12-13
  technical design, 9-12
  testing, 13-15
  UNIX-like filtering, 577-592
  writing, 21-25
prop_off function, 339
prop_on function, 340
pr_g_response function, 376
pr_g_yes_no function, 377
pseudocode, 11-12
  commands, 12
public, 154
push down stacks, 520-537
  clear_d, 535
  clear_i, 527
  empty_1, 525
  empty_d, 533
  full_d, 534
  full_i, 526
  getloc_d, 536
  getloc_i, 528
  getsize_d, 537
  getsize_i, 529
  gettop_d, 532
  gettop_i, 524
  header file, 520-521
  pop_d, 531
  pop_i, 523
  push_d, 530
  push_i, 522
push_d, 530
push_i, 522
putc( ) function, 283
putch( ) function, 113-114, 284
putchar( ) function, 285

Q

quart_liter function, 412

R

rand( ) function, 286
realloc( ) function, 287-288
register storage class, 208
remove( ) function, 289

rename( ) function, 290
repetition commands, 12
reset function, 341
return statement, 101-102
rewind( ) function, 291
Rvalues, 27-28

S

scanf( ) function, 48, 111-113, 292
sequential processing structure, 16
short data type, 33, 209
simulation testing, 14
sin( ) function, 293
sinh( ) function, 294
source code, writing, 12
sprintf( ) function, 295
square( ) function, 99-100, 103
srand( ) function, 296
sscanf( ) function, 297
stacks, push down, 520-537
statement block, 44
statements, 227-312
  break, 55-56
  char, 86-87
  continue, 57
  control, 41-59
  do, 242
  do-while, 17-19, 52-53
  for, 53-54, 254
  goto, 19, 57-59, 267
  if, 42-47, 268
  if-then-else, 16-17, 49
  return, 101-102
  switch, 47-48
  while, 51-52, 311
  while, 51-52
static storage class, 210
static variables, 106-108
stdeer, 120
stdin, 120
stdout, 120
storage classes, 199-214
  auto, 200
  extern, 203
  register, 208
  static, 210
  struct, 75-77, 211
  union, 213
strcat( ) function, 298
strcmp( ) function, 299
strcpy( ) function, 300
strien( ) function, 99
string arrays (see character arrays)
string functions, 348-358
  header file, 348
  str_convert, 349
  str_count, 350
  str_delete, 352
  str_index, 351
  str_lower, 353
  str_lpad, 354

str_rindex, 355
str_rpad, 356
str_swap, 357
str_upper, 358
strlen( ) function, 301
strncat( ) function, 302
strncmp( ) function, 303
strncpy( ) function, 304
struct storage class, 75-77, 211
structures, 75-84
  arrays of, 79-80
  arrays within, 82-83
  arrays within structures containing
    arrays, 83-84
  defining, 75-77
  initializing, 77-79
  pointers and, 92-95
  within structures, 81-82
str_convert function, 349
str_count function, 350
str_delete function, 352
str_index function, 351
str_lower function, 353
str_lpad function, 354
str_rindex function, 355
str_rpad function, 356
str_swap function, 357
str_upper function, 358
sub_off function, 342
sub_on function, 343
super_off function, 344
super_on function, 345
switch( ) function, 47-48, 305-
  306
syntax errors, 12

T

testing
  parallel, 13
  preliminary, 12-13
  prior, 13
  programs, 13-15
  simulation, 14
times( ) function, 100-101
tolower( ) function, 307
toupper( ) function, 308
Turbo C++, 313-322
  // (comment) operator, 314
  :: (scope resolution) operator, 319
  << (put to) operator, 321
  >> (get from) operator, 322
  array manipulation functions, 378-
    392
  class, 154, 317
  classes, 149-150
  const, 155, 318
  constructors/destructors, 151
  data input functions, 359-377
  data streams, 153-154
  default function arguments, 153
  Definition class, 150

  delete, 154, 316
  Dictionary class, 150
  encapsulation, 150
  enhancements, 149-155
  friend functions/classes, 152
  function overloading, 152
  inline, 155, 320
  inline functions, 150-151
  keywords/operators, 154-155
  member functions, 150
  new, 154, 315
  objects, 149-150
  private, 155
  public, 154
  public/private class members, 151
typedef data type, 212

U

unary expressions (see arithmetic
  operators; bitwise operators)
under_off function, 346
under_on function, 347
ungetc( ) function, 309
union storage class, 213
UNIX-like filtering programs, 577-592
unlink( ) function, 310
unsigned data type, 34, 214
uxcat, 582
uxcountc, 586
uxcountl, 584
uxcountw, 585
uxcut, 590
uxdouble, 588
uxhead, 578
uxlinesz, 583
uxlower, 587
uxpack, 591
uxprefix, 580
uxstrip, 579
uxsuffix, 592
uxtee, 581
uxupper, 589

V

variables, 27
  automatic, 106-108
  data types, 29-35
  global, 105-106
  list, 109
  name formats, 28-29
  static, 106-108
vmath1 function, 517
vmath2 function, 518
vmath3 function, 519

W

while statement, 51-52, 311

Y

yards_met function, 413

RESERVE
ROOM

DATE DUE